I0577189

James Heron

The Celtic Church in Ireland

The Story of Ireland and Irish Christianity from the Time of St. Patrick to the

Reformation

James Heron

The Celtic Church in Ireland
The Story of Ireland and Irish Christianity from the Time of St. Patrick to the Reformation

ISBN/EAN: 9783337310646

Printed in Europe, USA, Canada, Australia, Japan

Cover: Foto ©Lupo / pixelio.de

More available books at **www.hansebooks.com**

THE CELTIC CHURCH
IN IRELAND

THE CELTIC CHURCH
IN IRELAND

THE STORY OF

IRELAND AND IRISH CHRISTIANITY FROM
BEFORE THE TIME OF ST. PATRICK
TO THE REFORMATION

BY

JAMES HERON, D.D.

PROFESSOR OF ECCLESIASTICAL HISTORY IN THE
ASSEMBLY'S COLLEGE, BELFAST

AUTHOR OF "THE CHURCH OF THE SUB-APOSTOLIC AGE," ETC.

London
SERVICE & PATON
5 HENRIETTA STREET
1898

Printed by BALLANTYNE, HANSON & Co.
At the Ballantyne Press

PREFACE

It is beyond question that even among Irishmen much ignorance prevails respecting the history of Ireland. It is nothing short of scandalous that the study of Irish history has been excluded from the programme of the National Schools of the country, with the inevitable result that the larger proportion of our young people grow up knowing little or nothing of the formative influences and chequered experiences through which Ireland has passed, and how she has come to be what she is to-day. The primary object of the author in giving the following pages to the public is to awaken or stimulate a keener interest in this subject in the circles to which his volume may have access. Partly for this purpose, but also because ecclesiastical history is inseparable from civil, he has combined a picture of the social and civil state of Ireland with the story of the Celtic Church. The work is thus a rapid sketch of Irish affairs generally, with special attention to the ecclesiastical department, through a period of much more than a thousand years.

Wherever it was in his power to do so, he has gone to the sources, and, while he has been careful to avail himself of the results of the best and most recent criticism of early documents, he has, at the same time, endeavoured to invest the narrative with as much life and interest as possible.

The study of the organisation of the Celtic Church in Ireland has suffered greatly from having been pursued almost invariably in the light of modern Church systems, and with a constant effort to reconcile it with them. The effect has been to obscure or to keep out of sight its altogether unique features. If any justification is needed for another book on Irish history, the best apology the present writer can offer is that he has at least tried his utmost to regard and represent the facts with an unbiassed mind, and from an independent point of view.

It is right to add that the substance of the chapters that compose this volume was given as a series of lectures in connection with the Carey Foundation during the past winter. The lectures were delivered to somewhat varying audiences, and at considerable intervals; and, as a consequence, a few repetitions occur here and there which might otherwise have been avoided. They did not, however, seem to be of such moment as to require to be cancelled in the proofs. The writer is also conscious that some of the discussions that arise in connection with the life of St. Patrick—such as the attempt to prove that he was not a myth but a real historical personage; the summary of arguments in support of the genuineness of his reputed writings; the remarks upon the later Lives of the saint, and the criticism of

PREFACE

the evidence adduced in favour of a Roman mission —interrupt somewhat the course of the narrative, may try the patience of the reader, and might have been better relegated to notes or an appendix; but in addressing an intelligent audience these discussions were found necessary, and not uninteresting; they have been allowed, therefore, to retain their place in the text.

It only remains to add that the volume is published in response to the repeated and urgent request of those who heard the substance of it.

J. H.

ASSEMBLY'S COLLEGE, BELFAST,
September 1897.

CONTENT

PART I

IRELAND BEFORE PATRICK CAME

CHAP.   PAGE
I. RACIAL CHARACTERISTICS AND SOCIAL OR-
   GANISATION   3
II. EDUCATION, ARCHITECTURE, AGRICULTURE,
    AND RELIGION   28

PART II

THE COMING OF PATRICK

III. THE SOURCES FOR PATRICK'S HISTORY   .   53
IV. FROM PATRICK'S BIRTH TO HIS CALL   .   68
V. THE MISSIONARY CAREER OF PATRICK   .   101
VI. PATRICK'S TEACHING AND INFLUENCE   .   119

PART III

THE CHURCH OF ST. PATRICK

VII. THE FUNDAMENTAL FEATURE OF THE
     CHURCH OF ST. PATRICK—ITS MONASTI-
     CISM   131
VIII. SOME FAMOUS MONASTERIES AND MONKS .   151

CONTENTS

CHAP.   PAGE

IX. THE ORGANISATION OF THE CHURCH OF ST. PATRICK 161

X. PROCRUSTEAN METHODS OF TREATING EARLY IRISH CHURCH ORGANISATION . 192

XI. THE EDUCATIONAL ACHIEVEMENTS OF THE CHURCH OF ST. PATRICK . . . 207

XII. THE MISSIONARY ACHIEVEMENTS OF THE CHURCH OF ST. PATRICK : BRENDAN AND COLUMBA 215

XIII. THE MISSIONARY ACHIEVEMENTS OF THE CHURCH OF ST. PATRICK : COLUMBANUS . 253

XIV. DEFECTS IN THE CHURCH OF ST. PATRICK 274

PART IV

LATER FORTUNES OF THE CHURCH OF ST. PATRICK

XV. THE COMING OF THE DANES . . . 291

XVI. THE COMING OF THE ANGLO-NORMANS . 322

PART V

SUPPLEMENTARY

XVII. ON THE TITLE "THE CHURCH OF IRE-LAND" 355

XVIII. "APOSTOLICAL SUCCESSION" . . . 382

APPENDIX 408

INDEX 409

x

PART I

IRELAND BEFORE PATRICK CAME

CHAPTER I

RACIAL CHARACTERISTICS AND SOCIAL ORGANISATION

" LOVE of country is to peoples what love of life is ^{Love of} to individuals," says Lamartine. But as love of life ^{country necessary} is a self-regarding instinct which does not necessarily ^{to civilised} contain any element of generosity in it, I should ^{life.} prefer to say that love of country is to peoples what love of family is to individuals. Love of family withdraws the individual from himself, and prompts to that sacrifice of personal interests for the sake of others, which is recognised as the divinest attribute in human character. Love of country does this on a larger scale, and thus tends to extend the horizon and to broaden the sympathies of a people. Thin and cold must be the civic life that is not enriched and ennobled by this feeling. Without it even the sentiment of loyalty becomes a mere commercial consideration, and has that " curse of hardness " on it which Mr. Matthew Arnold says rests on the patriotism of the typical Ulsterman. A feeling of ardent patriotic devotion attaches the Scotsman to the land that gave him birth, and his loyalty to the throne is not diminished, but stimulated thereby. Why should it not act similarly in the case of Irishmen ?

What country is better calculated than Ireland to evoke and nourish such a sentiment ? We know of none whose historic past is touched with a more

3

The history of Ireland fitted to excite this sentiment.

The Celtic Church of Ireland especially has a unique interest.

pathetic or enchaining interest. Turn almost where we may, our feet tread on ground which, to him who brings to its contemplation an educated eye, teems with romantic and stirring associations. What early Church of any country has a story more suggestive and fascinating than the ancient Celtic Church of Ireland? In many respects it is quite unique, with peculiarities that have almost no parallel elsewhere. As compared with most contemporary Christian communities, it was exceptionally evangelical in its teaching. For many a day it guarded its distinctive customs and characteristics with jealous care, and refused to part with its independence. In the centuries of its prime it won a great reputation for the cultivation of both sacred and secular learning, and the world-wide renown of its schools drew numerous students from all parts of Europe. It sent forth distinguished educators and brave and devoted missionary pioneers, who stand out on the page of mediæval history and contributed in some measure to the making of our modern world. It gave Christianity to a large part of Scotland; and when, after the Augustinian mission, almost the whole of Anglo-Saxon England had relapsed into paganism, it was Irish missionaries sent from Iona that re-evangelised and recovered it.[1] It was a powerful Christianising agent on the Continent of Europe; several European countries turn to it as one of the tributary influences that went to make them what they are; and German and French scholars are to-day among the most eager students of its history. Shall we incur the reproach of being

[1] "Not Augustine, but Aidan, is the true apostle of England," says Bishop Lightfoot.

content to remain in ignorance of its story and achievements, and leave research in its literature to Frenchmen and Germans?

It is to a rapid survey of the planting and planters, the organisation and labours, the earlier and later fortunes of this primitive Church of Ireland—a survey which will afford many glimpses into the civil and social condition of the country—that I invite the reader. But to enable him to appreciate duly the work done by its renowned apostle and founder and his associates and successors, it will be necessary, first, to convey in the briefest way possible some fair idea of the state in which Ireland was when its illustrious evangelist landed on its shores.

Far back in a remote and legendary past a series of races is represented as having taken possession of the country, each subjugating or driving out its predecessors. Successive colonies, called Partholonians, Nemedians, and Fomorians or sea-rovers, are, in the legendary tales, the first to enter and take possession; but it is far from certain whether they are much more than mythical. It is, by the way, from the legend touching these Fomorians that the Giant's Causeway (of which we have been hearing so much of late) derives its Irish name, *Cloch-an-na-bh-Fomharigh*, which means the Causeway or Stepping-stones of the Fomorians, who in popular imagination became magnified into giants, and so gave rise to the designation "Giant's Causeway."

Then come in several successive waves the Celtic settlers: first, the Firbolgs or Bagmen, so called from the leathern wallets in which, when in bondage to the Greeks, they are said to have carried soil from the lowlands to the rocky and rugged hillsides,

Prehistoric races.

The Celtic Settlers: 1. The Firbolgs.

5

and who are supposed to have come from the Belgic coasts across South Britain and Wales; next, the

2. The De-
dannans.

Dedannans, who came through Caledonia, and who, in Dr. Skene's judgment, answer to the large-limbed, red-haired Caledonians of Tacitus;[1] and lastly, the

3. The
Milesians.

Milesians, who are said to have come from Spain under the command of the eight sons of Miledh or Milesius—the dominant and ruling race when legend passes into history. The difference between these three races is noted by MacFirbis in his Book of the Genealogies, in a statement which he says he has taken from "an old book." Here is what it says:—

Wherein
they dif-
fered.

"Every one who is white (of skin) and brown (of hair), bold, honourable, daring, prosperous, bountiful in the bestowal of property, wealth, and rings, and who is not afraid of battle or combat: they are the descendants of Milesius in Erinn.

"Every one who is fair-haired, vengeful, large; and every plunderer; every musical person; the professors of musical and entertaining performances; they who are adepts in all Druidical and magical arts: they are the descendants of the Tuatha De Dannan in Erinn.

"Every one who is black-haired, who is a tattler, guileful, tale-telling, noisy, contemptible; every wretched, mean, strolling, unsteady, harsh, and inhospitable person; every slave, every mean thief, every churl, every one who loves not to listen to music and entertainment, the disturbers of every council and every assembly, and the promoters of discord among the people: these are the descendants of the Firbolgs, of the Gailiuns of Liogarné, and of the Fir Domhnaans in Erinn. But, however, the

[1] See Skene's "Celtic Scotland," vol. i. p. 179.

6

descendants of the Firbolgs are the most numerous of all these."[1]

The picture here given bears evident marks of having been drawn by a Milesian hand; but, making due allowance for the bias and prejudice which it betrays, it indicates, along with another not so prominent, two distinctly marked and contrasted racial types; and everywhere these two types are clearly recognisable among the early inhabitants of Ireland: a smaller, slighter, black-haired, dark-eyed, pale-skinned, lithe-limbed, small-boned, aquiline race, quick in perception and fluent in speech, of Iberian and apparently Firbolg origin; and a much taller, bigger-boned, larger, fair-haired, often red-haired race, with blue or grey-blue eyes and more angular features. Dr. Sullivan thinks that, so far as the ancient tales enable us to judge, the Firbolgs, the Dedannans, and the Milesians all alike belong to the second type.[2] But there are reasons for believing that the Firbolgs contained an Iberian element. It is significant and noteworthy that the early Spanish records agree with the Irish respecting the fact of an early emigration from Spain to Ireland. Colmenar, in the "Annals of Spain and Portugal," says: "History informs us that two hundred years before Jesus Christ the Biscayans plied on the sea in vessels made of the trunks of trees hollowed and covered with leather, and, with a fleet thus constructed, they went to Hibernia, now called Ireland, and took possession of it."[3] Grimm, moreover, dis-

(margin note: Two types recognisable.)

[1] O'Curry's "Lectures on MS. Materials," p. 223.
[2] Introduction to O'Curry's "Manners and Customs of the Ancient Irish," p. lxxii.
[3] "Annals of Spain," &c., vol. ii. p. 55; see also "Proceedings of the Royal Irish Academy," vol. viii. p. 371 *et seq.*

covered that the language of Aquitaine in the fourth century had a Gaelic element in it.[1] It is curious, however, and not without suggestiveness, that the true Milesian type, the larger, more angular, fair or red-haired race, is said to be best represented not among the native Irish, who have been softened and enlivened by a large infusion of Iberian blood, but among the Scottish colonists in Ulster.

The races amalgamated at the opening of the historic period.

At any rate, it seems to be quite certain that at the opening of the historic period, whatever race distinctions had existed among the inhabitants of Ireland were practically obliterated; the people appear to have spoken one language, to have become in a great degree fused and amalgamated, and, under a common social system, reduced to unity of thought and feeling—a unity strikingly and beautifully expressed in the legend of Nemedh and his sons, which represents the three races as sprung originally from a common ancestor; that after having parted, and been scattered over Europe in three bands, they returned, one after the other, at first to fight as foes, but to discover afterwards that they spoke a common language and owned a common lineage, and to be reconciled to each other and to dwell together.

But the question naturally arises, Where did these Celts, of whatever type, originally come from ?

Whence and when the Celtic wave of migration flowed westwards.

At a far-distant prehistoric period Central Asia must have been a veritable hive of human life. It was the pressure of growing numbers there, and the struggle for existence, thereby made more difficult, that, from a date antecedent to the dawn of history, began to propel immense hordes of human beings

[1] Sullivan's Introduction to O'Curry's "Manners and Customs of the Ancient Irish," p. lix. *et seq.*

westwards from that centre, in search of new abodes, where they would have more room to live. Issuing from that teeming womb, huge masses of humanity, each driven forward at once by the exigencies of life and by the pressure of other masses from behind, continue through many centuries subject to a continually shifting, perpetual movement, which has been called by German writers " the wandering of the nations" (*Volkerwanderung*). One of the earliest waves of this mighty, ever-flowing tide of migration from the east westwards, earlier than that of the Goths and other Teutonic tribes, which at length overran and submerged the Roman Empire, was that of a people called *Celts* (Κελτοί, *Celtæ*, *Galatæ*, *Galli*, *Gauls*, *Gaels*). They are mentioned by Herodotus, and when first heard of have found their way to the north-west of Europe, and are occupying a large tract of the Continent west of the Rhine. From this region some of them recross the Rhine, and seek a home on the banks of the Danube; some pass farther westward into a country which, after them, long bears the name of Gaul, and thence spread northwards into Britain and Ireland; others, making their way southwards, pass over the Alps into Northern Italy, and in 390 B.C. sweep like a deluge over Rome herself, sacking and overthrowing the city; a few generations later Greece and Macedonia are overrun by them; and a fragment of the same wave about the same time rolls into Asia Minor, settles in its interior, and becomes known to history as Galatians.

Of the Celts who settled in the British Isles there were two main divisions—the Gaelic and the Cymric. To the Cymric stock belonged the ancient Britons,

Two divisions of Celts: the Gaelic and Cymric.

9

who were ultimately driven back into Wales and Cornwall, and the Bretons; while those who settled in Ireland belonged to the Gaelic stock. Of the Gaels, again, there were two branches—the Milesians and the Cruithne or Picts. The name "Cruithne" is believed to come from a word which means colour, of which the name "Picti," given them by the Romans, seems to have been the Latin rendering. The Cruithne or Picts took possession of Alban and of Ulster, although in Ulster they were at length confined to the district called Dalaradia; the Milesians spread over the other parts of Ireland. It is true that in the "Annals of Ulster" the Albanian Picts are called "Pictores" and the Irish Picts are named "Cruithne," but in the Irish records generally the name "Cruithne" is applied indiscriminately to both.

The Irish people as a whole were in the historic period called *Gaels, Milesians, Hiberni, Hiberionaces, Scoti.* The last two designations are employed by St. Patrick. The country was named by the Greeks *Ogygia* or *Ierne,* by the Romans it was called *Scotia,* and *Hibernia* or *Hiberio,* which latter was only the Latin form of *Eriu.* "Hiberio, which is the designation of Ireland in the 'Itinerary of Antonine,'" says Dr. Whitley Stokes, "is the Latin form of the native name of Eriu. The *b* sounding as *v* gave Iverio (*h* being omitted as not a distinct letter of the Irish alphabet), and, by a phonetic law, *v* between two vowels disappearing, it became *Ierio, Ieriu,* and finally *Eriu.* The modern *Erin* is the dative case." Of course *Eire, Eire-land, Ireland,* are but different forms of the same word. Besides these, quite a variety of names are in ancient native poetry given to the country, as, for example, *Inisfail* (or Isle of

Marginal notes:
Two branches of Gaels: Milesians and Picts.

Early names of Ireland and the Irish.

Destiny), *Inis Ealga* (the Noble Island), *Inis-na-beeva* (Island of the Woods), *Inis-na-naomb* (Island of the Saints), *Inis Fodhla* and *Inis Banbha*. There is a legend that when the Milesians came to Ireland they found three kings of the Dedannans ruling over it, that their three queens were *Eire*, *Fodhla*, and *Banbha*, and that the country was called by these several names after them. It is certain that *Fodhla* and *Banbha* frequently occur in ancient Irish poetry as names of Ireland. Of course this derivation rests only on a shadowy legend. Dr. Whitley Stokes suggests that *Eriu*, probably a contracted form of *Iberiu* or *Iveriu*, may be connected with the Sanscrit *avara*, which means posterior, western. But so far as the name "Scotia" is concerned, it should not be forgotten that originally it belonged exclusively to Ireland, and the term "Scoti" to the Irish, and to them only. Wherever the words "Scotia" and "Scoti" occur down till about the eleventh century, it is invariably Ireland and the Irish they are intended to designate. Subsequently Alba, the country which we now know as Scotland, got the name of "Scotia Minor" through a portion of it being colonised by Scots from Ireland, while Ireland was known as "Scotia Major;" for, in fact, Scotland got both her name and, in great part, her Christianity from Ireland; and, curiously, that thrifty country, which is said not only to keep the Sabbath but everything else she can lay her hands on, at length appropriated the title "Scotia" to her own exclusive use, and the land from which she took it had to fall back upon and be content with her still earlier name of Erin, or at least the Anglo-Saxon form of it, "Iraland" or "Ireland."

It is remarkable that in the earliest glimpses we get of the Celtic race, they exhibit the same mental and moral characteristics as distinguish them to-day. Cæsar notes their love of change, and the elder Cato says, "To two things are the Celts most attent: to fighting and adroitness of speech." Two modern historians have delineated the more prominent features of their character in lines fundamentally similar, though with some differences.

The first of these, Thierry, says in his " History of the Gauls : " "The characteristics of the Gaulic family—those which distinguish it the most, in my opinion, from other human families—may be summed up as follows : personal bravery unequalled amongst ancient nations, a spirit free, impetuous, open to all impressions, remarkably intelligent ; but, side by side with this, an extreme susceptibility, want of perseverance, marked dislike to the idea of discipline and order (so strong among the German nations), extreme ostentation, and, in fine, perpetual dissension, the fruit of excessive vanity. If we desire to compare, in a few words, the Gaulic nation with the Germans, of whom we have just been speaking, we might say that among the former the personal sentiment, the idea of self, is too much developed, and among the latter it is too little so. Thus in every page of the history of the Gauls we find original characters which vividly excite and concentrate upon themselves our sympathies, while they cause us to forget the existence of the masses of the nation. It is otherwise in the history of the Germans, where it is from the masses generally that great national movements originate."

The portrait of the Celtic race drawn by Mommsen,

in his " History of Rome," is less sympathetic and
more severe : " In the mighty vortex of the world's
history, which inexorably crushes all nations that are
not as hard and flexible as steel, such a nation could
not permanently maintain itself. With reason, the
Celts of the Continent suffered the same fate at the
hands of the Romans as their kinsmen in Ireland
suffer down to our own day at the hands of the
Saxon—the fate of becoming merged as a leaven
of future development in a politically superior
nationality. On the eve of parting from this remarkable nation, we may be allowed to call attention
to the fact, that in the accounts of the ancients as
to the Celts on the Loire and Seine, we find almost
every one of the characteristic traits which we are
accustomed to recognise as marking the Irish.
Every feature reappears; the laziness in the culture
of the fields, the ostentation, the droll humour, the
hearty delight in singing and reciting the deeds of
past ages; the most decided talent for rhetoric and
poetry; the curiosity—no trader was allowed to
pass until he had told in open street what he knew
or what he did not know; the extravagant credulity
which acted on such accounts; the childlike piety
which sees in the priest a father, and asks him
for advice in all things; the unsurpassed fervour of
national feeling, and the closeness with which those
who are fellow-countrymen cling together, almost
like one family, in opposition to a stranger; the
inclination to rise in revolt under the first chance
leader that presents himself, and to form bands,
but at the same time the incapacity to preserve the
self-reliant courage, equally remote from presumption and from pusillanimity—to perceive the right

time for waiting and for striking—to attain or even to tolerate any organisation, any sort of fixed military or political discipline. It is, and remains in all times and all places, the same indolent and poetical, irresolute and fervid, inquisitive, credulous, amiable, clever, but, in a political point of view, thoroughly useless nation; and, therefore, its fate has been always and everywhere the same."

Social organisation of early Ireland: the tribal system.

It is impossible to judge either individuals or peoples rightly without taking account of the circumstances and surroundings, the institutions and customs, that control and regulate their daily life. To appreciate early Irish society and the primitive Church of Ireland, it is of the first importance to observe the principle on which society, both secular and ecclesiastical, was organised. Now the root idea of the Irish social system was *kinship, blood-relationship*. The unit of that system was the family, which consisted in theory of the parents, children, and immediate relatives, but included also slaves, retainers, or sojourners not related by blood. When the father died, the eldest son, or the most capable of his blood, succeeded him, and the family continued in a sort of corporate capacity. A group of families from a common ancestry made a *sept*; a still larger group was called a *clann*, which means children; while a *tribe* or *tuath* consisted of several such clanns, septs, and families descended, or supposed to be descended, from a common ancestor, with their slaves and retainers, and occupying.a definite territory, which was the common property of the tribe. The right of any one to share in the tribe-land depended on his descent from the common progenitor and his kinship to the other members

14

of the tribe. Mere residence within a territory gave
no title to it. And so far from being unparalleled
and anomalous, "the Irish tribal system was merely
the western survival of the original form adopted
by all the races of the Aryan branch of the human
race." The tribe, however, really consisted of two
classes: (a) those who were recognised as real
members through kinship, and who were called
nemé; (b) and those who, not being members of
the tribe by blood-relationship, had no recognised
rights or position, except through those members
of the tribe whose slaves or retainers they were.
They were called *féini*. The former were what may
be designated "freemen," the latter the "unfree."
As regards the "freemen," the rank and place they
took depended on the number of retainers they were
able to support, and the number of armed men they
could bring into the field on any emergency. The
lowest in this class was the "*oc-airè*," who had a
house and some slight claim upon the common
pasture. If he owned ten cows, he rose into the
next rank, and became a "*bo-airè*," or cow-possess-
ing freeman. Neither of these grades was recognised
as "noble." The "nobles" or "flaiths" possessed
not only cattle but "deis," that is, rights or lordship acquired over persons who borrowed cattle from
them, and thereby became their dependants. Besides,
the "flaiths" at an early date acquired private property in land outside that which belonged to the
tribe, by means of which they were able to support
retainers. Some of this land they held in their own
hands, and employed the "unfree" class in its cultivation; some of it they let to tenants—the beginning
of the system of landlord and tenant in Ireland.

Chiefs and sub-kings with *Ardri*, or supreme king over all.

Each group, whether sept, clan, or tribe, had its "flaith" or chief. When the territory occupied by a tribe was of considerable extent, its chief was called a "*Ri*" or king. There were in Ireland one hundred and eighty-four *tuaths* or tribal territories, which corresponded in a great measure with the modern baronies. Then several tribes combined together made a sub-kingdom; a few sub-kingdoms united to form a provincial kingdom, and at the head of all was the "Ardri," or supreme king of Ireland, whose royal palace was at Tara in Meath, and to whom Meath was given as a sort of mensal territory. It was in the second century that Meath was formed into a separate and central realm, by taking a portion from each of the four provincial kingdoms of Ulster, Leinster, Munster, and Connaught. The chieftainships and kingships were in part hereditary and in part elective; that is to say, while there was a right of selection, the choice was limited to the relatives of the ruling chief or king. The eldest son was not necessarily elected, but generally the ablest and most capable man among the connections of the ruler; the successor was chosen during the lifetime of the existing chief or king, and the person on whom the choice fell was known as the *Tanist*.

There was from early times a distinct recognition of the supremacy of the Ardri or over-king of Ireland. Dr. Richey points out that while "the conquest of Britain was effected by numerous and perfectly independent settlements of Teutonic tribes, and the Heptarchy itself represents the consolidation of many previously independent communities, . . . it is remarkable that all the Irish legends acknowledge a common nationality and central government. Amidst all the

16

constant hostilities and civil wars which form the
staple of Irish history, there is a recognition of the
sovereignty of the Ardrigh as the head of a dimly
conceived nationality; and the palace of Tara and
the surrounding district of Meath (until the decay
of Tara, begun in 565) are in some sense regarded
as the centre and symbol of the national unity, the
metropolis of the Gaelic race."[1] But the tribal constitution of Irish society was so deep-rooted, and the
tribal feelings, feuds, and separations so inveterate,
that the central sovereignty was impaired, and in a
great measure paralysed. When a strong man like
Niall of the Nine Hostages, or Brian Boroihme
(Boru), the breaker of the Danish yoke, was supreme
sovereign, his controlling power was everywhere felt;
but it often happened that a provincial king was,
personally and through the combinations he was able
to effect, more powerful than the Ardri, in which
case the central control was little more than nominal.
The full development of Irish nationality and of a
strong central government was thus arrested by the
greater strength of the tribal system.

A brief notice of the more prominent and cele- The more
brated of the supreme sovereigns of pagan Ireland famous
Irish kings
may interest the reader, and enable him to realise before
better the state of things before the light of Chris- Patrick.
tianity dawned upon the country.

The over-king at the opening of the Christian era Conary the
was Conary the Great, and the chief event that marks Great.
his reign was the seven years' war between Mebh
(Maive), Queen of Connaught, and Conor MacNessa,
King of Ulster. About two miles west of the city
of Armagh is still to be seen an ancient rath called

---

[1] Richey's "Short History," p. 34.

Navan Fort. This was the royal fort, and here was the palace of Emain or Emania, where Conor Mac-Nessa resided. From her palace in Croghan—the remains of which are still extant and visible at Rath-croghan near Roscommon—Queen Maive set out to avenge some grudge which she had against the north. With her men of arms she had made her way as far as the region now known as North Louth, then called Cuailnge or Quelnè,[1] when her progress was arrested by the great hero Cuchullin, who, under King Conor MacNessa, had organised a sort of militia for the defence of the kingdom. They are renowned in Irish story under the name of the Red Branch Knights, and their chief leaders under Cuchullin were Keltar of the Battles, whose residence was at Rath Keltar, a great fort beside where Downpatrick now stands; the bard Bricriu of the venom tongue, whose fort is still conspicuous on a hill above the lake beside Loughbrickland, which takes its name from him; Conall Kernach, Fergus MacRoig, and the three sons of Usna. Cuchullin's own residence was at Dundalgan, now Castletown Fort, two miles west of Dundalk. After many single-handed combats be-tween Cuchullin and the most stalwart heroes of Queen Maive, the great Ulster chieftain was at length enabled so to rally the men of Ulster, who had been hitherto smitten with impotence, that Queen Maive and her invading army were utterly defeated and put to rout. The most famous of all the Irish epic tales, the *Tain-bo-Cuailnge*, has for its subject the battles, single combats, and incidents of this great campaign, of which Cuchullin is the chief hero; much

[1] Now Cooley. It derived its name from Cuailnge, a Milesian chief.

18

of the literature connected therewith has been published by noted scholars both in Germany and France.

About the beginning of the second century reigned King Tuathal, by whom the supreme monarchy was established on a firmer footing. It was in his time that the new province of Meath was formed, as mensal or demesne land for the maintenance of the Ardri, by appropriating a part of each of the other provinces; the three forts of Tlachtga near Athboy, Ushnagh in West Meath, and Tailltenn (now Telltown) between Navan and Kells, were built by him, and great annual fairs instituted at these centres. By this king the famous *Feis*, or Triennial Convention of Tara, is said to have been held with exceptional pomp and splendour. According to the "Annals of the Four Masters," the *Feis* at Tara was originated by the monarch Ollamh Fodhla, who also appointed a chief over every barony, and a farmer over every townland. The *Feis* was an assembly of all the kings, chiefs, ollamhs, and other leading men, and lasted for seven days, three days before and three after *Saman, i.e.* the 1st of November. Matters of importance were discussed, and all who attended were sumptuously banqueted and entertained by the Ardri. A full account of the *Feis* of Tara will be found in Dr. Petrie's "History and Antiquities of Tara Hill," pp. 29 *et seq.* Of the nature of the gathering the most ancient record, according to Petrie, is that contained in an old poem, quoted by Keating and printed by Petrie. It is as follows:—

King Tuathal and the Feis.

> " The *Feis* of Temur each third year,
> To preserve laws and rules,
> Was then convened firmly
> By the illustrious kings of Erin.

19

Cathaoir of sons-in-law convened
The beautiful *Feis* of regal Temur;
There came with him (the better for it)
The men of Erin to one place.
Three days before *Saman*, always,
Three days after it—it was a goodly custom—
The host of very high fashion spent,
Constantly drinking during the week.
Without theft, without wounding a man
Among them during all this time;
Without feats of arms, without deceit,
Without exercising horses.
Whoever did any of those things
Was a wretched enemy with heavy venom;
Gold was not received as retribution from him,
But his soul in one hour."

Conn of the Hundred Battles.

The next most renowned king of Ireland was Conn Ced-Cathach, or Conn of the Hundred Battles, who ascended the throne about A.D. 123. His great enemy was Eoghan-Mor (Owen More), also called Mogh-Nuadhat, King of Munster, with whom he was engaged in interminable war, and to whom he was compelled to yield half of Ireland. They divided the country into two halves, the dividing line having been a low range of sandhills extending from Dublin to Galway. The northern division was called Leth-Chuinn (Leth Conn), or Conn's Half, and the southern Leth-Mogha (Leth-Mogh), or Mogh's Half. Eoghan was at length defeated and slain, and Conn resumed the sovereignty of the whole country.

Conary II. and Cairbre Riada.

He was succeeded by his son-in-law, Conary II. (A.D. 157). It was Conary's son, Cairbre Riada, who led a colony of Scots out of what is now County Antrim into Alban or Caledonia,[1] where they settled

[1] The country north of the wall of Antoninus, extending from the Firth of Clyde to the Firth of Forth, was called Alban or Caledonia; the whole island south of that wall was called Britain.

on the western coasts and islands, and subsequently gave the name of Argyleshire (*Airer Gael*, *i.e.* the territory of the Gael or Irish) to the region where they settled, and at length the name of Scotland to the whole country.

By far the most renowned of the Irish kings of the pagan period was Cormac MacArt (A.D. 254), who was grandson of Conn of the Hundred Battles. As Cormac appears to have come under Christian influences, I shall have more to say of him and of his exploits when I come to speak of the traces of Christianity in Ireland before the time of Patrick. But as nearly all the still existing remains at Tara belong to the time of Cormac, it may be fitting here to give some brief account of them.

Cormac Mac-Art and the remains at Tara.

The Hill of Tara itself, as Dr. Petrie mentions, is not remarkable for either altitude or picturesqueness of form. It commands, however, a very extensive and pleasant prospect, and excels even the most interesting spots in a country full of scenes of intense interest in the historic memories associated with it. Dr. Petrie compares it in these respects with the Hill of Aileach near Derry, and the Hill of Emania near Armagh, famous residences of the Ulster kings. According to the traditions preserved in the ancient bardic literature, it became the chief residence of the Irish kings on the first establishment of a monarchical government in Ireland under Slainge, the first king of the Firbolgs.[1]

The most ancient monument still traceable is the *Rath-na-Riogh* (Rath of the Kings), which encircles the southern brow of the hill, and is assigned to the

---

[1] See Dr. Petrie's "History and Antiquities of Tara Hill," in "Transactions of the Royal Irish Academy," vol. xviii. p. 27.

Firbolgs. Its external diameter is 853 feet, its interior diameter 775 feet. Dr. Petrie supposes the parapet to have been originally built of dry stone, and the name Teamur (Tara) he derives from *teach*, "a house," and *mur*, "a wall" = "House of the Walls." Within this large rath are several minor ones and other monuments. To the south-east are the ruins of the house of Cormac, facing *Rath Laoghaire*, which is situated to the south and outside the *Rath-na-Riogh*. Alongside of the house of Cormac are the remains of the Forradh, which is thought to be coeval with the Rath-na-Riogh; and between the Forradh and the house of Cormac is the *Mur Tea*, or Wall of Tea. In addition to these there are the Mound of the Cow, the Mound of the Hostages, and the Lia Fail, or coronation stone.

On the east of the hill, and outside the Rath-na-Riogh, is a spring or well (*neambuach*) from which a stream flowed, on which Cormac built the first mill in Ireland; and a mill still stands on the reputed site of the ancient one.

Immediately to the north of *Rath-na-Riogh* is the *Rath of the Synods* (*Rath-na-Seanadh*), where certain ecclesiastical synods from the time of Patrick are said to have been convened.

To the east of the Rath of the Synods, and within the boundary of a churchyard, is the shaft of a cross, known as the "Cross of Adamnan;" and not far from this beautiful torques, or twisted circular collars, were found in 1810. They no doubt belong to a period anterior, perhaps long anterior, to the desertion of Tara in the sixth century.

Farther north still are the foundations of the Banqueting Hall, called the House of Heroes, and

celebrated in Irish bardic story—an immense hall
759 feet in length, and originally 90 feet in breadth.
It is stated in the records to have had fourteen
doors, and twelve or fourteen doors are still visible.
It was here that the *Feis*, or great assemblies, were
held, and here also that the kings and chiefs were
feasted and entertained by the Ardri or supreme
sovereign.   The statements in the ancient literature
respecting it are fully corroborated by the ruins.

Other raths lie to the north-west, such as *Rath
Caelchu* (Caelchu having been a contemporary of
King Cormac MacArt) and *Rath Graine*.   Graine
was a daughter of Cormac, and wife of the celebrated
Finn MacCumhaill, to whom she proved unfaithful,
and eloped with Dermot.

The next most illustrious of the Irish kings was Niall of
Niall of the Nine Hostages, who, according to the the Nine
"Four Masters," began to reign in A.D. 379; and
the most remarkable event in his reign was the great
invasion which he led against Britain.   By means
of a vast fleet, which the poet Claudian says made
"the ocean foam with their hostile oars," he landed
in Wales and carried off much spoil, but was compelled to withdraw by the celebrated Roman general
Stilicho.   Niall had fourteen sons, eight of whom
became the ancestors of many great and illustrious
families.   Four of them settled in Meath, and their
posterity were known as the Southern Hy Niall (*i.e.*
race of Niall), and four secured a territory in Ulster,
and their descendants were called the Northern Hy
Niall.   From this time forward almost all the kings
of Ireland were descended from one or other of these
branches of the great family of Niall.   While leading
an expedition to the coast of Gaul, Niall of the

23

Nine Hostages was killed by an arrow, said to have been aimed at him by the King of Leinster, on the shore of the river Loire. His immediate successor was his nephew Dathi, who was killed by lightning at the foot of the Alps, whither he had gone on a plundering expedition. On his death in 428, a son of Niall, called Laoghaire (Leary), became Ardri. He was reigning sovereign at Tara when St. Patrick went there on his famous visit of evangelisation.

Dathi.

Laoghaire.

Closely related to the social organisation were the ancient laws of Ireland, with regard to which a word must here be said. They are generally known as the Brehon Laws, because they were administered by the Brehons, who were the lawyers and judges or arbitrators in primitive Ireland. To qualify him for his profession the Brehon had to go through a long course of training. He needed to be acquainted with all the minute rules and ceremonies necessary to institute an action, as well as with the traditions, customs, and precedents of the tribe, and as these were often very complicated, great skill was required to interpret and apply them. The Brehons were naturally held in great esteem— in pagan times they were both priests and lawyers ;— kings and chiefs were accustomed to have Brehons attached to them, and free lands were given them for their support. The office was recognised as a very responsible one, for the Brehon was himself liable to a penalty if he gave a wrong or unjust decision.

The ancient laws of Ireland.

These old laws, it should be noted, were not the result of legislation, but had grown up through the accumulation of immemorial customs and of interpretations and decisions of the Brehons. And as they were not the enactments of any legislative body like our Parliament, so there was no state authority with force at command pledged to ensure obedience. There was no state power behind the laws requiring an offender to submit to the decision of a Brehon. The only compulsion was that of public opinion. Where the parties were strong and influential and jealous of their own rights, the natural, legal, and too common course was to bring their cause to the arbitrament of private war. But the deep reverence for law and the respect for public opinion were ordinarily sufficient to secure submission on the part of litigants. This reverence for law among the Irish was so developed that even in the time of James I., and at a time of much trouble and disturbance, it attracted the attention of Sir John Davies, a not over-friendly, but cool and clear-eyed observer. ."I dare affirm," he says, " that for the space of five years past there has not been found so many malefactors worthy of death in all the six circuits of this realm (thirty-two shires) as in one circuit of six shires, namely, the Western Circuit, in England. For the truth is that in time of peace the Irish are more fearful to offend the law than the English, or any other nation whatsoever. There is no nation under the sun that doth love equal or indifferent justice better than the Irish, or will rest better satisfied with the execution thereof, although it be against themselves."

The Brehon system of law knew nothing of a wrong against the state: every offence was against an individual, and, no matter what the offence was, the penalty took the form of a fine, to be paid by the offender, or, if he failed to pay it, by his family. Even for homicide or murder the penalty was a fine, called "*eric*," which was adjusted by the Brehons. It is a prevalent popular opinion that the laws of the Brehon codes were quite peculiar to Ireland, and were unknown elsewhere. This is a complete mistake. As Sir Henry Maine has shown, they are exactly similar to the laws of all the Aryan tribes, including the early English, at the same stage of social progress, modified somewhat of course by time and circumstances.[1] The ancient laws of Ireland were collected into tracts, the most noteworthy of which are those called the *Senchus Mor*, which in a general way may be said to be concerned with civil law; the "Book of Acaill," which deals with criminal law and law referring to personal injury; and the "Book of Rights," which "gives an account of the rights of the monarchs of all Ireland, and the revenues payable to them by the principal kings of the several provinces, and of the stipends paid by the monarchs to the inferior kings for their services. It also treats of the rights of each of the provincial kings, and the revenues payable to them from the inferior kings of the districts or tribes subsidiary to them, and of the stipends paid by the superior to the inferior provincial kings for their services."[2]

These ancient laws were, of course, adapted to a primitive state of society, but were on the whole singularly just and sympathetic towards the people, and tended to protect the weak against the strong and the wealthy, opening a way to the highest ranks from the lowest. They are said to have been revised

[1] Maine's "History of Ancient Institutions," p. 19.
[2] "Book of Rights," Introduction, p. vi.

and reorganised by the great reforming king, Cormac Macart (A.D. 218–260).

We are informed in the old introduction to the *Senchus Mor* that after the entrance of Christianity the ancient laws were revised by a committee of nine persons, appointed by King Laoghaire, and that the committee consisted of three kings, namely, Loaghaire himself, Corc, King of Munster, and Daire, King of Ulster; three ecclesiastics, namely, Patrick, Benen, and Cairnech; and three poets and historians, namely, Rossa, Dubhthach, and Fergus. It is stated that this committee of revision removed everything ·inconsistent with Christian morality and doctrine, and that the revised code was called *Senchus Mor* or Cain Patrick, *i.e.* Patrick's law. This statement, however, has been seriously questioned. Professor Richey, who had given special attention to the subject, and taken part in their publication, says that "the tradition that the Brehon laws were revised and codified on the introduction of Christianity is unsupported by evidence, and improbable in the highest degree;" yet he admits that "the Church, when once established, affected them to a large extent, and through the influence of the Church and the study of civil law a considerable element of equity was introduced, which largely modified, by the introduction of the ideas of equity, the form of the later Brehon writers."[1]

[1] "Short History," chap. iii. p. 57.

CHAPTER II

EDUCATION, ARCHITECTURE, AGRICULTURE, AND RELIGION

THE next question that naturally arises is, What was the state of education in pre-Christian Ireland? Was there such a thing as literary culture of any sort? Now there is ample evidence that from very early times learning of a sort was held in high honour in ancient Erin. The person who had attained the highest degree of knowledge, which included law, history, language, but especially the recitation of tales and verses, in which all forms of knowledge were apt to be clothed, was constituted an *ollamh* (pronounced *ollave*), or *doctor*, and many and great were the privileges which that degree brought with it. The *ollamh* was entitled to sit next the king at table; his person and property were inviolable; he had a stated income secured to him of twenty-one cows and their grass in the chief's territory; abundant means of support for himself and his retinue to the number of twenty-four, including pupils, tutors, and servants, and a title to be supplied at need with two hounds and six horses. When he travelled, he was accompanied by his pupils, to whom he stood very much in the relation of a parent, and he was not at liberty to accept of hospitality at the house

28

of any one below the rank of a *flaith* or noble. He also carried with him the privilege of sanctuary. But lest he should abuse the rare privileges which he thus enjoyed, he was required to be not only pure in morals and unstained by crime, but civil of tongue. It was in the infringement of this latter condition that his besetting sin lay. The *ollamh* was bound to master history and to teach it. He was the legal referee on all points in dispute respecting genealogies, on which rights of property so much depended. To obviate difficulties with regard to the right of succession, he kept the pedigree of the royal family, as well as of the families of the provincial kings and territorial chiefs; and not only the central monarch, but each provincial king and smaller chief had his *ollamh* attached to his court. Again, no one could act as a *brehon* or judge without the degree of an *ollamh*, whose education extended over a period of twelve years. During these years he had to pass through a successive series of courses, each of which secured an additional degree. Among other things, he was expected to be competent to teach the four divisions of the knowledge of poetry, which included the reciting of tales, skill in the seven kinds of verse, and the gift of improvising verses and reciting them without having thought of them beforehand. The *ollamh* was indeed a formidable personage. The lash of his satire seems to have been more feared than the blow of the sling-stone or the point of the " broad-green " *laighin* (or spear), or the edge of the long " flame-flashing sword." The satire of one of them called Laidcenn is said to have had such a scorching influence on his enemy, that, after he had been exposed to it, "neither his corn, grass, nor foliage would grow for a whole year!"[1]

Conor MacNessa, who was King of Ulster in the first century of our era, was a noted friend and patron of the poets and historians. The taste for learning and poetry had at that time taken such possession of the national mind, that it is said that more than one-third of the men of Erin gave themselves up to their cultivation ; and by finding entrance into the ranks of the *Ollamhs* and the *Fileadh* (or poets), they were invested with legal privileges, which raised them to high rank and secured them a liberal maintenance at the expense of the unlearned portion of the community. The latter soon began to groan beneath the heavy burden of supporting so large a section of the population, and their complaints soon became loud and threatening, especially in the south and west. The chief poets called a meeting of their profession to consider what they should do, when King Conor MacNessa, having heard of their situation, invited them to Ulster with the full consent of his people, where a multitude of the learned men and poets of the time were hospitably and regally entertained for a period of seven years. It was not the only occasion on which the same class found a similar asylum in Ulidia.

Irish epic literature.

I have said that one acquirement necessary to the *Ollamh* was familiarity with a large number of historic and other tales, which he was expected to recite at feasts and other gatherings. He was required to know at least three hundred and fifty such tales, so

[1] See O'Curry's "Manuscript Materials of Ancient Irish History,": pp. 2, 3, 204, 239 ; and his "Manners and Customs of the Ancient Irish," p. 70.

as to be able to relate them off-hand at any moment. It was in this way that so many of these tales, just like the legends of King Arthur and his Table Round, partly based on history and partly legendary, have been—improved doubtless and embellished in their progress—handed down, many of them singularly beautiful and impressive. A large number of them cluster around the history and exploits of Conor MacNessa and his *Red Branch Knights*, and especially of Cuchullin, the most renowned of the heroes of ancient Irish romance. A second great cycle of tales are those which gather around Finn MacCumhall and his Fianna, who served under King Cormac MacArt, and won much glory in the third century.

Of the dwellings of the ancient Irish, and of their architecture generally, we have next to speak. It has been found that on primitive communities passing over from paganism to Christianity, Christian tombs and other structures have, as a rule, been adopted and developed from the buildings to which, as heathen, they have been accustomed. In the new instalment of his work on the "Cities and Bishoprics of Phrygia," just published, Professor W. M. Ramsay states that the evidence of the epitaphs goes to show that the new faith had so fully blended with the old there, that the distinction between Christian and pagan tombs is recognised only by some variation of the symbol or the name. It was precisely so in Ireland. In cemeteries connected with the earliest Irish monasteries graves after the pagan model are quite common. Cromlechs and cromlech-like tombs, as well as carns surrounded by circular walls, have been found in churchyards. In a graveyard beside an ancient church at St. John's Point, in County Down,

Pre-Christian architecture.

and in other places, cists are found arranged in a circle after the pagan method, the feet of the skeletons pointing to the centre. Ecclesiastical buildings in like manner follow the models with which, before becoming Christians, the Irish were familiar. "Within the stone fort, now become Christian," says Miss Margaret Stokes, "or the cashel built in imitation of it, the first Christians found shelter for their little oratories, their round beehive huts, their wells, gardens, and *leachta*, or burial-grounds—or *leaba-na-marabham*, beds of the dead, as they are called, where the practice of the primitive Irish Church was a transition from the primitive pagan practice of raising a circle of upright stones, for they enclosed a green oblong space with pillar-stones set close together, each stone of the enclosure being marked with a cross. The oratories of this period, and within these cashels, are angular, oblong structures, with walls either sloping in a curve towards the roof, or built in steps, and often formed like up-turned boats. They measure on an average 14 feet by 9 feet wide and 12 feet high."[1] A few words on the primitive and pre-Christian architecture of Ireland must, therefore, here be added.

Cromlechs. The structures which reach back to the most remote antiquity are the megalithic monuments called *cromlechs* or *dolmens*. The cromlech consists of an immense slab or roof-stone, varying from twelve to thirty feet in length, of considerable breadth and thickness also, and of an average weight of 110 tons, resting on three or more upright blocks of stone, and usually surrounded by a circle or circles

[1] "Early Christian Art in Ireland," by Margaret Stokes, Part ii. p. 38.

of upright stones from 150 to 160 feet in diameter. There seems no room to doubt that they were erected as sepulchral monuments, and doubtless to the memory of distinguished chiefs. Underneath all the cromlechs that have been examined human bones have been found, with stone hatchets, flint arrowheads, sling-stones, and rings of shale and jet; and under some cinerary urns have been found. We have just seen that imitations of cromlechs occur in Christian burying-grounds, confirming the conclusion that their object was such as has been stated. There is evidence that the builders of the cromlechs were acquainted with the use of fire for cooking food and for making pottery, and that they grew cereals and kept domestic animals, so that a certain degree of civilisation had been attained by them. On the other hand, there is no trace in them of sculpture or of ornament. It is doubtful if any metal has been found in a cromlech.

The *cist, cistvaen,* or stone chest—a rectangular Cista. chamber formed by four or more slabs, with rudely flagged floor, roofed with flat stones, and sometimes having the sides formed by similar stones, and containing cinerary *fictilia*—seems to mark a somewhat more advanced stage in the development of the cromlech. Weapons and ornaments of bronze have been discovered in them, proving them to be of later date than the cromlechs.

The covering of chambers and cists with *carns* Tumuli. or *tumuli,* mounds of either stone or earth, seems to mark a still later stage in the development. Not only implements of stone, but beautifully formed weapons of bronze, and articles of iron, glass, and amber have been found in them. The word "carn" forms the whole or beginning of the names of three hundred townlands, and there are many others of which it forms the beginning or end. Each of these probably contained a carn, and so originated the name. In the Irish Annals the tumuli or dome-shaped tombs or mounds are described as royal cemeteries. The most remarkable are those of New Grange, Dowth, and Knowth on the banks of the Boyne, and the locality where they stand is called *Brugh-na-Boyne*, which means "the dwelling-place of the Boyne." There are some twenty mounds altogether in this immediate vicinity, besides raths, caves, circles, and pillar-stones, and the most famous are those just named. New Grange stands on two acres, and Knowth on about an acre of ground. The writer has visited these wonderful monuments, and explored the still more interesting chambers in their interior. That of New Grange is a large dome-shaped chamber formed of great blocks of stone, the roof at the centre, which is the highest point, being about twenty feet from the floor, with three recesses opening off it, and entered by a narrow passage, barely permitting a man to creep in on hands and knees at the entrance, but soon rising to a height of six feet, and sixty-three feet in length from the out-side to the centre of the chamber. Carved on the faces of the slabs which form the walls of the chamber are scribings of cups, circles, concentric circles, spirals, half-moons, zigzags, lozenges, rhomboids, dots, and stars. From the fact that iron has been found in these tumuli in juxtaposition with gold ornaments and Roman coins, and from other circumstances, their date has been assigned to the period between the first century and the third.

The earliest buildings of a non-sepulchral char- Duns and beehive stone huts. acter have been assigned by the best authorities to the period between 200 B.C. and the opening of the Christian era. On the western shores of.Kerry, Clare, Galway, Sligo, and also in Mayo, Donegal, and Antrim, great stone forts or duns have been found. These duns or fortresses are amphitheatres encircled by outer walls. The walls, which are in many cases eighteen feet in thickness, are built without mortar, of masses of stone, varying in size, but sometimes of great magnitude, and undressed by tools, yet closely fitting and compacted and admirably constructed, the centre of the wall being composed of rubble. In the walls themselves are passages and chambers, and inside the dun in some cases are little stone huts of beehive shape or long-roofed, like boats upturned. The principle of the arch was still unknown to the builders when they were erected. They are supposed to belong to the legendary heroic period before the introduction of Christianity into Ireland, and are associated with Ængus, Conor, Muirbhech Mil, Fergus, and Cuchullin. They continued in use, however, after the introduction of Christianity, and were, in fact, often given by kings or chiefs for Christian purposes. Conall Gulban, brother of King Laoghaire, for example, gave his dun at Tailtenn to St. Patrick. The fortress of Dun Lughaidh was similarly given to him. The cathair or stone fortress of Aodh Finn, the son of Feargna, King of Breffny, was put at the service of St. Caillin for his monastery, and the Dun of Muirbhech Mil, in the island of Arran, is to this day occupied by the beehive-shaped cells of the early monks.

Raths or forts.

Ramparts of earth, called *raths* or *forts*, are still very numerous in Ireland. It is calculated that there are not less than 40,000 of them still existing in the country. Some have a single "ring" or rampart, some two, and some three. The space of ground enclosed within the rampart varies from a rood to five acres. The raths are often popularly spoken of as Danish, but they existed in Ireland many centuries before the Danes were heard of. They continued to be built, however, till the twelfth or thirteenth century. They were, in fact, erected for shelter and protection, the residences of the owners being inside them. These latter were usually made of wood or wattles. The smaller forts with a single rampart appear to have belonged to the wealthier members of the community, and afforded shelter both for their own dwellings and for their flocks and herds: the larger ones, with two or three circumvallations, belonged to the flaiths or chiefs. The

Cathairs.

cashels or *cathairs* differed from the raths in being constructed of stone. Where water was available, the surrounding fosse or ditch was flooded with it. Hence the term *lis*. There are twenty-eight townlands called Lissanisky or Lissaniska, which means "the fort of water." A king's residence needed to be a dun, and was required by law to have three

Wooden and wattled houses of beehive pattern.

concentric ramparts. Beside the duns or royal dwellings were usually grouped the wooden or wattled houses of their retainers or dependants. The houses were almost all round-shaped, after the beehive pattern. Posts were driven into the ground, and the spaces between the posts filled with woven wattles or wicker-work, stanched and plastered with clay, and covered over with a conical roof of thatch

36

of some sort. After the introduction of Christianity, the churches, like the dwellings of the people, were also made of wood and wattles, although from the earliest times there were instances of stone churches, oblong in shape and very small and rude of construction. I shall have occasion to note the origin and use of the Round Towers when I come to speak of the Danes.

To the same period as the "duns" and "raths" Souterrains. belong the *souterrains*, or subterranean houses, or passages and chambers which most of the raths and cathairs have underneath their interior area, the chambers being generally after the beehive pattern, with, in some cases, ventilating shafts. In some instances the chambers are very large. They were evidently intended as keeps for storing treasures and things of value in, and where the residents of the raths might take refuge in case of sudden attack. At a place called Dysart, near Mullingar, what has been called a subterranean village of ten beehive-shaped chambers, with connecting galleries, has been exposed to view by the removal of the surrounding rath and superincumbent earth. These souterrains contain no traces of Christianity, and evidently belonged to the pre-Christian period. Inscriptions in the Ogham character have been found on the walls of many of them, a form of writing which seems to have continued to the period of transition from paganism to Christianity.[1] The souterrains

[1] Ogham characters consist of groups of incised lines and dots along a stem-line, which stem-line was in many cases the angle of a stone. The consonants are formed by lines of from three to five inches long when above or below the line, or from four to seven inches when across it. The vowels are formed by strong, oval, or round dots on the angle or stem.

were indeed known both to the Christians and to the Danish invaders of Ireland. In the Irish Annals we read that in the year 866 Leinster and Munster were plundered by the Danes, and that "they left not a cave there underground that they did not explore . . . neither was there in concealment underground in Erinn . . . anything that was not discovered by these wonderful Denmarkians."

Crannogs.   Still more remarkable was another sort of structure, which was very common in Ireland in primitive times, though not confined to this country. A considerable portion of the population resided in dwellings situated on islands artificially constructed in lakes. Between two and three hundred such island-dwellings have been discovered, and these are believed to be but a small proportion of what at one time existed. It is certain that many of these belong to a very remote antiquity, but many continued to be used till comparatively recent times. Their Irish designation is " crannog," from "crann," a tree or timber,¹ because trees were so much used in their construction. Much ingenuity and toil must have been expended in the making of them. Posts or stakes were driven into the bottom of the lake so as to form a circle of from fifty to eighty feet in diameter, the stakes being of such a length that they stood up out of the water, and formed a sort of stockade which at once sheltered and defended the island. They were secured to each other and made fast by means of horizontal beams. The space within the circle was then filled up with trunks and branches of trees, stones, gravel, and earth, the whole being stayed and strengthened by piles. Over this was laid a layer of beams similarly

secured, and over it again stones and gravel; and
on this, when high enough above the water, the
dwelling was erected, slabs of stone being laid down
for the hearth. There is clear evidence of the
existence of these lake-dwellings at a very remote
period, but also that their use has continued far
into historic times. Implements of stone, bronze,
and iron have been found in them, and several
have been discovered buried at the bottom of deep
bogs, which have grown over them since they were
made. In the Bog of Drumkelin, in County
Donegal, one of the most complete of such structures of this character has been discovered, with a
dwelling twelve feet in length and width and nine
feet in height, made of split logs of oak, and with
half-burnt peat, charred wood, and ashes on the
hearth. The apartment was divided into two
storeys. Its great antiquity appears not only in
the implements of flint, stone, and wood that have
been found in it, but in the fact that thirty or
forty feet of bog had grown up around it since it
was constructed.

But perhaps the most singular of primitive Irish Sweat-
structures is the *Teach-an-alais*, or " sweat-house," houses.
in which the Irish were accustomed to have what
we now call a "Turkish bath." The "sweat-house"
was usually beehive in form, about six feet wide and
six feet high, with a low entrance, resembling the
stone huts that still remain in cashels. It was filled
with peat which was set on fire and burned. When
the ashes were removed and the chamber had cooled
a little, the floor was covered with rushes, and the
person desiring the bath entered, and the door was
closed. It seems to have been usually placed near

a pool of clear water, wherein the bather could cool himself by means of a plunge-bath. It was often had recourse to as a cure for rheumatism as well as enjoyed as a luxury.

Transition. It was between the sixth and eighth centuries that the transition took place from undressed stones built without mortar to dressed and chiselled stones built with mortar, which consisted of shells and sea-sand or of mud and gravel. The mortar in a liquid state was at first poured on the top of the wall, whence it filtered downwards, but in the course of the tenth century the stones begin to be laid in a bed of mortar.

Aspect of country: covered with forests. Very different too was the general aspect of the country in the pre-Christian times to which I refer from what it is to-day. It should be remembered that a large proportion of it was covered with dense forests, in which oak predominated, and where wild boars and wolves and other wild beasts roamed. It was the vast extent of its forests which in early times gained for Ireland the name of *Inis-na-Beeva*, or Island of the Woods. It may be inferred that hunt-

Agricul- ing was common, but the arts of agriculture had ture. made some progress. Water-mills existed from a very early period : they are said to have been introduced by Cormac MacArt in the third century. There appears to have been one in connection with each *ballybetagh*, or ancient townland, owned by a number of the inhabitants in common. The Brehon Code has special laws with regard to them. In almost every house too there was a *quern*, or hand-mill for grinding corn, in the use of which the female members of the household were expert. And as to roads, they were both better and more numerous than any one would imagine. There were five main roads, leading in various directions over the country from Tara, and numerous roads of minor importance, but each known by a distinctive name, are referred to in the Irish Annals. The Brehon laws provide for keeping them in repair.

But the religion of pre-Christian Ireland now de- The religion mands some brief notice.

The religion of the ancient Irish was Druidical, but the popular idea of that form of heathen religion is quite erroneous. It included belief in the immortality of the soul and in the doctrine of a day of judgment — doctrines doubtless which, along with others, made them more ready to accept of Christianity. As the Scandinavian had his Walhalla, so the Irishman had an Elysium of his own, and curiously enough the pig was as conspicuous in the Irishman's Elysium as he is to-day in the cabin of the Irish peasant! " There are three trees always bearing fruit; there is one pig there always alive, and another pig ready cooked, and there is a vessel full of excellent ale."[1]

The old metrical " Life of St. Patrick," ascribed to Fiacc of Sleibhte, says "the Tuatha (or people) adored the *Sidhe*." Who were the *Sidhe* thus described as the objects of the people's worship ? The *Sidhe* (as appears from the " Book of Armagh ") were supernatural beings, supposed to dwell in the earth, the sea, the rivers, in valleys and hills, in fountains, wells, and trees. Both they and the natural objects in which they were supposed to dwell were invoked and conciliated. The belief still survives in the popular superstition with regard to fairies, and in

[1] " Book of Leinster."

41

the virtue still ascribed to sacred trees and wells.
The supernatural beings were, in fact, the personified
powers of Nature, and belief in them was a sort of
fetishism which tenanted all natural objects with
malignant beings, to whose agency natural phenomena were attributed, and who were supposed to be
conciliated by the spells and incantations of a sacred
caste called Druada or Magi. The Banshee, of which
we still hear, is just the *bean-sidh* (pronounced *banshee*), or female sprite or fairy, the legends about
which in Irish story are legion. Mullaghshee, the
hill on which the church stands in Ballyshannon, is
the hill of the *sidh* (shee), or fairy palace. *Shane* is
another form of the same word, which occurs constantly in combination with the names of places, and
points out the places so named as supposed dwelling-
places of the fairies.

Patrick himself, near the close of his " Confession,"
refers to sun-worship. "For that sun which we see,
by command of God, arises daily on our account;
but he shall never reign, nor shall his splendour
continue; but all even that worship him, wretched
persons, shall come unhappily into punishment."
Connected with this perhaps were the primitive fire-
customs which we know obtained in Ireland. At
Tlachtga, in Meath, there was an annual fire-festival,
beginning on the eve of the 1st of November, and in
the fires then kindled the Druids were accustomed to
burn their sacrifices. On Beltane, or May-Day also
it was the custom to light bonfires. Such a festival
fire was about to be lit at Tara on Easter Eve, when
the fire lit by Patrick and his associates was seen
ablaze on the Hill of Slane, in violation of the law
that while the sacred fire was burning no other, on

pain of death, should be kindled throughout the country; and as a lighted brand from the sacred fire was employed to light all other fires, so still in remote districts if the fire goes out in the house of a peasant before the morning of the 1st of May, he is anxious to get a lighted turf from the priest's hearth to kindle it.

A great fair was held in May of each year in West-meath, and at that time it was usual to light fires all over Ireland, and to drive the cattle through them as a preservative against disease during the ensuing year. Some of these customs still continue. There was a pagan oath by the sun and moon, water and air, day and night, sea and land, an oath which was regarded as being peculiarly solemn, and for violating it King Laoghaire is said to have been "killed by the sun and wind, and by the other guarantees, for no one dared to dishonour them at the time."[1]

The great national idol, called *Crom Cruach*, over-laid with gold, stood on the plain called *Moy-Slecht* (or Plain of Adoration), in what is now known as the County of Cavan. It was surrounded by twelve lesser idols. It is stated in the "Book of Leinster" that the Irish people were accustomed to offer their children in sacrifice to this idol.

I should fail, however, to convey an adequate idea of the condition of Ireland on the arrival of its great Christian apostle if I did not intimate that there are traces of Christianity having in some degree found its way into the country before he came. Traces of Christian-ity before Patrick.

I have referred already to King Cormac MacArt,

1 "Book of the Dun Cow," p. 118.

Cormac
MacArt.

who flourished in the third century, and who was in some respects the greatest of the kings of Ireland. He was distinguished in many ways. The Annals tell us that in the year 222 "the large fleet of Cormac MacArt went over the sea for the space of three years," on an expedition to the British coasts. But his domestic reforms were more important than his attempts at foreign conquest. He established a Military College, a College of Law, and a College of Literature. The "Book of Ballymote" cites this statement from the "Book of Navan," which is no longer extant : "The monarch of Erin [the reference is to Cormac] appointed an army over the men of Erin; and over it he appointed three times fifty royal Fenian officers, for the purpose of enforcing his laws, and maintaining his sovereign rule, and preserving his game; and he gave the command of the whole and the high stewardship of Erin to Finn na Baiscné (that is, Finn MacCumhal)." This was none other than the famous Finn MacCumhal, the Fingal of Macpherson's "Ossian," and the subject of a vast collection of ancient bardic literature; and the army which he commanded was the *Feni* or *Fianna*, renowned in story, a sort of police or militia organised by King Cormac MacArt, and from whom the modern Fenians have, with singular incongruity and inappropriateness, derived their name. Their purpose seems to have been the preservation of internal order rather than to resist foreign invasion. Finn himself is represented not only as a warrior but as a poet, learned in bardic lore, and with a poet's insight into, and enjoyment of, the world of nature. Here is Mr. Standish O'Grady's version of Ossian's picture of him : "The music that Finn loved was that which

44

filled the heart with joy and gave light to the countenance, the music of the black bird of Letter Lee,
and the melody of the Dord Fian, the sound of the wind
in Droum-derg, the thunderstorm of Asseroe, the
cry of the hounds let loose through Glen Rah, with
their faces outward from the Suir, the Ton Rury
lashing the shore, the wash of water against the sides
of ships, the cry of Braan at Knock-an-Awr, the
murmur of streams at Slieve-Mish, and oh! the
blackbird of Derry Carn. I never heard, by my soul,
sound sweeter than that. Were I only beneath his
nest!"[1] Internal dissensions, however, broke out
among the Feni. Finn, who was Cormac's son-in-law,
with his militia, quarrelled with the king; the
people, on whom they were wont to be quartered
from November to May, were probably weary of them
also; the people sympathised with the king in his
effort to overthrow them, and they were finally
broken up and dispersed.

More enduring was the service done by Cormac in
the reorganisation and revision of the ancient laws,
already hinted at. The "Saltair of Tara," a manuscript no longer extant, is ascribed to him, and a
portion of the "Book of Aicill," which is part of one
of the Brehon law tracts. It is evident that the reign
of Cormac made a profound impression on the
national mind, both for its well-ordered rule and its
general beneficence. "The world was full of all
goodness in his time," says an old manuscript; "there
were fruit and fatness of the land, and abundant
produce of the sea, with peace and ease and happiness
in his time. There were no killings nor plunderings in

[1] Mr. Standish O'Grady's "History of Ireland," vol. i.
chap. xii.

his time, but every one occupied his lands in happiness."

His wise, firm, and kindly rule, and the reforms which he inaugurated, are the more noteworthy because there is good reason to believe that he had adopted the Christian faith. In his expeditions to Britain he was brought into contact with the British, by whom, or through some of the captives whom he carried away to Ireland, he was likely to have the Christian verities pressed on his attention. In whatever way it was brought about, it is practically certain that he came under Christian influences. In the "Annals of the Four Masters," under the year A.D. 266, we are informed that "forty years was Cormac the son of Art, the son of Conn, in the sovereignty of Ireland when he died at Cleiteach, the bone of a salmon sticking in his throat on account of Siabhradh (genii) which Maelgen the Druid incited against him, after Cormac had turned against the Druids on account of the adoration of God in preference to them. Wherefore a devil attacked him at the instigation of the Druids." The representation is that because he forsook Druidism and worshipped the true God, the Druids stirred up the evil spirits against him, and brought about his death in the manner recorded. It is also added in the "Annals" that he "told his people not to bury him at Brugh, because it was a cemetery of idolaters; for he did not worship the same God as any of those [i.e. the pagan kings] interred at Brugh; but to bury him at Ross-na-Righ, with his face to the east. He afterwards died, and his servants held a council, and came to the resolution of burying him at Brugh, the place where the kings of Tara, his predecessors,

were always buried. The body of the king was
thrice raised to be carried to Brugh, but the Boyne
swelled up thrice, so that they could not cross.
They afterwards dug his grave at Ross-na-Righ, as
he had ordered." In his "Lays of the Western
Gael" Sir Samuel Ferguson has celebrated this
occurrence in a picturesque and stirring poem, of
which one stanza may be given as a specimen :—

> "Crom Cruach, and his sub-gods twelve,
>   Said Cormac, are but lawen treene ;
> The axe that made them haft or helve
>   Had worthier of your worship been ;
> But He who made the tree to grow,
>   And hid in earth the iron stone,
> And made the man with mind to know
>   The axe's use, is God alone."

Again, the ruins of several primitive churches are
still to be seen in Ireland, some of them complete,
with walls sloping upwards till they meet, showing
that the principle of the arch was still unknown to
their builders. The late Dr. Petrie believed these
churches to have been the work of Christians earlier
than the time of Patrick.

With one attempt to evangelise Ireland prior to Mission of
the coming of Patrick history has made us familiar. Palladius.
Prosper of Aquitaine testifies in his "Chronicon"
that in A.D. 431 Palladius was "ordained Pope by
Celestine, and sent to the Scots believing in Christ
as their first bishop." It is known that in this year,
431, Prosper was in Rome on business connected
with the Church of Gaul, and had thus a special
opportunity of obtaining information with regard
to the mission of Palladius. In another work of his
—the *Contra Collatorem*—Prosper states that the

result of the mission of Palladius was to "make the barbarous island Christian." Here, however, Prosper has fallen into error, and set down to the credit of Palladius what was afterwards due to Patrick. The locality where the Irish records represent Palladius as landing in Ireland has been identified as the spot where the town of Wicklow now stands. The Scholiast on Fiacc's hymn affirms that before he left he "founded there some churches," but "was not well received by the people, and was forced to go round the coast of Ireland towards the north." The author of Colgan's second "Life of Patrick" gives the name of the hostile chief as Nathi, specifies the names of the three churches which Palladius founded, and adds that in one of them, whose name is mentioned, he (Palladius) deposited books and relics which the writer describes as existing "even to the present day." There are some curious coincidences between what is said of Patrick and what is recorded of Palladius, which seem to show that by some early writers the one has been confounded with the other. Thus it is remarkable that St. Patrick, on his first arrival as a missionary in Ireland, is described as landing in the same region in Wicklow, as meeting with a similarly unfavourable reception, as having been driven away by the same chief, Nathi, and compelled to betake himself to his coracles and to sail round the coast northwards. In the "Collections of Tirechan," again, we are told that Palladius "was by another name called Patricius." Nor is it less singular that the Roman authorities, such as Prosper and Bede, who record the mission of Palladius, never so much as mention that of Patrick; that precisely the same success is attributed to the

CHAP. II]   **RELIGION**

mission of Palladius by Prosper as the Irish Lives
assign to Patrick; that an ancient record quoted
by Ussher represents Palladius as having been, like
Patrick, a Briton; that while, according to Prosper,
Palladius was concerned in the mission of Germanus
to Britain to counteract the Pelagian heresy, the
Irish represent Patrick as concerned in it, and that
both Palladius and Patrick are, in different writings,
said to have brought the very same relics of the
Apostles from Rome. For these and other reasons
it has been supposed by some that Palladius is only
another name for Patrick. If that position is untenable, it is at least certain that some things which
properly belong to the one have got transferred to
the other.

However that may be, to the Patrick whom we
now always recognise by that name belongs the
indubitable honour of having been the true "apostle
of Ireland," the founder of the Church there, and, as
the Tripartite Life expresses it, "the father of the
baptism and the belief of the men of Erin." In
spite of occasional and isolated efforts, Ireland was
virtually unevangelised, Christianity practically unknown when he came: before he died, the gospel
was preached, multitudes were converted, ministers
in great numbers ordained, and churches built in all
parts of the country. The material was ready for a
skilful hand to work in. The bard had long been in
the land. Imaginations, already stirred by the tale
of heroic deeds, were ready to be moved by a tale
still more wonderful, and to be touched to sympathy
with a nobler, purer type of moral beauty than they
had yet dreamt of. The man destined and prepared
of God to awaken and enkindle that interest was

none other than St. Patrick, the story of whose heroic enterprise, even stripped of its legendary marvels, is intensely interesting—a veritable romance of history. That story I have to tell in the succeeding chapters.

PART II

THE COMING OF PATRICK

CHAPTER III

THE SOURCES FOR PATRICK'S HISTORY

I⊤ has been said that the best part of the history of a nation consists in the biography of its great men. " Universal history," says Carlyle, " the history of what man has accomplished in this world, is at bottom the history of the great men who have worked here. They were the leaders of men, these great ones; the modellers, patterns, and in a wide sense creators, of whatsoever the general mass of men contrived to do or to attain; all things that we see standing accomplished in the world are properly the outer material result, the practical realisation and embodiment of thoughts that dwelt in the great men sent into the world : the soul of the whole world's history, it may justly be considered, were the history of these. . . . Could we see *them* well, we should get some glimpses into the very marrow of the world's history."

Although Carlyle's way of putting the matter is characteristically exaggerated, there is a considerable amount of truth in the representation. There have been few nations or great national movements in which exceptionally great men have not had a paramount and controlling influence. We have only to recall the part played by Paul in the fortunes of primitive Christianity, or the work done by Luther in Germany, by Calvin at Geneva, or by Knox in Scotland at the time of the Reformation, to recognise the use which God makes of individual genius and energy in the furtherance of His kingdom. The introduction of Christianity into the different races and nations of Europe, and the organisation of the Churches planted by them, were in each case due primarily to some great and self-consecrated missionary. The predominant spirit and activities of the early Churches were concentrated in and promoted by devoted and distinguished leaders, aflame with Christian zeal and piety, and took mould and form at their hands. It was emphatically so in Ireland. Ulphilas is not more fittingly recognised as the apostle of the Goths, or Augustine of Saxon England, or Columba of the northern Picts and Scots, or Boniface of Germany, or Willibrord of Frisia, or Anskar of Sweden and Denmark, than Patrick is of Ireland. As we gaze back into the remote vistas of our country's religious past, his is one of the most conspicuous figures that meet the eye.

If any truth in this, it must be profitable to study the life of St. Patrick.

If it be true, as Carlyle says, that "great men, taken up in any way, are profitable company, that we cannot look, however imperfectly, upon a great man without gaining something from him," that "he is the living light-fountain which it is good and pleasant to be near," it cannot be otherwise than quickening and stimulating to us to keep company for a little while with St. Patrick.

But his existence called in question.

From the circumstance that Patrick is not mentioned by either Prosper or Bede, who notice the mission of Palladius, and for other reasons, the very existence of our apostle has indeed been called in

54

question. In his "Antiquities of Ireland" Ledwich long ago made a laborious attempt to show that he never existed except as a mythical personage, and the view advocated by Ledwich has been occasionally revived since his time. It may be well, therefore, to make sure that he actually existed before sketching his history. That the sceptical position taken by this writer and a few others is altogether untenable, that Patrick was a real person who left his mark deep in the history of Ireland, a brief statement will, I think, be sufficient to convince the unbiassed reader.

The argument from silence is of little value when writers have very obvious reasons for their silence. Thus, it is no matter of surprise that while Prosper of Aquitaine records in his Chronicle that "Palladius was ordained by Pope Celestine, and sent to the Scots (*i.e.* the Irish), believing in Christ as their first bishop," he says nothing of Patrick. Prosper was the panegyrist of Celestine and the chronicler of his doings. His silence with respect to Patrick is a good proof that the Irish apostle was not sent by Celestine, that Patrick's mission had no connection with Rome, and that the records that Prosper consulted at Rome had no reference to him: it is no proof that Patrick did not exist. To the advocate of the Roman mission, Prosper's silence is indeed a serious difficulty. But if, as we shall see by-and-by, Patrick's mission had no connection with Rome, why should Prosper be expected to refer to it? To expect this is to forget the purpose Prosper had in view in writing his Chronicle and the materials within his reach. As to Bede, he too was a strong supporter of the Roman obedience,

The argument from silence of little value.

and as such his strong antipathy to the Celtic Christians, who stood aloof from Rome, is constantly apparent. It is easy, therefore, to see why in his " Ecclesiastical History " he in a single brief sentence repeats the statement of Prosper with regard to Palladius having been sent by Pope Celestine, but omits reference to Patrick, who not only was not sent from Rome, but whose Church was at the time Bede wrote (he died in 735) in strong antagonism to Rome. But while Bede is thus reticent in his History, we have the means of knowing that he was well aware of the existence of Patrick, and of Patrick's position as the "apostle of Hibernia." In his *Martyrologium*, at "XVI. Kal. Apr.," he has these words: "In Scotia S. Patricii Confessoris;"[1] and in the Calendar in his *De Rerum Natura*, he has again at "XVI. Kal. Apr." the words: "Patricii episcopi et Apostoli Hiberniæ."[2] Even if Bede had been altogether silent, it would prove nothing in the circumstances. Just as contemporary Roman writers refer to Palladius but fail to mention Patrick, so the Irish Annalists, while abundant in their references to Patrick, are equally reticent with respect to Palladius. That Patrick *did* really exist will, I think, be apparent from the following considerations:—

That he did exist proved.

(1.) The evidence in favour of the genuineness of the "Confession" and "Epistle" attributed to him is so complete and overwhelming, that scholars generally—it may be even said universally—find it irresistible. That evidence will be placed before

[1] See Dr. Whitley Stokes' Introduction to the "Tripartite Life," p. cxx. Of course "Scotia" here means Ireland.
[2] "Tripartite Life," as before, vol. ii. p. 502.

56

the reader immediately. Now in the "Confession" and "Epistle" we have a detailed and circumstantial account of St. Patrick, his parentage, his early abode, his captivity, his escape from bondage, his wanderings, his return to his relatives, his call, and his work in Ireland, with such a picture of a modest, humble, shrewd, courageous and fearless, generous and energetic missionary, with strong passions under firm control, conscious of imperfect education, and writing in a rude and broken style, yet intensely sensitive to unjust charges, as bears the evidence of its own genuineness on the face of it.

(2.) We have the Hymn of Sechnall or Secundinus, Patrick's own nephew and disciple, also admitted to be genuine by careful and critical scholars generally. It contains a somewhat detailed account of Patrick in twenty-three stanzas of four lines each. The testimonies just mentioned are contemporary, belonging to the fifth century.

(3.) In the sixth century we have Columba's subscription to the "Book of Durrow" in which he appeals to the "holy presbyter Patrick:" "I pray thy blessedness, O holy presbyter Patrick, that whosoever shall hold this book in his hand may remember the writer, Columba, who have myself written this Gospel in the space of twelve days by the grace of our Lord."[1] Even supposing that the subscription was not written by Columba himself, it is traceable back to an early date.

(4.) We have Cummian's letter written to Segienus, Abbot of Iona, in the year 634, expressly referring to

[1] See Reeves's "Life of S. Columba," p. 242, note, and the Introduction to the "Tripartite Life," by Dr. Whitley Stokes, p. cxiv.

the example of "Sanctus Patricius, papa noster"
("holy Patrick, our pope").[1]

(5.) We have the record in the Luxeuil Calendar
(end of seventh century, according to Piper): "XVI.
Cal. Apr. Depositio S. Patricii episcopi."[2]

(6.) We have Muirchu's memoir of St. Patrick
in the "Book of Armagh," purporting to be
written at the dictation of Bishop Ædh, who died
in 698.

(7.) We have the Hymn of St. Cummine Fota,
assigned by Dr. Whitley Stokes to the seventh
century, and making special mention of Patrick.[3]

(8.) We have Adamnan's reference to Patrick in
his "Life of Columba," in which he describes Maucteus
as "*Sancti Patricii episcopi discipulus*" ("a disciple
of the holy bishop Patrick).[4] Adamnan died in
A.D. 704.

(9.) Again, in Fiacc's Hymn, in Ninnine's Prayer,
in the Liturgical tract, in Alcuin's Poem, in Bede's
"Martyrology" (already mentioned), in the Basel
Hymn on Brigit, and in the Catalogue of Saints, all
of them assigned by Dr. W. Stokes to the eighth
century, we have express references to Patrick. See
also the list of numerous Lives and documents
relating to Patrick which Stokes gives, belonging
to the succeeding centuries.[5] It is easy, of course,
for a mere special pleader or faddist to make out a
case more or less plausible for any theory, but we
cannot conceive how any one of fairly balanced mind,

[1] See Ussher's "Sylloge," Ep. xi.
[2] See "Tripartite Life," by Dr. W. Stokes, vol. ii. p. 493.
[3] "Tripartite Life," Introduction by Dr. W. Stokes, pp. cxv.,
cxxix.
[4] "Vita Sancti Columbæ," ed. Reeves, Dublin, 1857, p. 6.
[5] "Tripartite Life," p. cxxx. *et seq.*

and with a true apprecation of evidence, can, in the face of the evidence thus briefly summarised, and in view of the universal Irish tradition, and of the innumerable traces left by him in the country and in the history of the Church which he founded, deny that Patrick was a real historical personality.

For the story of Patrick's life we must depend primarily and chiefly on his own writings, described by the late Sir Samuel Ferguson as "the oldest documents in British history." These are his "Confession" and his "Epistle" to the Christian subjects of Coroticus, now universally admitted to be genuine; and to these may be added the well-known canticle or hymn attributed to him. Dr. Whitley Stokes has shown that Coroticus is identical with Coirthech regem Aloo, i.e. Coirthech, King of Ail or Ail-Cluade, "Rock of Clyde," of the "Book of Armagh," that he was King of Ail-Cluade or Dumbarton, that "he seems to have made a descent on Ireland, killed some neophytes on the day after their baptism, carried off prisoners to be sold as slaves, and derided the clerics whom Patrick had sent to implore that part of the plunder or some of the baptized captives might be restored." Dr. Whitley Stokes adds that "the statements of Professor G. T. Stokes ("Ireland and the Celtic Church," p. 28), that 'the Irish invaded the principality [of Wales] and conquered it,' that 'Coroticus organised his countrymen,' 'defeated the invaders, and pursued them across the Irish Sea,' are more imaginative than accurate."[1] "Tirechan seems to have had before him a work (now lost) entitled *Commemoratio Laborum*, which was ascribed

The original sources for his life: "the oldest documents in British history."

[1] "Tripartite Life," vol. i., Introduction, p. c., and vol. ii. p. 271.

to Patrick himself."[1] The evidence in favour of the authenticity of the " Confession " and the " Epistle " is so diversified and so strong as to be irresistible. Let me briefly summarise it.

(1.) Both the " Confession " and the " Epistle " quote from a Latin version of the Bible older than that of Jerome.

(2.) In his " Epistle " Patrick represents his father as a " decurio," or member of what has been called the " local town council "—a form of local government that obtained in towns and villages under the Empire, and that existed in Britain in the fourth century. When in A.D. 410 the Romans withdrew from Britain, the institution collapsed there. Had this " Epistle " been written later by a forger, he would have known nothing of such a form of local government.

(3.) The passage in the " Epistle " which says, " It is the custom of the Roman and Gallic Christians to send holy and suitable men to the Franks," " proves that it must have been written while the Franks were pagans, i.e. before A.D. 496, and before they had crossed the Rhine and settled in Gaul, i.e. before A.D. 428. On the other hand, the references to the apostate Picts point to a date after A.D. 412, when Ninian converted the southern section of that nation."[2]

(4.) In two different places in the " Confession " Patrick employs the plural form " the Britains." He says: " After a few years I was in the Britains (in Britanniis) with my parents;" and again, " I had been most willingly prepared to proceed to the Britains as to my country and parents." Now, in Patrick's early life Britain was divided into five

[1] Dr. Whitley Stokes, " Tripartite Life," p. xci.
[2] Ibid., vol. i. p. ci.

provinces — *Britannia Prima, Britannia Secunda, Britannia maxima Cæsariensis, Flavia Cæsariensis,* and *Valentia*—and was habitually designated by the plural form of the word, *Britanniæ,* just as Patrick here designates it. Of course, this method of describing it soon ceased. Here again we have a most striking note of genuineness.

(5.) Patrick's father and grandfather were clergymen, and yet were both married. This certainly would not have been suggested in a forgery at a time when the feeling had grown strong in favour of the celibacy of the clergy.

(6.) The whole spirit and tenour of the two documents leave on the reader the impression of simple, earnest truthfulness, and at the same time of rugged force, inconsistent with the hypothesis of a forgery. It is inconceivable that any one could have forged the picture of a rude, uncouth, uneducated, but simple and vigorous personality which these writings set before us.

(7.) The ungrammatical and barbarous Latin in which both these documents are written is exactly what we might expect from a missionary with such an early history as that of Patrick was.

(8.) While all the later Lives of Patrick abound in the thaumaturgical and the miraculous, the absence of this element from the "Confession" and the "Epistle" is conspicuous, and is another attestation to their trustworthiness.

(9.) The scribe who wrote the copy of the "Confession" in the "Book of Armagh" professes to have transcribed it into the "Book of Armagh" from the manuscript which was written by Patrick himself. "Thus far," he says, "the volume which Patrick

61

wrote with his own hand." He complains of its having been illegible and difficult. We mention this not because it is in itself convincing, for the credulity of those times was boundless, but as a fact of some interest.

The "Lorica," or "Deer's Cry." The hymn attributed to Patrick, and said to have been composed by him as a *Lorica*, or defensive armour on the occasion of his visit to the court of King Laoghaire, has also strong probability in its favour. It was known in early times as "the Deer's Cry," a title originated by the legend that Patrick and his eight companions escaped the evil designs of King Laoghaire by assuming the form of deer. Dr. Todd points out that "it is written in a very ancient dialect of the Irish Celtic," and that "it was evidently composed during the existence of pagan usages in the country. . . . Internal evidence is in favour of the antiquity and authenticity of this composition. The prayer which it contains for protection against 'women, smiths, and Druids,' together with the invocation of the power of the sky, the sun, fire, lightning, wind, and other created things, proves that, notwithstanding the undoubted piety and fervent Christian faith of the author, he had not yet fully shaken off all pagan prejudices. But this class of superstition lingered longer than any other in men's minds, and was with greater difficulty eradicated."[1]

Dr. Whitley Stokes, referring to this hymn, says: "Its references to the 'black laws of heathenism,' the 'craft of idolatry,' and 'the spells of women, smiths, and wizards,' obviously point to a time before Christianity had been fully established in Ireland."[2]

[1] Todd's "St. Patrick," p. 430.
[2] "Tripartite Life," vol. i., Introduction, p. ci.

Of the hymn itself Dr. Sigerson has said in a recent lecture : " The great devotional feeling of this hymn, its original power, vehement sincerity, and fine lyric rhythm, at once command attention. It was not his only essay in poetry. There are other shorter pieces in which he loves to bless each region of his adopted land. We cannot well overrate this desire for literary expression on the part of the apostle of Ireland. It must unquestionably have given an impulse in the same direction not only to his immediate disciples, but to all their successors for many centuries."

On these writings, then, with the Hymn of Secundinus, Patrick's nephew and disciple, we must mainly depend for information with regard to the Irish apostle. By these all later representations respecting him must be tested. Later Lives of him The later indeed we have in abundance: never was there a Patrick. Lives of better example of the "embarrassment of riches." But the very earliest of them was written nearly two centuries after Patrick's death, most of them several centuries later; all of them have been constructed in a most unhistorical spirit—a spirit of extreme credulity, embellished with the most absurd legends and miracles, and framed with a too obvious purpose of connecting Patrick's coming to Ireland with a mission from the Roman See. They have to be read with the utmost discrimination and caution. A brief summary of the most notable of them must here be given.

The two oldest Lives are those contained in the The two "Book of Armagh," which is deposited in Trinity Lives: their earliest College, Dublin. The earliest of the two is probably date. that by Muirchu Maccumatheni, which claims to have Muirchu's been written at the dictation of Ædh, Bishop of memoir.

63

Sleibhte (Sletty). Ædh died in 698. If the claim thus made for it is conceded, this memoir belongs to the end of the seventh century, and was composed more than two centuries after the death of Patrick. The other Life in the "Book of Armagh" is designated by Dr. Whitley Stokes the "Collections of Tirechan." They purport to have been written by Bishop Tirechan from the mouth or book (*ex ore vel libro*) of Bishop Ultan, who died in 657. If they were written about this date, they are still earlier than the memoir of Muirchu. But Dr. Reeves has given valid reasons for believing that they belong to a much later period. True, the manuscript of the "Book of Armagh" itself states that the Gospel of Matthew, which it contains, was finished in September 21, A.D. 807. Dr. Petrie, too, has affirmed that "there is no part of the manuscript older than the close of the seventh century, or perhaps than the eighth;"[1] and he has expressed the opinion that the "Collections" in the "Book of Armagh" with regard to the life of Patrick were written in the seventh century.[2] But, as Dr. Reeves has pointed out, "from the mention made by Tirechan of the removal of St. Columbkille's bones from Britain, compared with the 'Annals of Ulster,' 841, 877, it may be concluded that Tirechan's part of the work was not composed till near the close of the ninth century, and that the transcript in the 'Book of Armagh' is not earlier than the beginning of the tenth, being executed but a short time before 937, the year in which, according to the 'Four Masters,' the 'Canon Patraic,' or 'Book of Armagh,' was covered."[3] This reference in the

The Collections of Tirechan.

---

[1] "Round Towers," p. 330.   [2] "Essay on Tara," p. 107.
[3] Reeves's "Antiquities," p. 224.

" Collections of Tircchan " to an event which took place, according to the Annals, in 877, is fatal to the early date to which they have been commonly assigned, and shows, as Dr. Reeves indicates, that they cannot have been composed earlier than the close of the *ninth* century.

In addition to the two Lives just mentioned, Dr. John Colgan, a Franciscan of the seventeenth century, made a collection of seven Lives, which he published in 1647 in his *Trias Thaumaturga (i.e.* the Wonder-working Triad). The triad were Patrick, Brigit, and Columba.

The seven Lives in Colgan's *Trias Thauma-turga.*

(1.) The first of Colgan's " Seven Lives " is a bio-graphical hymn, which recites the principal events in the career of Patrick. It has been attributed to Fiacc, Bishop of Sleibhte (Sletty), who was a disciple of Patrick. It refers, however, to the desolation of Tara, and could not, therefore, have been written before the middle of the sixth century. Dr. Todd ascribes it to the ninth century ;[1] Dr. Whitley Stokes to the eighth.[2]

(2.) The second of Colgan's Lives is anonymous. It was written later than the " Book of Armagh," and belongs probably to the ninth or tenth century.

(3.) The third Life in Colgan's collection is also anonymous. It is largely taken from that of Probus, referred to below, and Probus wrote in the tenth or beginning of the eleventh century.

(4.) The fourth Life, which is anonymous, was written after the " Book of Armagh," and belongs to the ninth or tenth century.

(5.) The fifth Life is by Probus. It belongs to the tenth or eleventh century. It employs the term

---

[1] " Liber Hymnorum," Part ii. p. 287.   [2] " Tripartite," cxxx.

"Scotia" as a designation of North Britain, which itself shows that it cannot be earlier than the end of the tenth or the beginning of the eleventh century. It combines the two accounts given by Muirchu and Tirechan in the "Book of Armagh."

(6.) The sixth Life, by Jocelyn of Furness, was written between 1183 and 1185.

(7.) The seventh and last in Colgan's collection is the "Tripartite Life," which, according to Dr. Whitley Stokes, cannot be older than the tenth century.[1] The "Tripartite Life" is so called from the three parts into which it is divided. It is based on the Life of Patrick in the "Book of Armagh," but greatly enlarges on it, and, as indeed the Lives generally do, revels in the miraculous. Dr. Whitley Stokes's two volumes entitled "The Tripartite Life of Patrick, with other Documents relating to that Saint," published by the authority of the Government, and under the direction of the Master of the Rolls, is in itself a library of Patrician literature. It is a complete repertory of all documents bearing upon the life of Patrick, and one which no student of his history can afford to neglect.

Dr. Whitley Stokes's edition of the "Tripartite."

Dr. J. H. Todd's Memoir.

By far the most elaborate, critical, and scholarly modern Life is that by Dr. James Henthorn Todd, entitled "St. Patrick, Apostle of Ireland, a Memoir of his Life and Mission." But Dr. Todd's Memoir is not so much a biography as a very able and detailed criticism of the documents and materials available for his Life. Indeed, the criticism in Dr. Todd's work is out of all proportion to the bio-

[1] Dr. Whitley Stokes shows conclusively that the "Tripartite" was compiled in the eleventh century. See Introduction to "Tripartite," pp. lxii.–lxxxix.

66

graphical account of the Saint. It is like Falstaff's two gallons of sack to his one halfpenny-worth of bread. A well-written Life of Patrick, based on a critical and careful estimate of the material, but with the critical processes less obtrusive, is still a desideratum.

The chronology of Patrick's life is, at least in its details, somewhat difficult to determine. Dr. Whitley Stokes supposes him to have been born in 373, to have gone on his mission to Ireland in 397, and to have died in 463. When Patrick visited the royal court at Tara, we know that Laoghaire was the reigning over-king there, and that the period of his rule was A.D. 428–458. Taking this as the basis of calculation, Dr. Skene assigns Patrick's birth to the year 387 and his death to 461. Dr. Todd suggests a somewhat later series of dates for the Saint's career. Dr. Todd points out that the Irish Annals, which belong to the time of the Roman obedience, assume his mission by Pope Celestine in 432, and are compelled to arrange their chronology with reference to that date; whereas, he says, there are traces in the older documents of an earlier tradition and a different chronology, guided by which he supposes Patrick to have been born between the years 395 and 415, to have come on his mission to Ireland between 440 and 460, and to have died in 495. The reasons given by Dr. Todd for transferring Patrick's first visit to Tara to a time not far from the end of his life are to our mind far from convincing. On the whole, for many reasons which we cannot wait to mention here, we think the earlier dates for the chief events in Patrick's life the most feasible.

The chronology of Patrick's life.

CHAPTER IV

FROM PATRICK'S BIRTH TO HIS CALL

WITH the help of such material as I have indicated
a rapid sketch of the career of Patrick has now to
be attempted, and the most fitting words wherewith to begin our narrative are those with which he
himself opens his autobiography :—

"I, Patrick, a sinner, the rudest and the least of
all the faithful, and most contemptible to very many,
had Calpornius, a deacon, for my father, son of
Potitus, a presbyter, who dwelt in the village of
Bannavem Tabernæ, for he had a small farm close
to the place where I was taken captive. I was then
almost sixteen years of age. I did not know the
true God ; and was taken in captivity to Ireland
with many thousand men, in accordance with our
deserts, because we were living far from God, and
did not observe His commandments, and were dis-
obedient to our priests, who admonished us with
regard to our salvation."

It may be mentioned here that in quite a number
of the documents it is stated that Patrick had been
called by four different names—that his baptismal
name received from his parents was "Succat," that
the name given him when he was in bondage in Ireland was "Corthraige," that the name "Magonius"

68

was given him in Gaul when with Germanus, and that he was called Patricius at his ordination.

In the sentences just quoted from the "Confession" several points demand attention before we can proceed. The first question to be determined is, Where was this village of "Bannavem Tabernia," Birthplace. whence, Patrick tells us, he was carried captive? Some excellent writers, following the lead of the able Roman Catholic historian Dr. Lanigan, have identified it with Boulogne in Gaul, and much can be said on behalf of that identification. But the case made for it is, in our judgment, outweighed by other considerations. The theory that identifies "Bannavem Tabernia" with Boulogne requires us to assume that Bannavem is a mistaken reading for Bononia, Tabernia a mistake for Tarabenna, that Nemthur stands for Neustria, and that the plural "Britanniæ" is applicable to [that part of Gaul. We cannot but agree with Dr. Skene that it always raises a strong presumption against an argument when it begins by assuming violent emendations of the text of documents. In the present instance Patrick's own words seem to me quite decisive against any place in Gaul, and in favour of Britain as having been at least his native country. He says in his "Confession:" "Though I could wish to leave them (his converts in Ireland), and had been most willingly prepared to go to the Britains, as to my country and parents, and not that only, but even to go as far as to the Gauls, to visit the brethren, and to see the face of the saints of my Lord." He here clearly distinguishes "the Britains," which he calls his country and the home of his parents, from Gaul. In another place he

69

says : "Again, after a few years, I was in the Britains with my parents, who received me as a son, and earnestly besought me that now at least, after the many hardships I had endured, I would never leave them again." Now in the fourth century, as has been already pointed out, Britain was divided into five provinces—Britannia Prima, Britannia Secunda, Valentia, Maxima Cæsariensis, and Flavia Cæsariensis—and these were called *Britanniæ* in the plural. The plural designation employed by Patrick is thus historically accurate, can mean no other country than Britain, and as applied to it is a significant mark of genuineness, for shortly after this such a title would have been out of date and inappropriate. Dumbarton, with its great basaltic rock (Dun Bhreatuin[1]) rising up sheer two hundred feet and more from the banks of the Clyde, so familiar to travellers to Glasgow, was included in the Roman *Britanniæ*, standing as it did at the end of the great Roman wall built by Agricola. We see no reason, then, to doubt the testimony of the early writers, who place Bannavem Taberniæ in that neighbourhood, and the less so as we know that that was a centre of attack in the predatory expeditions made by the Scoti or Irish, and that a place called Kilpatrick still exists in the neighbourhood, where an ancient church was called after him, and which, as the present writer recently learned on the spot, a local tradition identifies as his birthplace. In the Hymn of Fiacc it is stated that Patrick was born at Nemthur, and the scholiast adds in the margin, that "that is a city which is in North Britain,

---

[1] Dumbarton = Dun Bhreatuin = fort or city of the Britons.

viz., Ailcluaide," or "Rock of Clyde," the ancient name of Dumbarton. The " Lebar Brecc " likewise seems to identify " Nemthor " with " Ail-Cluaide." Joceline (twelfth century) describes Nempthur as being in the valley of the Clyde, and as usually called by the people Dunbreaton, or *Mons Britonum*, the Hill of the Britons. A very old poem in the " Black Book of Caermarthen " speaks of the same place under the name of *Nevtur*, while Probus in his Life makes the place of Patrick's birth the village of Bannauc of the Taburnian region in the Roman province (*in Britanniis*).

There is evidence that a good deal of intercourse went on between Ireland and Britain during the Roman occupation of the latter. Roman coins of the period between the first century and the fifth have been found all round the Irish coast. In 1831 two hundred Roman coins were found at the Giant's Causeway belonging to the years between A.D. 70 and A.D. 160, and in 1854 two thousand such coins of the fourth and fifth centuries were discovered at Coleraine, some of them bearing the name " Patricius." How in the third century Cormac MacArt undertook expeditions against Britain, we have already seen. In the fourth century especially, when the Roman power was on the wane, sustained and determined attacks were made by the Irish on the British coasts. In the year 360, in conjunction with the Picts, Saxons, and Attacotti, they actually took possession of Britain, and held it for ten years under an Irish king called Crimthann. Suppose they had been able to hold it permanently, how different its future might have been ! How suggestive to

How Patrick came to be taken captive to Ireland.

71

think of England groaning for centuries under the oppressions of Irish kings, and pathetically pleading or desperately fighting for self-government! But Crimthann and his allies were expelled by the Roman general Theodosius in 369. The Roman power indeed did not long maintain its sway in Britain. Troubles nearer home—those barbarian invasions which by this time were approaching the very heart of the empire and threatening the Eternal City herself—compelled the withdrawal of the Roman legions, and left Britain open to those desperate raids of the Irish, in one of which our youthful hero, with many thousands besides, was carried away and consigned to a life of slavery in Ireland—that sea-girt island whose isolation had enabled it to escape the grip of the iron hand of the Cæsars, and to retain its native institutions in their primitive simplicity, untouched by Roman civilisation.

How Patrick's father and grandfather came to be Christian office-bearers.

The reader will have noticed in the sentences just quoted from the "Confession" that both Patrick's father and grandfather were not only Christians, but office-bearers in the Christian Church, and, as the mission of Augustine to the Anglo-Saxons did not begin till 597, two centuries later, may naturally ask how Calpornius and Potitus came by their Christianity, and how there came to be an organised Church at this time in Britain and in the neighbourhood of Dumbarton.

Let it be remembered that before the influx of Angles and Saxons, the inhabitants of Britain were Celts, whose religion before they became Christians was, just like that of their Irish kinsfolk, Druidical. It is not possible to fix the exact date of the introduction of Christianity into Britain. Its subjugation to the Romans was completed by Agricola towards the close of the first century, and it could hardly fail that individual members of the Roman legions occupying the country would be Christians, and would take the opportunity to make Christ known to those among whom they lived. It is now practically certain that Pomponia Græcina, the wife of Aulus Plautius, the conqueror of Britain under Claudius (A.D. 43–47), was a Christian. Tacitus mentions[1] that she was arraigned before the Senate for a "foreign superstition," a phrase employed by him, there is little doubt, to designate the Christian religion. In one of the catacombs at Rome, constructed in the first century, a sepulchral inscription has been found bearing the name of Pomponius Græcinus, while other neighbouring inscriptions record the names of members of the Pomponian gens, or of families allied to it. As Bishop Lightfoot, who discusses the matter with his wonted scholarship and moderation, says, "It is clear that this burial-place was constructed by some Christian lady of rank, probably before the close of the first century, for her fellow-religionists; and that among these fellow-religionists within a generation or two a descendant or near kinsman of Pomponia Græcina was buried."[2] As Bishop Lightfoot shows, there is little doubt of its having been made by Pomponia Græcina herself. In her, then, we see one example of an agency through which at a very early date the knowledge of Christ might have found its way into Britain. But the Britons were not dependent upon Roman Christians merely for acquaintance

[1] "Annals," Lib. xiii. cap. 32.
[2] "Apostolic Fathers," Part i., "Clement of Rome," vol. i. p. 31.

with the gospel. The first really trustworthy testimony we have on the subject is that of Tertullian, who, writing about the beginning of the
third century, states that "places in Britain not yet
visited by the Romans were subject to Christ."
Tertullian here implies that Christian truth had
reached them through other channels than Roman
Christians. Many indications make it probable that
it was to her kinsmen of the same race in Gaul that
Britain chiefly owed her knowledge of Christian
truth. Early British Christianity, just like early Irish
Christianity, differed in many of its usages from the
Roman type, and had close affinities with Eastern
Christianity, which had, we know, at an early period
in the second century, found a firm footing in Gaul.
There is hardly any room to doubt that from Gaul
it passed into Britain. From the time when both
Churches come into the clear light of history there is
abundant evidence of close intercourse between them.

It is remarkable indeed how little we know of
the history of the British Church under the Roman
dominion. "Perhaps no Church in the world has
left in the region which it once occupied so few
traces of its existence" (Cheetham). There is, however, ample proof of the existence of an organised
Church in Britain prior to the time of St. Patrick.
Gildas mentions St. Alban and other martyrs whom
it gave to the Diocletian persecution, although,
through the friendly attitude of Constantius, there
was no general or prolonged immolation of the Christians. Eusebius refers to it as having its churches.
It has been made probable that the British had
their own Latin translation of the Scriptures.[1]

[1] "Councils and Documents," by Haddan and Stubbs, i. 170 ff.

Jerome speaks of Christian pilgrims from Britain visiting the holy places in Palestine from the end of the fourth century. Three British bishops attended the Synod of Arles, in Gaul, in 314, and some were also present at the Council of Nicæa in 325. Pelagius, who gave his name to the heresy which he originated, and which gave such trouble to Augustine, Jerome, and others, was from Britain, his native name having been Morgan ; while his friend Celestius, whom Jerome in his truculent and abusive style described as " an Alpine cur reared on Scotch porridge," was an Irishman. It was not by Pelagius, however, but by the son of a Pelagian bishop from Gaul that the heresy was introduced into Britain, when Germanus of Auxerre and Lupus were sent from Gaul to oppose it. About the beginning of the fifth century the British Church had begun to evangelise the still pagan Picts of Galloway. Ninian, who at this time built the church and monastery called *Candida Casa* in Galloway, is described by Bede as " a holy man of the British nation." All this enables us to understand how it came to pass that both Patrick's father and grandfather were office-bearers in a British Church.

But it has been noted also that they were not only clergymen, but married men with families, and that Patrick mentions or implies this as a matter of course. In fact, the celibacy of the clergy was not insisted on in Ireland till long after Patrick's time. The canons of an Irish synod gave directions with respect to the dress of a clergyman's wife.[1] The Brehon Laws, revised as they were after the introduction of Christianity, constantly assume the marriage

Patrick's father and grandfather married clergymen.

[1] Haddan and Stubbs, voL ii. Part v. p. 328.

of the clergy. In the case of a bishop falling into sin, he may be restored to office by doing penance within three days if he is the husband of one wife; if unmarried, he cannot recover his position.[1] So that those in a state of matrimony had the advantage. This continued to be the law till the twelfth century, when the Irish Church was brought into conformity with the Roman. "Conn of the Poor," Bishop of Clonmacnois, was married,[2] and his father, grandfather, and great-grandfather, who were clergymen, were all married men.[3]

His father held a secular office. It is also interesting to observe that Patrick's father, though a clergyman, held a secular office. The fact that Calpornius held a farm, and was a *decurio* or local town-councillor, conflicts in no way with the usages of the time. On the contrary, it is certain that deacons, presbyters, and even bishops, continued in the early centuries to earn their bread by their own toil, as Paul did. We hear of them cultivating farms, keeping shops and banks, acting as physicians, shepherds, smiths, and artificers of all kinds. A record in the Cemetery of Callixtus, in the Roman Catacombs, describes Dionysius, the presbyter, as a physician. We read of one bishop who was a weaver at Maiuma, of another who tended sheep on the mountains of Cyprus, of another who practised in the courts of law, of one presbyter who was a silversmith, and of another who was an innkeeper at Ancyra.[4] Patrick's own sister's son, Lugnædon, though a presbyter, was a pilot; and

[1] "Senchus Mor," i. 55.
[2] "Chronicon Scotorum," Rolls ed., p. 209.
[3] "Annals of the Four Masters," 1022, 1031, 1056, 1079, 1103, 1128.
[4] See Hatch's "Bampton Lecture," p. 147 *et seq.*

of the presbyters who attended on the apostle, one was a smith and another a maker of book-satchels. Patrick often speaks of his poverty, and of his performing the functions of his calling gratuitously, like Paul. In early Christian literature we find no trace of the idea that the pursuit of a secular calling is incompatible with the office of the Christian ministry. Quite the contrary. When the Montanists proposed to pay a fixed salary to their clergy, the proposal was condemned as an innovation alien to Catholic usage. The withdrawal of the clergy from secular callings was part of the same movement that introduced enforced celibacy and monasticism. It was one of the higher tidemarks in the progress of sacerdotalism.

In the " Confession," as we now possess it, Patrick Patrick's makes no mention of his mother. But the author of mother. the fourth Life in Colgan's collection quotes the " Confession " as stating that his mother's name was Conches or Conchessa (which Todd thinks may represent the Latin *Concessa* or *Conquesta*). It is possible that an earlier copy of the " Confession " than any now extant may have contained the statement. This Conchessa is said to have been daughter of Ecbatius or Ochmus, a Frank. The scholiast on Fiacc's Hymn, Jocelin, and the " Tripartite Life " also speak of her as sister (the word may mean niece or relative) of St. Martin of Tours, but the testimonies are too late to carry much weight, and all the less because they are not unanimous. An ancient writing " On the mothers of the Saints of Ireland," attributed to Ængus, the Culdee (ninth century), gives Ondbahum or Gondbaum of the Britons as the name of Patrick's mother. Quite a number of the Lives also refer to the sisters and brothers of St. Patrick. The scholiast on Fiacc states that he had five sisters, namely, Lupait and Tigris, and Liamain or Limania, and Darerca and Cinnenum, and that he had a brother called Sannan. Limania is said to have married Restitutus, a Longobard, by whom she had seven sons, the eldest having been Secundinus, author of the hymn in praise of Patrick, and the youngest Lugna or Lugnaid. In these statements with regard to Patrick's sisters and their sons there is mixed up a vast deal which we know to be blundering and mistaken, and much that is quite fabulous. But they are not to be treated perhaps as entirely and purely legendary. The late Dr. Petrie discovered on the island of Inchaguile, in Loch Corrib, County Galway, a tombstone with an inscription in characters not later then the beginning of the sixth century, and in these words : " The stone of Lugnaed, son of Limania." It should be added, however, that Dr. Whitley Stokes gives a somewhat different reading.

I have spoken of the freebooting forays of the North of Ireland Scots upon North Britain in the fourth and fifth centuries, and of the evidence of this still extant in the Roman coins that have been found round the Irish coast. In one of those raids, Patrick informs us, he, with many thousands besides, was carried away captive to Ireland. He was nearly sixteen years old at the time, he says. It was probably about the year 390. Although his father was a Christian and an office-bearer in the Church, and he himself had been brought up in the knowledge of Christianity, his penitent admission is that he was living far from God and in disregard of His precepts.

He recognises his captivity as having been a Divine judgment for his sins, and a discipline to bring him to repentance. He was sold to a master called Miliuc, Milchu, or Milcho, son of Hua or Hy Buain, King of North Dalaradia, whose residence was at the foot of Slemish, in the valley of the Braid, a little beyond Broughshane, going from Ballymena, and only a few perches from the Presbyterian church of Buckna. The reader is to distinguish carefully between the ancient Dalaradia and Dalriada. Dalaradia or Dal-araidhe extended from Slemish or Sliebh Mis in County Antrim to Newry, in the south of Down, and took its name from Fiacha Araidhe, who was King of Ulster in 236. As a territorial designation, however, a considerable part of Down was not included in it, and the name by which this territory was known was the "Country of the Cruithne," or the " Picts."

Place of Patrick's captivity near Broughshane, in ancient Dalaradia.

Dalaradia.

On the road leading from the town of Antrim to Parkgate, half a mile or so from Dunadry, is a townland called Rathmore, which derives its name from a large ancient rath or circular entrenchment, locally known as "the Trench," measuring inside 138 feet in length and 108 feet at its narrowest part. It was formerly surrounded by a deep fosse, which is now almost filled up. It was in ancient times the residence of the chiefs of the Dalaradian Picts, and, from the frequent references to it in the Annals, was manifestly a place of great importance. Thus we hear of a great battle having been fought there between the army of Ecgfrid, King of Northumbria, under his general Berct, and the Irish, a battle in which Cumasgach, the chief of the Picts, was slain. In the " Annals of Innisfallen " it is related that in

79

THE COMING OF PATRICK [PART II

987 the celebrated Brian Boroimhe paid a visit to it, and carried away with him the hostages of Dalaradia. The "Annals of. Connaught" state that in 1315 "Edward, son of Robert Bruce, Earl of Carrick, came to Ireland [disembarking] in the land of Ulster, in the north, a fleet of 300 ships his number: so that the heroes of valour and fight of all Ireland in general, both Gall and Gael, shook and trembled. And he soon plundered the best part of Ulster; and *he burned Rathmore* of Moylinney and Dundalk." There was once a church at the place, for in the "Ecclesiastical Taxation of 1306," given by Dr. Reeves in the "Antiquities," "the church of Rathmore," as well as the tax imposed on it, are mentioned. Close by the rath is a garden, one of the fences of which is "a portion of a very ancient wall, which, judging from its position and masonry, appears to have been part of the north wall of a religious edifice." Colgan, in his *Trias Thaumaturga*, also mentions the church by name.

Dalriada. Dalriada (written briefly "Riada," "Reuta," "Ruta"—hence the modern "Route," in which the word still survives) is from *Dal*, which means "posterity," "descendants," and then "the territory occupied by descendants," and "Riada," the name of a chief. His full name was Cirbre Righfada or Riada, that is, "Cairbre the long-armed." He was son of Conaire II., King of Ireland, and flourished near the middle of the third century. His descendants and followers settled in, and gave their name to, the whole district, extending from the Ravel, the Cloughwater, and the Main River to the river Bann. The three rivers first named were the boundaries between Dalaradia and Dalriada. Many of the

80

descendants of Cairbre Riada passed over to Alba, and settled in what is now called Argyleshire, which became known as the Albanian Dalriada. It was they who also took with them from Ireland the name of "Scotia," which in due time they gave to the whole country. Slemish, at the foot of which Patrick was now to serve a captivity of some six years, was near the boundary between Dalaradia and Dalriada. The passage in which he gives an account of his captivity is exceedingly interesting :—

"After I had come to Ireland I was wont daily to feed cattle, and I prayed often during the day; the love of God and His fear increased more and more, and faith became stronger and the spirit was stirred ; so that in one day I said about one hundred prayers, and in the night nearly the same; so that I used even to remain in the woods and in the mountain (*i.e.* Slemish); before daylight I used to rise to prayer, through snow, through frost, through rain, and felt no harm ; nor was there any slothfulness in me, as I now perceive, because the spirit was then fervent within me. And there indeed one night, in my sleep, I heard a voice saying to me, 'Thou fastest well; thou shalt soon go to thy country.' And again, after a very short time, I heard a response saying to me, 'Behold, thy ship is ready.'"

(marginal note: How Patrick spent his captivity.)

"There," says Dr. Sigerson, referring to his sojourn in that region, "face to face with nature, in the silence of the hills, his character became strong and spiritualised." Several traces of him are still found in the locality, which I spent a pleasant day in exploring a couple of years ago. His name still survives in the name of a townland which is called

Ballyligpatrick, or "the town of Patrick's hollow."
The parish is called "Skerry" (*sciric* = "rocky")
from a basaltic hill, which was the site of its
ancient church. Tradition represents St. Patrick
as the founder of it, and the voice of tradition is
supported by some early records. The scholiast
on Fiacc's Hymn, already mentioned, and the "Tripartite Life" both refer to it. There are the ruins
of a larger and less ancient church; but close
beside them are the traces of a smaller building,
which the late Dr. Reeves regarded as answering
to the primitive one. Colgan, writing of it in
1647, calls it, or rather says it was called in his
time, *Skerry-Patrick*, and states that as a place of
pilgrimage it was frequented by a great concourse
of people. The site on which the residence of
Milchu stood is pointed out in a field near the
centre of the valley, and a few perches from Buckna
Presbyterian church. A little south of the hill of
Skerry, on the other side of the Glenarm road, is
Tubernacool "Holy Well," called by Colgan "*fons
miraculosus.*"

Ever after, Patrick seems to have regarded this
region with feelings of peculiar interest; and no
wonder. It was at once the place of his captivity
and of his emancipation—the spot where, like the
prodigal, he came to himself and said, "I will arise
and go unto my father." Here, too, during his
six years' bondage, he had a good opportunity of
seeing the condition of the Irish, learned to speak
their language—indeed, his native British tongue
was but another dialect of it—and, as both his
"Confession" and his life spent in their service
afford abundant proof, a deep and abiding sym-

pathy and pity for them were awakened in his soul.

Moved, as we have seen, by a voice which seemed to address him in vision while he slept, he fled to the sea-coast with a view of returning to his own country, and, after a journey of 200 miles, reached a port where he found a ship which, not without some demur of the captain, who was a pagan, took him on board. After three days' sailing they came to land—somewhere, probably, on the coast of Gaul, for he goes on to say, "After a few years I was in the Britains with my parents," implying that the country where he landed was *not* the Britains—and for twenty-eight days they journeyed through a desert, and he had abundant opportunity of displaying his faith in God and of proving the efficacy of prayer.

Having, "after a few years," reached Britain again, and been received by his parents as a son, they besought him that he would never leave them. He was a man of deeply affectionate nature, who evidently felt keenly the pain of separation from his relatives. But a crisis now arrived in his history when he heard the voice of duty irresistibly calling him away from home and friends; and Patrick never for a moment hesitated to prefer what was dutiful to what was agreeable when the two were in conflict. He was a man of simple, childlike faith, full of the primitive Christian spirit. His writings show him to have been in an exceptional degree familiar with the sacred writings, and imbued with their teaching; and as Scripture speaks much of visions and dreams, and of holy men of God having been much influenced thereby, so one cannot but be struck with the large place which they had in Patrick's life, and with the determining effect which they had upon him at critical moments in his career. Many in this dry, hard age would set such experiences down to superstition, but Patrick thought he heard in them the voice of God. Accordingly, while he was now staying with his parents—the "Tripartite Life" says he was in his thirtieth year—he beheld in a night vision a man coming as from Ireland, Victoricus by name, who handed him a letter containing the "voice of the Irish" inviting him to Ireland. He thought also that he heard the voice of those near the wood of Foclut, not far from the Western Sea—identified as a place near Killala, in County Mayo—saying, "We entreat thee, holy youth, that thou come and walk among us."

His call to the evangelisation of Ireland.

The question here arises, By what external authority, if by any except that of his Divine Master, did St. Patrick enter on his great enterprise? Roman Catholic writers allege that before he went to Ireland he repaired to Rome, and received his commission and episcopate directly from the Pope. The question is not one of any vital importance. No matter how it is decided, no one will change or should change his Church principles in consequence; and even though it did involve principles of the most vital moment, it is a matter to be determined solely in the light of the evidence available on the subject. Prejudice in favour of some particular Church cannot justify one-sided treatment of the evidence. The one question is, In what direction does the weight of the evidence point?

Did he receive his commission from the Pope?

There is one recognised rule with respect to An im-portant criterion of historical testimony. historical testimony which, in looking at this matter, it is necessary to carry with us. Sir George Cornewall Lewis, in his "Enquiry as to the Credibility of Early Roman History," says: "As all original witnesses must be contemporary with the events which they attest, it is a necessary condition for the credibility of a witness that he be a contemporary; though a contemporary witness is not necessarily a credible witness."[1] In his "Critical History of Early Christian Literature," Dr. Donaldson takes similar ground. He lays it down as a fundamental axiom that "the only proper historical evidence is contemporary." He says: "As we move away from the particular period into testimony of a later period, we must remember the marvellous proneness of human beings to mistake one thing for another, especially when they are under any influence which may blind them to the naked truth."[2] He might have noted also the tendency in an age of credulity for huge fables and legends to grow up around the simplest facts, and the habit, amounting almost to a law, by which tradition gradually substitutes what it thinks *ought to be* for what *was*. In the case before us, not only the contemporary evidence, but all the evidence we possess within the first two centuries and more from the date of his death points unanimously in one direction. The simplest and best course will be to take the witnesses as nearly as possible in chronological order.

1. First, then, both in chronological order and

[1] "Enquiry," &c., vol. i. p. 16.
[2] "Critical History," vol. i. p. 13.

Patrick's own testimony. in intrinsic value is the testimony of St. Patrick himself. What *he* has to say bearing on the question outweighs a cartload of testimony which dates some centuries later than his time, and which has a too manifest motive behind it. Observe, then, that Patrick's "Confession" is literally an *Apologia pro vita sua.* His chief object in writing it was to justify his action in entering on so great and holy an undertaking as the evangelisation of Ireland—to vindicate it in the face of detractors who were branding his coming as a piece of presumption. If the contention on behalf of a Papal commission is just, no vindication could have been so natural or so effective in the circumstances as that he had received his commission from the Pope, or from some representative of his. That, if the Roman advocates are right, should have silenced all gainsayers. Had he been sent by the Pope, or by some one in his name, he could not have failed to mention it. But he never so much as hints at it. On the contrary, he is careful to affirm that his mission was "from God" Himself, and he relates in detail the circumstances in which the Divine voice spake to him when he was in the Britains with his parents. "I testify in truth and in joy of heart, before God and His holy angels, that I never had any reason, except the gospel and its promises, for ever returning to that people from whom I escaped with difficulty." How could he have spoken thus had he been commissioned by the Pope? How could he have failed to refer to such a commission? The truth is, the independence of the early Irish Church with respect to Rome is one of the most indubitable facts of history—an

independence given up only after an intense struggle
which continued through centuries.

But what about the so-called " Irish Canon " So-called
"Irish
Canons."
attributed to Patrick, in which he is represented
as laying down the rule that " if any questions
arise in this island, let them be referred to the
Apostolic See ? " This " Canon of Patrick " occurs
in a collection of sayings, &c., gathered with great
want of accuracy from various sources by some compiler, and first published in 1874 by Wasserschleben
under the title *Irische Kanonensammlung*. The
compiler did not know the original sources from
which the extracts are taken, and in many cases
wrong authors are given. These " Irish Canons "
were compiled and produced at a time when, and
by a person or persons by whom, it was desired
to bring the Irish Church into conformity with
Rome. For example, one of the canons attributed
to Patrick is that " any cleric whose hair is not
tonsured after the Roman fashion ought to be
excommunicated." The introduction of the Celtic
tonsure from ear to ear into Ireland is ascribed to
the swineherd of Loigaire, son of Neil ! Now Bede
and other authorities make it quite certain that
this tonsure imputed to the swineherd of King
Laoghaire was universal in the Irish Church from
the time of Patrick, and that the Roman tonsure was
persistently opposed till the beginning of the eighth
century. Curious that this so-called Canon of St.
Patrick was so utterly set at nought for nearly three
centuries ! In the same collection there is another
Canon, also fathered upon Patrick, condemning ordination by a single bishop, although this is known
to have been the practice of the Irish Church all

87

along her history, and although so late as the twelfth century Anselm and Lanfranc feel called upon to denounce it as a still prevalent custom. The same remarks apply to the so-called Canon of Patrick, "that if any questions arise in this island, let them be referred to the Apostolic See." Many questions arose, like the two just mentioned, in which the Irish Church differed from the Roman; and they not only did not think of referring them to the "Apostolic See," they strongly resented and resisted its interference. These Canons imputed to Patrick are manifestly the handiwork of some friend or friends of the Roman obedience at a later age, whose desire it was to bring Ireland into line with Rome, and who astutely employed for this purpose the influence of Patrick's great name. As Dr. Whitley Stokes says, they are "certainly not older than the eighth century." But it may be replied that the same Canon appears in a more enlarged form in the "Book of Armagh." In the "Book of the Angel," contained in the "Book of Armagh," we have the following decree: "Whatsoever cause shall arise, very difficult and unknown to all the judges of the Scottish nations, it is rightly referred to the chair of the Archbishop of the Irish, that is, of Patrick, and to the examination of its prelate (*hujus antestitis*). But if by it with his wise men such a cause of the nature aforesaid cannot be healed, we have decreed that it be sent to the Apostolic See, that is, to the chair of the Apostle Peter, having authority in the city of Rome. These are those who have decreed concerning this, namely, Auxilius, Patricius, Secundinus, Benignus." Dr. Lanigan admits this to be simply an expansion of the Canon above referred to. Assuming, as it does, the existence of an episcopal hierarchy in the Irish Church, it evidently belongs to a much later age than that of Patrick. Both it and the others just noticed come manifestly from a Romanising source. Hadden and Stubbs refer it to the eighth century.[1]

Of the collection of Canons as a whole, Wasserschleben says: "The compilation of the collection must probably be placed at the end of the seventh or the beginning of the eighth century, at a time at which the Irish Church, after a long struggle, had become more closely related to Rome, and it is not improbable that the author of the collection had endeavoured by the same to secure and maintain as far as possible the acceptance of the national canon law, and the national recognition and approval of the canon and decree of the Roman Church."

2. The testimony of the next witness is of a negative sort, but nevertheless very weighty and significant. It is that of Prosper of Aquitaine, who died A.D. 433, and who, as we have seen, records under the year 431 that "Palladius was ordained by Pope Celestine, and sent to the Scots believing in Christ as their first bishop," but it is absolutely silent with regard to any mission of Patrick by Celestine. Now the significance of Prosper's silence arises, as has been already suggested, from the fact that he was the chronicler of Pope Celestine, and as such sets down everything he can in praise of him. If Celestine had really ordained and commissioned Patrick, Prosper would have known of it, and could not have failed to record

The testimony of Prosper.

---

[1] "Councils and Documents," vol. ii. Part ii. p. 332, note.

it, as, owing to the immensely greater results of Patrick's mission, it would have reflected very much more credit on his master than the sending of Palladius.

"Liber Pontifi-calis." 3. Not less significant is the fact that the writer of the Life of Celestine in the "Liber Pontificalis" is equally reticent with respect to any mission of our apostle by Pope Celestine.

Secundinus. 4. Sechnall, or Secundinus, was St. Patrick's nephew and disciple, as well as his successor at Armagh. The hymn of twenty-three stanzas in praise of his uncle is regarded by scholars generally as a genuine work of his. "The evidence for the antiquity of this hymn is strong," says Dr. Whitley Stokes.[1] Now this hymn of Secundinus refers expressly to Patrick's mission to Ireland, but, just like the Saint himself, attributes it exclusively to God, and never hints at a mission from Rome. It states that he "received from God the apostleship of the Church," that "God chose him to teach barbarous nations," that "God chose him to take care of His people," that "God for his merits advanced him to the high-priesthood," that "Christ elected him as His vicar in the land (*in terris*) of Ireland." Had Patrick been ordained and sent by the Pope, it is most unlikely that Secundinus in this hymn in praise of the apostle would have so utterly ignored it.

Muirchu. 5. The Life by Muirchu Maccumachtheni, preserved in the "Book of Armagh," claims to have been written about the close of the seventh century. The writer mentions that it was Patrick's intention to go to visit the Apostolic See at Rome, but

[1] "Tripartite Life," Introd. cii.

that, meeting with Germanus in Gaul, he went
no farther; that he had already set out on his
mission to Ireland without being raised to the
pontifical order, because Palladius, who had already
gone to Ireland, was a bishop; that, meeting with
certain disciples of Palladius at Ebmoria, who told
him of their master's death, he went out of his way
a little to Amathorex, by whom he was ordained
a bishop, and then went to Ireland without going
to Rome.   Here then the legend of a journey to
Rome and a commission from the Pope is expressly
contradicted.   It is true the narrative of Muirchu
is full of absurd errors and anachronisms and im-
possibilities; but that is true of all the later
Lives.

6. The hymn attributed to Fiacc, another disciple Fiacc's
of Patrick, has been shown by Dr. Todd to belong Hymn.
to a much later age, probably the ninth century.
Though biographical in character, it has no reference to Pope Celestine or a commission from him.
It represents Patrick as coming to Ireland through
the admonition of an angel, and of a voice in
which he seemed to hear the voices of the youths
of Ireland from the woods of Fochlut.   It is thus
an echo simply of what Patrick had stated in his
"Confession."

7. In fine, Bede, who wrote his History about Bede.
the year 731, although he is careful to relate how
Palladius was sent by Celestine, gives an account
also of Ninian, and was most diligent and pains-
taking in procuring facts for his History from the
Roman archives, never so much as mentions Patrick,
or hints that there was such a person.   Zealous
friend as he was of the Roman obedience, such

silence could not have been maintained by Bede had Patrick been sent from Rome or submitted to her jurisdiction.

Thus every particle of evidence we have from Patrick himself and his contemporaries, and for several centuries after him, is against the legend of a Roman mission. Let us now turn to the writers who affirm it.

A Roman mission first affirmed by "Tirechan's Collections."

(1.) The earliest testimony in favour of it is that contained in the " Collections of Tirechan " in the " Book of Armagh." The scribe asserts that Tirechan wrote these notes from the mouth or from the book of Bishop Ultan, who died in 656 or thereabout; but the reader has already seen that the " Collections " themselves are inconsistent with so early a date, and that the late Bishop Reeves for good reasons assigns their composition to the close of the ninth century, *more than four centuries after the death of Patrick*. The writer states that Laoghaire, who died in 463, reigned two or five years after the death of Patrick ; that Patrick was taken captive in his tenth year, served four years, studied thirty years, taught seventy-two years, and died at the age of one hundred and twenty. In four points he resembled Moses, one of them having been his age. Then he adds: " In the thirteenth year of Theodosius the Emperor, Patricius the bishop was sent by Bishop Celestine, Pope of Rome, for the instruction of the Irish, which Celestine was the forty-second bishop of the Apostolical See of the city of Rome after Peter. Palladius the bishop was the first sent, who is otherwise called Patricius, and suffered martyrdom among the Scots, as the ancient saints relate. Then the second Patricius was sent by an angel of God named Victor, and by Pope Celestine, by whose means all Ireland believed, and who baptized almost all the inhabitants." Writing more than four centuries after Patrick's death, at a time when the Irish Church had come into touch with Rome, and when it was felt to be most desirable to connect its great founder and apostle with Rome, the author of these " Notes " transfers to Patrick the statement he found applied to Palladius, that he was sent by Celestine. It is impossible to attach the slightest historical value to an assertion which comes so late and in such circumstances.

(2.) This statement in Tirechan's " Collections " The statement in Tirechan repeated by later writers. that Patrick was sent by Celestine is of course repeated in the subsequent Lives, as, for example, in Colgan's " Fourth Life," which is certainly later than the " Book of Armagh," and which Dr. Todd assigns to the ninth or tenth century. In like manner, the life by Marcus the Anchorite, annexed to Nennius's " History of the Britons," shows acquaintance with the Lives in the " Book of Armagh," and, following Tirechan's " Collections," takes Patrick to Rome, where it says he " remained a long time studying the sacred mysteries of God." It mixes up in the most impossible manner the statements of Muirchu and Tirechan, adding that Patrick was for eighty-five years "apostle of the Irish." Similarly Probus in the tenth century reproduces the account of Muirchu, adding to it that of Tirechan with respect to the Roman mission, but, seeing the inconsistency of the two versions, represents Patrick as in the first instance coming to Ireland without a commission from

93

Rome, and as, after he had laboured for thirty years to no purpose, at length going to Rome and obtaining the sanction of the Pope, and then returning to Ireland and speedily converting the whole nation. The chronological impossibility of Patrick being thus commissioned by Celestine does not appear to have given any concern to this biographer. The " Third Life " of Colgan is taken from Probus, and was later than the tenth century. The account in Tirechan's " Collections " is also reproduced in *Marianus Scotus* (died 1084), as well as in the later Irish Annals. The " Tripartite Life," which its editor, Dr. Whitley Stokes, after an elaborate examination of its statements and vocabulary, demonstrates was compiled in the eleventh century, likewise combines the two records thus : " Patrick went to Rome to have orders given him, and Celestine, Abbot of Rome, he it is that read orders over him, Germanus and Amatho, King of the Romans, being present with them. . . . And when the orders were being read the three choirs mutually responded, namely, the choir of the household of heaven, and the choir of the Romans, and the choir of the children from the wood of Fochlut in Ireland. This is what they all sang : ' All we Irish beseech thee, holy Patrick, to come and walk among us and free us.' " [1] An extraordinary choral union truly! Observe, the writer of the " Tripartite " brings Germanus, the Bishop of Auxerre, to Rome, and Amathorex, who is represented by Muirchu as a bishop of Gaul, and who is generally identified with Amator, who was Bishop of Auxerre before Germanus, and had

[1] " Tripartite Life," pp. 32, 33.

died before Germanus succeeded, is also brought to Rome along with Germanus by the "Tripartite," which, misled by the termination "*rex*," describes him as "King of the Romans!" The Life by Jocelyn was compiled in 1185, and of course follows its predecessors.

This simple chronological record of the testimony relating to a Roman mission is quite sufficient to discredit it in the eyes of any unprejudiced inquirer accustomed to test and weigh historical testimony in a scientific spirit. Coming so late, traceable to a common source, and originating at a time when it was felt to be desirable to show that the early Irish Church had a connection with Rome, the testimony in favour of a mission from Rome is altogether outweighed by the earlier testimony. Professor Zimmer connects the genesis of the legend of a Roman mission with the labours of Adamnan, at the close of the seventh century, to introduce the Roman mode of celebrating Easter, which the Irish Church so long and so strenuously opposed. He thinks that Adamnan sought to connect Ireland with Rome through St. Patrick.[1]

The "Tripartite" and other Lives allege that after his call by God, and before setting out to Ireland, Patrick spent some thirty years in Gaul or on the Continent under the instruction of certain distinguished teachers, such as Germanus and Martin of Tours. But this is quite inconsistent with what he himself says at the close of his life about his ignorance, rusticity, and rudeness, and his lack of the means of education. He describes himself as "now in his old age, striving after what he did

Alleged thirty years' stay on the Continent.

Inconsistent with other facts.

[1] "Keltische Studien," vol. ii. p. 183.

not learn in his youth, and as blushing for his
ignorance and unskilfulness." And what he says
is abundantly confirmed by the rude and ungrammatical character of his writings. How could he
have exhibited such rudeness, and so pathetically
deplored his lack of means and opportunity of
removing it, if he had enjoyed for so many years
a course of training in the best and most famous
schools of the Continent?

Such a delay of thirty years on the part of one
so moved by compassion for the Irish, so much
aflame with missionary zeal as Patrick evidently
was, is indeed inconceivable. We learn, in fact,
from several intimations in his writings that he
was still a young man when he came to Ireland as
its missionary. "You know," he says to the Irish,
"how I have conducted myself among you *from
my youth, both in the faith of the truth and in
sincerity of heart.*" He speaks of a certain holy
presbyter, sent by him on an important embassage,
"whom he taught from his infancy," showing that
at the time when he wrote he must have been
some thirty or forty years in Ireland, and that
therefore he must have been a comparatively young
man when he came.

Uncertain
by whom
ordained.
As to the person or persons by whom he was
ordained there is complete uncertainty. Germanus,
Amathorex, Martin of Tours, and others have severally, in different Lives and documents, got credit
for it; but when the date and real character of
the testimony are examined, it is found to be worthless. The testimony comes so late, and is so conflicting and self-contradictory, as to be valueless.
The conflict of testimony reflects the complete

uncertainty that existed on the subject. He himself
does not give us the slightest hint on the matter,
except that his "Confession" leaves the impression
that it was neither in Gaul nor in Rome, but in the
Britains that he was ordained to the episcopate. In
these circumstances, to assert, as some do very positively, that Patrick's succession can be traced back
by sure and certain steps to the Apostles, is to
betray a singular want of appreciation of the nature
of valid historical testimony.

Patrick mentions that, when he was about to be
designated to the episcopate, a sin which he had
committed in boyhood, and which, long before—
apparently when he was going to be made a deacon
—he had confessed to an intimate friend, was brought
against him by the friend to whom he had confessed
it, so that opposition arose to his being made
a bishop. "After thirty years they found me, and
brought against me a word which I had confessed
before I was a deacon." He states that, during the
night succeeding the day on which this reproach
was brought against him, he seemed in a night
vision to have a communication from God, express-
ing displeasure with the charge made against him,
and assuring him, "He that toucheth you toucheth
the apple of mine eye." "I grieve more for my
most valued friend," he adds, "to whom I intrusted
my life, that we should have deserved to listen to
such statements. And I learned from several brethren
before that defence (apparently the Divine defence
of him), that when I was not present nor in the
Britains, nor did it originate with me, that even he
in my absence contended for me. He himself said
to me with his own mouth, 'Behold, thou art to

Charge brought against him at his appointment to the episcopate.

be granted the dignity of a bishop,' of which I was not worthy. Wherefore then did it come to him afterward, that before all, good and bad, he should publicly dishonour me, although before, of his own accord, he joyfully granted that honour to me?" Now, when he says, "After thirty years they found me, and brought against me the word I had confessed before I was a deacon, and which I had, through perplexity and with a sorrowful mind, made known to my dearest friend, what I had done in my boyhood on one day, nay, in one hour, because I was not yet to overcome. I know not, God knows, if at that time I was fifteen years of age," the question arises, from what point of time are the thirty years to be reckoned? From the time of his commission of the sin? or from the time of his confession of it to his friend, a confession which appears to have been made when it was proposed to make him a deacon? It is difficult to determine which is intended. If the thirty years are to be counted from his fifteenth year, when he fell into the fault, thirty years added to the fifteen would make him forty-five years old when he was ordained a bishop. This, with the sixteen years of his age when he was carried captive, the six years of captivity, and say three years between his escape from slavery and his call to Ireland, would leave twenty years between his call and his being made a bishop. If, on the other hand, the thirty years are to be calculated from the date of the confession of his sin, and if that confession was made shortly before his appointment as deacon, let us see the earliest date at which that appointment could have occurred. He was sixteen years old when he was taken captive to Ireland; he was six years in captivity; allow three years for the "few" which came between his escape and his return to his parents when he received the call to Ireland, and seemed to hear the voice of the Irish crying, "We entreat thee, holy youth, that thou come and henceforth walk among us." When he adds, "After very many years the Lord granted to them according to their cry," are these "very many years" to be taken as including his years of missionary labour in Ireland, in which they had such an answer to their cry? This is perhaps more likely than that one so aflame with earnestness and zeal as from the moment of his call he evidently was, should delay for a long series of years before setting out on his mission. It is manifest, too, from what he says of his ignorance and rusticity, that he could not have spent a long series of years in study and preparation in schools on the Continent. If he means that "very many years" elapsed before he set out on his mission to Ireland, we cannot allow less than ten for what he describes as "very many years;" and perhaps ten years are hardly adequate, except that a few years would seem many and long to one so impatient as he must have been to enter on his work. He would in that case be thirty-five years old when he went on his evangelistic enterprise, and we should conceive of him as having been made a deacon before going. Indeed, his own words leave the impression that he laboured in Ireland for many years as a deacon, perhaps also as a presbyter, before he was made a bishop. Now, thirty years added to the thirty-five already counted would make him sixty-five years old when he became a bishop. There is nothing impossible in this. His going to Ireland at thirty-five might perhaps be reconcilable with his own statement, "You know, and God also, how I have conducted myself among you from my youth, both in the faith of the truth and in sincerity of heart." The impression made by the whole passage from which the foregoing sentences are taken is that it was in the Britains that Patrick received his appointment to the episcopate.

CHAPTER V

THE MISSIONARY CAREER OF PATRICK

WE can easily see by the spirit of the man as mani- How well fitted
fest in his writings, as well as by the result of his Patrick was
labours, how eminently fitted St. Patrick was for the for his mission.
work to which he now devoted his whole soul and
strength. His writings are indeed rude and broken
utterances, sometimes setting grammar at defiance ;
but, not unlike Cromwell's letters, they reveal a
strong and rugged personality, in presence of which
even princes and kings are subdued and awed, a
decision of character and an intrepidity and mag-
nanimity of spirit distinctive of great men, and these
set on fire by an intense ardour that no difficulties
or discouragements can cool, sustained by an indomitable courage that can look danger and death
in the face without flinching, throbbing with a tremu-
lous sympathy and yearning compassion for the
objects of his mission, chastened by a deep humility
and modesty, and baptized by a spirit of prayer, and
a trust in God that to a remarkable degree pervade
his whole life.

Setting out, then, in this spirit on his great mission Lands at Wicklow ;
to Ireland, St. Patrick appears to have landed first but, driven
on the coast of Wicklow, at the mouth of the river away, passes northwards
Vartry, but, as he was received inhospitably, his to County
stay there was brief. Sailing northwards round the Down.

coast, touching at an island off the Skerries, now
called, after him, Holmpatrick; calling also for a
short time at the mouth of the Boyne, he made his
way past Carlingford Bay, and, entering Strangford
Lough, he landed in the barony of Lecale, at the
mouth of a small river called Slany, about two miles
from the place now known as Saul. Here our
apostle and his companions were brought into the
presence of a chief called Dichu, descendant of an
ancient Irish king, who, taking them for pirates,
came out against them armed; but, soon discovering
his mistake, Dichu listened while Patrick preached,
and he and his whole family became Christians. He
gave Patrick a barn (*sabhall*) to be used as a church,
or, according to the more probable account, he gave
him ground on which to build a church, which, at
Dichu's request, was not turned from west to east,
but from north to south, and for some reason became
known as *Sabhall Padhrig* (Saul-Patrick) or Patrick's
Barn, and the place is known as Saul to this day.
It is about two miles from Downpatrick. This was the
first church founded by Patrick. It is remarkable,
however, that the same name, *sabhall*, was applied to
a church of similar construction at Armagh. The
late Bishop Reeves supposed that it was a technical
term for churches with some such peculiarity as
marked these two, also called *transverse* churches.

Returns to scene of early captivity. From Lecale our missionary passed to the scene of
his early captivity at Slemish; but if there is any
basis of truth in the legend, as doubtless there is,
his old master, Milchu, must have feared being overcome by some magical influence on his part, for,
according to the story, he set fire to his house and
perished in the ruins. To Dr. Whitley Stokes "it

seems to be an instance of *dharna* or of propitiatory
self-sacrifice." The true version of the incident has
probably got distorted in its transmission. It is certainly very unlike what one would expect from a
rough warlike Irish chieftain that, on seeing the
approach of his former slave, he should collect his
treasures and store them in his house, and then set
fire to it, leap into the flames, and perish in the
ruins. Whatever the truth may be, Patrick's visit
to that neighbourhood was far from fruitless.
Milchu's son, Guasacht, became a bishop at Granard ;
two daughters of his became consecrated virgins ;
and a grandson—son of a daughter of Milchu—a
young man called Mochay, became a bishop and
abbot also, and founded a monastery, including a
church, on Nendrum, in Strangford Lough, which
the late Bishop Reeves identified as Inis Mochaei or
Mahee Island, which to this day shows the remains
of a round tower, and of a cashel surrounding the
foundations of an old church. Mochay survived till
497. Another grandson of Milchu, called MacErc,
a brother of Mochay, became the founder and first
bishop of a church at Donaghmore in County Down,
near Newry.

Patrick soon returned to Maghinis, the region Comes back
near what we now call, after him, Downpatrick, where to Dichu:
his labours
he had won his first triumph, and whose chief, Dichu, in Down.
was so friendly, and remained there for some time
(*diebus multis*, the "Book of Armagh" says), preaching and spreading the faith, until, says the "Tripartite Life," "he brought all the Ulster men by the
net of the Gospel to the harbour of life." It is
significant and noteworthy that from the time of
our apostle churches, monasteries, and bishops were

very numerous in all that district about Strangford Lough, where he first landed and laboured,
and round Dundrum Bay towards the Mourne
Mountains. There was, at a comparatively early
date, a monastic establishment and a bishop at
Movilla, near Newtownards, another at Mahee Island,
another at Killinchy, another at Raholp, where he
first landed, three miles north-east of Downpatrick;
another at Downpatrick itself, which of course took
its modern name from Patrick; another at Bright,
two or three miles south-east of Downpatrick, and
another still at the foot, as well as one on the
summit, of Slieve Donard. One of Patrick's disciples
in that district was Domhanghart (Donart), son of
Eochy, who was king of Ulidia or Ultonia (Ulster)
in the time of our apostle. Domhanghart became a
bishop and abbot too, and founded two churches (or
monasteries rather), one at the place now known as
Maghera, not far from the foot of Slieve Donard.
Its original name was Rath-Muirbhuilg; sometimes
it was known simply as Rath, and then as Machaire-
Ratha (the plain of the fort), hence Maghera. The
name " Murlough," the modern form of Murbhuilg,
is applied to two townlands on Dundrum Bay. At
Maghera there still exist the ruins of an ancient
church and the stump of a round tower. The other
was built on or near the summit of Slieve Donard—
as Colgan has it, " in vertice ejusdem altissimi montis,
longe ab omni humana habitatione posita "—and was
still standing a century ago. Harris says: " On the
summit of this mountain are two rude edifices (if
they may be so termed), one being a huge heap of
stones piled up in a pyramidical figure, in which are
formed several cavities, wherein the devotees shelter

themselves in bad weather while they hear mass; and in the centre of this heap is a cave formed by broad flat stones, so disposed as to support each other without the help of cement. The other edifice is composed of many stones, so disposed in rude walls and partitions, called *chappels*, and perhaps was the oratory and cell erected by St. Domangard before hinted. Sir William Petty mentions in his maps a *chappel* on the north-east side of Slieve Donard, which he calls *Leniord's Chappel*; but, probably for want of due information, he has corrupted the name, and the true name of it is *Donard's Chappel*."[1] It was this Domhanghart (Donard) who gave its modern name to the mountain. The ancient name was Slieve Slainge, and it was so called from a bardic hero who was buried on its summit, the cairn raised over him being still a conspicuous object on the top of the mountain, and a goal for tourists. A name intermediate between the two was Beanna Boirche, which means "Boirche's Peaks." Boirche was a shepherd who used the surrounding summits as his points of outlook.

It should be noted that anchorite or monastic establishments were placed in the early time, not only on islands, but for the same reason on high mountain tops and on lofty sea-cliffs. Thus Slieve Gullion, Slieve Liag, and Brandon Mountain in Kerry are still crowned by the cashels and beehive cells of Æd and Brendan. But the most inaccessible and singular of the monasteries is that on the Skelligs, supposed to have been founded by Finan. "This rock rises perpendicularly out of

[1] Harris's "Down," p. 121.

THE COMING OF PATRICK [PART II

the sea to a great height. It stands twelve miles
from the nearest land out in the Atlantic Ocean,
and on a ledge or platform of the summit of one
shoulder the monastery was erected. It is approached from a landing-place on the north-east
side. There are still remaining six hundred steps
cut by the monks in the cliff, which rises to 720
feet above the level of the sea, the lower part of
this ascent being now broken away. The island
has been the scene of annual pilgrimages for many
centuries, and the service of the Way of the Cross
is still remembered here; different points and turn-
ings in the cliffs being named after the different
stations, such as the Garden of the Passion, Christ's
Saddle, the Stone of Pain, the Rock of Woman's
Wailing, &c. The plateau occupied by the monastic
buildings is about 180 feet in length, and from
80 to 100 feet in width. These buildings consist
of the Church of St. Michael, two smaller oratories,
and six cells or beehive dwelling-houses, two holy
wells and five *leachta* or burial-grounds, with many
rude stone crosses. They are all enclosed by a
cashel or wall running along the edge of the preci-
pice, which in its whole character strongly resembles
the wall of Staigue Fort on the mainland. 'It is
astonishing,' writes Lord Dunraven in his 'Notes
on Irish Architecture,' vol. i. p. 30, 'to conceive
the courage and skill of the builders of this fine
wall, placed as it is on the very edge of the preci-
pice, at a vast height above the sea, with no possible
standing ground outside the wall from which the
builders could have worked; yet the face is as
perfect as that of Staigue Fort, the interstices of
the greater stones filled in with smaller ones, all
106

fitted as compactly, and with as marvellous firmness and skill.'"[1]

The policy of St. Patrick all through his ministry was to approach in the first instance the kings and chiefs, and to endeavour to win them over to his side, knowing that, as a result of the tribal constitution, if they could be secured, the gain of their followers would be easy; but that, if they were hostile, an insuperable barrier would be put in the way of his missionary operations. It is sometimes made a reproach against the early Church that it had no martyrs. The assumption is not correct. Patrick's own life was repeatedly threatened, and in one case his charioteer was slain for himself. The Druids were deeply exasperated against him, and he was compelled to travel with an escort, and to surround the churches and monasteries built by him with ramparts or forts for self-defence. He speaks of having been delivered from twelve dangers by which his life was imperilled, and says he daily expected murder, or slavery, or mishap of some kind.[2] All the more, had he not secured, as a rule, the countenance and protection of the king or chief, the case would have been worse, and success almost impossible.

His rule first to approach chiefs and kings.

Acting on this plan, our skilful missionary pilot now determined to steer his course towards the royal court at Tara, to attack the pagan system in its stronghold, effect if possible the conversion of King Laoghaire and his retinue, and obtain their approval and assistance. As has been already in-

Visits accordingly the royal court at Tara.

[1] "Early Christian Art in Ireland," p. 42, by Miss Margaret Stokes.

[2] "Confession," 4, 15; 5, 23.

dicated, we do not think the reasons adduced by Dr. Todd for postponing Patrick's visit to Tara to the close of his career at all conclusive. Sailing from Strangford Lough round the County Down coast past Carlingford Lough and Dundalk Bay, Patrick and his eight companions landed at the mouth of the Boyne. Leaving there their coracles, or basket-boats covered with hide, they made their way up the valley of the Boyne past the famous "graves of the sons of Feic," or royal burying-places at Brugh-na-Boyne, to the Hill of Slane. A series of sepulchral mounds, raths, caves, circles, and pillar stones invest this locality, which is within sight of Tara, with intense historic interest. The writer spent a most delightful time in visiting and examining these memorials of 'a remote antiquity, a few summers ago. He can recommend the reader who wishes a few days' pleasant and instructive holiday to spend it in this entrancing region, with Sir W. Wilde's "Beauties of the Boyne" and Dr. Petrie's "History and Antiquities of Tara Hill" in his hand. As has been already mentioned, the greatest of these huge mounds is that called New Grange, which stands on two acres of ground, the central chamber underneath it being 19 feet 6 inches high at the centre, 22 feet long, and 18 feet wide. It is entered by a low-mouthed, narrow passage, along which at the entrance the visitor has to crawl on his hands and knees, and if he has any tendency to stoutness, I would advise him to be content with an outside view.

Passes up the Boyne valley to Slane.

Where he kindles the Easter fire. It is stated that the time when Patrick and his little company reached the Hill of Slane was Easter Eve, and that by way of celebrating it they kindled the Easter fire. It so happened that Laoghaire and his Druids were just then celebrating a great heathen festival, part of the ceremonial of which was the lighting of a fire at Tara; and there was a most stringent law that while the sacred fire was burning no other should be lighted by the people on pain of death. The king, therefore, on seeing the fire on the Hill of Slane, easily visible at Tara, though nine miles distant, was much incensed, and with his horses and chariots he set out to punish the impious transgressor of the sacred rule. When he reached Slane, Patrick was summoned to his presence, and com- Interview manded to appear at his court next day, and give with the king and an explanation of his profane and daring violation. his court. As he and his attendants proceeded to obey the summons, they are said to have sung the words of the psalm, "Some trust in chariots and some in horses; but we will remember the name of the Lord our God." It was on this occasion, too, according to the Lives, that Patrick composed his famous hymn as a "Lorica," or armour to protect him from his foes, both spiritual and fleshly. There is doubtless much that is legendary in the details of the story of this visit, and of the extraordinary miraculous feats performed by the saint; that, for example, which represents him and his clerics as assuming the form of deer, and as bounding safely through the midst of those who lay in wait for them, who saw only eight deer bounding away and a fawn behind them. But there is no reason to doubt the substance of the story, that Patrick and the clergymen who accompanied him presented themselves before the king and his assembled courtiers, Druidical priests, and bards, when Dubhthach (Duffa), the chief bard, rose

and welcomed them. Patrick expounded and enforced the doctrines of Christianity. The priests
and magicians did their best to oppose and thwart
them in their object, but Dubhthach and many
others were converted. The king professed to
acquiesce, but his conversion was only nominal. At
all events, he not only permitted St. Patrick to
preach the gospel throughout his realm, but extended over him the shield of his protection—a
boon of which the evangelist was not slow to avail
himself. He was a consummate missionary—a man
of immense force and energy of character—a man
evidently too of intense ardour of spirit, of quick
sensitiveness, warm affection, and great magnetic
power, which drew men towards him, and through
him to his Master, and commanded their reverence,
confidence, and love.

At Tailtenn. He and his friends next went to Tailtenn (now
Telltown), not far off, where the national games
were being celebrated, and where immense multitudes assembled continuously for some weeks. On
many successive days he preached to the swarming
crowds of natives, made many converts, including
Conall Gulban, a brother of the king, and ancestor
of the celebrated Columba. At a later date we
find him at Moy Slecht, in County Cavan, then the
seat of the great national idol, called *Crom Cruach*,
which, having won over the people to the Christian
faith, he was permitted to demolish. The idol appears also to have been called *Cromdubh*, and to
have given rise to the name of *Cromduff Sunday*,
by which title the last Sunday in summer is known
among the Irish. It is certain that the eve of 1st
November, the first day of winter, was the festival

of Crom Cruach.[1] The Irish Church would seem to have substituted a Christian solemnity for the old pagan festival.

Our missionary now went to Connaught, where he spent seven years, preaching, founding churches and monasteries, and appointing clergy. It is said that in the province of Connaught alone he was the means of converting 12,000 men. *In Connaught.*

It was there—in the vicinity of the royal palace of Croghan—that he had the famous interview with King Laoghaire's two daughters, Ethnea the Fair and Fedelma the Ruddy. They had been sent there, it would appear, to be educated by the Druid priests. The story of the interview is given by Tirechan in the "Book of Armagh"; and although it bears marks of having been somewhat touched up and embellished, it is generally accepted by scholars as being true in substance. The simple, artless questions put by them to Patrick, and his answers, are natural and lifelike, and as the incident is picturesque and striking, and affords an illustration of the methods of the great Irish missionary, it may be proper to relate it. *Conversion of the King's daughters.*

"Whence are you, and whence have you come?" they said to Patrick and his company, as they found them seated beside a spring to which the maidens had come to wash at break of day. "It were better for you to believe in God than to inquire after our origin," said Patrick. Then the first virgin said: "Who is God? and where is God? and of what is God? And where is His dwelling-place? Has your God sons and daughters, gold and silver? Is He ever-living? Is He beautiful? Did Mary foster

[1] See Todd's "St. Patrick," p. 128.

His Son? Are His daughters dear and fair to the men of the world? Is He in heaven or in earth? In the sea? In rivers? In the mountains? In valleys? Declare unto us the knowledge of Him. How shall He be seen? How is He to be loved? How is He to be found? Is it in youth or in age?"

But St. Patrick, full of the Holy Ghost, answered and said: "Our God is the God of all men—the God of heaven and earth, of the sea and rivers, the God of the sun, the moon, and all stars, the God of the high mountains and of the low valleys, the God who is above heaven, and in heaven, and under heaven. He has His dwelling in heaven and earth, and the sea, and all things which are in them. He inspires all things; He gives life to all things; He is over all things; He sustaineth all things. He giveth light to the light of the sun, and to the light of the moon. He hath made springs in dry land, and dry islands in the sea, and hath set stars to minister to the greater lights. He hath a Son co-eternal and co-equal with Himself. The Son is not younger than the Father, nor is the Father older than the Son. And the Holy Spirit breathes in them. The Father, the Son, and the Holy Ghost are not divided. But I desire to unite you to the Heavenly King, as you are daughters of an earthly King. Believe in Him." And the virgins said; "Teach us how we may believe. Show us how we may see Him face to face." Then Patrick taught them repentance and faith, and the life after death, and the resurrection, and the judgment. And they believed, and were baptized, and had white raiment put upon their heads. And they received the Eucharist, and slept in death—by which some understand their death to the world, and their consecration to a religious life.

It is very manifest that the story in its present form has passed under the hand of the artist. The questions and answers are just a little too finished and elaborate to have taken shape at an incidental interview. But the romantic tale is probably true enough in substance.

It was during this sojourn in Connaught that Patrick is said to have paid his memorable Whitsuntide visit to Crochan Aigle, the lofty mountain overhanging Clew Bay, Westport, County Mayo, now called after him Croagh-Patrick, and to have driven from thence all the serpents, venomous reptiles, and demons. We have here an excellent example of the manner in which a legend grows with the lapse of time. The visit to Crochan is not recorded at all by Patrick's earliest biographer, Muirchu. In the " Collections of Tirechan " (ninth century) we are told that Patrick spent forty days and forty nights on Crochan Aigle fasting, and that "noxious birds (*graves aves*) came about him, and he could not see the face of heaven or earth or sea." The " Tripartite Life " (eleventh century) represents the mountain as " filled with black birds, so that he knew not heaven and earth, and he sang maledictive psalms at them; but they left him riot because of this. Then he strikes his bell at them, so that the men of Erin heard its voice ; and he flung it at them, so that its gap broke out of it, and that bell is ' Brigit's Gapling.' Then Patrick weeps till his face and his chasuble in front of him were wet. No demon came to the land of Erin after that till the end of seven years, and seven months, and seven

Margin note: Legend of visit to Croagh-Patrick, and expulsion of serpents, &c.

days, and seven nights." Observe the circumstantial additions of the "Tripartite," its interpretation of the birds as being demons, and their banishment for seven years, seven months, and seven days. But this is not all. According to the "Tripartite," an angel appears to Patrick, from whom the saint makes a series of the most extraordinary requests, all of which are conceded, the whole being framed after the model of Abraham's intercessions for Sodom. Then, more than a century later, comes Joceline, who represents the saint as gathering together all the demons, serpents, and venomous reptiles in Ireland on the top of the mountain, and by means of his *baculum* or staff driving them into the sea. There is, of course, distinct evidence that long before Patrick's time such reptiles were unknown in the land. Solinus, for example, a Roman writer on geography in the third century, mentions the fact in the 22nd chapter of his "Polyhistor."

Ulster, Leinster, and Munster were in turn visited by our indefatigable missionary. The kings and chiefs, according to his usual policy, were first won over, and everywhere he went large numbers of people were converted, churches were founded, and a numerous clergy ordained.

His work in Dalriada and Dalaradia.
It is of course quite impossible to go into details; but as a specimen of his method of procedure, as recorded in the "Tripartite Life," I may quote a passage from it with reference to a visit of Patrick to Dalriada and Dalaradia. After referring to "Bishop Olcan of Patrick's household in Airthir Maige,[1] a noble city of Dal Riatai," and

---

[1] Armoy.

to Bishop Macc Nisse, who founded "Condire" or
Connor, the "Tripartite" proceeds :—
"Patrick found a welcome in the land with Erc's
twelve sons; and Fergus the Great, son of Erc,
said to Patrick : 'If my brother respects me in
dividing his land, I would give it to thee.' And
Patrick offered to Bishop Olcan that part, to wit,
Airthir Maige. Said Patrick to Fergus : 'Though
thy brother hath not much esteem for thee to-day,
it is thou that shalt be king. The kings in this
country and over Fortrenn shall be from thee for
ever.' And this was fulfilled in Ædan, son of
Gabran, who took Scotland by force."

"Patrick left many churches and cloisters in the
district of Dal Riata. He founded Fothrad,[1] and
left therein two of his household, namely, Presbyter Cathbad and Dimman the monk. And he
founded Raith Mudain.[2] He left Presbyter Erclach
therein. He left Bishop Nehemiah in Telach Ceneoil
Œngusa,[3] two Cennfindans in Dormach Cainri, in
Cothraige,[4] Enan in Drumman Findich,[5] Bishop
Fiachra in Cuil Echtrann.[6] And Patrick blessed
Dun Sobairci,[7] and Patrick's well is there, and he
left a blessing thereon."

"After this he went into Dal Araidi. He found
Coilbad's twelve sons before him. He proposed to
take the place wherein Cell Glass,[8] stands now. He
was refused, and yet he hath it still. And he left
therein two of his household, namely, Glaisinc and
Presbyter Libur, and he proposed, moreover, to take

---

[1] Now unknown.
[2] Ramoan.
[3] Probably Drumtullagh.
[4] The barony of Cary.
[5] Now probably Drumeeny.
[6] Culfeightrin.
[7] Now Dunseverick.
[8] Now unknown.

the place in which Lathrach Patraic is now. Therein is Daniel who is called 'the angel,' and 'Patrick's dwarf.' By him is Patrick's well—Slan ('healthful') is its name. There Patrick's new key was found. Now, Saran, son of Coelbad, expelled him thence, and Patrick deprived him of heaven and earth."

" Howbeit, Conlae, son of Coelbad, received Patrick with humility, and offered to him Domnach Combair.[1] And Patrick blessed him, and left as a benediction that there would be kings and princes of his race for ever. And he founded many churches in Dal Araide, namely, Domnach Mor Maige Damoerna,[2] and Raith Sithe,[3] and in this he left two of his household, and Telach, that is Cell Conadain,[4] and Gluaire[5] in Latharna (Larne)—and Macclessi is therein. And he founded Glenn Indechta,[6] and Imlech Cluane in Semne[7]—Coeman is therein—and Raith Epscuip Findich in the country of the Hui Darcachein."[8]

Patrick founds Armagh.

It was near the close of his career that Patrick, according to Muirchu and the "Tripartite," laid the foundations of Armagh. Emania, now represented by Navan Fort, near the present city of Armagh, was, as has been already mentioned, the royal residence of the kings of Ulster. Patrick, the "Tripartite" says, went to the fortress of Dare, son of Findchad, son of Eogan, son of Niallan, and asked him for a site

[1] Comber, then in Dalaradia.   [2] Magheramorne.
[3] Rashee.   [4] Possibly St. Cunning, Carncastle.
[5] *Glore* is the name by which the old churchyard of Tickmacrevan is commonly known (Reeves).   [6] Glynn.
[7] Ransevyn, the ancient name of Island Magee, Reeves thinks, may include the name of "Semne" (Shevny).
[8] A district, Dr. Reeves thinks, on the confines between Down and Antrim.

116

for his cell on a great hill to which he pointed—the hill on which the Protestant Cathedral now stands. Dare at first refused, but gave him a site in a strong rath below, where Patrick founded his cell, and remained for a long time. Later, however, Dare, through the entreaties of his wife, took the death of two horses which ate the grass of the graveyard around the church, and an attack of colic which came upon himself, as an admonition that he had acted wrongly, and so relenting, he gave Patrick the site which he sought on the hill; and there within an earthen fort was built an oratory, and the usual monastic appurtenances.

When Patrick began to realise that his departure Patrick's death at Saul. was at hand, he is said to have retired to Saul, the scene of his earliest success, and there to have terminated his great career. Keen debate has been held over the place of his burial. Muirchu and the third Life in Colgan's Collection declare that his place of sepulture was *Dun-leth-glass* (*i.e.* Downpatrick). Giraldus Cambrensis, writing in the twelfth century, relates how the remains of Patrick, Brigit, and Columba were found, and laid in one grave in Down by John de Courcy, and he quotes the verse :—

> "In burgo Duno, tumulo tumulantur in uno,
> Brigida, Patritius, atque Columba pius."

Which has been thus rendered :—

> "Patrick, Columba, Brigit rest in glorious Down,
> Lie in one tomb, and consecrate the town."

The whole affair of the discovery and transfer seems to have been a political device of De Courcy.

117

It is not mentioned by any Irish writer; indeed, the Annals of the Four Masters tell of a rival discovery, by an Irish primate, of the remains of the three saints, not at Down, but at Saul. Tirechan in his Life says where Patrick's bones are no one knows, but remarks afterwards that Columbkille had, under the guidance of the Spirit, pointed out Saul as the place where he was buried. Nennius also states that his sepulchre was unknown; while the "Tripartite Life" assigns it, like Tirechan, to Saul, which seems the more likely spot. But amid the conflict of testimony we shall not undertake to decide the question, which is in no sense a vital one.

CHAPTER VI

PATRICK'S TEACHING AND INFLUENCE

FIACC's hymn says that at Patrick's death "to a Legend of a year's radiance. year's end bided radiance, this was a long continuous day. At the battle fought at Bethoron against Canaan's folk by Nun's son, the sun rested at Gibeon, that is what history tells us. Since the sun rested with Joshua at the death of the wicked, though it be thrice as strong, meet is radiance at the decease of the saints."

The "Tripartite," as usual, carries the legend further and embellishes it : "For the space of twelve nights, to wit, the time during which the elders of Israel were watching him with hymns and psalms and canticles, there was no night in Maghinis, but an angelic radiance therein. And some say that angelic radiance abode in Maghinis till the end of a year after Patrick's death. And no one doubts this came to pass in order to make manifest the merits of so great a man. And so night was not seen in the whole of that region during the days of lamentation for Patrick, just as, when Hezekiah was sick, the sun went back ten degrees on the sundial of Ahaz, as a manifest sign of his recovery. And even so the sun stood over against Gibeon, and the moon over against the valley of Ajalon."

"On the first night the angels of the Lord of the

elements were watching Patrick's body with spiritual songs. The odour of divine grace which came from the holy body, and the music of the angels, brought sleep and joy to the elders of the men of Ireland who were watching the body on the nights afterwards."

This beautiful legend may at all events be taken as a representation of the spiritual radiance which flowed from his teaching, and of the fragrant memory and influence of a holy life which the good man left behind him.

Patrick's doctrine.

But to understand and appreciate these better it will be necessary to pause at this point for a little in order to ascertain and note what the doctrine was which was preached by the great Irish apostle. It would indeed be very unjust to our noble evangelist to raise our expectations with regard to this too high. Not a few of the great men who have set vast movements agoing, have turned the current of national life in a new direction, and been in an exceptional degree makers of history, have been undistinguished as writers. They have been content to be actors, and for the most part have left to others the task of reporting and interpreting their actions. St. Patrick was a man of this type. He was not a writer of books, much less of elaborate and systematic theological treatises. What writings of his have come down to us do not extend beyond a few pages. The most important is his " Confession," which is a short apology for one so unlearned and insignificant as he was presuming to come to Ireland as a missionary. The other is a spirited and at times scathing letter with reference to the cruel conduct of Coroticus, who, while professing to be a Christian, inflicted massacre, rapine, and robbery on some Irish Christians, and carried many away captive. Add to this the hymn attributed to him. We cannot expect to find much theology in such short incidental utterances, written for a practical purpose. Yet as Patrick is an earnest Christian man, whose soul is in every word he writes, it is wonderful what insight even these fragments afford us into the innermost thought of the Irish apostle on the great Christian verities. And here, indeed, we come upon one secret of the extraordinary power and influence of his teaching. It had its root in, and drew its inspiration and vitalising energy from, his own personal experience of its saving power. What he had seen and heard and touched and handled of the word of life, *that* declared he to men. As it was this that gave life and power to his doctrine when he preached it, it is from this also that it derives its interest for us to-day. A rapid survey of the chief truths taught by this successful evangelist may not be devoid of interest.

His one authoritative standard of appeal for doctrine and life is Holy Scripture. For him the supreme source of authority is not the Bishop of Rome, nor tradition, nor Church councils—he never once hints at any of these as authoritative—but Holy Writ. He is perpetually appealing to it; his familiarity with it is quite remarkable; he interweaves it constantly with his remarks and exhortations. He is on this account designated "the man of the enduring language, *i.e.* the Holy Canon."[1] When he founded a church, one present he was accustomed to make to it was "the Books of the

Place assigned to Scripture.

[1] " Tripartite Life," ii. 566.

Law and the Books of the Gospel."[1] It should be added that he quotes from the Apocryphal books as well as from the canon of inspiration.

Teaches the doctrine of the Trinity. Both in the "Confession" and in the Hymn he applies the term "Trinity" to the Godhead. The expression of his faith in the sacred Trinity contained in the "Confession" takes very much the form of a creed, and is perhaps the echo of some early formula, though, as it occurs, it follows a reference to his conversion, and is a warm outpouring of his faith in God. It is as follows:—

"Because there is no other God, neither ever was, neither before, nor shall be hereafter, except God the Father, unbegotten, without beginning; upholding all things, as we have said.

"And His Son Jesus Christ, whom indeed with the Father, we testify to have always been, before the origin of the world, spiritually with the Father, in an inexplicable manner begotten before all beginning, and by Himself were made the things visible and invisible, and was made man, and, death having been vanquished, was received into the heavens to the Father. And He has given to Him all power 'above every name of those that are in heaven, on earth, and under the earth, that every tongue should confess to Him that Jesus Christ is Lord and God,' in whom we believe, and expect His coming, to be ere long 'the Judge of the living and of the dead,' 'who will render to every man according to his deeds.'

"And He hath poured upon us abundantly the Holy Spirit, a gift and pledge of immortality, who makes the faithful and obedient to become 'sons of God and joint-heirs with Christ.'

[1] Colgan, "Trias Thaum.," c. xxiii. p. 521.

"Whom we confess and adore—one God in the Holy Trinity of the sacred name." Although the *homoousian* doctrine is not expressly affirmed in it, this creed of Patrick runs closely parallel to the Nicene, and has several terms and phrases not unlike the Athanasian, which by some good authorities is supposed to have originated in Gaul in the fifth century.

Patrick's teaching with respect to the *way of* salvation is strikingly evangelical. There is no trace in it of the doctrine of the *merit of good works.* On the contrary, all goodness in man is traced to the sovereign, free grace of God. He compares himself to a stone lying in the mud, till God by His mercy has raised him out of it, and set him on the wall of the Christian temple. "From God I have received what I have;"[1] "I have no power unless He had given it to me."[2] *(And the Evangelical doctrine of grace.)*

Salvation by faith in Christ is very emphatically taught by him. One text which he is specially fond of quoting is, 'He that believeth and is baptized shall be saved, but he that believeth not shall be condemned."[3]

The necessity of regeneration and sanctification by the Spirit is pressed with equal urgency.

How the Lord's Day is now secularised and dishonoured throughout Ireland by the express sanction and countenance of the Roman priesthood is but too well known. By Patrick and the early Irish Church this day was devoted to the Divine service, and its sanctity most carefully guarded. By the Brehon Law the people were required to *(Scrupulous observance of the Lord's Day.)*

[1] "Corot.," i.   [2] "Confess.," v. 24.
[3] "Confess.," iv. 17 ; "Corot.," ii.

give every seventh day of the year to God's service. The "Tripartite Life" informs us that "from vespers on Saturday night until the third hour on Monday, Patrick used not to go out of the place where he was staying."[1] Saturday night, it should be remembered, was in the early Irish Church treated as part of Sunday. "Once, when Patrick was resting on the Lord's Day near the sea, he heard a tumultuous noise of heathens who were toiling in forming a rath. St. Patrick, calling them, ordered them not to work on the Lord's Day; but as they disobeyed his command, the sea broke in and destroyed their work."[2]

Celebrates Communion in both kinds.

Patrick and the early Celtic Church observed the Lord's Supper in both kinds. A hymn in the Antiphonary of Bangor, sung while the people were communicating, begins thus: "Come, ye saints, take the body of Christ, drinking His holy blood, by which you were redeemed." In the "Life of St. Molling of Luachair" it is related how on one occasion he administered the chalice to a person who was a leper. In the "Stowe Missal," the earliest known Irish liturgy, assigned to the eleventh century, it is prescribed that the wine should be mixed with water. Even Dr. Lanigan, the Roman Catholic historian, is constrained to admit "that in old times it [Communion in both kinds] was practised in Ireland as well as elsewhere."[3]

Auricular confession, invocation of saints, prayers for the dead, and the doctrine of purgatory are all conspicuous by their absence from the teaching of Patrick and the early Irish Church. How long will the Irish people groan under the oppressive yoke

[1] Vol. i. p. 125.   [2] "Tripartite," vol. ii. p. 289.
[3] "History," iii. 310.

of a system which their ancestors stoutly and long resisted, which was not indigenous to the Church planted by Patrick, but at a later time imported from Italy, and imposed on them by foreigners?

It is true, however, and should be borne in mind, that at the time of St. Patrick's death the whole of the Irish had not accepted of the Christian faith, and that a large proportion of those who had outwardly accepted of it were far from being what they ought to have been. By several chiefs and tribes he was strenuously opposed and thwarted in his missionary enterprise; even in Brigid's time—she was ten years old when Patrick died—there were many unconverted heathen, and a large proportion of the conversions were only nominal. Still, making every allowance, his success was certainly remarkable, and was helped by several secondary causes. One was his policy, already noticed, of skilfully adapting his methods to the tribal system, and the care he took to secure in the first instance the adhesion of kings and chiefs. Another was the appointment from the first of a native clergy, taken largely from the highest ranks of society. *Secondary causes of Patrick's success.*

He did not absolutely confine himself to the native Irish. In the "Catalogue of the Saints of Ireland," it is said of the bishops of the first order or period that "all these bishops were sprung from the Romans and Franks, and Britons and Scots." It was no doubt those who came from the Roman province of Britain who are called here Romans and Britons. Many thousands of such, some of whom doubtless were Christians, were carried away captive at the same time as Patrick, and others appear to have accompanied him when he returned on his mission of evangelisation. By Franks is probably meant persons who had come from Gaul. The extent to which the staff of Irish clergymen was made up of such material appears in the " Litany of Angus." As, however, those first referred to had settled in Ireland and intermarried with the Irish, they cannot properly be called foreigners. At any rate, it is quite remarkable how many of Patrick's clergy were the sons of kings and chiefs. This, by reason of the tribal constitution and the usages of the time, would immensely enhance their influence with the people. But a third explanation of the large number of conversions must be candidly admitted—the toleration of the numerous pagan customs which the converts brought over with them on their conversion. Dr. O'Donovan, a very high authority, says that " Patrick engrafted Christianity on the pagan superstitions with so much skill that he won the people over to the Christian religion before they understood the exact difference between the two systems of belief; and much of this half-pagan, half-Christian religion will be found, not only in the Irish stories of the Middle Ages, but in the superstitions of the peasantry of the present day." In the serious relapse towards paganism that took place a few generations later, Irish Christianity had to pay dearly for permitting the importation of so many pagan practices. But notwithstanding all drawbacks, the success of Patrick was truly pheno-menal, and, under God, has won for him immortal renown. What need in our time of men with the indomitable faith, and consuming zeal, and self-sacrifice of Patrick!

The " Tripartite Life " thus epitomises his character : " A righteous man, verily, was this man, with purity of nature like the patriarchs; a true pilgrim, like Abraham; mild, forgiving from the heart, like Moses; a praiseworthy psalmist, like David; a student of wisdom, like Solomon; a choice vessel for preaching righteousness, like Paul the apostle; a man full of the grace and favour of the Holy Spirit, like John the child; a fair herb garden with plants of virtue; a vine branch laden with fruit; a flashing fire with fervour to warm and heat the sons of life, to kindle and inflame charity; a lion for strength and might; a dove for gentleness and simplicity; a serpent for prudence and cunning as to good; gentle, humble, merciful unto the sons of life; gloomy and ungentle to the sons of death; a slave laborious and serviceable to Christ; a king for dignity and power in binding and loosing." [1]

The story is that towards the close of his life our apostle prayed to be certified of the future of Hibernia, and that in answer he saw the whole island wrapped in a flame of fire. He looked again, and saw cone-like mountains of fire rising heavenwards. He looked again, and this time saw candles burning here and there, scanty lights with darkness intervening, and coals lying hidden in their ashes, but still alive. Such, he was assured, would be the future experience of Ireland. Then, weeping bitterly, he cried, " Will God cast off for ever, and will He be no more entreated ? " Then he was directed to look towards the north, when, raising his eyes, he saw a tiny light arising in Ulidia, struggling with the darkness, but at length dispersing it, and illumining the whole island with its rays. Then the

[1] "Tripartite " vol. i. p. 257.

heart of Patrick was filled with joy, and his tongue
with exultation, and he gave thanks for what God
had showed him. May Patrick's vision be realised
in our time. May there go forth from Ulidia (from
Ulster) to Munster, from the north to the south—
not spreading clouds of darkness, but the very light
of life; not hate, but love; not notes of war, but
peace through the Prince of peace.

PART III
THE CHURCH OF ST. PATRICK

CHAPTER VII

THE FUNDAMENTAL FEATURE OF THE CHURCH OF ST. PATRICK—ITS MONASTICISM

I HAVE now to try to convey some just idea of the Church that was set up by Patrick and his companions, and of the institutions and agencies by means of which it sought to evangelise the people and edify its members. In doing this, it is absolutely necessary to begin with its monasticism, which it is not too much to say was its predominant characteristic. To overlook the monastic character of early Irish Christianity were to miss its most fundamental and comprehensive institution, that which dominated and coloured everything, and brought everything into subjection to itself—the keystone in the arch of its ecclesiastical order, or rather both arch and keystone, and the most distinctive note of its life. "The entire Church appears to have been monastic, and her whole clergy embraced within the fold of the monastic rule."[1] I have now to speak of this institution as it appeared in Ireland, the probable source whence it was derived, and its more salient features.

It would be almost impossible to draw too dark a picture of pagan family life at the opening of the Christian era. The marriage bond was lightly set

---

[1] Skene's "Celtic Scotland," vol. ii. Bk. ii. p. 42.

at nought; the ties that bound husband and wife, parents and children, masters and servants, were not, as a rule, ties of affection; the atmosphere that pervaded the dwelling—it cannot be called by the sacred word *home*—was too apt to be impregnated with impurity; and social life had equally lost its savour. Christianity gave men a new sense of the sanctity of marriage and of the family relations; purified, consecrated, and drew closer all family ties; cultivated the domestic and social affections; bound men in a common brotherhood, and encouraged a frugal but cheerful use of temporal blessings. From the first it inculcated a severe self-discipline, a sitting loose to worldly advantage, a spirit of self-renunciation, and a readiness, often exemplified, to sell all one's goods to give to the poor. Luxury was condemned, and a certain aloofness from the amusements of the time distinguished Christians, due chiefly, however, to the fear of getting contaminated with the pagan impurities that were apt to mingle with them. "We are no Brahmins nor Indian Gymnosophists," says Tertullian, "no wild men of the woods, nor separatists from life. We are mindful of the gratitude which we owe to the Lord our God, and do not despise the enjoyment of His works. We only so moderate it as to avoid excess and abuse."[1] "Pleasantry is permissible," says Clement of Alexandria, "but not frivolity. Whatever things are natural to men we must not eradicate, but impose limits and times. One needs not be gloomy, but only grave."[2] As yet there is no disposition to regard the domestic and social life as an inferior ideal to that of complete withdrawal from the world,

[1] "Apol.," 42.   [2] "Pæd.," Bk. ii. ch. i.

renunciation of marriage and society, and an ascetic
self-mortification. But a dualistic philosophy derived
from Platonic and Pythagorean, as well as Oriental Origin of
sources, taught that there exists an irreconcilable cism.
antagonism between spirit and matter, soul and
body, that evil is inseparably connected with matter,
and can be got rid of only by an ascetic mortification
of the flesh. This philosophy was everywhere and
powerfully dominant, and reached deep and far.
Outside the Christian pale the ascetic spirit appears
in Brahminism, in Buddhist monasticism, in the
Indian Gymnosophists, and in the monk-priests of
Serapis in Egypt. Within the Christian pale, and
deeply affecting the Church, it works through Gnosti-
cism and Manicheism. The great Christian teachers,
like Clement of Alexandria, Origen, and his disciple
Hieracas, are profoundly imbued with the Neo-
Platonic philosophy, and its leaven spreads. As
Professor Sohm well says: "The theory that was
the supreme principle of pagan philosophy, that
sense as sense is immoral, and that the subjection of
the bodily passions through ' ecstasy,' that is, through
detachment from the body, can alone lead the spirit
of the wise man to God—this theory took captive
the Christian world also. Asceticism was now declared to be a duty of life; nay, more, to be the
highest duty of life, inasmuch as it was a means
to the vision and possession of God. Monasticism
arose in the moment when this thought was shared
by the masses of the people, and multitudes withdrew into the solitude of the deserts that they might
make asceticism the calling of their life."[1] The
approaches to that stage were, however, gradual.

[1] " Kirchengeschichte im Grundriss," p. 67.

Its gradual rise.

We see its beginnings in the esteem in which virginity has come to be held in the second century, and the feeling against second marriages amongst the Montanists and elsewhere.[1] This higher sanctity is especially demanded in the clergy, and hence the Canons of the Councils of Elvira, Neo-Cæsarea, and Ancyra. Then we find a class of ascetics arising who practise asceticism without external separation from their families, as in the case of Origen and Hieracas, and the society of ascetics he gathers around him.

First appears in Egypt.

It was in Egypt that Christian monasticism first appeared, and it is deeply significant that, as Weingarten appears to have established, Pachomius, one of the chief founders of the system, and a contemporary of Anthony, in the first half of the fourth century, was before his conversion a monk of Serapis. It is curious, too, that the form of monasticism introduced into Ireland was similar to that of Pachomius. Athanasius brought the knowledge of it to the West, and it is highly probable that St. Martin of Tours was the medium through whom, indirectly perhaps, Patrick became familiar with it. The tradition that Patrick's mother, Conchessa, was a sister of Martin is exceedingly doubtful, and not generally credited. As Martin appears to have died in 397, it is difficult to fit into any feasible chronology of Patrick's life the tradition that he spent some years under Martin's tuition. But that Ninian, the apostle of the Southern Picts, came in contact with Martin, that it was through Martin that Ninian was enabled to build the church called *Candida*

Is brought to the West.

[1] See Athenagoras, "Suppl.," 33 ; Clem. of Alex., "Quis dives salvetur;" and Tertullian.

Casa at Whithorn, dedicated to Martin, and that other monasteries of the same type were established in Britain, there is no doubt. If not in Gaul and by direct contact, at least in Britain, where Martin's monastic system was introduced and extended, Patrick could not fail to become familiar with it. That after Patrick's time close relations were maintained between Irish ecclesiastics and the *Magnum Monasterium* at Whithorn, and that some great and influential abbots were trained there, is well known.[1] There was, indeed, one marked difference between Martin's system and that of Patrick. The former was strongly averse to the society and service of women in the institutions founded by him, while Patrick was just as strongly in their favour. But the difference may have been due to the initiative of the Irish apostle.

At any rate, that monasticism existed in the Irish Church from the time of Patrick is quite certain. Both in the Confession and in the Epistle to Coroticus he refers to monks and virgins who had devoted themselves to the religious life as being numerous. In the letter he says : "The sons of the Scots and the daughters of princes are monks and virgins of Christ to an extent I cannot enumerate."[2] Before long, monastic settlements were established all over the country, and became, as I have said, the most fundamental and all-embracing institutions of the Irish Church. I must now endeavour to give the reader some idea of what an Irish monastery was like.

If he imagines a large building or cluster of

(margin note: Introduced by Patrick.)

[1] See Skene's "Celtic Scotland," vol. ii. Bk. ii. pp. 45 *seq.*
[2] "Epistle to Corot.," 7.

buildings in some populous town or city, such as those in which monks now find accommodation, he will be wide of the mark indeed. The primitive Irish monastery was rude and simple, and often in some remote and isolated situation. The most

The favour-
ite sites of
monasteries
were islands. favourite site appears to have been an island near the coast, or in some inland loch, or on the summit of a lofty mountain. I have already spoken of the monastery on Nendrum, now Mahee, in Strangford Lough. Similar institutions were set up on Rathlin, or Rechran (still called Raghery by the natives), off the Antrim coast, on another Rachrain (now Lambay) off the coast of County Dublin, on the three islands of Arran in Galway Bay—the largest of these, now called Arran of the Saints, having had no fewer than ten monasteries erected on it. On five islands in Lough Erne there were as many monasteries. In Lough Ree, formed by the Shannon, there were also five, and in Lough Derg, formed by the same river, and Lough Corrib, there were five more. Islands were chosen not only on account of their isolation and solitude, but for the sake of the greater safety and freedom from molestation which they afforded. The larger establishments, however, as a rule, appear to have been placed upon the mainland. In the latter case, a rath was sometimes given by a chief for the purpose, or a site was found on the outskirts of a forest, which had first to be cleared

How the
monastery
was built. of its trees and brushwood. The monks needed to be handy with the axe and other tools, and so many of them were. We read of a bishop, for example, who always went abroad with his axe slung over his shoulder. The next step was the erection of a church or oratory, which was wont to be very

small, and rarely built of stone; most generally it was made of wood or wattles. We are told of Mochai, the abbot of Nendrum (Mahee Island), that on one occasion he went with seven score young men to cut wattles wherewith to make the *ecclais* or church.[1] It was in this manner, we are informed, that St. Kieran of Saigir constructed his church and the huts for his monks; and it is eminently characteristic of the monkish method of writing history when it is added, that when he went into the forest to procure the materials, a wild boar assisted him by biting off with his teeth the branches which he required. Both church and hut were constructed on the simplest plan. Stakes were driven into the ground, rods or wattles were woven between the stakes, very much as baskets are made, only in ruder fashion; moss was stuffed between the wattles, and the whole stanched and plastered with clay. Stone buildings were rare till the end of the eighth century, when the Danes began to penetrate and ravage the country, and to burn the wattled or wooden houses. But in addition to The monastic build-the little church, there would also be the common ings. room or refectory, in which the monks took their meals, and off it the kitchen. They generally took care to settle by a stream of water, beside which they would build a mill, with a kiln for drying the corn. Grouped around would be the cells or bee-hive huts, made of wattles, each by itself, and very small, in which the monks lived. For shelter and protection the whole group of huts would be surrounded by a rampart or circular enclosure made of earth or stones. The number of huts would vary

[1] "Martyrology of Donegal," p. 177.

with the number of monks and their pupils to be accommodated : the smallest of which we hear contained 150. The monastery on Nendrum, under the rule of Mochai, contained "nine times fifty monks." In cases where the monastery became famous as a seminary, the numbers in residence would rise to thousands. The great monastery of Clonard in Meath, when Finian presided over it (A.D. 530), is said to have contained 3000, while Bangor, under the rule of Comgall (A.D. 550), contained 4000. Indeed, there was no limit to the accommodation, so far as residence was concerned. When a new pupil arrived, he had only to go to the neighbouring wood, cut down some wattles, and his hut would be completed in an hour or two. Such were the students' chambers of those days! It was in such huts, in which they could hardly stand erect, with no light but what came from the door, and no table but the knee, on which the book in which they wrote rested, that the beautiful Irish manuscripts were written and illuminated.

How the monks lived.

How were the monks sustained ? It is a problem how the innumerable hives of monks with which the land swarmed found support in such a poor country. But their mode of life was simple and abstemious. A single rough garment, a little coarse bread made from the corn grown on the patch of ground which their own hands cultivated, an egg from the fowl they kept, a few watercresses, and some water, solved the problem of living. Erc, one of Patrick's disciples who lived beside the Boyne, kept a flock of geese, and the half of one of their eggs did him for twenty-four hours. (We are here reminded how the monks sometimes tamed the wild animals and

birds of the wood, and turned them into pets. It
is related of St. Kieran of Saigir that a fox, a wolf,
a badger, and a wild boar were thus domesticated
by him, and that he was wont to call them his
monks, and himself their abbot. They were in
such subjection that when the fox committed a
theft, and St. Kieran required him to do penance,
he submitted as if he knew all about it! St. Kevin
of Glendalough is said to have had a blackbird that
laid her eggs and hatched her brood in his hand!
But this is only by the way.) When anything more
than their own resources supplied was needed, it was
got gratuitously from the neighbourhood. When
Adamnan, as a youth, was attending the great
monastic school of Clonard, he was one day carrying a cask on his back. He was overtaken by the
king and his cavalcade, when, hurrying to get out
of the way, he fell, and the cask was broken,
and the milk spilled which it contained. As he
appeared greatly troubled, the king asked him
what vexed him. He explained that there were
three noble students, and three lads (of whom he
was one) who attended on them, each going round
the neighbourhood in turn to collect provisions. It
was his turn that day, but what he had procured
was lost, and the vessel, which he had borrowed,
was broken. The king comforted the lad by more
than compensating him for the loss. Here were six
students whose wants were supplied by the bounty
of the surrounding neighbourhood.

Besides those referred to, there was, it should be
remembered, another source of revenue secured by
law. According to the Brehon law, "the right of
the Church from the *tuath* or tribe is tithes and

The Brehon
Law secured
tithes.

first-fruits and firstlings: these are due to a church from her members." It is probable that the law with regard to tithes dates from a comparatively late period. The law of first-fruits and firstlings appears to have belonged to an earlier time. The firstling is defined to mean every male animal that opens the womb. "First-fruits are the fruit of the gathering of every new produce, whether small or great, and every first calf and every first lamb which is brought forth in the year."[1]

The muintir or familia.

The total number of monks connected with a monastery was called its *muintir* or *familia,* although the term is applied sometimes not only to the community in each monastery, but to all the monasteries of which it is the parent, and over which it exercises jurisdiction. The monastic community was also called the "city" (*civitas*) of its founder. Thus the monastery founded by Brigid at Kildare

How employed.

is called the "city" of Brigid.[2] Those members of the monastic community who were advanced in life seem to have been chiefly occupied in conducting the devotional exercises, and in reading and transcribing the Scriptures. Thus of the sixty "seniors" under Mochta in the monastery of Lughmagh (Louth) it is said:—

> "Threescore psalm-singing seniors
> Were his household, royal the number;
> Without tillage, reaping, or kiln-drying,
> Without work, except reading."[3]

But the brethren not yet enfeebled by age found ample scope for their energy. Almost every sort

[1] "Ancient Laws of Ireland," vol. iii. pp. 39 *seq.*
[2] See Todd's "St. Patrick," p. 22.
[3] *Cf.* "Martyrology of Donegal," and Adamnan's "Vit. S. Col.," Bk. iii. ch. iv.

of industry known at that time was prosecuted.
Even in the *familia* of Patrick himself, which was
not stationary, we hear not only of his chaplain
and bishop and priest and psalmist and bell-ringer,
but of Bishop Erc his judge, of Bishop MacCair-
thinn his champion, of Coeman his chamberlain,
of Athcen his cook, of Presbyter Mescan his brewer,
of Presbyters Catan and Acan his waiters, of Odran
his charioteer, of Presbyter Manach his woodman,
of Rottan his cowherd, of MacCecht, Laeban, and
Fortchern his smiths, of Essa, Bite, and Tassach his
artisans, and of Lufait, Erc, and Cruimthiris his
embroideresses. Both mechanical employments within
doors, and the humblest forms of husbandry in the
fields, occupied the monks. It is evident that the
Irish monasteries must have been largely self-sup-
porting, as they were also able to minister to the
poor and the destitute.

In the earlier period, too, the society and service Society and
of women were not refused, but welcomed and service of
women
turned to account. The Irish monks, far from welcomed.
being compelled to exclude the gentler sex from
their society, were permitted to admit them, enjoy
their intercourse, and profit by their ministrations.
There appear to have been many women, like those
just named, who employed their skill in embroidery
and other feminine arts, and in the general service
of the brotherhood.

All these facts should be borne in mind when we Irish
speak of the Irish Church as having been dominated cloisters
social, edu-
and controlled by monastic institutions. After all, cational,
they partook more of the social, educational, and industrial.
industrial spirit than they did of the monastic; at
least the monastic element was modified, mitigated,

and humanised by these other influences. The Irish monasteries were really industrial colonies, devoted in a large degree to productive labour and to the cultivation of the useful arts—to some extent even of the fine arts and of learning, as well as to the practice of the rules of the "religious life."

Church organisation affected by the secular environment But to obtain an adequate idea of the position of the monastery as related to other institutions another most important feature in its constitution has now to be noticed. History has come to recognise in recent times, as it had not done before, to what a great extent church organisation has been affected by the external environment, and, in particular, by the constitution of the secular society in the midst of which it finds itself. Every one knows how the organisation of what we call the "Catholic Church" of the early centuries was laid on the lines and reflected the political divisions and subdivisions of It was so in the Roman Empire. the Empire. Hatch, in his "Growth of Church Institutions," has amply shown this. "The Contitution of the Church," says Professor Rudolph Sohm, in his admirable little "Kirchengeschichte im Grundriss," "was in the main modelled on the organisation of the Empire." He is speaking not of the primitive Apostolic Church, but of "Catholicism." "In its old age," he says, "the Roman Empire bequeathed its constitution to the young Church, struggling upward with all the forces of a new life. It was its last great legacy to the future. In the form of an ecclesiastical constitution, the imperial constitution outlived the fall of the Empire. To this day the diocese of the Catholic bishops is the copy of the Roman 'civitas'; the province of the Catholic archbishop the copy of the Roman imperial

province; and the Catholic Church, under a Pope,
declared omnipotent by law, the copy of the ancient
Roman Empire, with its Cæsars, who claimed the
world as its possession." Similarly, the organisation It was so in
of the Celtic Church of Ireland adapted itself to the Ireland.
civil and social condition of the people whom it
sought to influence. Just as the whole Church was
under the rule of the monks, so the monks in turn,
and the whole monastic system, were in Ireland
dominated by the tribal spirit and customs which,
as we have seen, then reigned supreme over Irish
society. As the unit of Irish society was the tribe, The Church
the members of which were bound together by order
                                                    affected by
common interests and customs, and occupied a defi- the tribal
nite territory under the chief, and as the tribes system.
were often in conflict with one another, and intercourse between them impossible, Patrick and his
successors were compelled to adapt the external
framework and organisation of the Church to the
tribal constitution of Irish society. As Montalembert puts it: "The monasteries in Ireland were
nothing else, to speak simply, than clans reorganised
under a religious form. From this cause resulted
the extraordinary number of their inhabitants, which
were counted by hundreds and thousands, and from
this also came their influence and productiveness,
which were still more wonderful." As Professor
Richey points out, the monastic family became an
artificial tribe, of which its founder was the chief;
with the land granted to the founder were conveyed
all the rights of the chief of the clan; and "the
family of the monastery comprised as well the monks
as the clansmen, vassals, and serfs living on the
territory of the Coarb." The artificial tribe thus

created was governed by the Coarb, or heir of the saint who founded it, who enjoyed all the rights of the original chief as well as the spiritual authority of the abbot, although the temporal and spiritual functions of the office were often divided. The grant of land on which a monastery was situated was, of course, obtained from the head of the tribe to which the land belonged, and, as a rule, the eccle siastic who founded the monastery placed it within the territory of his own tribe. It was, however, not always so. Sometimes he belonged to a different tribe from that in whose territory he planted it. When the founder belonged to the same family as the owner of the land on which his monastery was placed, the abbacy was always hereditary in that family; that is, some one was provided from among its members who was qualified to take the place of Coarb or successor on each vacancy of the abbacy. But when the saint founding the monastery belonged, as sometimes happened, to a different family from that of the head of the tribe owning the land, the Coarbship or succession to the abbacy was enjoyed by the clan or family to which the saint belonged. Here is how the Brehon law dealt with cases wherein " the tribe of the land " and " the tribe of the saint " were different:—

" The Church of the Tribe of the Saint; that is, the tribe of the saint shall succeed in the church as long as there shall be a person fit to be an abbot of the tribe of the saint; even though there should be but a psalm-singer of these, it is he that will obtain the abbacy. Where this is not the case, it is to be given to the tribe of the land until a person fit to be an abbot of the tribe of the saint shall be found;

and when he is, it is to be given to him if he be better than the abbot of the tribe of the land who has taken it. If he be not better, he shall take it only in his turn. If a person fit to be an abbot has not come of the tribe of the saint or of the tribe of the land, the abbacy is to be given to the tribe of the monks, until a person fit to be an abbot of the tribe of the saint or of the tribe of the land shall be found ; and where there is such, he is pre-ferable. If a person fit to be an abbot has not come of the tribe of the saint, or of the tribe of the land, or of the tribe of the monks, the *Annoit* (*i.e.* the parent monastery) shall take it in the fourth place ; the *Dalta* (or affiliated or disciple monastery) shall take it in the fifth place ; the *Compairche* (or monastery in the same ' parochia ') shall take it in the sixth place ; the nearest *Cill* (or Cella) shall take it in the seventh place. If a person fit to be an abbot has not come in any of these seven places, the *Deoruid De* (God's stranger or pilgrim, *i.e.* the anchorite who lived apart from his brethren) shall take it in the eighth place. If a person fit to be an abbot has not arisen of the tribe of the saint, or of the land, or of the monks together, and the *Annoit*, or the *Dalta*, or the *Compairche*, or the nearest *Cill*, or the *Deoruid De*, has the wealth, it must be given to the tribe of the saint, for one of them fit to be an abbot goes for nothing. The abbacy goes from them."[1] We have seen already how the monastery or Church could claim certain rights from the tribe— the right of tithes, first-fruits, and firstlings; but so, on the other hand, could the *tuath* or tribe claim certain rights from the Church. "The right of the

[1] " Ancient Laws of Ireland," vol. iii. p. 75.

tuath or tribe against the Church" is: "they can demand baptism and communion and requiem of soul, and the offering from every church to every person after his proper belief, with the recital of the Word of God to all who listen to it and keep it."[1] A tract on the legal constitution and rights of privileged classes, in MS. in the British Museum, says: " It is no *tuath* or tribe without three free dignitaries—the *eclais*, or church ; the *flaith*, or lord ; and the *file*, or poet."

It thus appears how intimately the monastic Church of Ireland was interwoven with, and was made to adapt itself to, the tribal constitution to which Irish society was subject.

The monastery an asylum for those in peril: privilege of sanctuary.

In those evil, rude, and troubled times, |when might often took the place of right, and violence ran riot, it cannot but have been an immense advantage to have the quiet and safe shelter of the monastery to flee to when danger threatened. The monastery possessed the privilege of sanctuary, and this privilege was most jealously guarded. According to a story told in a "Life of Columba" by Manus O'Donnell, Diarmaid, king of Ireland and head of the Southern Hy Neill, took Curnan, son of Ædh, king of Connaught, by force from under the protection of Columba in his monastery, and slew him. Thereupon Columba, who was also dissatisfied with Diarmaid for a decision which he gave respecting the ownership of a transcript of a copy of the Book of Psalms, stirred up the race of the Northern Hy Neill, to which both Curnan and Columba belonged, to punish Diarmaid for his violation of the privilege of asylum which belonged to the monastery, the

[1] " Ancient Laws," vol. iii. p. 33.

result of which was the great battle of Cooldrevny
(Culdremhne), in which Diarmaid was defeated.
This was not the only instance of a violation of
the right of sanctuary by this same Diarmaid. A
certain transgressor of the law called Guaire, a provincial king, had tried to escape the hand of justice
by taking refuge with Ruadhan, abbot of Lothra,
one of the "twelve apostles of Ireland;" but Diarmaid pursued him, and, in spite of the privilege of
sanctuary, which he naturally thought only abused
in such a case, he seized the offender, and carried
him off to his palace at Tara. Having refused to
surrender him, "Roadanus and a bishop that was
with him took their bells that they had, which they
rang hardly, and cursed the king and place, and
prayed God that no king or queen ever after should
or could dwell in Tarach, and that it should be waste
for ever, without court or palace, as it fell out
accordingly." So undoubtedly it "fell out." The
belief in the efficacy of the curse worked out its
fulfilment, and so, as an ancient Irish poem has it—

> "From the judgment of Ruadhan on his house
> There was no king at *Teamreagh* or Tara."[1]

An incident related in Adamnan's "Life of
Columba" affords another illustration of the way in
which the monastery served to befriend persons in
distress or danger. Referring to Columba, Adamnan
says: "When the holy man, while yet a youth in
deacon's orders, was living in the region of Leinster,
learning divine wisdom, it happened one day that
an unfeeling and pitiless oppressor of the innocent
was pursuing a young girl, who fled before him on a

[1] See Petrie's "Antiquities of Tara Hill," pp. 125, 127.

level plain. As she chanced to observe the aged Gemman, master of the aforesaid young deacon, reading on the plain, she ran straight to him as fast as she could. Being alarmed at such an unexpected occurrence, he called on Columba, who was reading at some distance, that both together might defend the girl from her pursuer; but he immediately came up, and, without any regard to their presence, stabbed the girl with his lance under their very cloaks, and leaving her lying dead at their feet, turned to go back. Then the old man, in great affliction, turning to Columba, said, 'How long, holy youth Columba, shall God, the just Judge, allow this horrible crime and this insult to us to go unpunished?' Then the saint at once pronounced this sentence on the perpetrator of the deed: 'At the very instant the soul of this girl whom he hath murdered ascendeth into heaven shall the soul of the murderer go down into hell;' and scarcely had he spoken the words when the murderer of the innocent, like Ananias before Peter, fell down dead on the spot before the eyes of the holy youth. The news of this sudden and terrible vengeance was soon spread abroad throughout many districts of Ireland, and with it the wonderful fame of the holy deacon." Indeed it was not "wonderful" in the circumstances! But the reader need not believe all the details of the story unless he pleases.

The monas- tery set an example of industry and self- denial. There were other directions, however, in which the influence of the monastery, and of the industrial community which it sheltered, was calculated to be less equivocal and more wholesome and salutary. In those rude and rough times, when the rights of different septs, families, and individuals were in

148

almost perpetual conflict, and when the temptations
to a selfish, idle, but predatory and violent life were
powerful, it was of immense advantage to a people
addicted to such a mode of living to have set before
them from day to day the example which they saw
in the monastic community.   That community lived
and moved before them continually as a little industrial Christian colony of persons who had severed
the ties that bound them to earthly friends and
interests, and lived a life of stringent self-discipline
and self-denial.   They were, as a rule, a pattern of
purity, temperance, and self-control.   The time that
was not spent in religious exercises was given to
reading, writing, teaching, preaching, or busy industry at some trade or handicraft, and the means
which they acquired by gift of others or by their
own diligence and thrift they spent in works of
charity and benevolence.   It was inevitable that
they should command the respect and reverence of
both chiefs and people, and that they should do
much to mitigate the evils and abate the injustices
and cruelties of the time, and wield on the whole
a civilising influence.   In course of time another But also
element was added to their influence, which was generated
neither so legitimate in its nature nor so wholesome stitious
in its effect.   " We know how readily a rude and dread.
primitive people invest with superstitious and supernatural power those claiming superior sanctity, and
the newly converted people soon surrounded these
saints, as they termed them, with the same old halo
of reverence and awe which had belonged to their
pagan priests, such as they were.   The power with
which the latter were supposed to be endowed of
influencing the action of their native gods was

transferred to the Christian missionary, who was believed to exercise a similar power with regard to the Christian Deity. Their intercession was sought for, their malediction dreaded, and the claims and rites of the Christian Church invested with superstitious sanctions which brought the people more readily and universally into subjection to her."[1]

[1] Skene's "Celtic Scotland," vol. ii. p. 74.

CHAPTER VIII

SOME FAMOUS MONASTERIES AND MONKS

PATRICK's immediate disciples, and the monasteries or churches founded by them, can be referred to only in the briefest terms. Most prominent among these was Mochay, son of Bronach, daughter of Milchu, already mentioned. Mochay was converted by Patrick about 433, founded his monastery on Nendrum or Mahee island, in Strangford Lough, about 450, and died in 497. In this monastery education was combined with monastic discipline. Finnian, the founder of Moville, and Colman, the founder of Dromore, both got their training under Mochay. Six brothers of his were ecclesiastics, one of them having been Bishop Mac Erc of Donaghmore, in County Down. Then there was Mochta, a Briton, who founded a monastery at Louth, which contained 300 presbyters, 100 bishops, and 60 or 80 singers, who "ploughed not, reaped not, dried not corn, laboured not save at learning only." There was Benen or Benignus of Kilbennan, near Galway, where the ruins of a monastery and a round tower are still to be seen. He was one of the nine said to have been appointed to revise the laws. There was Fiacc of Sleaty (Sleibhte), to whom a hymn in praise of Patrick is ascribed. There was Lomman, son of Gollit, a Briton, and of Darerca,

151

sister of Patrick, and therefore at once Patrick's nephew and disciple, who founded a church at Trim. He had four brothers—Manis, who was a bishop in Forgney, County Longford; Broccaide, whose church was at Imleach Each, in County Mayo; Brocan and Mugenog, whose churches were in the great plain of Bregia, in Meath. There was Mel, also said to have been a nephew of Patrick, who became abbot and bishop of Ardagh. There was Sechnall or Secundinus, still another nephew of Patrick, son of Restitutus and Liamain or Limania, a sister of the saint. Dunshaughlin takes its name from Sechnall. He was a bishop in Armagh, and had six brothers—Necktan, a bishop; Dabonna, a presbyter; Mogornan, a presbyter; Rioc, a bishop; Auxilius, a bishop; and Lugna, a presbyter; and there was Cianan or Keenan, founder of Duleek, near Drogheda.

It is of course impossible even to mention by name the almost innumerable monasteries that were established in Ireland in the centuries succeeding Patrick. But a few were so powerful and influential, and acquired such fame for the educational and evangelistic work accomplished by them, that a brief notice of them is necessary to a right appreciation of the history of the time.

St. Brigid founds Kildare.

1. *Kildare.*—Next to St. Patrick, the highest place in Irish hagiology and in the veneration of the Irish people is assigned to St. Brigid. The two principal Lives of her are attributed, the one to Bishop Ultan, and the other to Cogitosus. According to Dr. Petrie —and Dr. Todd agrees with him—the period when Cogitosus wrote was within the years 800–835.

Brigid was born about the year 455. Her father,

whose name was Duffack, was a chief of the race of
Ugaine Mor (Hugo the great), king of Ireland,
but she was an illegitimate child, her mother having
been Duffack's slave. The jealousy of his wife compelled him to part with the slave, whom he sold to
a Druid, and so it was that Brigid was born on a
farm belonging to this Druid at Faughart, between
Newry and Dundalk. The locality derives further
historical interest from another event which happened
there. It was beside Faughart that, near the beginning of the fourteenth century, a great and decisive
battle was fought between Edward Bruce and the
Irish on the one side and the English on the other.
Bruce was defeated and slain, and, according to tradition, his dust lies in a little graveyard picturesquely
situated on the summit of the hill on whose slopes
the battle was fought.

Brigid grew up to be a most kindly and earnest
Christian maiden; her heathen master and mistress
were converted through her agency; she obtained
her freedom from them, and then gave herself to a
"religious" life. It is thought not improbable that
it is to her Patrick refers in his "Confession" when
he says: "There was one blessed Scotic maiden,
very fair, of noble birth and of adult age, whom I
baptized; and after a few days she came to me,
because, as she declared, she had received a response
from a messenger of God desiring her to become a
virgin of Christ and to draw near to God. Thanks
be to God, on the sixth day from that she with
praiseworthy eagerness seized on that state of life
which all the virgins of God now adopt." From this
time Brigid laboured with great earnestness and success for the conversion of those still in heathenism.

It seems to have been between the years 480–490 that she laid the foundation of her great monastery in Leinster at a spot then called Drumcree. Her first church and hut were erected under the shadow of a large oak, whence they took the name by which the place is still known, *Kildare* (or Church of the Oak). Cogitosus states that innumerable people of both sexes flocked to her "from all the provinces of Ireland," bringing their voluntary offerings, and that thus she was enabled to raise on the plain of Liffey a monastery "which is the head of nearly all Irish churches, and the pinnacle towering above all monasteries of the Scots, whose jurisdiction, spread throughout the whole Hibernian land, reaches from sea to sea." In many parts of Ireland monasteries arose acknowledging Brigid's jurisdiction. How widespread her influence was may be inferred from the fact that, extending over all the four provinces of Ireland, there are thirty-five parishes and townlands called Kilbride (*Cill-Bhrighde*), or Brigid's Church. In connection with her monastery in Kildare, two or three points of interest may be noted. It is worthy of notice that the community that resided in it was composed of both sexes. In this age, marked by such a strenuous assertion of women's rights, it is interesting to observe the high place and privilege given voluntarily to woman in the early Irish Church, and that offices and dignities were open to her not yet conceded by modern society with all our vaunted progress.

The author of the "Scholia" on the Martyrology of Ængus the Culdee mentions the singular fact that Brigid was ordained a *bishop* by St. Mel or Moel, Bishop of Ardagh; and this accords strikingly with an expression of Cogitosus in his Life of her when he speaks of "her episcopal and virginal chair" (*cathedra episcopalis et puellaris*). It is not less singular to learn that she chose an anchorite "to govern the church with her in episcopal dignity." Who the anchorite was is not stated, but there is no reason to doubt that it was Condlaed, who was also her principal artificer in gold, silver, and other metals; and yet this Condlaed was very decidedly under her control, and came and went only at her bidding. He wanted very much to pay a visit to Rome, probably in connection with his art, but Brigid peremptorily forbade him ; and when he set out without her leave, it is related that he was devoured of wolves, and that "because he tried to go to Rome in violation of an order of Brigid." She died about 525, and became enshrined in the veneration of the early Irish Church as a sort of divinity. They applied to her the same titles as are now conferred on the Virgin Mary—"the mother of the Lord," "one of the mothers of the Lord," "the Queen of the true God," and "the Queen of Queens."

A singular custom was observed in the monastery at Kildare. Giraldus Cambrensis, writing in the twelfth century, refers to a "perpetual fire" that was kept burning at Kildare, and had never been permitted to go out from the time of Brigid till the date at which he wrote. In Irish history there are many references to such perpetual fires as being kept up in other places. There can be no doubt the custom was originally a heathen one.

2. *Clonard.*—The founder of the great monastery of Clonard was Finnian, who is said to have been of the race of the Cruithne or Picts, to have been Finnian founds Clonard.

instructed in early life by Fortchern of Trim and
Caiman of Darinis, an island in Wexford Bay, to
have crossed the Irish Channel in his thirtieth
year to Wales, where he came in contact with "the
three holy men"—David, Gildas, and Docus. For
thirty years, it is stated, he remained in Britain,
and then, accompanied by several British evange-
lists, he returned to Ireland "to gather together
a people acceptable to the Lord." After building
many churches, he at length settled at Clonard
(Cluain-Erard), a retired and beautiful spot on the
river Boyne, where the great monastery arose, and
continued to grow till it contained three thousand
monks, and became one of the most famous centres of
training and education in Ireland. Clonard appears
to have been founded about A.D. 530; but prior to
that time there had set in a sad decay of the faith
in Ireland and a widespread relapse towards Pagan
customs and superstitions. In the "Life of Gildas"
it is stated that he took a chief part in reviving and
restoring the faith in Ireland, and the part he took,
there is little doubt, was accomplished chiefly through
his great disciple, Finnian, and the pupils who were
trained at Clonard by Finnian in turn. Twelve of
those disciples became known as "the twelve apostles
of Erin," and doubtless they were so designated
because of the great work which they did in re-
evangelising Ireland, in planting monasteries all over
the country, and in infusing a new spirit of life and
missionary zeal into the Church—a spirit which, as
we shall see later, bore rich and memorable fruit.
In the "Martyrology of Donegal," Finnian is characterised as a "doctor of wisdom and a tutor of the
saints of Ireland in his time; for he it was that had

three thousand saints at one school at Cluain-Erard, as is evident in his Life; and it was out of them the twelve apostles of Erin were chosen." The "twelve apostles of Erin" were Kieran of Saigir, in Munster; and Kieran, "the son of the artificer," who in 548 founded the famous monastery of Clonmacnois in King's County; Columba, son of Crimthan, who founded Terryglass in Tipperary; Mobhi, of Glasnevin; Ninnidh and Sinnell, who founded monasteries on islands in Loch Erne, the one on Inis-mac-Saint, and the other on Cleenish; the two Brendans, Brendan of Birr, and Brendan who founded the monastery of Clonfert, and became renowned for his seven years' voyage in search of the land of promise; Molaise of Devenish; Canice of Aghaboe; Ruadan of Lorrha; and lastly, the greatest and most distinguished of the twelve, the great Columba, who went to Iona and became "the apostle of the northern Picts."

3. *Bangor.*—But not less renowned than Clonard was the monastery of Bangor in County Down, the founder of which was Comgall. Tigernach says that he was born in the year 517. He was a native of Magheramorne near Larne, a region then occupied by the Cruithne or Irish Picts, and Adamnan represents Columba as describing this people as Comgall's relations according to the flesh. It was about 559 that Comgall laid the foundations of the monastery at Bangor, which in course of time grew to be the largest in all Ireland, embracing no less than four thousand monks. St. Bernard describes it as "producing many thousands of monks, the head of many monasteries, a holy place fruitful in saints, one of whom, named Luan, alone is reputed to have been the founder of a hundred monasteries." The ancient

Comgall founds Bangor.

THE CHURCH OF ST. PATRICK [PART III

service-book of the Abbey of Bangor is still extant
in the Ambrosian Library at Milan. It is entitled,
Antiphonarium Benchorense, or "Antiphonary of
Bangor," and is a deeply interesting survival from
a remote past. At the close of it, among other
hymns, is one entitled *Memoria Abbatum Nos-
trorum*, in which the names of fifteen abbots are
recorded and commemorated, abbots who lived prior
to the year 691. This ancient service-book has been
(as Dr. Reeves points out) away out of Ireland for
more than a thousand years, and yet the record
it contains exactly corresponds with the register
contained in the "Annals," the two being quite
independent of one another. Let me present a
specimen of this ancient "In Memoriam" poem :—

"The holy valiant deeds of sacred fathers,
    Based on the matchless church of Benchor ;
    The noble deeds of abbots, their number, times, and names,
    Of never-ending lustre—Hear, brothers, great their deserts,
    Whom the Lord hath gathered to the mansions of His
        heavenly kingdom.

Christ loved Comgill ; well, too, did he the Lord
    He held Beogna dear ; He graced the ruler Ædh ;
    He chose the holy Lillan, a famous teacher of the world,
    Whom the Lord hath gathered to the mansions of His
        heavenly kingdom.

He made Finten accepted, an heir generous, renowned ;
    He rendered Maclaisre illustrious, the chief of all abbots ;
    With a sacred torch He enlightened Segene,
    A great physician of Scripture,
    Whom the Lord hath gathered to the mansions of His
        heavenly kingdom.

Bercenus was a distinguished man ; Cumine also had
        grace ;
    Columba, a congenial shepherd ; Aidan, without complaint ;
158

Baithene, a worthy ruler; Crotan, a chief president,
Whom the Lord hath gathered to the mansions of His
heavenly kingdom.

To these so excellent succeeded Caman, a man to be
beloved by all;
Singing praises to Christ, he now sits on high.   That
Cronan,
The fifteenth, may lay hold on life, the Lord preserve him,
Whom the Lord will gather to the mansions of His
heavenly kingdom.

The truest merits of these holy abbots,
Meet for Comgill, most exalted, we invoke,
That we may blot out all our offences,
Through Jesus Christ, who reigns for ages everlasting."[1]

Cronan, the last of the fifteen, was still living
when this poem was written.   He died, we know, on
November 6, 691, so that it must have been written
prior to that date.

If for nothing else Bangor deserved distinction,
the illustrious men whom it trained and sent forth
would be enough to win renown for it.   It was at
the monastery of Bangor that Columbanus, who
founded the famous abbeys of Luxeuil, in Burgundy,
and Bobbio, in the Apennines; and Gallus, who
founded St. Gall, in Switzerland; and Scotus Erigena, who astonished the scholars and thinkers of
Europe with his genius, were trained and inspired.
Comgall died in 602.

The " Annals of Innisfallen," under the year 810,
which answers to 824 according to our modern
reckoning, have this record :   " Bangor laid waste
by the Danes, and the shrine of Comgall broken
open by them, and its learned men and bishops were

---

[1] Reeves's "Antiphonary of Bangor."

smitten by the sword." It seems never to have recovered again its early prosperity.

Another Finnian founds Movilla.

4. *Movilla.*—The monastery at Movilla (Maghbile), near Newtownards, was founded by Finnian or Find-barr, who is to be distinguished from Finnian of Clonard. He was connected with the royal family of Ulidia (Ulster), and was first sent to Nendrum to be instructed under Mochay; but from Nendrum he went to the "Magnum Monasterium" of Whithern, founded by Ninian, in Galloway, where for several years he was trained and instructed in the monastic life. It was about 540 that he founded the abbey at Movilla, and it was there that the celebrated Columba was for a time one of his pupils. The "Annals of Innisfallen" refer the death of Finnian to the year 572.

Other distinguished founders.

But I cannot pursue this monastic history farther in detail. Time would fail me to tell of Carthach and his monastery in Lismore, of world-wide fame, celebrated by Moronus in striking verses; or of Brendan and his monastery at Clonfert; or of his namesake of Birr; or of the two Molaises, him of Inishmurray, in Sligo Bay, and him of Leighlin; or of St. Kevin and his establishment at Glendalough, with its seven churches; or of St. Kieran and Clon-macnois; or of Mobhi and Glasnevin; or of St. Buite or Boetius of Monasterboice, with its magnificent ruins of two churches, a round tower, and three exquisitely carved stone crosses; and of a multitude besides which I cannot even name. Their work, influence, and history may be measured and appreciated by conceiving a repetition of those I have described.

CHAPTER IX

THE ORGANISATION OF THE CHURCH
OF ST. PATRICK

It now becomes our duty to examine more closely
than we have yet done into the form given to the
Church founded by the Irish apostle; how its officials
were related to one another; where the paramount
authority resided; in a word, how it was governed
and its affairs administered. It is a most interesting *In entering*
study, but one of a somewhat difficult and delicate *on this study we*
nature, which requires us resolutely to divest our *must divest*
ourselves of
minds of every vestige of prepossession and prejudice. *drepossession.*
To many people the difficulty of conceiving of an *sion.*
ecclesiastical order radically different from their own,
a state of things which ignores or subverts principles which they have been accustomed to regard as
essential, is almost insuperable.   That difficulty
exists in this case. The organisation of the primitive Church of Ireland was widely and radically different from that of any Church which exists to-day,
and its abnormal and quite remarkable features have
been hopelessly obscured and distorted by regarding
them through denominational spectacles, and by the
effort to construe and colour them in a denominational interest. Dr. Bright, the Regius Professor of
Ecclesiastical History at Oxford, in his recent book
on "The Roman See in the Early Church," very

THE CHURCH OF ST. PATRICK [PART III

appropriately describes the work which he is critici-
sing—"The Primitive Church and the See of Peter,"
by the Rev. Luke Rivington, an advocate of the
Roman claim—as "a bold attempt to Vaticanise
antiquity." The same thing may be said, *mutatis
mutandis*, of the treatment to which the early ecclesiastical history of Ireland has been subjected. The
Roman Catholic historian "Vaticanises" it, and sees
in it an exact copy of his own relation to the Papacy.
The Protestant Episcopalian "Anglicises" it, reading into it the forms of modern Episcopacy.
Presbyterians, I am sorry to say, have tried to make
it speak in *their* language, and in theirs exclusively,
and have written books or pamphlets to prove that
St. Patrick was a true blue Presbyterian. I happen
to have in my possession a volume of considerable
bulk written by an American Baptist, who demonstrates to his own satisfaction that Patrick was an
out and out Baptist; and in view of the evangelical
warmth and fervour of our Irish apostle, I am not
sure that our Methodist friends would not have
equally valid grounds to claim him as a forerunner
of John Wesley. But, seriously, to treat the facts
thus—to ignore them when they are inconvenient
and do not suit our theory, or to twist and colour
them to make them conform to our modern Church
patterns—is not to write history, but to pervert it,
and to make real insight into ancient affairs and
institutions impossible. And after all, what is gained
by such methods? We may depend upon it that
sooner or later somebody will have eyes to see and
honesty to reveal the true state of the case. The
organisation of the primitive Church of Ireland was
in many respects quite unique. It had peculiarities

162

that have no parallel in any modern Church, and no modern Church whatever can claim that it repro- duces or resembles them. *Episcopal government was absolutely unknown in it.* It was governed by abbots, who were frequently presbyters, and sometimes lay- men; and the office of abbot was in a sense heredi- tary, that is, it continued in the family of the original founder. It was not in submission to the Roman See, and in many points both of doctrine and practice it differed from the Roman ecclesiastical type. But, on the other hand, as it was funda- mentally monastic, no Protestant Church now existing corresponds to it. If we are to have any real insight into the state of things which obtained in the Church founded by St. Patrick, if its study is to be of any practical value to us, we must frankly take the facts as we find them, and not force them to conform to our preconceptions, or with much ingenuity read into them the modern institutions with which we are familiar. In this spirit must we enter on this study.

The organi- sation of the early Irish Church unique: no modern Church re- produces it.

Taking a broad and comprehensive as well as a close and intimate view of the organisation of the early Irish Church, one cannot but be struck with the absence of such hierarchical grades and dignities as constitute to-day the most salient feature in the Church of Rome and in the Anglican Churches.

1. It is necessary, however, to be more particular, and to note in the first place that in the primitive Church of Ireland there was *no Papal jurisdiction,* and no submission to the authority of the Roman See. I have already touched on this point when dealing with St. Patrick. But the independence of the Irish Church in relation to Rome was main-

Papal jurisdiction not recog- nised in Ireland.

163

tained long after Patrick's time. It has been shown in a previous chapter that the so-called "Irish Canons," including the one that states that "if any questions arise in this island, let them be referred to the Apostolic See," belong to a much later age than that of Patrick, and are the manifest handiwork of a writer or writers anxious to bring the Irish Church into conformity with Rome. It is very significant of Irish independence that the first Roman legate in Ireland of whom we have any record is Gillebert, who lived in the twelfth century. St. Bernard in his "Life of Malachi" states that Gillebert was regarded as the first legate who represented Rome in Ireland. Cardinal Baronius in his "Ecclesiastical Annals," under the year 566, and referring to the time of Columba, says that "the bishops of Ireland were all schismatics, separated from the Church of Rome." The extant Irish Liturgies show that even in the matter of liturgical forms respecting the celebration of the Lord's Supper, Baptism, and other rites and services, there was a marked difference between the Irish and the Roman Uses.[1] It has been already pointed out how in the Irish Church the Eucharist was administered in both kinds. So late as the twelfth century Gillebert, as he mentions in the prologue to his book "*De Usu Ecclesiastico*," set down in that work "the Canonical custom in saying of hours, and in performing the office of the whole ecclesiastical order," "to the end that those diverse and schismatical orders, wherewith in a manner all Ireland is deluded, may give place to one Catholic and Roman office."[2]   And St. Bernard in his "Life

[1] See Warren's "Liturgy and Ritual of the Celtic Church."
[2] Ussher's "Religion of the Ancient Irish," chap. iv.

of Malachi " relates how the effort of Gillebert was
seconded by Malachi, who "established in all the
churches the apostolical constitutions and the decrees of the holy fathers, but especially the customs
of the holy Church of Rome."[1]

. The long-continued controversy between the Celtic
Church—Irish and British—on the one side, and the
Anglo-Saxon Church representing Rome on the
other, with regard to Easter and other usages, the
persistent refusal of the Celtic Church to submit to
the Roman customs, and the embittered relations
between them—the refusal of the one to have any
communion with the other—are among the most
familiar and indubitable facts of history. Bede
testifies that the British not only deviated from
Rome in their mode of celebrating Easter, but
" were in the habit of doing several other things
which were against the unity of the Church ; " and
that when Augustine, the Archbishop of Canterbury,
and agent of Rome, met with the British bishops at
the place afterwards known as Augustine's Oak, with
a view to persuade them to " preserve Catholic unity
with him," they " preferred their own traditions
before all the churches in the world ; " and when, on
a later occasion, he besought them to act " according
to the custom of the holy Roman and Apostolic
Church," they refused to do so, or to submit to his
jurisdiction.[2] Augustine's successor, Laurentius, in
the opening of the seventh century, writes thus to
the Irish bishops and abbots : " When the Apostolic
See, according to the universal custom which it has
followed elsewhere over the globe, sent us to these

[1] Ussher's "Religion of the Ancient Irish," chap. iv.
[2] See Bede's "Eccles. Hist.," ii. 2.

western parts to preach to pagan nations, we happened to come into this island, which is called Britain, without possessing any previous knowledge of its inhabitants. We held both the Britons and the Scots [Irish] in great esteem for sanctity; but when we came to know the Britons, we supposed the Scots must be superior to them. We have, however, learned from Bishop Dagan [an Irish bishop], coming into this island [Britain], and the abbot Columbanus, coming into France, that the Scots [or Irish] differ not at all from the Britons in their behaviour. For Bishop Dagan, when he came to us, not only refused to eat with us, but even to take his repast in the same house with us." Bede immediately adds : " The same Laurentius and his fellow-bishops wrote a letter also to the priests of the Britons, worthy of his high station, in which he endeavoured to persuade them to Catholic unity; but how much he gained by these efforts the state of things to this present day sufficiently shows."[1] This was about 606. In the letter just quoted Laurence says that "the Scots [i.e. the Irish] were in no respect different from the Britons in their ways." What these "ways" were we learn from a poem written about the year 620 by the chief of the bards of the Britons, in which these lines occur :—

> " Woe be to him that doth not keep
> From Romish wolves his sheep
> With staff and weapon strong."[2]

About the middle of the seventh century in the south of Ireland, and at the opening of the eighth century in the north, the Irish Church was at length

---

[1] Bede's "Eccles. Hist.," ii. 4, 98.
[2] See Ussher's "Religion of the Ancient Irish," chap. x.

induced to conform with the Roman method of observing Easter; and from this time forward there
is a Roman party in the Irish Church, and a gradual
approximation to Roman customs. It was not, however, till much later that the Roman jurisdiction was
definitely recognised and the Roman hierarchical
organisation introduced, and this recognition began
among the Danish invaders when they became Christianised. Farther on in the history we shall have
the opportunity of seeing how the Danes, who were
kinsmen of the Normans of England, took steps to
connect themselves with the Anglo-Norman Church,
which, of course, was subject to the Roman See.

2. Not only was there no Papal, there was no
metropolitan jurisdiction in the Irish Church. The
abbot of Armagh was regarded as Patrick's Coarb or
successor, and as such he was held in honour; but,
as Dr. Todd has shown in his Memoir of St. Patrick,
he had " no primatial jurisdiction." " There was no
special jurisdiction in Armagh," he points out.[1] The
abbot of Armagh had no jurisdiction over other
abbots, such as those of Clonard or Bangor. He might,
as Dr. Todd indicates, exercise a moral influence,
but " this did not amount to a primatial jurisdiction."
We shall see in a moment that the rulers of the Celtic
Church of Ireland were the abbots, that the bishops
were entirely subject to them, and that there was no
such thing as episcopal jurisdiction, or, in other words,
that episcopal church government was absolutely
unknown in it. Even the Coarb or successor of St.
Patrick in Armagh was not necessarily a bishop, but
was often a presbyter, and even a layman. The
word " Ard-bishop " does sometimes occur in Irish

No metro-
politan
jurisdiction

[1] " St. Patrick," Introduction, pp. 43, 94.

records; but, as Dr. Todd makes clear, this word "did not imply anything of jurisdiction," but "denotes only an eminent or celebrated bishop." There might be several "ard-bishops" in the same place.[1] A Synod of the English Church, held at Cealcythe in 816, refused permission to the Irish clergy to exercise their ministry in any of their dioceses, because it was uncertain whether or by whom they were ordained (*quia incertum est nobis, unde, et an ab aliquo ordinentur*), and also because they had no metropolitan jurisdiction (*cum quibus nullus ordo metropolitanis*).

From this passage Dr. Todd concludes that the peculiarity of the Irish Church, "that there were no dioceses properly so called, no regular episcopal or archiepiscopal jurisdiction, and no limit or canonical restraint upon the consecration of bishops," was well known in England. "And," he adds, "we know this to have been the case from the native records of Irish Christianity."[2] Giraldus Cambrensis affirms positively that "there were no archbishops in Ireland" till the time of John Paparo.[3]

No diocesan episcopacy. 3. What will perhaps surprise the reader still more is that *diocesan episcopacy* was equally unknown. The word bishop now means a prelate who rules over a district called a diocese, and over the parochial clergy included in it. In that sense episcopacy had no existence in the early Irish Church. Episcopal writers are agreed in frankly admitting this. In the work already quoted Dr.

[1] Todd's "St. Patrick," p. 16.
[2] Ibid., p. 43.
[3] "Archiepiscopi vero in Hibernia nulli fuerant."—"Topograph. Hibern.," distinct. 3. cap. 17. *Cf.* also Ussher's "Religion of the Ancient Irish," c. viii. p. 320.

Todd says: "'The normal state of episcopacy in Ireland was, as we have described, *non-diocesan*, each bishop acting independently, without any archiepiscopal jurisdiction, and either entirely independent, or subject only to the abbot of his monastery, or in the spirit of clanship to his chieftain. The consequence of this system was necessarily a great multiplication of bishops. There was no restraint upon their being consecrated. Every man of eminence for piety or learning was advanced to the order of bishop as a sort of *degree* or mark of distinction" (p. 27). Again he says: "We know this to have been the case from the native records of Irish Christianity:" "that there were no dioceses properly so called, no regular episcopal or archiepiscopal jurisdiction."[1] Skene says: "'There was episcopacy in the Church, but it was not diocesan episcopacy."[2] The most recent writer on "The Church of Ireland," the Rev. Thomas Olden, Vicar of Ballyclough, writes to the same effect. "From this it will be seen," he says, "that diocesan episcopacy did not exist in the early Church, and no attempt was made to introduce it until the Synod of Rathbreasil in 1118, which proposed a division of Ireland into dioceses. There were, in fact, neither dioceses in the ordinary sense, nor parishes, until the twelfth century."[3] The diocesan system was introduced through the Danish invaders at the same time as the Roman jurisdiction, and as part of the hierarchical system of Rome. The first bishop of the Danes of Dublin was Dunan, and, as

[1] Todd's "St. Patrick," p. 43.
[2] Skene's "Celtic Scotland," vol. ii. Bk. ii. c. ii. p. 44.
[3] "The Church of Ireland," chap. vii. p. 117.

Mr. Olden says, "Dunan was the first bishop in Ireland who possessed diocesan jurisdiction, limited as it was."[1] Somewhat later, at the Synod of Rathbreasil in 1118, called and presided over by Gillé, the Papal legate, Ireland was divided into twenty-four dioceses, with two archbishops, and so the diocesan system, first begun among the Danes, was extended to the whole of Ireland. Diocesan episcopacy thus came in with the Papal system, and was set up in Ireland by the Pope's representative.

4. That there were bishops of a sort in Ireland, however, from the time of Patrick is quite certain; and what manner of officials they were we have now to ascertain. This will be best learned from a simple statement of the facts as they are set forth in ancient Irish records.

Bishops very numerous. (1.) Now the first thing that strikes the inquirer is the *vast number* of the bishops in the early Irish Church in proportion to the population.

There is a remarkable document, assigned by Dr. Todd and others to the middle of the eighth century, and believed to be the work of Tirechan, entitled "A Catalogue of the Saints in Ireland according to their different periods," first published by Ussher. It divides the time between the age of St. Patrick and the year 666 into three periods, describing the character of each. The first period extended over about one hundred years from the time of Patrick till about 543 A.D.; and here is what the " Catalogue " says of it: " The first order of Catholic saints was in the time of Patrick; and then they were all bishops, famous and holy, and full of the Holy Ghost, 350 in number, founders

[1] "The Church of Ireland," p. 192.

of churches. They had one head, Christ; and one leader, Patrick." It is added that "they rejected not the service and society of women." "The second order was of Catholic presbyters. For in this order there were few bishops and many presbyters, in number 300. . . . They refused the services of women, separating them from the monasteries." This second period or order continued from 543 to 572. This was the time when so many distinguished missionaries, such as Columba and Columbanus, went forth to evangelise Europe. "The third order of saints was of this sort. They were holy presbyters, and a few bishops, one hundred in number, who dwelt in desert places, and lived on herbs and water, and the alms; they shunned private property." It is worthy of note, too, that the first period, when the bishops were most numerous, 350 in number, is represented as superior to the others. The first is "most holy" (*sanctissimus*), the second "very holy" (*sanctior*), and the third only "holy" (*sanctus*).

Several early writers agree substantially with the "Catalogue" respecting the number of bishops and churches. In an ancient poem in the *Leabhar Breac*, attributed to Aileran, who died A.D. 664 at a very advanced age, Patrick is said to have ordained 350 bishops and 300 presbyters, and to have consecrated 700 churches. The writer of the "Tripartite Life" puts the number at 370 bishops and 5000 presbyters. Nennius states that Patrick founded 365 churches and ordained 365 bishops. But the "Four Masters" give the number as 700 churches, 700 bishops, and 3000 presbyters.

The statements of these early writers with respect to the large number of bishops in the Celtic Church

of Ireland are abundantly confirmed from other
sources; as, for example, by the facts and figures
culled by the late Bishop Reeves from ancient documents and annals, and given to the public in his
"Ecclesiastical Antiquities of Down, Connor, and
Dromore." Let me lay before the reader a few
examples gleaned from this scholarly work. From
the evidence printed in it we find that there was a
bishop at Downpatrick; another at Raholp, three
miles north-east of Downpatrick; another at Bright,
two or three miles south-east of Downpatrick;
another at Maghera, on the Newcastle side of it;
and another on Mahee Island, off Killinchy in Strangford Lough. Here were five bishops in the same
immediate neighbourhood. Again, Loughbrickland
and Donoughmore in County Down closely adjoin
each other; there was a bishop in each. Passing
to County Antrim, there was a bishop in Coleraine;
one at Armoy; one at Ramoan; one at Culfeightrin
close by; and one on the adjoining island of Rathlin.[1]
There was a bishop at Kilroot; another at Rashee,
the next parish; another at Connor, the parish next
to that; and another at Muckamore, only a few
miles off. Very significant results surely from the
scanty records that are extant. Dr. Reeves himself
states that, in addition to five others whose names
he gives, "there are within the jurisdiction of the
modern see of Meath *sixteen* churches which are
recorded as having been the seats of bishops;" that
is, *twenty-one* altogether.[2]

It has been computed by Sir William Petty that at

---

[1] There were other bishops, too, in the same neighbourhood,
at places which cannot now be identified.
[2] "Antiquities," p. 128.

the time of the English invasion in the twelfth century the population of Ireland was little above 300,000. Covered as the country then was with extensive forests and unreclaimed bogs and marshes, it could hardly have been so great in the time of Patrick. That is to say, the population of all Ireland was hardly equal to the population of Belfast or Dublin at the present time ; and yet a population hardly so large as we have now in Belfast had more bishops than Belfast has of clergy of all denominations, even taking the lowest number of 350 given above as the number of bishops in ancient Ireland. St. Bernard was, therefore, within the mark when he said " that one episcopal district was not content with one bishop, but almost every church had its separate bishop."[1]   Lanfranc adds that " in towns or cities many (*plures*) bishops were ordained ;"[2] and Anselm complains that " bishops were made without any fixed place at all."[3]   Skene remarks that " he (Patrick) appears to have placed a bishop consecrated by himself in each church which he founded," and calls the system established by him " a congregational and tribal episcopacy."[4]   This accords with what is implied in the statements already given from early writings which represent the number of bishops as corresponding with the number of churches. The " Annals of the Four Masters " give the names of upwards of one hundred churches, each of which had a bishop.[5]

[1] "Ita ut unus episcopatus uno non esset contentus, sed singulæ pene Ecclesiæ Singulos haberunt episcopos." — " De Vita Malachiæ," c. x.

[2] See Ussher's " Religion of the Ancient Irish," p. 322.

[3] Ibid.   [4] " Celtic Scotland," Bk. ii. c. i. pp. 21, 22.

[5] Reeves's " Antiquities," p. 126, note.

Many groups of seven bishops each living together.

But the whole facts are not yet before the reader. I have now to direct attention to a series of facts still more singular. One is a little surprised at discovering that a provincial king (Ængus, king of Munster) had *two bishops* and *ten priests* in his household;[1] and that, as Lanfranc testifies, towns or cities had many bishops. More remarkable still were the immense number of bishops that lived together in groups of seven, all the seven being connected with a single church. The "Martyrology of Donegal" mentions six such groups, each group containing seven bishops, who were connected with a single church, the seven in each of three of these groups being brothers, sons of one father. "The Litany of Ængus the Culdee," contained in the *Leabhar Breac* and in the "Book of Leinster," gives 153 such groups of seven each, and here too in very many instances the seven are sons of one father; and the testimony of the "Litany of Ængus" with regard to this has striking corroboration from other sources.[2] In addition, the "Litany of Ængus" mentions (according to Mr. Olden) two sets, each of 150 bishops, and two more of 350. And more marvellous still, St. Mochta, the abbot of Louth, a disciple of St. Patrick, is described in the same work as having with him in his monastery, and as part of his "family" there, one hundred bishops. It would seem from these figures that those writers who speak of 700 as the number of bishops ordained by St.

---

[1] Reeves's "Antiquities," p. 123.

[2] See Todd's "St. Patrick," pp. 32–34, and Skene's "Celtic Church of Scotland," vol. ii. Bk. ii. p. 25. The number of groups mentioned by Ængus is differently represented. Skene states it to be 153, Todd 141, and Olden 138.

Patrick are nearer the mark than those who put it at 350.

In the facts and figures I have just adduced there is much food for reflection, which, however, it will be better to reserve till the whole case is before the reader. Inductions which fail to recognise and embrace all the phenomena are valueless.

In the meantime, the question naturally occurs and solicits an answer, How came there to be, with such a sparse population and in such a rude and primitive society, such an immense supply of bishops and other clergy as at this time not only swarmed the Irish Church at home, but, as St. Bernard says, sent them "like a flood" over other countries? The answer is at hand. It was due in part to the earnest religious spirit that prevailed and the high regard for the clerical office; but, as a fruit of this, there was a remarkable law in the Brehon Code, unparalleled, so far as we know, in any other Church in Christendom, a law which declared "that every first birth of every human couple, the mother being a lawful wife," belonged to the Church; and that if there were eleven or more children, of whom less than ten are sons, the Church was entitled to a second son.[1] It was manifestly a republication in the Christian Church of the Mosaic law, which declared that the first-born of every creature, including the first-born of man, was to be presented to the Lord, and given to Aaron and his successors (Exod. xiii. 2; Numb. xviii. 15). And this law was no dead letter in the Irish Church. From its operation there were no exemptions. It applied to the sons of kings and chiefs, as well as to

[marginal note:] How the clergy were so numerous: every first-born belonged to the Church.

---

[1] "Senchus Mor," vol. iii. p. 57.

THE CHURCH OF ST. PATRICK [PART III

the humblest in the land. And the young, dedicated to God in pursuance of this law, were put
under training in the great monastic schools, which
were the colleges of that time. Let me give a case
in point. It is related that Kellach, son of Eoghan
Bel, king of Connaught, was put under the care of
St. Kieran of Clonmacnois, in accordance with this
law. But his father was mortally wounded in battle,
and, having no other son or relative old enough to
take his place, the chieftains asked St. Kieran to
permit the young man to leave the monastery and
become king. Kieran declined to give the permission sought; but Kellach, at the instance of the
chiefs, left clandestinely, and was cursed by the
saint. After a time, the young man repented, returned to Clonmacnois, was received by St. Kieran,
and became eminent for sanctity, but (according to
the story) the curse could not be removed, and at
last he died a violent death. The editors of the
Senchus Mor truly remark that "rights such as
these were never claimed as against the whole body
of the laity by any other Christian Church in
Europe."

The bishops had no juris-diction. (2.) The bishops of the primitive Church of Ireland had *no jurisdiction*. We have seen that they
had no dioceses. "Dioceses and diocesan episcopacy had no existence at all" in it.[1] It should
never be forgotten by any one who wishes to realise
and to appreciate the organisation of the Irish
Church that its government was not in the hands
of the bishops, but in quite other hands. *There is
nothing more absolutely certain than that the govern-*

[1] Professor G. T. Stokes in "Ireland and the Celtic Church,"
p. 338.

176

ment of the primitive Church of Ireland was not the episcopal form of government. The bishops had no governmental power. The real rulers were the abbots, or *Coarbs*, as they were called, who were often only presbyters, and sometimes laymen. This is a fact of prime significance in connection with early Irish Church organisation, and authorities are happily una- **The abbots** nimous with regard to it. It was the abbots who **were the** exercised jurisdiction, and the bishops were in com- **real rulers** plete subordination to them. Bede says of Iona that **of the** "that island was wont to have always as ruler a **Church.** presbyter-abbot, to whose jurisdiction the whole province,. and even the bishops themselves, were, contrary to the usual method, bound to submit, according to the example of their first teacher, who was not a bishop, but a presbyter and monk."[1] Again, in his "Life of Cuthbert," he says, in reference to Lindisfarne, of which Iona was the parent : "All the presbyters, with the deacons, cantors, lectors, and other ecclesiastical orders, along with the bishop himself, were subject in all things to monastic rule."[2] But the state of things which thus obtained at Iona and Lindisfarne was simply a reproduction of what we know obtained throughout the whole Church in Ireland. Even when the head of a monastery was a woman, the bishops and other clergy were subject to her. In the case of Brigid, who founded and ruled over the monastery of Kildare, although it included both men and women, we have an instance in point. She made Condlaed a bishop, but he was entirely under her jurisdiction, and could do nothing but as she directed. He was, as we have seen, chief

[1] Bede's "Eccl. Hist.," Bk. iii. c. 4.
[2] Bede's "Life of Cuthbert," c. 16.

worker or artificer in gold and silver and other
metals, and it would seem, in connection with his
art, wished to pay a visit to Rome, but she refused
permission, and when he persisted in going, contrary
to her desire, a Divine judgment is represented to
have come upon him by way of punishment. As
Skene says, referring to Ireland: "The entire
Church appears to have been monastic, and her
whole clergy embraced within the fold of the
monastic rule."[1] In the words of Mr. Olden, the
most recent writer on the subject: "The true
heads of the Church were the Coarbs. . . . The
Coarbs of the principal monasteries formed a council,
who debated questions, and spoke the voice of the
Church." He then goes on to justify this statement by evidence.[2]

How the
bishops
were em-
ployed.

(3.) As the bishops in the Irish Church at the
time I speak of had no jurisdiction, as its government was in the hands of the abbots, the question
naturally arises, How did such a vast number of
bishops find employment?

Mr. Olden makes the curious remark that their
duties were "exclusively spiritual."[3] By this he
seems to refer especially to their "transmission of
orders," which Dr. Reeves describes as "the essence
of their office." Now, if this was "the essence of
the office," and if, as we know it was, ordination
by a single bishop was recognised as valid, it is
strange to find so many bishops often in the same
neighbourhood, connected with the same monastery,
and even with the same church. If this was their

[1] "Celtic Scotland," vol. ii. Bk. ii. p. 42.
[2] "The Church of Ireland," p. 117.
[3] Ibid.

essential and chief duty, very few of them can have
had the opportunity of performing it at all; an idle
time of it they must have had, and very unneces-
sarily burdened with such an army the Celtic Church
must have been. For the purpose of ordaining and
of consecrating churches and the like, one out of
every fifty would have easily sufficed.

But where do we learn that the "transmission of
orders" is the essence of the office of the bishop as
distinct from that of presbyter? To see what the
"essence of the office" was originally conceived to
be, we naturally turn to the title employed to describe
it. Now ἐπίσκοπος means literally an "overseer,"
and undoubtedly *oversight* was one of the essential
duties of a bishop, although it brought with it
others, such as *teaching*. To the elders of Ephesus,
Paul says: "Take heed unto yourselves, and to all
the flock in which the Holy Ghost hath made you
bishops, to feed [*lit.* to *shepherd*, to act the part of
pastors to] the Church of God, which He hath
purchased with His own blood" (Acts xx. 28).
Again Peter says: "The elders, therefore, among
you I exhort, who am a fellow-elder . . . Tend [*lit.*
shepherd] the flock of God which is among you,
taking the oversight"[or episcopate—ἐπισκοποῦντες]
(1 Peter v. 2). In 1 Tim. iii. 2, 4, 5, both *teaching*
and *ruling* are clearly indicated as belonging to the
office of a bishop; *compare* also 1 Tim. v. 17 and
Titus i. 9, where the bishop is required to "hold to
the faithful word which is according to the teaching,
that he may be able both to exhort in the sound
doctrine and to convict the gainsayers." Oversight, or
rule, and teaching are thus regarded by both Peter
and Paul as the "essential" duties of the episcopal

THE CHURCH OF ST. PATRICK [PART III

office. And as to ordination, or what Dr. Reeves calls "the transmission of orders," where is it said to be the essence of the office of the bishop as distinct from the presbyter? In the passages just quoted, "presbyter" and "bishop" are names for the same officers, and the functions of the episcopate are to be discharged by the presbyters. Nay, this very function of ordination or "transmission of orders" is expressly stated to belong to and to have been performed by presbyters (1 Tim. iv. 14), and continued to be performed by them long after the time of the Apostles. Bishop Lightfoot shows that in Alexandria and Egypt, down to the beginning of the fourth century, the bishop was ordained by the presbyters; [1] and Canon Gore is, under the irresistible pressure of the evidence, constrained to admit the validity of presbyterial ordination.[2] The idea that ordination belongs exclusively to the bishop as distinct from the presbyter is post-apostolic; it is a later ecclesiastical development, and belongs to the sacerdotal and hierarchical accretions that began to grow and accumulate upon apostolic Christianity towards the end of the second century, and as a result in large measure of its contact with Paganism. In any case, it is certain that ordination or the "transmission of orders" formed but a very small part of the duties that devolved on the great army of bishops that belonged to the Church founded by Patrick.

How then were so many of them employed? There is one duty of a spiritual kind which, according to

[1] "Philippians," p. 231.
[2] See Gore's "Ministry of the Christian Church," pp. 73, 324, 339.

the New Testament, is an essential duty of the episcopal office, and which there is no doubt some of
the Irish bishops at all events performed, namely,
the work of the preacher and evangelist. Bede informs us how the English king, Oswald, asked "the
elders of the Scots" at Iona to send him a bishop to
minister to his people, and how an "assembly of the
elders" turned their eyes towards Aidan, and "concluded that he deserved to be made a bishop, and
ought to be sent to instruct the unbelievers and
unlearned, since he was found to be endued with the
grace of a singular discretion, which is the mother
of other virtues, and *so ordaining him they sent him
to preach.*"[1] Aidan, we know, too, did go and preach
and evangelise among the English, and there is no
doubt that a good many bishops were similarly
employed in Ireland.

There was one rather remarkable functionary in
the Irish Church, called the *Anamchara* or "Soul-
friend," who acted the part of a spiritual adviser,
and gave counsel in perplexing circumstances. After
the battle of Cooldreevny, and after Columba (according to the story) had been excommunicated by the
Synod of Telltown, he sought the advice of his
"soul-friend," and on his advice it was that Columba
went, with his companions, on his mission to Iona.
It was quite common for kings and chiefs to have
their "soul-friend" residing with them. Sometimes
the "soul-friend" was a presbyter, sometimes, as in
the case of Aidan, the "soul-friend" was a woman—
Molua, the mother of Choche"—but very often the

---

[1] "Sicque illum ordinantes ad prædicandum miserunt."—Bede's
" Eccl. Hist.," Bk. iii. c. 5.

office was filled by a bishop. Many bishops were employed thus.

Not a few, again, were engaged in the communication of sacred learning, and, so far as we can gather, of secular knowledge also. Reference has been made to the great monastic schools, which reached the zenith of their fame in the eighth century. This was another department of work in which bishops occupied themselves.

In those early times, before printing was invented, the copying and illumination of manuscripts of the Sacred Scriptures and of other books were regarded as a work of very great importance, one of the most honourable tasks in which any one could engage. Only those who have seen such manuscripts as the " Book of Kells," the " Book of Durrow," or the " Book of Armagh," can form any idea of the exquisite beauty of their ornamentation and illumination, and of the patient artistic skill expended on them. The work of transcribing and preserving ancient records was a necessary work, and its necessity brought about the evolution of a special functionary devoted to it, who was known as the *Scribhnidh* or *Scribe*. Bishops, in many instances, found employment in the practice of the scribe's art.

The making of shrines, reliquaries, bells, covers of sacred books, and other ornaments, was regarded as hardly less honourable, and was almost exclusively in the hands of the clergy. It is beyond question that bishops devoted themselves to such work. Condlaed, the bishop appointed by Brigid, was her " principal artist," that is, her artificer in metalwork of gold or silver. Bishop Erc, of Slane, acted in the capacity of a Brehon or judge. Bishop

Etchen was engaged as a ploughman in the field
when Columba went to him for ordination.[1] But
the most singular post which we have found filled
by a bishop is that of "Champion," or strong man.
St. Patrick, in his missionary journeys, we are told
by Jocelinc and in the "Tripartite,"[2] was accompanied by a "champion," or strong man, who, in
his old age, carried him on his shoulders and defended him in peril; and the "champion" who
attended St. Patrick was Bishop MacCarthinn, who
at length got tired of the work, complained that he
had been "a long time on the pad," asked to be
relieved, and to have a church assigned to him, as
some of his comrades had.   Patrick yielded to his
request, appointed him to Clogher, and gave him a
copy of the Gospels, which may still be seen in the
Royal Irish Academy of Dublin.   Life was exposed
to such risks in those times, and fighting so common,
that even ecclesiastics found it expedient to learn the
art of self-defence, and monasteries had their cham-
pions and armed retainers; but it is startling to our
modern notions to find bishops acting in that capacity.

It should not be forgotten that in rank and dignity the bishop held a subordinate position in Ireland,
and was regarded as inferior not only to the abbot,
but even to the lector.   Dr. Skene points out that
"inferior functionaries of the monastery . . . appear
to have united the functions of a bishop with their
proper duties."[3]

In view of such facts as I have recited, it is surely
putting it rather strongly, and in a way calculated

---

[1] Todd's "St. Patrick," p. 71.
[2] See Stokes's "Tripartite," p. 175.
[3] "Celtic Scotland," vol. ii. Bk. ii. c. ii. p. 44.

to mislead, to say that the duties of the bishop were "exclusively spiritual." I believe it was the Marquis of Dufferin who, when Chancellor of the Duchy of Lancaster, described himself as the "maid-of-all-work" to the Government. The bishop held a somewhat analogous position in the Irish Church. He was very much the "maid-of-all-work" to the monastic community, and a great deal of the work imposed on him appears to have been secular.

Ordination in the Irish Church.

A word with regard to *ordination* in the Irish Church. And what strikes one here is what may be called the laxity which characterised the rite. In view of the rules generally regarded as canonical, the Church in Ireland was certainly not rigorous or stringent. Ordination to the episcopate was not regarded as being irregular when it took place *per saltum*, that is, without requiring the person ordained to have been previously a deacon and a presbyter. Again, one bishop was thought sufficient to confer it. Still more extraordinary, women were not excluded from the episcopate. It is stated by the author of the "Scholia" on the Martyrology of Ængus, that "the form of ordaining a bishop was read over Brigit by Bishop Mel," and that she was actually ordained a bishop—a statement confirmed by her biographer, Cogitosus, who speaks of her "episcopal and virginal chair" (*cathedra episcopalis et puellaris*). Then we have the case of Findchan and Ædh Dubh. Findchan was an Irish ecclesiastic, a presbyter abbot, who founded a monastery on the island of Tirce. He had brought with him from Ireland a person called Ædh (Hugh), whose previous reputation had been somewhat shady. But Findchan thought he had induced him to quit his bad ways, and brought a bishop to have him ordained a presbyter. When the ceremony was about to be performed, the bishop insisted that Findchan, who was only a presbyter, should lay *his* hands on the head of the candidate first, the bishop then laying on his. The canonical rule was that when a presbyter was ordained the bishop's hand was to be first laid upon his head, and then the presbyters present were to lay their hands beside the bishop's. It is evident that the Irish ecclesiastics were not confined to methods elsewhere regarded as canonical. Much has been written on the case of Aidan, to which reference has been made already. When Oswald became king of England, Bede tells us that he " sent to the elders of the Scots " at Iona, among whom he himself had been well received and instructed in the faith, desiring them to send him a bishop who would labour among the English. The person first sent, however, was of too severe a temper to be acceptable to the English. At " an assembly of the elders " (*conventu seniorum*) in Iona it was debated what was to be done; but Aidan having addressed the council, " all who sat with him, turning on him their eyes, began diligently to weigh what he had said," and finally decided on sending him, " and so ordaining him, they (the elders) sent him to preach " (*sicque illum ordinantes, ad prædicandum miserunt*).

Over these words there has been much and keen debate. To the present writer it is a matter of complete indifference what conclusion is drawn from them: his mind is perfectly open on the subject. But the conclusion must not outrun the evidence. It is quite possible that the " assembly of elders " at Iona called in a bishop to ordain

THE CHURCH OF ST. PATRICK [PART III

Aidan. It is remarkable, however, that this is not
stated—that what is stated is that the "assembly
of elders" or "seniors" "ordained him and sent him
to preach." "It seems only reasonable to suppose,"
says Dr. Reeves, "that one or more bishops were
constantly resident at Hy, or that they were sent for
from the neighbouring coast when it was required to
confer the orders of the ministry, otherwise a forced
interpretation will be put upon Bede's words."[1] As
Bede states that Aidan was ordained by the assembly
of elders, it is difficult to see how a forced interpretation would be put upon his words by supposing
that they mean literally what they say—that he was
ordained by the "assembly of elders," and not by
a bishop. Is it not rather a forced interpretation
to make them state that Aidan was ordained by a
bishop or bishops without a particle of evidence that
there was a bishop at Iona at this time ? "It seems
only reasonable to suppose," says Dr. Reeves, "that
one or more bishops were constantly resident at Hy."
On the contrary, the inference seems most unreason-
able in view of the evidence which Dr. Reeves himself
supplies. On a succeeding page he admits the want
of evidence to support his statement : "That Columbkille associated a bishop with the brotherhood is not
expressly mentioned, but that bishops from Ireland
occasionally visited Iona is directly stated in Adamnan's Life of that saint," he affirms. But in the
"Chronicon Hyense," given in the Appendix to Dr.
Reeves's "Adamnan," there is no trace of a bishop
residing at Hy *from the arrival of Columba in 563
till long after the ordination of Aidan.* Aidan was
ordained in 635 and died in 651. And the first

[1] "Eccl. Antiq.," p. 131.
186

resident bishop we hear of in this Chronicle of Hy
is Cellach, of whom we are told : "654. Cellach,
relicto episcopatu, reversus est ad insulam Hii."
Cellach had been labouring as bishop among the
Mercians and Midland Angles. The "Chronicon
Hyense" contains a record not only of Hy, but of
the monastic communities connected with it. We
do read in Adamnan's " Life of Columba" of the visit
of Bishop Cronan from Munster. It is quite true
also that in a few instances in Ireland or in North
Britain, where ordination is referred to, a bishop is
described as being called in to take part in it; but
one of these instances—the ordination of Columba
by Bishop Etchen—is characterised by Dr. Reeves
himself as "the fiction of a later age," and Dr. Todd
takes the same view of it. It is not safe, where
Ireland is concerned, to impute the custom of a later
age to an earlier. In the case of Ædh Dubh, the
bishop called in by Findchan insisted on the latter,
who was a presbyter, laying his hand first on the
head of the candidate, showing great laxness from
the canonical point of view. It should be remembered farther that in the early period ordination by
presbyters was recognised as valid, and continued at
Alexandria and in Egypt, as Bishop Lightfoot has
shown, till the beginning of the fourth century.
Besides, the power of ordination appears to have
been expressly given to presbyter-abbots by more
than one monastic rule. In the Rule of Aurelian,
a French bishop contemporary with Columba, it is
laid down that "when the abbot wishes, he has
power to ordain."[1]   The Rule of Benedict gave

[1] " Et quando (abbas) voluerit, ordinandi habeat potestatem,"
cap. 46.—Migne, " Patrol.," Curs. lxviii. 392.

THE CHURCH OF ST. PATRICK [PART III

the same power.[1] Cassian speaks of a monk called
Daniel as having been ordained first a deacon, and
then a presbyter, by the presbyter-abbot Paphnutius.[2]
An old ritual, in use before the time of Theodore
of Canterbury, assumes that abbots ordained.[3] As
regards the case of Aidan, therefore, it seems better,
in view of all the facts, not to be too positive either
way, and not to allow denominational predilections to tempt us to conclusions which outrun the
evidence.

THE LAW OF SUCCESSION IN THE
IRISH CHURCH.

The
abbacies
hereditary.

There is one other point in connection with this
subject of Church organisation which must not be
overlooked—the singular law of succession which
obtained in the Celtic Church of Ireland. Many
of our readers will be surprised to learn that the
most important Church offices were *hereditary*, and
yet this was literally true. The chief functionaries
and real rulers of the early Church of Ireland were
the abbots, and the abbots succeeded one another,
not by election, but by a hereditary law. What
that law was has been already indicated. When a
monastery was founded, a portion of land, or in
some cases a royal rath, was made over by the head
of the tribe to which it belonged to the founder,
who was usually connected with the same tribe.
In that case the abbacy always remained in the
family, and the abbot was provided from among

---

[1] Reg., cap. lxv., Migne's "Latin Fathers."
[2] Cassian, " Collatio," iv. cap. i.
[3] " Patrol.," Curs. clvi. 1113, ed. Migne.

188

its members. When the founder belonged to a different tribe from the chief by whom the site was granted, the succession to the abbacy was always retained by the family to which the first abbot belonged, and the successive abbots were called the "coarbs"—*i.e.* the heirs or successors of the original founder. For many generations, for example, the coarbs, or heirs, or successors of Comgall, who founded the great monastery of Bangor, were lineal descendants of the family to which he belonged. The hereditary principle came to have an extended application in Ireland. Even the office of Brehon became hereditary in certain families, although all who held it had to comply with certain fixed conditions of study and preparation. Free election of the abbot by a monastic community was unknown, and, as we have seen, the abbot was often not a bishop, but only a presbyter, or a layman. "It did not follow," says Dr. Todd, "that these coarbs were always bishops, or even priests. In the case of Kildare the coarbs were always females; and there is an instance on record, although in a different sense, of a female coarb of St. Patrick at Armagh. But it is evident that the abbot or coarb, and not the bishop as such, inherited the rights of chieftainship and property, and was, therefore, the important personage in the ecclesiastical community. Hence we have in the Annals a nearer approach to a correct list of the abbots or coarbs than to a correct list of the bishops. The bishop or bishops—for there were often more than one bishop connected with the monastery, or with what afterwards became the episcopal see—were in subjection to the coarb-abbot, and did not necessarily succeed each other, according to our modern

A regular succession of bishops in Ireland it is impossible to trace.

notions of episcopal succession. There were frequent breaks in the chain." [Dr. Todd refers here to Reeves, "Eccl. Ant.," p. 136 in proof.] . . . "Considerable difficulty," Dr. Todd proceeds, "has therefore been created by the attempt to make out a regular succession of bishops in Armagh and elsewhere. *The truth is there was no such thing.* The names handed down to us as successors of Patrick are many of them called abbots. Some are called bishops as well as abbots, some are styled bishops only, and some coarbs of St. Patrick. But there is nothing in this last title to indicate whether the personage so designated was a bishop, a priest, or a layman."[1]

"Hence," also remarks the Rev. Thomas Olden, "catalogues of successive bishops of Irish sees, from their founder to the present day must be illusive."[2]

Hence also, we may add, the absurdity of asserting in the most cocksure manner, as many do, that they are able to trace their apostolical succession up to St. Patrick, and through him to the apostles. The confidence with which such assertions are made is usually in inverse proportion to the information of those who make them. A course of reading in early Irish Church history would considerably abate their confidence.

How the state of things which thus existed in the Irish Church was regarded in England we have seen from the decision of the Synod of Cealcythe to exclude the Irish clergy from their dioceses ; how they were regarded by contemporary ecclesiastics on the Continent we learn from St. Bernard. In his

---

[1] Todd's " St. Patrick," pp. 171, 172.
[2] "The Church of Ireland," c. vii. p. 120.

" Life of Malachi " he says : " There had been introduced by the diabolical ambition of certain people of rank a scandalous usage whereby the Holy See (Armagh) came to be obtained by hereditary succession.   For they would allow no person to be promoted to the bishopric except such as were of their own tribe and family.   Nor was it for any short period that this succession had continued, nearly fifteen generations having been already exhausted in this course of iniquity."   He mentions that before the time of Celsus eight of these coarbs, or successors of St. Patrick in Armagh were married, and not in orders at all—mere laymen.   He appears to have regarded the case of Armagh as quite exceptional, whereas we have abundant evidence to show that the law of succession was the same everywhere throughout Ireland.

CHAPTER X

PROCRUSTEAN METHODS OF TREATING EARLY IRISH CHURCH ORGANISATION.

THE facts which I have been recounting with regard to the constitution of the early Irish Church
—its thoroughly monastic character; the universal
rule over it of the abbots; the complete absence of
anything in the shape of episcopal government; the
vast number of bishops in proportion to the population; their connection in so many instances with
single churches; their absolute subjection to the
abbots, and (where the two offices of abbot and
bishop were not combined) their inferior and
humble status in the monastery—have been a sore
trial to some writers. Instead of taking the facts
as they find them, a certain class of historians have
put forth painfully laborious efforts to reconcile
them with modern church systems. The ingenuity
that has been expended in reading Anglicanism,
with its diocesan episcopacy and hierarchical grades,
into the organisation of the Celtic Church of Ireland,
and in making out the former to be identical with
the latter, might have yielded magnificent results
had it been brought to bear on some fruitful field
of study. To any one whose eyes have once been
opened to the real state of the case they are as
puerile as they are futile. But by a species of

"apostolical succession" the most extraordinary analogies and arguments to this end are handed down from one writer to another. Dr. Todd and Dr. Reeves get hints from Bishop Lloyd; the ingenuities of Dr. Todd and Dr. Reeves are appropriated by minor compilers; and the comic futilities of compilers are retailed by other scribes still as heaven-inspired oracles.

The late Bishop Reeves has done immense service, *Valuable researches of Dr. Reeves.* especially in his learned volumes on the "Ecclesiastical Antiquities of Down, Connor, and Dromore," and in his edition of "Adamnan's Columba," in collecting and making available to the reader from out-of-the-way and often obscure sources so much that serves to throw light on the early ecclesiastical history of this country. For the patient labour which he devoted to this task, and for the valuable fruit of it embodied in these volumes and in other publications, he has earned the gratitude of every student of Irish history. But when Dr. Reeves quits research and proceeds, as he does in the Appendix to *His explanation of the anomalies in the early Irish Church not satisfactory.* his "Antiquities," to explain the anomalies of the primitive Irish Church organisation, and to reconcile them with modern Anglicanism, his success is not conspicuous. It may be interesting and instructive to notice briefly some of the ways in which he seeks to account for the peculiarities of the Celtic Church.

1. One reason which he gives for the extraordinary *Bishops multiplied, he says, to secure perpetuity of orders.* multiplication of bishops is that it was "more the object to secure to the Church the perpetuity of orders than to parcel it out into accurately defined dioceses."[1] So far as we have means of knowing, the "securing to the Church the perpetuity of orders"

[1] "Antiquities," p. 123.

seems to have given those old Irish ecclesiastics precious little anxiety—much less than it does to a modern Anglo-Catholic—much less than it did to their English Papal contemporaries, who refused to admit them into their dioceses, and declared by a solemn synodical canon that it was quite "uncertain by whom they were ordained, or whether they were ordained at all." "To secure to the Church the perpetuity of orders," was it necessary to have a bishop in every church, where the churches were not more than a mile or two apart? Was it necessary for this purpose, from the "Catholic" point of view, to have a series of 140 or 150 collegiate churches, with seven bishops attached to each, and to have not one, but in some cases a numerous staff of bishops in each monastery? "The perpetuity of orders," if that had been the object, could have been secured quite as well, as it was elsewhere, at a much cheaper rate—by at least one out of every fifty of the staff of bishops that was kept up.

Patrick appointed suffragans!

2. Dr. Reeves reproduces, and appears to adopt, Bishop Lloyd's suggestion that, besides the bishops ordained by St. Patrick, he appointed as many suffragans as there were rural deaneries at a later time.[1] But to conceive of "suffragans" as existing in the early Celtic Church is to perpetrate a very palpable anachronism, which it is strange that Dr. Reeves should for a moment countenance. The metal which an astronomer once imagined he detected in one of the heavenly bodies turned out to be but an element in his own atmosphere, or a part of his own spectroscope, which had to be removed before he could see the orb truly. The "bishops'

[1] "Antiquities," p. 124.

sees " and " suffragans," with which Dr. Lloyd credits
the primitive Church of Ireland, were but motes
floating in that good Bishop's atmosphere. We must
remove these from our line of vision before we can
see just as they were past times and institutions.

3. Conscious that the explanation just given was
far from satisfactory, Dr. Reeves next supposes the
great multiplication of bishops to be " due to the
sudden accession of great numbers to Christianity "
in Patrick's time.[1] Now, if the Irish bishops were,
as they seem to have been, very much like ordinary
clergy of our own time, missionaries or ministers of
congregations, the sudden accession of large numbers
to the Christian faith would no doubt make their
increase necessary. But if they were anything like
modern bishops, with similar duties, no such multiplication was required as took place. There was the
same sudden accession of great multitudes of converts in England through the mission of Augustine;
there was a like sudden and vast accession in many
Continental countries, but in none of them did it
lead to the appointment of such an immense army
of bishops. It necessitated an increase in the staff
of the ordinary clergy.

Sudden accession of large numbers said to explain the large number of bishops.

4. The next cause to which Dr. Reeves attributes
the large proportion of bishops in the Irish Church
is a much more feasible one. He thinks that " the
civil condition of the country "—its division and sub-
division into so many tribes and principalities—may
have had much to do with it.[2] Dr. Todd assigns a
similar reason for their increase: " When one of the
petty kings or chieftains embraced Christianity, he

A more feasible explanation

[1] "Antiquities," p. 125.   [2] Ibid., p. 126.

provided a bishop, sometimes more than one bishop, and other clergy for the benefit of his clan. The district which owed allegiance to the chieftain, and was inhabited by his followers, became the proper field of labour to *his bishops* and clergy, and this was the first approach made to a diocesan or terri- torial jurisdiction in the Church of Ireland."[1] And Dr. Skene makes a like remark. Patrick, he says, " founded churches wherever he could obtain a grant from the chief of the sept, and appears to have placed in each *tuath,* or tribe, a bishop ordained by himself, who may have had one or more presby- ters with him. It was, in short, a congregational and tribal episcopacy, united by a federal rather than a territorial tie under regular jurisdiction."[2] Now it is no doubt perfectly true that the ecclesi- astical arrangements and the distribution of monas- teries and clergy were much affected by the tribal divisions, and these divisions might have been ade- quate to account for the multiplication of bishops had the bishops in Ireland been only as numerous as the tribes or septs, each tribe or sept having its bishop ; but its insufficiency to explain the appointment of so many bishops appears from the fact that there was often quite a number of them within the terri- tory of a single sept—in the extract from Dr. Todd given above, he unwittingly but quite correctly speaks of the district of the chieftain becoming the proper field of labour to his *bishops*, not his bishop ; that we find a large number of bishops in a single monas- tery where one would have been sufficient for con- ferring orders, consecrating churches, and the like ;

[1] Todd's " St. Patrick," p. 38.
[2] Skene's " Celtic Scotland," vol. ii. Bk. ii. p. 22.

that in adjacent churches in the same immediate neighbourhood we find a bishop in each, and that in a multitude of instances we have seven bishops attached to a single church. The seven could not have been all needed for the purposes just indicated.

5. Once more, following Dr. Lanigan, Dr. Reeves attributes the large number of bishops in the Church of St. Patrick to "the existence of the order of Chorepiscopi, or country bishops."[1] But there is no trace whatever in the early records of any difference in this respect between country bishops and city bishops. On the contrary, it is the express complaint of Lanfranc that "in *towns or cities many* bishops were ordained" (*quod in villis, vel civitatibus plures ordinantur*). But in this reference to the Chorepiscopi Dr. Reeves appears to me to have been on the track which would have led him to the natural solution of the problem had he pursued it far enough. The numerous Chorepiscopi, which synods of the fourth century passed decrees to reduce or suppress, were a survival of a primitive state of things to be noticed presently, in which each bishop was simply the chief minister of a congregation. "There is good reason to believe," says Dr. Todd, "that the ancient *Chorepiscopi*, although enjoying the name, and in part exercising the jurisdiction of bishops, were in reality no more than presbyters."[2]

6. But Dr. Reeves is conscious that he has not yet hit on the true secret of such a multiplication of bishops, and feels it necessary to look around to see if he cannot find other causes. "The increase of bishops in Ireland," he says, "was further owing to

Explained by the alleged existence of Chorepiscopi?

A sixth attempt at explanation.

[1] "Antiquities," p. 127.
[2] Todd's "St. Patrick," p. 76.

the custom which prevailed from the commencement, of combining the episcopal and abbatial offices in the founders or superiors of religious houses, or of associating a bishop in the brotherhood where the rector was only a priest." This, however, goes but a short way in accounting for the state of things which has been laid before the reader. It in no way accounts for the presence of a number of bishops in the same monastery or church, nor the presence of a bishop in each of a number of closely adjacent churches.

A seventh attempt.

7. Both Dr. Reeves and Dr. Todd ascribe the consecration of so many bishops without sees to the missionary character of their duties.[1] Now, it is quite true that some bishops went abroad as missionaries, and others doubtless laboured at home in that capacity, although it is not to be forgotten that some of the greatest, most eminent, and successful missionaries, like Columba and Columbanus, were not bishops but presbyters. But what needs to be explained, and what all that has hitherto been adduced fails to explain from the episcopal point of view, is the existence of so many bishops who were not "ambulatory," but fixed to particular churches, which in many cases were quite near to one another.

The true explanation: the bishops of the primitive Church pastors of congregations.

8. At one point Dr. Reeves seems to me to light upon the true solution of the problem, although he fails in some measure to appreciate its full significance. When he quotes Bingham for the purpose of showing that the nearer you go back to primitive times bishops are found to be relatively more numerous, he has really got his hand on the clue to

[1] "See Reeves's "Antiquities," pp. 134, 135 ; and Todd's "St. Patrick," pp. 36, 47.

the labyrinth. The chief explanation of the mystery, which after all is no mystery at all, is doubtless to be found here. All through the second century, and in many quarters even in the third century, the bishop was simply the presiding pastor of a single congregation. There is extant a very notable law-book of the Egyptian Churches, entitled "The Apostolic Canons," or "Apostolic Church Order." It has been edited by Dr. Harnack, and discussed by him with great knowledge and acumen. The work is a compilation, and as such is assigned by Dr. Harnack to the year 300 or thereabouts, but it is made up of some earlier documents, among others of portions of the *Didache*. Here is a suggestive passage from it : " If there are in one place few men and not twelve persons who are fit to vote at the election of a bishop, the neighbouring churches should be written to, where any of them is a settled one, in order that three selected men may come thence and examine carefully if he is worthy." Here, then, it is laid down that even *where there are less than twelve Christians in a place competent to vote, a bishop must be chosen by them.* Direction is given also respecting the appointment of presbyters, and also deacons, readers, and widows. But other things even more striking come out in this old " Code of Discipline." I prefer to give them in the words of Dr. Harnack. " From its statements it appears without doubt," he says, " that the bishop, at least in one view, although *primus inter pares*, is con-sidered the superior of the presbyters." But on the other hand, Dr. Harnack shows that there is *a superintendence of the bishop by the presbyters.* " It is to be observed that of the relation of the pres-

199

byters to the bishop the same word is used
($\pi\rho o\nu o\widehat{\epsilon}\iota\sigma\theta a\iota$) which shows their relation to the
congregation. This is the technical term for the
function of the care and of the 'rule,' and that of
the presbyters." [In a note Dr. Harnack gives evidence of this from both profane and ecclesiastical
inscriptions.] "Thus also *the bishop stands under the
care of the presbytery*. That is information of the
first importance; for what we hitherto might only
have guessed at, we now receive incontestable proof
of. We discover that even in the time when from
a plurality of bishops there has come to be only one,
*a kind of supervision by the presbyters over the
bishop's actions has continued*. The episcopal
monarchy has thus not yet had, even at the beginning, the significance of an autocracy; rather
has the supreme control of the presbyters continued
at times." The bishop is described as "the pastor,
the liturgist, and representative of the congregation
to the outer world."[1] We have already seen that
in Egypt the bishop was ordained by the presbyters.

The immense number of bishops as compared with
the population in Proconsular Africa and in other
countries, has been often noticed, and was itself
sufficient to suggest that each bishop must have
been the presiding pastor of a single community or
congregation. At a conference in Carthage between
the Donatists and the Catholics there were present
altogether 565 bishops from a comparatively limited
area, and of course there must have been many
absent. Somewhat later a contemporary, who was
himself a sufferer, mentions that 466 Catholic

[1] Harnack's "Sources of the Apostolic Canons," pp. 29, 32, 33.

bishops presented themselves on one occasion before the king of the Vandals at Carthage. Dupin reckons up about 690 bishops in Africa about this time; the greater number of these must have been in the position of pastors in small towns and villages.

This is precisely the position of the Ignatian bishop: he is the chief pastor of a congregation, with his presbyters and deacons around him. He presides and administers the sacraments just as, for example, any non-Episcopal minister does. Candid Episcopal scholars fully admit what is implied in these facts. "The whole position of the bishop," says Professor Sanday, "was very similar to that of the incumbent of the parish church in one of our smaller towns." Dr. Sanday is perhaps, since the death of Bishop Lightfoot, the highest Episcopal authority on this subject. He adds that in some respects "the Nonconformist communities of our own time furnish a closer parallel to the primitive state of things than an established Church can do. Christianity itself was an instance of non-conformity."[1] Later still, Dr. Sanday says: "The Church passed through a congregational stage, and (if we exclude the activity of the apostles as something exceptional) it passed through a presbyterian stage. If any one wishes to single out these stages, and to model the society to which he belongs upon them, he is zealous for a pure and primitive polity; he clings to the Bible and what he finds in the Bible; he will not allow himself to wander far from that ideal which he thinks Christ and His apostles have left him. Can we condemn him for this? Shall

[1] "The Expositor," Feb. 1887, p. 113.

we not rather say, εὐδοκιμείτω καὶ ἐπὶ τούτῳ?" Dr.
Sanday very justly thinks that, he sees here the
basis of an eirenicon between the Churches. One
of the most recent Anglican Church historians, who
is by no means of so scientific a spirit as Dr. Sanday,
and who often exhibits an Anglican bias and gives
an Anglican colouring to the facts, nevertheless
fully admits the *congregational* character of episcopacy in the early period. He says: "Every city
[he might have said every village] in which a church
was formed had its bishop, whose position in many
respects resembled that of the rector of a parish
surrounded by his assistant clergy rather than that
of the modern bishop of a diocese, containing perhaps several large towns. To him it belonged to
preside over the assemblies, whether of the presbyters
or of the brethren at large; to decide finally on the
reception or exclusion of members; to grant com-
mendatory letters to members of his flock passing
into other dioceses; to maintain correspondence
with other churches: to ordain, to preach, to administer the sacraments; the two latter offices he
might, and often did, delegate in case of necessity
to his presbyters." [1] Why, this is just the position
of a Presbyterian minister. He is the "pastor" of
the congregation; there can be no regular meeting
of the elders without him in the chair; he only can
ordain and administer the sacraments.

Now the primitive Church of Ireland was detached
and isolated from the empire, cut off from the influences and changes at work in the great "Catholic
Church" throughout the empire. Some features of
the primitive organisation, therefore, persisted longer

[1] Cheetham's "Church History," p. 128.

in Ireland than in most other countries. What need is there to travel farther afield than this to account for the fact that in the Celtic Church of Ireland the bishops were so numerous—as numerous as the churches? If, along with this, one recognises the effect of the tribal system, and the predominant and controlling influence of the monasteries and their abbots, what more is needed to read the riddle of early Irish Church organisation?

And may we not find here the basis of an eirenicon between Episcopal and non-Episcopal denominations, a common meeting-ground where Episcopalians cannot but be delighted to stand beside their non-Episcopal brethren? As Episcopalians, of course, they have a warm admiration for bishops—such a love for them and such a faith in them that they cannot object to increase their number. Now what I suggest is, that they should multiply their bishops till they are as numerous relatively as they were in primitive times—till they are as numerous as the congregations, and every pastor is a bishop. Our Episcopalian friends cannot object to that. In view of their own contention that their Church polity is identical with that of the early Church, wherein Episcopacy was congregational and bishops as numerous as the churches, they cannot hesitate to welcome the proposal. It would be a union, too, on the basis of the "historic Episcopate." Why then should we not have it?

9. There was one feature in the ancient Church of Ireland which has given great scope to the inventive faculty of some writers—the fact that its bishops had no dioceses, no jurisdiction, no part in the government of the Church, were in such complete *Subordination of bishops to presbyter-abbots: analogies adduced.*

203

and universal subjection to the abbots, and held such
a humble place. Dr. Reeves refers to a supposed
parallel instance adduced by Bishop Lloyd, who
points out that the government of the University of
Oxford is exclusive of the Bishop of Oxford, that the
Chancellor and his deputy have precedence of the
Bishop, and that the students are exempt from his
cognisance and jurisdiction.[1] Dr. G. T. Stokes reproduces Bishop Lloyd's instance in a slightly modified form. He supposes a fellow or professor of the
University of Dublin appointed a bishop while still
retaining his fellowship or professorship. As professor or fellow, he would be subject to the provost,
though the latter were merely a presbyter (or, for
that matter, though he were merely a layman), who,
however, would acknowledge his superiority as bishop.
Dr. Stokes also cites the case of a returned Colonial
bishop acting as curate to a rector who is only a
presbyter, and, as his curate, subject to the presbyter. And such instances are sufficient to prove, it
seems, that modern diocesan episcopal government
is substantially identical with that of the early Irish
Church !—Q.E.D. ! It strikes an ordinary mind
that, accepting the instances as they are given, the
parallel is slightly imperfect, and scarcely sufficient
to bear the weight of the inference. No doubt some
odd cases like those adduced may now and then occur
as a quite abnormal and exceptional arrangement.
To make the parallel complete and to justify the
inference, the exception must become the rule, the
abnormal instance universal. Let us suppose this
taking place. Suppose all primatial, archiepiscopal,
and episcopal jurisdiction to be done away with, not

[1] Reeves's "Antiquities," p. 133.

in one or two exceptional cases only, but in the
whole Protestant Episcopal Church of Ireland; that
dioceses and diocesan bishops were completely abolished, and deans, canons, and the like entirely swept
away; *that there was no such thing as episcopal government left in it;* that the government of the Church
was put entirely into the hands of the heads of universities; that the functionaries known as "bishops"
were simply pastors of congregations, or missionaries,
or humble servants of the provost, who employs
them in teaching, or in copying old manuscripts, or
in brewing his ale, in cultivating his garden, cutting
down his trees, rowing his boat, grinding his corn,
driving his carriage, or, if he is old, carrying him
about on their back—*then* you would have a parallel,
or something approaching a parallel, to the ecclesiastical polity and government of the ancient Church
of Ireland; but the change that should bring that
state of things about *would be a revolution,* in which
episcopal government would be utterly swept away!
To argue that, because the subordination of a modern
bishop to the provost of a university, or to the rector
of a parish for whom he acts as curate, might occur
as *an abnormal and isolated arrangement, therefore*
the modern Episcopal Church is in government and
polity identical with one in which such a system was
universal, is only to trifle with the subject. To
establish identity, the exception must become the
rule, and in making the exception the rule you do
away with episcopal government altogether. If it
be alleged that there were the three orders of
"bishop," "presbyter," and "deacon" in the early
Irish Church, the reply is that the very same distinction is made in other Churches. There is a wide

and deeply-marked difference, for example, between the Presbyterian minister and his presbyters or elders. *He only* can preside, ordain, and administer the sacraments. We are inclined to share in the regret of a friend, who is a master in these matters, that Calvin did not reserve for him the sole right to the title of " bishop." ·

CHAPTER XI

THE EDUCATIONAL ACHIEVEMENTS OF THE CHURCH OF ST. PATRICK.

REFERENCE has been made to the schools or colleges Endowed set up by the illustrious King Cormac MacArt in university colleges the third century. But Professor O'Curry shows and inter- that even during the Christian period there were mediate schools in endowed educational establishments, which were in primitive Ireland. fact great national colleges, quite distinct from the ecclesiastical schools of the time.[1]   Such a system was devised by Dallan Forgaill, the *ard-ollamh*, chief poet and doctor of Ireland.   The scheme received the approval of the great convention of Drumccatt in 574, and provided that there should be what O'Curry describes as equivalent to a modern university in each of the five provinces, and something like what we now call an intermediate school in each *tuath*, or territory of a tribe, and they were well endowed.   To each *ollamh* were assigned free lands from his chief, as well as free common lands for the gratuitous education of such men of Erin as were without means of their own.   It reminds us somewhat of the system of universities, of colleges in the chief provincial towns, and of parish schools pro-

---

[1] O'Curry's "Manners and Customs of the Ancient Irish," pp. 77, 78.

jected, and to some extent set up, in Scotland by Knox.

With regard to such public schools in Ireland, the Brehon laws had the following among other prescriptions:—

"The poet (or tutor) commands his pupils. The man from whom education is received is free from the crimes of his pupils, if they be the children of natives [*i.e.* of the district], even though he feeds and clothes them, and they pay him for their learning. He is free, even though it be a stranger he instructs, feeds, and clothes, provided it is not for pay, but for God that he does it. If he feeds and instructs a stranger for pay, it is then he is accountable for his crimes."[1]

"However it may surprise us," says Sir Henry Maine, "that the connection between pupil and teacher was regarded as peculiarly sacred by the ancient Irish, and as closely resembling natural fatherhood, the Brehon tracts leave no room for doubt on the point. It is expressly laid down that it created the same *patria potestas* as actual paternity, and the literary foster-father, though he teaches gratuitously, has a claim through life upon portions of the property of the literary foster-son. Thus the Brehon with his pupils constituted not a school in our sense, but a true family. While the ordinary foster-father was bound by the law to give education of some kind to his foster-children—to the sons of chiefs instruction in riding, shooting with the bow, swimming, and chess-playing, and instruction to their daughters in sewing, cutting out, and

[1] O'Curry's "Manners and Customs of the Ancient Irish," vol. ii. p. 79.

embroidery—the Brehon trained his foster-sons in learning of the highest dignity, the lore of the chief literary profession. He took payment, but it was the law which settled it for him. It was part of his status, and not the result of a bargain."[1]

It may be added that the staff of masters or pro- Staff of fessors in a lay school or college included (according professors. to Professor Eugene O'Curry) the following :—

"1. The *Caogdach*, or 'fifty man;' who was the lowest, having only to chant the 150 Psalms.

"2. The *Foghlantidh*, or scholar; who taught ten out of the twelve books of the college course or native education.

"3. The *Staraidh*, or historian; who had also, besides history, thirty lessons of divinity in his course.

"4. The *Foircetlaidh*, or lecturer; who professed grammar, orthography, criticism, enumeration, the courses of the year, and the courses of the sun and moon (*i.e.* astronomy).

"5. The *Saoi Canoine*, or professor of divinity; who taught 'the canons, and the Gospels of Jesus, that is, the Word of God, in the sacred place in which it is; that is, who taught the Catholic Canonical Wisdom.'

"6. The *Drumchli*, or chief head; a master who knew the whole course of learning."[2]

But our business just now is with the monastic The great schools, which, it should be remembered, imparted monastic secular as well as religious education. It was quite schools. common for the sons of chiefs and kings at home

---

[1] Sir Henry Maine's "Early History of Institutions," Lect. viii. p. 242.
[2] "Manners and Customs of the Ancient Irish," vol. ii. p. 84.

and abroad to receive their training in them. As Dr. Skene says, the monasteries generally were "educational establishments to which the youth of the tribe were sent, not only to be trained to monastic life, but also to receive secular education. Each monastic institution had, besides its community of monks, a body of young people who received secular education. Even in the smaller monasteries the number of scholars was usually fifty. In the larger, of course, a much greater number were taught."[1] It is highly interesting to learn that it was to Ireland that the better classes, and even the nobility and royal families in England, sent their sons to be educated. Referring to the year 664, Bede says: "There were many of the nobility, and of the middle classes too of the English people, who, in the time of Bishops Finan and Colman, had left their native isle and retired thither [i.e. to Ireland], either for the purpose of studying the Word of God, or to live a stricter life. And some devoted themselves to the monastic life, others chose to apply themselves to study, going about from one master's cell to another. The Scots [i.e. the Irish] most cordially received them all, and took care to supply them gratuitously with daily food, as also to furnish them with books to read and instruction without charge. Among these were Ædilhun and Ecgbert, two youths of excellent parts, of the English nobility. The former was brother to Ædilvini, a man no less beloved of God, who himself also afterwards went over to Ireland for the sake of study, and having been well instructed,

The sons of the English nobility educated in the Irish schools ;

---

[1] Skene's "Celtic Scotland," vol. ii. p. 75.

returned to his own country."[1] Similarly, Bede says of Aldfrid, son of King Oswin, afterwards king of Northumbria, that "he was a man most learned in Scripture," that "he at that time lived in exile in the islands of the Scots for the sake of studying letters," and that before he came to the throne "he had for a considerable time gone into voluntary exile in the regions of the Scots [or Irish], for the sake of acquiring learning, through the love of wisdom."

But it was not from England only that students and scholars flocked in those times to Irish schools, but from all come parts of Europe. It might be thought that Italy from all parts of the was at the very source and centre of light in the Continent. days of which I speak, and yet even Italy sent large numbers to be educated and trained in Ireland. In the "Life of Senan" we read of "fifty Roman monks who came to Ireland for the purpose of leading a life of stricter discipline, or improving themselves in the study of the Scriptures, then much cultivated in Ireland, and became pupils of those holy fathers who were most distinguished for sanctity of life and the perfection of monastic discipline."[2] There is no doubt whatever that of all the countries of Europe, the remote island of Ireland was the one which was regarded as holding the highest place for learning and devotion. How great must have been the fame of the great monastic school of Lismore to justify these words of Moronus, who, it should be noted, was not an Irishman, but a foreigner. They are quoted by Ussher, and have been thus rendered :—

---

[1] Bede's "Eccl. Hist.," Bk. iii. c. 27.
[2] "Colgan, "A.SS.," p. 533.

> " Now haste Sicambri from the marshy Rhine ;
> Bohemians now desert their cold north land ;
> Auvergne and Holland, too, add to the tide ;
> Forth from Geneva's frowning cliffs they throng.
> Helvetia's youth by Rhone and by Säone
> Are few : the Western isle is now their home.
> All these from many lands, by many diverse paths,
> Rivals in pious zeal, seek Lismore's famous seat."

In fact, the Irish monastic schools appear to have been crowded with students. There were three thousand at one time under Finnian at Clonard. The city of Armagh was divided into three parts, and one of them was called *Trian Saxon*, from the great number of Saxon students who dwelt in it. We learn again that in the eighth century seven streets of a town called Kilbally, in King's County, were wholly occupied by Galls and foreigners who had come to attend its school.[1]

The sort of education given in them. Nor are we without the means of becoming acquainted with the sort of knowledge which Irish scholars at that time possessed. Fergil, known on the Continent as Virgilius, and bearing the honourable title of "the geometer," originally abbot of Aghaboe in Queen's County, was great both as a man of science and as a missionary. On the Continent he came into serious collision with Boniface, the " apostle of Germany," and incurred the condemnation of Pope Zachary himself for affirming the rotundity of the earth and the existence of the antipodes ; but he was held in high honour by Pepin, who made him bishop of Salzburgh. Sedulius in the eighth century wrote on a great variety of subjects, on grammar, on government, and on theology, and his works prove him to have been familiar with

[1] "Petrie's "Round Towers," p. 355.

Latin, Greek, and Hebrew. In his commentaries he is able to quote with freedom both the Latin and Greek Fathers. Clement, an Irishman, was employed by Charlemagne along with Alcuin in his great palace school and for the promotion of learning in his realm; another Irishman, Albinus, he sent to Italy to establish a school near Pavia; and Dicuil, a third Irishman, the author of a geography entitled *Liber de Mensura Terræ*, in which he gives evidence of wide and singularly accurate information, was not improbably a teacher under Charlemagne also. Nor should Johannes Scotus Erigena, the brilliant genius and wit, the profound thinker and scholar, who has left ample proof on record of his knowledge of Greek, be forgotten. He appears to have been educated in the monastic school of Bangor, in County Down. Of the cultivation of both Greek and Hebrew learning in the Irish schools, Dr. G. T. Stokes has given copious proof and illustration.[1]

No wonder, then, that the monastic schools of Ireland and their teachers were held in the highest respect by the great scholars of the Continent.

The growth and development of education in Ireland seem to have created the necessity for a new functionary, who appears to have superseded the scribe. This was the *Ferleighinn*, a word composed of two terms, which mean "a man of erudition." Colgan renders it by the word "*Prælector*, vel potius *scholasticus*." One of the earliest to whom the title is applied was Colcu of Clonmacnois in the eighth century—the "Annals of the Four Masters" connect his death with the year 789—and he is there described

[1] See his "Ireland and the Celtic Church," Lect. xi., and the "Expositor" for June and August 1889.

as the " supreme moderator (or head) and prælector of the school of Clonmacnois," while it is added that " he had arrived at such eminence in learning that he was called chief scribe and master of the Scots in Ireland."[1] A letter is still extant addressed to this Colcu by Alcuin, the renowned English scholar, who was employed by Charlemagne as his trusted friend and counsellor, and chief adviser in all ecclesiastical and educational affairs. Alcuin addresses Colcu as " *lector* in Scotia," calls him " pater sanctissime," and himself as " filius tuus ; " employs other language which implies deep veneration and respect ; mentions that " all thy friends who are with us serve the Lord in prosperity," and sends to certain persons whom he mentions a present of money from King Charles, himself, and others.[2] There could be no more striking proof of the high esteem in which Irish scholars were held by the most distinguished men of the time.

[1] " Annals of the Four Masters," vol. i. p. 396, note *e*.
[2] See Ussher's " Veterum Epistolarum Hibernicarum Sylloge, Epistola xviii., where the letter is given in full.

CHAPTER XII

THE MISSIONARY ACHIEVEMENTS OF THE CHURCH OF ST. PATRICK

The noble service done by the Irish Church, not for Ireland only, but for Europe, in the department of education, has been briefly touched on. But the Irish monasteries were not more renowned for their seminaries of learning than for the missionary zeal which they inspired, and the bands of earnest and successful missionaries they sent forth to evangelise those still living in sin and ignorance, and to carry their peculiar type of Christianity to both North and South Britain, and over the broad Continent of Europe.

If one of the surest signs of life in a Church is her missionary spirit—her desire to share the blessings which she herself enjoys with those less privileged in other lands—this symptom of spiritual vitality and energy was now exhibited in the Irish Church to an extraordinary degree. It was very natural, too, that the first to awaken her benevolent ardour and move her to self-denying missionary enterprise should have been her own kinsmen who had crossed the Channel and settled on the opposite coasts and islands of North Britain. Soon, however, her operations were extended beyond these to the Picts of the North, and before long the whole Continent of

If mission-ary activity is a sign of life, the Irish Church was a living Church.

215

Europe was being traversed by missionaries from Ireland. They generally went in companies of twelve.

I. ST. BRENDAN.

St. Brendan goes in search of the Promised Land. The first who went forth from his own country on such an errand appears to have been St. Brendan of Clonfert (483–577). He was born at Annagh, near Tralee, and, like so many Irish ecclesiastics, was descended from a noble ancestry. He is said to have been brought up under the care of St. Ita, and to have been educated and ordained by Bishop Erc, having spent some time with St. Jarlath at Tuam. On the occasion of his ordination he would seem to have been profoundly impressed by the words of our Lord, "There is no man that hath left house, or parents, or brethren, or wife, or children for the kingdom of God's sake, who shall not receive manifold more in this present time, and in the world to come life everlasting;" and in the spirit of these words he resolved to spend the remainder of his life. One night, according to his biographer, he dreamt that an angel appeared to him and said, "Arise, O Brendan, for God hath given thee what thou soughtest, even the land of promise." He then arose, ascended the mountain close by, looked forth, and saw the vast ocean stretching out on every side, and imagined that away in the mists of the far distance he caught a sight of the veritable Land of Promise. He determined to set out in search of it, and the voyage on which he now entered (it is said to have been in 545) with the hope of reaching it earned for him the name of "the Navigator." Having made a wicker vessel, strong and firm, and carefully covered it with skin, "in this," according to the story, having induced some friends to accompany him, "he sailed over the wave-voice of the strong-maned sea, and over the storm of the green-sided waves, and over the mouths of the marvellous, awful, bitter ocean, where they saw the multitude of the furious red-mouthed monsters, with abundance of great sea-whales."

Such is the pretty romance that poetry, in the form of legend, has created out of an earnest missionary life. One poet, Cumin of Connor, represents him as spending seven years on a whale's back, remarking naïvely that "it was a difficult mode of piety!" Let us not attempt to vulgarise the story by stripping it of its poetry. Does not every true missionary still set out in his "coracle" in search of the "Promised Land"? Do not we all, at one time or another in our lives, sally forth in search of our Promised Land? Nay, are we not, most of us, every day going out in quest of it? Those especially still in the morning of life, are they not, even in their waking dreams, forming visions of a "Promised Land," and preparing for a voyage of exploration? Let them be thankful that, instead of the coracle and the whale's back, they have now the railway train, and the motor-carriage, and the steamship to carry them! If nothing else will do but to divest this exquisite legend of its poetic halo, then the reader must be told in sober prose that the solid kernel of truth at the heart of this romance about Brendan is that it is beyond question, and a well-ascertained fact of history, that he did literally go to the Western Islands of Alba, evangelising their inha- *Brendan plants Churches in the Western Islands.*

bitants, and planting churches and monasteries on them, as Columba went and did a little later. In one island, for example, he founded a monastery called Ailech, and in another, which is described as having been "in Britain in the region of Heth," we are informed that he built a church with its village of huts around it. Bishop Reeves has shown, in his edition of "Adamnan's Life of Columba," that this was the island of Tiree. The situation of the other is not definitely known; but the name of Brendan is connected with several of the Western Islands. Fordun, in his Chronicle, tells us that St. Brendan constructed a booth and shrine on the island of Bute. His name still survives in the Kilbrandan Sound. The principal church in the island of Seil, off the coast of Lorn, is dedicated to Brendan, and one of the group of Garveloch isles bears the name of Culbrandan, or the retreat of Brendan. The last-named island is next to that called *Eilean-na-Naoimh*, or the Island of the Saints, which appears also to have been called *Elachnave*. This was probably the place on which Brendan built the monastery of Aileach, referred to a moment ago. You see, in Brendan's voyage of discovery in quest of his Promised Land it was no mere "will o' the wisp," or fiction of a holy grail that he was pursuing, but a sober Christian purpose of giving the benefits that had come to him to his fellow-men.

Founds Clonfert, &c.

On his return to Ireland he is said to have founded the monasteries of Clonfert and Annadown, and to have built many cells and monasteries throughout Ireland. His Life, edited by Bishop Moran, states that he was in his seventy-seventh year when he

founded Clonfert. As he was born in A.D. 583, this
would make the date of the foundation of Clonfert
to be A.D. 560. It is remarkable that the "Annals
of Innisfallen" fix the date of its foundation on the
very day of the battle of Culdreimnhe, which took
place in 561.

II. COLUMBA.

The most illustrious name in the Irish Church
after Patrick's is that of Columba, described by the
"Four Masters" as "the apostle of Alba, head of
the piety of the most part of Ireland and Alba after
Patrick," depicted in the old Irish Life as "the
renowned presbyter of the island of the Gael" (or
Irish), "the battlebrand endowed with talents and
various gifts of the Holy Ghost," "the bright, clear
luminary," "eminent above all clerics," but generally
designated by moderns as "the apostle of the
Northern Picts." In learning and culture, and probably also in intellectual power, Columba was
superior to Patrick. From his biographers we learn
that he was a man of majestic and commanding
presence, tall and stately, of pleasing countenance—
Adamnan says "he had as it were the face of an
angel"—with a voice at once soft and sonorous, and
so powerful that it could be heard distinctly chanting
a psalm a mile and a half away, and sounding the same
whether near or far,—the symbol of a personality at
once gentle and strong, combining the stern, fierce
qualities of a soldier with the mildness of a saint,
endowed with a poetic genius which was sensitive
to the tenderest feelings and touched to the finest
issues, yet surging with restless practical energy,
and capable of being stirred into tempestuous

passion; a master-mind, a born leader of men, who would have come to the front in any age and in any department of human activity. It is of him that I am now to speak.

The legendary character of the Lives of Columba. In dealing with Columba, we labour under the same difficulty as that which we had to encounter in the case of Patrick. It was the fate of every man and woman of any note in Ireland, and especially of the most distinguished, that in the minds of their superstitious admirers of succeeding generations a huge mass of legendary matter of the most puerile and absurd sort grew up around their name, rank and copious as ivy on an old ruin; and their successive monkish biographers, steeped to the lips as they were in superstition and credulity, have so interwoven the legendary and miraculous with the authentic facts of their lives, that it is no easy, in some cases an impossible, task to disentangle what is fictitious from what is genuine history. This is true of all the biographies we possess of Columba, from the earliest to the latest. His two earliest biographers, who were both successors of his at Iona, were indeed sufficiently near his own time to gather up and embody in their works the chief events of his career; one of them, Cumine, having become abbot of Iona sixty years and the other, Adamnan, eighty-two years after Columba's death. Even they, however, are panegyrists rather than historians, and seek to glorify their hero by imputing to him all sorts of stupendous prodigies in the way of prophecy and miracle, many of which would be the reverse of creditable if they were true. Adamnan's Life is in three books, the first book being a record of some fifty " prophecies " delivered

Cumine's Life.

Adamnan's Life.

by Columba, the second an account of about the
same number of "miracles" wrought by him, and
the third book a record of more than twenty
"visions of angels" seen by him. It is out of
such a legendary heap of prophecies, miracles, and
visions that we have to sift the grains of fact that
are mixed up with them. On scores of interesting
questions and matters of fact Adamnan is wholly
silent. "What were the predisposing causes which
led to this great movement [the acceptance of the
faith by whole nations] among the Gothic and
Celtic tribes? What was the condition of their
own belief? What were to them the attractive
elements in the new religion? What were the
arguments addressed to them by Columba? . . .
It is really afflicting that Adamnan gives us no
ray of light on these questions, so interesting and
so profoundly dark," says the Duke of Argyll. As the
Duke adds, "the imperishable interest of Adamnan's
book lies in the vivid though incidental touches of
life and manners which he gives us in the telling of
his tales—of life and manners as they were in that
obscure but most fruitful time."

This also is the character of what is known as the The "Old
"Old Irish Life," which has been translated by Mr. Irish Life."
W. M. Hennessey, M.R.I.A., and appended to the
second volume of Dr. Skene's "Celtic Scotland." It
is a discourse which was composed, Dr. Reeves
thinks, as early as the tenth century, and delivered
as a eulogy of Columba on the occasion of his
festival. The Life of the saint by Manus O'Donnell, Life by
compiled in 1532, professes to be made up from all O'Donnell.
previously existing records. Where it supplements
and embellishes the facts in the earlier Lives, as it

does to a considerable extent, we are safe in largely
discounting the later accretions. Adamnan's "Life
of Columba" has been edited by the late Dr. Reeves,
with most learned and valuable notes and discussions,
which, however, are somewhat hard reading to any
but scholars specially interested in the subject. In
Skene's second volume, just referred to, and in Dr.
Fowler's recent edition of Adamnan's "Life of
Columba," there is an excellent digest of the researches of Dr. Reeves. By careful criticism it is
not difficult to separate what is legendary in these
lives from what is true and trustworthy, and to obtain a vivid portraiture of Columba and his romantic
career. And altogether what the Duke of Argyll
says may be taken as correct: "Not one historical
character of the time is in any similar degree known
to us. On one spot, and one spot only, of British
soil, there shines in this dark time a light more vivid
even than the light of common history—the light
of personal anecdote and of domestic narrative.
When we land upon Iona, we can feel that we are
treading in the very footsteps of a man whom we
have known in voice, in gesture, in habits, and in
many peculiarities of character; and yet of a man
who walked on this same ground before the Heptarchy, when Roman cities still stood in Britain, and
when the ancient Christianised Celts of Britain
were maintaining a doubtful contest with Teutonic
heathenism."[1]

His birth and education. Columba was born at Gartan, a townland and
parish in the barony of Kilmacrennan, in County
Donegal. It was on December 7, 521. The name
given him was Colum, which in its Latin form is

[1] The Duke of Argyll's "Iona," p. 56.

Columba, but later he became known as Columkille, or "Colum of the Church," either because of his constant attendance at the church of *Tulach Dubh-glaise,* now Temple Douglas, near where he was born, or because so many churches were founded by him. His mother, Eithne, was descended from a famous Leinster king; his father, Fedhlimidh, was the son of Fergus, who was the son of Conall Galban, brother of Laoghaire, the over-king at Tara at the time of Patrick's visit. He was thus the great-great-grandson of Niall of the Nine Hostages, a scion of the royal house of Niall, and a near kinsman of the reigning families in Ireland. The "Old Irish Life" informs us that he was not only "eligible to the kingship of Erin according to family, but that it was actually offered to him, only he had abandoned royal honours for God."

Having spent his childhood and youth under the guardianship of a priest or presbyter called Cruith-nechan, he went to Maghbile (now Movilla, near New-townards), where he became a pupil of Finnian, or Finnbarr, of whom I have already spoken. Here he was ordained a deacon. Thence he passed to Leinster, where he studied under Gemman, an aged bard, of whom we know but little, but to whom doubtless he was drawn by his innate love for poetry, in the cultivation of which Gemman would at once stimulate and guide him. Leaving Gemman, we find him next under the famous Finnian at the great monastic seminary of Clonard, near the source of the Boyne, of which Ussher has said : " From the school of Clonard (*Cluain-Eraird*) scholars of old came out in as great numbers as Greeks from the side of the horse of Troy." The usual number of pupils in

At Movilla.

Under Gemman.

At Clonard.

223

attendance is set down at 3000, so that the ancient Annalists call St. Finnian himself a "doctor of wisdom and tutor of the Saints of Ireland in his time." Here Columba was trained as one of that famous band, already spoken of, who afterwards became known as "the twelve apostles of Erin." Both here and at Movilla he no doubt perfected himself in the art of copying and illuminating manuscripts, in which we learn that he was specially proficient. It is stated that he wrote with his own hand three hundred copies of the New Testament, one of which he gave to each of the churches which he founded. It was at this stage in his career that he is said to have been ordained a presbyter. His ordination. The story (as related in the Scholia or Annotations on the Martyrology of Ængus) is, that Columba was sent to Etchen, bishop of Clonfad, in West Meath, to be ordained to the episcopate. Having found Etchen ploughing in the field, Columba, it is said, duly tested him by giving him the opportunity to work some miracles. He was then ordained a presbyter by Etchen, although, according to the legend, it was the order of a bishop that Columba wished to have conferred; yet, having been made a presbyter, he would not permit the error to be rectified, but remained a presbyter to the end of his life. Adamnan, however, knows nothing of the legend; and, as Todd suggests, "it was most probably framed to account for the fact that so eminent a saint as Columkille had never risen beyond the rank of a presbyter; and that he had vowed, as was believed, never to accept episcopal consecration, or to permit any of his abbots to be bishops."[1]

[1] Todd's "St. Patrick," p. 72.

The double impulse which Columba must have received, first under Finnian of Movilla, and next under Finnian of Clonard, should be taken into account to understand his later career. Through Finnian of Moville he would get at second hand Gets a the impulse that Finnian himself had derived from double impulse. the great monastic centre of Candida Casa; and from Finnian of Clonard he would share in the reviving influence which we know the latter had obtained from David, Gildas, and Cadoc in Wales. Bidding farewell to Finnian and Clonard, as the "Old Irish Life" puts it, he went to the monastery of Glassnaoidhen (Glasnevin) near Dublin, which At Glas-nevin. had been founded by Mobhi (Movi), one of his fellow-disciples at Clonard, and where he also found his old Clonard companions Kieran and Cainnech, as well as Comgall, the future founder of Bangor. The "Old Irish Life" mentions that Movi warned his *protégés* to leave his monastery on account of a terrible and deadly plague that was approaching. It was called the *Buid Chonaill* or *Crom Chonaill*, that is, the "yellow plague," and appears to have been exceptionally fatal, and to have swept over and desolated the country between the years 543 and 560. Mobhi himself died of it in 545. But just before the advent of this terrible pestilence Columba had left Glasnevin, and was about to enter on a career of extraordinary activity.

What immediately follows is best told in the Enters on "Old Irish Life" of Columba. Leaving Glasnevin active life. (it says), he "proceeded to Cenel-Conaill [*i.e.* the district now known as County Donegal, then called Tir-Conaill, or territory of Conaill. The Conaill from whom it took its name was Conaill Gulban,

Columba's great-grandfather, who had taken up
his abode there]. The way he went was across
the river, the name of which is Biur. [Dr. Reeves
has identified this river with the Moyola, which
flows into Lough Neagh.] Colum-Cille went after-
**Founds
Derry.** wards to Daire [*i.e.* Derry, then called Daire Calgaig,
or 'Calgach's oak-wood'], namely, the royal *dun* of
Ædh, son of Ainmire. He was king of Erin at that
time. The king offered that *dun* to Colum-Cille,
and he refused it because of Mobhi's command.
As he was coming out of the *dun*, however, he
met with two of Mobhi's people, and they had
Mobhi's girdle for him, and permission to accept
a grant of land, Mobhi having died. . . . Colum-
Cille then settled in the fort of Ædh, and founded
a church there." This Ædh, who was king of Erin,
was a near kinsman of Columba, who was cousin-
german of his father, Ainmire. In that royal fort
given him by Ædh, surrounded by an oak-wood,
which belonged originally to some chief called *Cal-
gaich*, and hence called *Daire-Calgaich*, Columba
founded his first monastery, and at the same time
laid the foundations of the city now called Londonderry. Six hundred years after Columba's time the
oak-wood from which the city took its name was still
standing; for at the year 1178 the "Four Masters"
have this record: "A violent windstorm occurred
this year; it caused a great destruction of trees; it
prostrated oaks. It prostrated 120 trees in Derry-
Colum-Kille." The old pagan name of the place
was, as I have said, *Daire-Calgaich*, and this name
it retained till the tenth or eleventh century, when
it began to be called Derry-Columkille, after its
Christian founder, and this name it continued to

bear till James I. gave it to a company of London
merchants, and in the charter which contained the
grant imposed on it the name of "Londonderry."
Thus from two different sources this city has derived
a title to distinction which other towns might envy;
one of them, the heroic defence by her own citizens
against the famous siege, characterised by Macaulay
as "the most memorable in the annals of the British
Isles;" the other the laying of her foundations in
the year 546 by the renowned and royal missionary
Columba. At two remote points in her history
that famous city was the centre of two great deliver-
ances. From Derry it was that Columba "sailed
away" to Alba to emancipate the Northern Picts from
the yoke of pagan bondage and degradation, and,
through his successors at Iona, a large portion of
Anglo-Saxon England; while, by their heroic defence and glorious victory, the besieged residents
of Derry broke the chains of political despotism
and ecclesiastical tyranny by which it was sought
to enslave these British and Irish lands.

Columba seems to have had a special attachment His love for
to Derry. The "Old Irish Life" says he "loved that "Beautiful
city very much;" and in one of his poems he him- Derry."
self thus hymns its praise:—

> "Were all the tributes of Scotia mine,
> From its midland to its borders,
> I would give all for one little cell
> In my beautiful Derry.
> For its peace and for its purity,
> For the white angels that go
> In crowds from one end to the other,
> I love my beautiful Derry
> For its quietness and purity,
> For heaven's angels that come and go

Under every leaf of the oaks,
I love my beautiful Derry.

My Derry, my fair oak grove,
My dear little cell and dwelling,
O God, in the heavens above!
Let him who profanes it be cursed.
Beloved are Durrow and Derry,
Beloved is Raphoe the pure,
Beloved the fertile Drumhome,
Beloved are Swords and Kells!
But sweeter and fairer to me
The salt sea where the seagulls cry,
When I come to Derry from far,
It is sweeter and dearer to me—
  Sweeter to me."

Let us hope that the maiden city by the Foyle is still true to her ancient character as Columba here portrays it, that she has not lost altogether her "peace and purity," and that she is still "full of angels white"!

Founds Raphoe; It was about this time that Columba founded the church of Raphoe (Rath-Both), where the Irish Life represents him as resuscitating from death the carpenter, who had been drowned in the mill-dam, and as performing other miracles.

and Durrow; Ten years after establishing the institution at Derry, he founded what Bede calls the "noble monastery of Durrow," in County Meath. With Durrow also he must have had pleasant associations; for in after years, when residing on the sea-girt island of Iona with his monks, his mind (he tells us) often wandered back to Durrow with wistful longing, and his memory recalled the wind sighing among its oak-groves, and the notes of the cuckoo and the and Kells; blackbird. At Cenandas, or Kells, in Meath, the king gave him his own *dun*, where he set up a

monastery, and it is said marked out the form or
outline of the city that would be built there. At
Clonmore in County Louth, on Rechra, now Lambay,
off the coast of Dublin, at Drumcliffe near Sligo,
at Swords in County Dublin, on Tory Island, off
the coast of Donegal, and at many other places *and many*
too numerous even to name, Columba founded *besides.*
monasteries and churches. He is said to have
erected three hundred in Ireland altogether. As a
poem quoted in the Irish Life says :—

> " Three hundred he measured without fault,
>   Of churches fair, 'tis true ;
>   And three hundred splendid, lasting books,
>   Noble-bright he wrote."

Columba was a born poet. Weird strains often *His poetic*
break from him, which reveal a spirit of true poetry. *vein.*
" One day Colum-Cille and Cainnech were on the
sea-shore. There was a great storm on the sea.
'What sings the wave?' said Cainnech; which
reminds us of little Dombey's query to his sister,
'What are the wild waves saying?' 'My people
were in peril on the sea a while ago,' said Colum-
Cille, 'and one of them has died; and the Lord will
bring him to us in the morning to-morrow, to this
shore on which we are." That, Columba told his
companion, was the sad and dirgeful song of the
wave.

But Columba has now arrived at a great turning-
point in his career, which the " Old Irish Life " thus
approaches and refers to : " When Colum-Cille had
made the circuit of all Erin, and when he had sown
faith and religion ; when numerous multitudes had
been baptized by him; when he had founded

churches and establishments, and had left in them seniors and reliquaries and relics of martyrs, the determination that he had determined from the beginning of his life came into his mind, namely, to go on pilgrimage. He then meditated going across the sea to preach the Word of God to the men of Alba, and to the Britons, and to the Saxons. He went, therefore, on a voyage. His age was forty-two when he went."

Meditates a pilgrimage across the sea.

Here we are told that from the beginning of his life he had determined on the expedition to Alba on which he now set out. A very different reason for his going is given by some of the later Lives, especially that of Manus O'Donnell.

His motive discussed.

A bloody battle was fought at a place called Culdreimhne (Cooldreevny), near the boundary between Ulster and Connaught. On the one side was the Northern Hy Niall under their respective chiefs, and on the other was Diarmid or Dermot, king of Ireland, and head of the Southern Hy Niall. The latter was defeated, and the slaughter was great and terrible. By Manus O'Donnell the battle is attributed to Columba, who, according to O'Donnell, had a double grievance against Diarmid. O'Donnell states that in a visit paid by Columba to Finnian of Movilla, Columba secretly made a copy of a Latin Psalter which Finnian valued highly, and the use of which Columba had obtained from him. When Finnian became aware of what Columba had done, he claimed the copy that the latter had taken, which, however, he refused to surrender. It was agreed to leave the matter to the arbitration of King Diarmid, who decided against Columba on a principle contained in the

Brehon Code, that as to every cow belongs its calf, so to every book belongs its copy. The representation is that Columba was deeply offended at King Diarmid because of this verdict. But a still deeper cause of offence is said to have been given him by the latter. It has been already referred to in another connection. At a royal feast at Tara, Curnan, son of the king of Connaught, had a quarrel with another young man and killed him, and then fled to Columba and put himself under his protection in the monastery where he was; but the king pursued Curnan, and, in spite of the sanctuary which Columba offered him, seized him and inflicted the punishment which he thought he deserved. It is alleged that Columba was deeply wounded by Diarmid's hostile action in connection with both these incidents, and stirred up his kinsmen of the Northern Hy Niall, and united all their leaders in a determination to inflict chastisement on the king. But soon after a Synod was convened at Taillten which held Columba guilty of the blood spilled at the battle of Cooldreevny, and laid on him the obligation of delivering as many souls from pagan darkness as had been slain in it; and the penance put upon him was perpetual exile from Erin, and that his eyes should never again look upon its hills, nor his feet tread its strands. It is added that, when he departed for the Western Isles, he first disembarked on Colonsay, but finding that from its heights Ireland could be seen, he then made for Iona, where he was out of sight of his native country. The tradition of the quarrel between Columba and Finnian of Movilla about the copy of the Psalter seems to be purely legendary. It is quite inconsistent with the cordial feelings of mutual esteem and love which continued to be cherished between him and Finnian. Adamnan does mention that Columba was excommunicated by a Synod at Taillten, but he speaks of the charge as trivial and unjust, and of the excommunication as not being persisted in. It is possible, and even probable, that Columba may have had some hand in the bloody conflict at Cooldrcevny. The right of sanctuary was a much-prized privilege in the Celtic Church of Ireland. Columba would naturally resent the action of King Diarmid. The former belonged to the royal line, was a man of imperious and even passionate nature, and may have been too active in inciting to revenge. It is thought that the Irish temperament even to this day delights in nothing more than a good sturdy fight. It is certain that in those times clergymen, and even women, took part in battle. "The clergy of Ireland," MacFirbis says in his "Annals," "went to their synods with weapons and fought pitched battles." Such a battle was fought, we know, between the monasteries of Clonmacnois and Durrow. It is thus not improbable that Columba may have felt himself justified in active interference against Diarmid. But the whole history of Adamnan and of the earlier Lives goes to contradict anything like a sentence of perpetual exile against Columba. Not less than ten different visits of his to his native shore after he had gone to Iona are recorded by Adamnan, and he is always received with the greatest reverence and honour. Thus when, after an absence of many years, he paid a visit to Clonmacnois, Adamnan tells us : " As soon as it was known that he was approaching, the whole people flocked from their lands near the monastery, and joining those who were within it, followed with enthusiasm the Abbot Alitherus; then passing beyond the enclosure of the monastery, they went forth, united as one man, to meet Columba, as if he were an angel of the Lord; humbly bowing down with their faces to the earth, they kissed him very reverently, and singing hymns and praises as they went, they conducted him with honour to the church. And that the holy abbot Columba might not be troubled by the pressure of the multitude thronging on him, a canopy of wood was upheld over him as he walked by four men keeping step by his side." [1]

He was probably influenced by a twofold motive in the mission to Alba on which he now embarked. Let it be remembered that he was closely related to the colony of Scots from Dalriada, who now occupied Cantyre and the Western Isles of what we now call Scotland, from these very Irish Scots. [Curious reversal of things; we now call those who have come from Scotland to settle in Ireland "Scotch-Irish."] Of their settlement in North Britain the venerable Bede thus informs us : " In process of time Britain received, in addition to the Britons and Picts, a third nation, the Scots, who, migrating from Ireland under their leader, Reuda, secured for themselves those settlements among the Picts which they still possess. From the name of their commander they are to this day called Dalreudini; for in their language *dal* means a part. Ireland, in breadth, and for wholesomeness and serenity of climate, far surpasses Britain; for the snow scarcely ever lies

His motive probably twofold :
(1) To assist his kinsmen.

―――――――――

[1] Adamnan's " Life," Bk. i. c. 3.

there above three days; no man makes hay in the summer for winter's provision, or builds stables for his beasts of burden. No reptile is found there, and no snake can live there; for, though often carried thither out of Britain, as soon as the ship nears the shore, and the scent of the air reaches them, they die." Then he tells how the Scots, migrating from Ireland, settled in Britain to the north of the bay on which stands Alcluith, the strong city of the Britons. Some of my readers, no doubt, have stood on Fairhead, near Ballycastle, which was in the Irish Dalriada, and looking across the narrow channel of only sixteen miles, have distinctly seen the white houses sparkling in the sunlight on the Mull of Cantyre in Argyleshire. It is probable, therefore, that pretty constant intercourse was kept up between the Irish Dalriadians and their kindred across the channel. Just about the time when Columba was born, another band of them passed over from the Antrim coast, under the leadership of six sons of Erc, namely, two Ferguses, two Lorns, and two MacNisis, also descendants of Cairbre Riada, driven from Ireland apparently by the pressure of both plague and famine, and settled in the same region. The district colonised by them became known by the name of *Airer-Gaedhil*, *i.e.* the territory of the Gael or Irish; and the name still survives in the abbreviated form of Argyle, a living, extant witness to that early colonisation. The descendants of the two Lorns, sons of Erc, were called *Cinel-Lorn*, *i.e.* the race or family of Lorn, from whom the Marquis of Lorne derives his title. It was from this colony of Irish Scots (as I have said) that Scotland got its name.

Now, after the withdrawal of the Romans the whole country was exposed to the desolating incursions of the Northern Picts, who were still heathens. In Columba's time they had a powerful king called Brude, whose royal residence was near where Inverness now stands. In the year 560 this Pictish sovereign had inflicted a heavy blow on the Scots in Alba, slain their king, and threatened to drive them from the country. The battle of Cooldreevny took place in 561, and in the same year we find Columba residing in Cantyre with his relative King Conall, the successor of Gabran, who had been slain by the Picts. Adamnan says it was "in the second year after the battle of Culdreimhne, that is, in the year 563, and in the forty-second of his age, that Columba, resolving to seek a foreign country for the love of Christ, sailed from Scotia or Ireland to Britain." It was no doubt partly to assist and cheer his brethren in their difficulties, but also with a view to evangelise and convert their (2) To evangelise the Picts. terrible enemies the Picts, that he had turned his back on his native land, and had taken up his residence in Britain.

We have seen that in Ireland the favourite site Iona. for a monastery was an island. It was such a spot that Columba now selected as the site of the church and monastery he wished to found, and as the centre of his operations. Iona, or Hi (Dr. Reeves has shown that "Iona" was the mistake of some transcriber for Ioua, the ancient name having been "I," "Hi," or some form of this)—Iona, I say, a little Its extent, island three and a half miles long and one and a and suitability for half mile broad, lying a mile off Mull, on the west Columba's coast of Scotland, was admirably situated for his purpose.

purpose, with its picturesque little bays and beautiful white strand, quiet dells, hills both green and
rugged, and fruitful plains. From its higher eleva-
tions some thirty islands are in sight, and Mull seems
like the mainland, for which possibly in the first
instance Columba mistook it.

Here Columba would have many an opportunity
of indulging that delight in the ever-varying aspect
and music of the sea to which he gives expression
in one of his poems (see Skene, p. 92). There is
a certain rocky elevation on the island which is
called " Torr-Abb," or the " Abbot's Knoll," on
which the saint was wont to take his stand, and
to survey the scene that spread out before him.
" From its isolated position," says the Duke of
Argyll, " from its close proximity to St. Oran's
Chapel and to the ancient place of sepulture—
from its rising beside the old path which runs
along the foot of the rocky hills, from the splendid
view it commands over the sacred objects close at
hand, over the sloping fields, the sound, the opposite coast, and the distant mountains—this knoll
must have been a favourite resort of all the generations of men who lived and worshipped on Iona.
. . . How often from this very hill must the monks
have watched for their abbot's returning barque
rounding the red rocks of Mull from the south-
ward, or speeding with longer notice of approach
from the north. From the same spot, we may be
sure, has Columba often watched the frequent sail—
now from one quarter, now from another, bringing
strange men on strange errands, or old familiar
friends to renew the broken intercourse of youth.
Hither came holy men from Erin to take counsel

(margin) The " Abbot's Knoll :" what Columba was to see from it.

236

with the saint on the troubles of clans and monasteries, still dear to him. Hither came also bad men,
red-handed from blood and sacrilege, to make confession and do penance at Columba's feet. Hither,
too, came chieftains to be blessed, and even kings to
be ordained, for it is curious that on this lonely
spot, so far distant from the ancient centres of
Christendom, took place the first recorded case of a
temporal sovereign seeking from a minister of the
Church what appears to have been very like formal
consecration. . . . Nor can we fail to remember with
the 'Reilig Oran' at our feet, how often the beautiful galleys of that olden time came up the sound
laden with the dead—'their dark freight a vanished
life.' A grassy mound, not far from the present
landing-place, is known as the spot on which bodies
were laid when they were first carried to the shore.
We know from the account of Columba's own burial
that the custom was to wake the body with the
singing of psalms during three days and nights before
laying it to its final rest. It was then borne in
solemn procession to the grave. How many of such
processions must have wound along that path that
leads to the 'Reilig Oran'! How many fleets of
galleys must have ridden at anchor on that bay
below us, with all those expressive signs of mourning
which belong to ships, when kings and chiefs who
had died in distant lands were carried hither to be
buried in this holy isle!"

Those who have read Boswell's "Life of Johnson"
will not forget the account therein given of the visit
of Johnson and his biographer to this island in 1773.
There was then no landing-place, and through the
tide they had to be carried on the backs of natives

to the shore. Boswell informs us that Johnson was "much affected" on the occasion. His words are well worth recalling: "We are now treading," said the great lexicographer and literary king, "we are now treading that illustrious island, which was once the luminary of the Caledonian regions, whose savage clans and roving barbarians derived the benefits of knowledge and the blessings of religion. . . . That man is little to be envied whose patriotism would not gain force upon the plains of Marathon, or whose piety would not grow warmer amid the ruins of Iona."

The ruins now seen by the visitor are the remains of buildings which have been erected on the island long subsequent to the time of Columba, and during the Roman Catholic period. *His* were formed chiefly of wood and wattles, and have disappeared long since, although the outlines of the original monastery, its rampart, its kiln, its mill-dam and stream, its ancient cemetery, are still traceable. The monastery established by him in Iona consisted, as appears to have been usual in island monasteries, of 150 monks. The old Irish Life thus describes them :—

> " Illustrious the soldiers that were in Hii,
> Thrice fifty in monastic rule,
> With their curacles across the sea ;
> And for rowing threescore men."

The community or *familia* of Iona consisted of three classes : the *seniors*, who read and copied the Scriptures and led the religious services ; the *working brethren*, who cultivated the fields, looked after the cattle, or prepared the food, and plied the necessary trades within doors ; and the pupils, or *alumni*, who

238

were under training. Their dress was a white tunic
or under-garment, and an upper garment which was
made of wool, and which constituted an overcoat
and hood in one. Sandals were worn upon the feet
in travelling. A part of each day seems to have been
given to the recitation of the Psalter, and on the
Lord's Day and on stated festivals the Eucharist
was celebrated. A severe penitential ascetic discipline was imposed upon the brethren; and in
government, as in all else, the usages of the mother-
church in Ireland were reproduced. The words in
which Bede describes the mode of ecclesiastical rule
have been already given, but may be repeated here:
"That island is always accustomed to have for its
governor a presbyter-abbot, to whose authority both
the whole province, and even the bishops themselves,
by an unusual constitution, owe subjection, after
the example of their first teacher, who was not a
bishop, but a presbyter and a monk."

The first two years appear to have been spent
by Columba and his community in labouring among
the rural population near him in Mull, and what
Adamnan calls the "stony region" of Ardnamurchan, Morven, and Lochaber. It was in the
year 565, two years after his arrival at Iona, that
he made his way to the royal residence of Brude, Columba
the Pictish sovereign, which Adamnan describes visits and
as having been situated near the river Ness. The Brude, the
exact site of it is not certain. Dr. Skene conjectures king.
that it may have been on a gravelly ridge called
Torvean, a mile south-west of Inverness, and which
is still in part encircled with ditches and ramparts;
or an eminence east of Inverness called the Crown,
which tradition regards as the site of its most

ancient castle. The pagan system of these northern Picts was Druidical, and in no way differed from that which preceded the introduction of Christianity in Ireland. Just as in the case of Patrick's first visit to Tara, so Columba's attempt to find access to the Pictish king is in the Lives generally attended by a series of miraculous feats on the part of the saint, feats by which, of course, all barriers are broken down. According to Adamnan, King Brude refused to open the gates of his fortress, but "the blessed man approached the folding doors with his companions, and having first formed upon them the sign of the Cross, he knocked, and laid his hand upon the gate, which instantly flew open of its own accord, the bolts having been driven back with great force. The saint and his companions then passed through the gate thus speedily opened."[1] His associates were Comgall of Bangor and Cainnech of Achaboe. They were both of the race of the Irish Picts, and Columba had no doubt got them to accompany him because of the greater influence they were likely to have with a king of their own blood. Adamnan adds that "when the king learned what had occurred, he and his councillors were filled with alarm, and immediately setting out from the palace, advanced to meet with due reverence the blessed man, whom he gently addressed in the most conciliatory language. And ever after from that day, as long as he lived, the king held this holy and reverend man in very great honour, as was due." We may assume that no greater external miracle occurred than that due to the impressive presence and speech of three great ecclesiastics, whose visit,

[1] Adamnan, Bk. ii. c. 36.

by the blessing of God's Spirit, ended in the conversion and baptism of the king. How interesting
it would have been to possess a record of the
address given by Columba to the royal company,
and to have had some details of the manner in
which the missionaries pressed the claims of the
Christian faith! But not a hint is given with
regard to it. To put on record legends of incredible miracles was more in the line of the monkish
biographers.

Columba and his monks continued to spread the
faith far and wide among the Pictish tribes. In
the year 574—nine years after the conversion of
Brude—Conall, king of British Dalriada, died, and
was succeeded by Aidan, who, Adamnan tells us,
was ordained to the kingly office by Columba laying
his hand upon his head and giving him his benediction. It was very shortly after this, that is, in Columba
the year 575, that Columba, accompanied by Aidan attends the
and several of his clergy, went to Ireland to attend sembly at
the great convention, which in that year was held Drumceatt.
at Drumceatt, a mound now called Daisy Hill, on
the river Roe, near Limavady. The convention
was summoned by Ædh, son of Ainmire, king of
Ireland, and was attended by all the petty kings
and chiefs as well as abbots of Erin; and as British
Dalriada was a subject colony to Ireland, King
Aidan, Columba, and their retinue attended it also.
An ancient record mentions that Columba had Three
three reasons for attending this great national attending
assembly. One was in order to procure the release it.
of Scannlan Mor, son of the king of Ossory, with
whom he had gone in pledge; another was to
intercede for and prevent the banishment or sup-

pression of the ancient order of Ollamhs or Bards.
They had degenerated, and become very burden-
some in exacting what was called their *coinmed*
or refection for themselves and servants from the
tribes, and abused their privilege by lampooning
any who did not purchase their good-will by liberal
presents. It was proposed accordingly to suppress
or banish them; but Columba, who was himself
a poet, and had some touch of sympathy with his
fellow-bards, interposed on their behalf, remarking
that the wheat should not be pulled up with the
tares. The sentence of banishment was revoked,
but the number of their retinue was reduced, and
stricter rules were imposed on them.

But the main object of his going to the convention was connected with the interests of the
British Dalriada. As a subject state to Ireland, it
was liable to the same tribute as was payable by
the various principalities in Ireland. This was
felt to be a burden; and what Columba and its
king, Aidan, sought, was exemption from this
burden and relief from the subjection in which
they were to the king of Ireland. They secured
this object; from this date onward British Dalriada
became an independent kingdom, but continued in
friendly alliance with their kinsfolk in Ireland.
Aidan's descendants reigned over British Dalriada
till the year 842, when Kenneth MacAlpine, a
prince of the same line, united Picts and Scots,
Highlanders and Lowlanders, under one sovereign.
I may add that Aidan, who was himself a descendant of Niall of the Nine Hostages, was an ancestor
of Queen Victoria, so that her Irish subjects are
rendering allegiance to a sovereign in whose veins

flows the blood of their own ancient and most famous royal line.

During the thirty-four years of his life in Iona, Columba and his fellow-labourers succeeded in establishing monasteries and churches in the Western Isles and among the Northern Picts throughout the Highlands. And an event which at first may have seemed adverse was the means of opening the way to a still wider field of labour. On the death of King Brude in 584, he was succeeded by Gartnaidh, who belonged to the Southern Picts, and whose royal residence was on the river Tay. The Southern Picts (we have seen) had been in some measure evangelised by Ninian in the previous century, but almost all trace of Christianity had disappeared from among them. But there is clear evidence that Columba, assisted by his friend Cainnech from Achaboe in Ireland, co-operated with King Gartnaidh in planting churches and monasteries among the Southern Picts also, in what we call the Lowlands of Scotland. Iona, however, remained the parent monastery, to whose jurisdiction all the others were subject. The little island church is said to have been the mother of a thousand similar institutions. It thus became a centre of light and Christian influence to the greater part of North Britain. It has been affirmed, apparently on good grounds, that were beacon fires kindled on a winter night on the hills adjacent to the various centres of the mission enterprise which was carried on from Iona, there would be a complete chain of lights, visible one to another, extending from the Humber in the south to the Orkney Islands

in the north, and from Aberdeenshire in the east
to the remotest Hebrides in the west. The
Church thus founded by Columba was the national
Church of Scotland for one hundred and fifty
years.

The story of Columba's last day on earth is
eminently characteristic and very touching. With
Diormet, his attendant, he had paid a visit to the
barn where the monks stored their corn, and having
bestowed his blessing on it, he added : "I heartily
congratulate my beloved monks that this year also,
if I am obliged to depart from you, you will have
a sufficient supply for the year." As he made his way
back to the monastery, he found it necessary in his
weakness—he was now seventy-seven years old—to sit
down and rest when about half-way. While resting
there, an old white horse, which was employed to
carry the milk vessels from the byre to the monastery, came up to him and put its head on his
shoulder, while it foamed and wailed, its eyes moist
with tears. Diormet, seeing this, began to drive it
away; but the saint said, "Let it alone, as it is so
fond of me ; let it pour its grief into my bosom."
Then ascending a hillock that overlooked the monastery, he stood for a time upon its summit, and lift-
ing up his hands, he blessed the institution. After
this he returned to his cell, and resumed the occupation in which he so much delighted—that of
transcribing the Psalter. He was engaged in copying the 34th Psalm. When he came to the 10th
verse—"Inquirentes autem Dominum non deficient
omni bono "—he said, "I think I can write no more :
let Baithen finish it." It was Saturday night, June
9, 597. He then passed into the church to cele-

brate the vigils for the Lord's day, and returning
to his cell, lay down on his couch of stone. He
counselled the brethren who gathered round him
to have "peace always and unfeigned charity among
themselves," adding, "The Lord, the Comforter of
the good, will be your helper." When the midnight
bell rang he rose hastily, went to the church, and,
running more quickly than the others, reached the
altar, and knelt down in prayer beside it. Diormet, His death.
his attendant, entering, cried, "Where art thou,
father?" and feeling his way in the darkness, found
him prostrate. He raised him up a little, and
sitting down beside him, laid his head against his
breast. Meantime the rest of the brethren came
in, and seeing their father dying, burst into lamenta-
tions. He then moved his hand as if to give them
his benediction, turned on them a look of radiant
joy, and so passed away, Adamnan says, with a face
calm and sweet, like that of a man who in his sleep
had seen a heavenly vision.

His character has been often portrayed. Let me Three word-
present the reader with three brief but vivid word- pictures of
Columba.
pictures of him. The first is by one who knew him
personally. Dallan Forgaill was the chief of the (1) That of
order of the bards, whom Columba befriended at the Dallan
Forgaill.
National Synod of Drumceatt. As an expression of
gratitude for Columba's aid, Dallan wrote a poem
in praise of him, called the "Amra." In this poem
Dallan Forgaill describes him as "the soul's light,
and learned one" of his people, as "a harp without
a base chord, a perfect sage, who believed in Christ;
he was learned, he was chaste, he was charitable, he
was an abounding benefit to guests; he was eager,
he was noble, he was gentle, he was the physician of

the heart of every age; he was to persons inscrutable, a shelter to the naked, a consolation to the poor; there went not from the world one who was more continuous in the remembrance of the cross."[1]

(2) That of Adamnan.

The next picture is from Adamnan, his biographer, who says of him: "From his boyhood he had been devoted to the service of Christ and the study of wisdom, and by the grace of God had so preserved the soundness of his body and the purity of his soul, that, though dwelling on earth, he appeared to live like the saints in heaven. For he had, as it were, the face of an angel, was polished in speech, holy in work, excellent in disposition, and great in counsel; he lived during thirty-four years an island soldier. He never could spend the space even of one hour without study or prayer or writing, or even some manual labour. So incessantly was he engaged night and day in the unwearied exercise of fasting and watching that the burden of each of these austerities would seem beyond the power of all human endurance. And still, in all these he was beloved by all, for a holy joy ever beaming on his face revealed the joy and gladness with which the Holy Spirit filled his inmost soul."

3) That of Montalembert.

Along with these, perhaps, I ought to give the portrait drawn by a most eloquent modern writer, Montalembert, who, however, accepts without question all those representations of Manus O'Donnell which modern criticism has discounted, and has therefore given his picture a dash of truculence and fierceness which the earlier Lives do not justify. You require to bear this in memory in surveying it.

[1] From Mr. O'Beirne Crowe's translation.

246

"He was vindictive," says Montalembert, "passionate, bold, a man of strife, born a soldier rather
than a monk, and known, praised, and blamed as a
soldier—so that even in his lifetime he was involved in
fight; and continued a soldier, *insulanus miles*, even
upon the island rock from which he rushed forth to
preach, convert, enlighten, reconcile, and reprimand
both princes and nations, men and women, laymen
and clerics. He was at the same time full of con-
tradictions and contrasts — at once tender and
irritable, rude and courteous, ironical and com-
passionate, caressing and imperious, grateful and
revengeful, led by pity as well as by wrath, ever
moved by generous passions, and, among all passions,
fired to the very end of his life by two which his
countrymen understand the best—the love of poetry
and the love of country. Little inclined to melan-
choly when he had once surmounted the great
sorrow of his life, which was his exile; little disposed, save towards the end, to contemplation or
solitude, but trained by prayer and austerities to
triumphs of evangelical exposition; despising rest,
untiring in mental and manual toil; born for eloquence, and gifted with a voice so penetrating
and sonorous that it was thought of afterwards
as one of the most miraculous gifts that he had
received from God; frank and loyal; original and
powerful in his words as in his actions; in cloister
and mission and parliament, on land and sea, in
Ireland as in Scotland, always swayed by the love
of God and his neighbour, whom it was his pleasure to serve with an impassioned uprightness—
such was Columba."[1]

[1] "Monks of the West," vol. iii. p. 269.

He had great faults, but still greater virtues. Some tares, no doubt, mingled with the seed which his hand scattered far and wide, but rich and lasting was the harvest it produced.

> " Who are these who rise and hail him 'father,'
> Soldier-sons and all the lands ingather,
>   Isle and island, height and highland, shore and shore?
> 'Neath the shade of our great spirit parted,
> Mightier shadow of the mighty-hearted,
>   Strives a seed, and lives a deed for evermore."
>   —SKRINE'S " *Columba.*"

III. IRISH MISSIONARIES IN ENGLAND.

Irish mission- aries from Iona labour in England. How King Oswald, on the defeat of Penda, became king of Northumbria, and how, on finding almost all traces of Christianity obliterated, he sent to Iona, where he himself in his exile had found hospitable shelter and education, for a missionary of the Scots [Irish] there, to restore his people to the faith, and *Aidan.* how, in response, they sent him Aidan, after ordaining him a bishop, has been already related. Oswald assigned him the little island of Lindisfarne, now called Holy Island, on the east coast, a little south of Berwick, and not far from what is now known as the border between England and Scotland. It was then in the kingdom of Northumbria, which extended northwards as far as the Firth of Forth. "On the arrival of the bishop," Bede says, "the king appointed him his episcopal see in the Isle of Lindisfarne, as he himself desired; which place, as the tide flows and ebbs twice a day, is enclosed by the waves of the sea like an island, and again twice in the day, when the shore is left dry, becomes contiguous to the land." Here, then, Aidan esta-

blished a monastic institution after the model of
Iona, and from this centre he directed the extensive operations of the Irish mission among the
Anglo-Saxons. Bede, who does not attempt to
conceal his strong antipathy to the Irish type of
Christianity, is constrained to speak of Aidan in
the warmest terms. "It was the highest com-
mendation of his doctrine with all men," he says,
"that he taught no otherwise than he and his
followers lived; for he neither sought nor loved
anything of this world, but delighted in distri-
buting among the poor whatever was given him
by kings or rich men of the world. He was
wont to traverse both town and country on foot,
never on horseback, unless compelled by some
urgent necessity, and wherever in his way he saw
any, either rich or poor, he invited them, if unbelievers, to embrace the mystery of the faith; or,
if already believers, he sought to strengthen them in
the faith, and to stir them up by words and actions
to alms and good works. His course of life was so
different from the slothfulness of our times, that all
those who bore him company, whether they were
shorn monks or laymen, were employed in medita-
tion, that is, either in reading the Scriptures or
committing psalms. This was the daily employment
of himself, and all that were with him, wherever
they went; and if it happened, which was seldom,
that he was invited to eat with the king, he went
with one or two ecclesiastics, and having taken a
small repast, made haste to be gone with them,
either to read or to pray."[1] Aidan died in 651,
and was succeeded by Finan, who lived to see the Finan.

[1] Bede's " Eccl. Hist.," iii. 5.

Christian faith everywhere restored in those northern parts, and died in 661. And not in Northumbria only, but also in Wessex, Essex, and East Anglia, through the labours of the Irish missionaries, the Irish form of Christianity became the accepted form. In fact, only one of the seven kingdoms of the Anglo-Saxon confederation, namely, Kent, owed its conversion exclusively to Rome. In the case of three of them, the efforts of the Roman and Celtic Churches were combined; while the remaining three, comprising two-thirds of the whole extent of the country, owed their Christianisation entirely to the Celtic Church. At one period Christianity in its Celtic form was quite in the ascendant in England, and looked as if it was going to oust the Roman form introduced through the mission of Augustine. "For a time it seemed," says Green, "as if the course of the world's history was to be changed, as if the older Celtic race that Roman and German had swept before them had turned to the moral conquest of their conquerors, as if Celtic and not Latin Christianity was to mould the destinies of the Churches of the West."[1] But it fell out otherwise.

Controversy respecting Easter. In the time of Finan, Aidan's successor, a controversy broke out between the Celtic missionaries and certain ecclesiastics from Kent concerning the mode of celebrating Easter. Finan was succeeded at Lindisfarne by Colman, who had been "sent out of Scotia" (*i.e.* Ireland), and under him the controversy became intensified. King Oswald's successor, Oswy, who had also received his education at Iona, was in like manner in sympathy with its customs.

[1] Green's "Short History," chap. i. sec. 3.

But Oswy's queen, Eanfled, was a daughter of the
Kentish king, where the Roman usage obtained,
and both she and her son, Alfrith, were ardently
attached to it. It was no doubt through their
influence that a synod was convened at Whitby for
the purpose of discussing and trying to settle
the differences between the adherents of the Celtic
and the advocates of the Roman usage. The
chief leader on the one side was Colman, who had
succeeded Finan at Lindisfarne, and the champion
of the Roman practice was Wilfrith. Wilfrith had
himself been brought up at Lindisfarne, but anxious
to conform the customs of his Church with those
of the great Catholic world, he had gone to Rome
to study them, and came back aglow with zeal for
the Roman observances. Wilfrith insisted on the
authority of Peter, and asked if Columba, whom his
opponents followed, was to be preferred to the great
apostle on whom Christ had built His Church and
given him the keys of the kingdom of heaven?
The king said he would not like to oppose the
person who held the keys, "lest, perchance, when
I arrive at the gates of the kingdom of heaven,
there should be none to open to me, because I
have made an enemy of him who has been
proved to possess the keys." The result was
that Oswy and his people went over to the side
of Rome, and "Colman, perceiving that his doctrine was rejected and his sect despised, took
with him such as were willing to follow him and
would not comply with the Catholic Easter and
the coronal tonsure—for there was much controversy about that also—and went back into Scotia,
or Ireland, to consult with his people what was to

be done in this case."[1] About thirty years later a large portion of the Irish Church itself—the southern portion—was (through the agency of Adamnan, Columba's biographer) brought over to the adoption of the Roman usage. In a short time indeed Picts and Scots as well as the Britons of Wales submitted and conformed to Rome, and the English Church, although it never altogether lost the spirit of independence derived from Celtic Christianity, became in some respects, till the time of the Reformation, among the most zealous and devoted subjects of the Pope.

[1] Bede's "Eccl. Hist.," Bk. iii. c. 26.

CHAPTER XIII

THE MISSIONARY ACHIEVEMENTS OF THE CHURCH OF ST. PATRICK—*continued*

IV. COLUMBANUS.

But the missionary activity of the early Irish Church was not confined to Alba or to England. It was pre-eminently a Mission Church—in that respect not unlike the Moravians of modern times—and it sent forth its sons, on fire with unquenchable Christian ardour, and in the face of innumerable perils and hardships, far beyond the confines of the British Isles, to evangelise the Continent of Europe.

I have now to speak of the brave and indomitable leader of a missionary band who went on this wider and more distant mission, and one hardly less famous than Columba. I refer to Columbanus, who, though bearing a name so closely resembling that of Columba, is a very different person, to be carefully distinguished from Columba, who was his older contemporary. Columbanus was born twenty year later than the other (in 543), and whereas Columba hailed from the north, Columbanus was of southern origin, having been born in Leinster, and, as so many of the Irish ecclesiastics were, of noble parents.

We are fortunate in possessing a " Life of Colum-

Life by
Jonas, a con-
temporary.
banus" written by a contemporary of his own, Jonas, who was first his friend and companion, and then his successor in the Italian monastery of Bobbio, where Columbanus finished his career. His own writings also, a good many of which are still extant, are a valuable source of information with regard to him.

Educated at
Cleenish,
in Lough
Erne;
His early education he received in a monastery on Cleenish, an island of Lough Erne, where, Jonas says, he soon became proficient in " grammar, rhetoric, geometry, and the range of the Divine Scriptures;" and as evidence of his progress he mentions that "while yet a very young man he wrote an exposition of the 'Book of Psalms' in elegant language . . . and he also composed many other pieces suitable for singing or profitable for communicating instruction." The commentary still exists.

and at
Bangor,
Co. Down.
From Cleenish he betook himself to the great monastery of Bangor, in County Down, where, under Comgall, a very liberal education must have been given. Columbanus wrote excellent Latin verse (some of which is still extant), and such as only a well-grounded Latin scholar could produce. He knew Greek also, and shows himself familiar with the Greek poets. It is manifest that he was conversant, not only with the Greek and Latin fathers, but with the chief writings of classical antiquity. He appears even to have numbered Hebrew among his accomplishments, and all this learning he must have acquired in the two Irish monasteries I have named, for on leaving Ireland for the Continent his life was too busy and eventful to admit of his acquiring it there. Indeed, he had reached

middle age before his departure from the Irish shores.

He was more than forty years old when, probably stimulated and fired by the splendid example of Columba, who was an intimate friend of his abbot, Comgall, and had summoned Comgall over to Britain to assist him in his work, when he (Columbanus) determined, with a company of twelve companions, to set out for the shores of Gaul, and to devote the remainder of his life to the Christianisation of the vast populations of the Continent still in heathen darkness, or, if nominally Christian, living in practical paganism. This was about the year 585. *Sets out for Gaul.*

Landing in the north of Gaul, the little company of pilgrims went about disseminating the faith, but at length made their way southwards till they came to Burgundy. A picturesque band they must have been, that could not fail to excite the interest of the rude inhabitants of the regions through which they passed. It is not hard to picture them with their coarse, undyed woollen upper garment, in colour the same as when it grew upon the sheep's back, on their head a cowl of the same material, and sandals on their feet, with forehead tonsured in front to a line drawn from ear to ear in the way I have already described, and the long hair flowing down behind; a wallet on their back, which constituted at once their pantry and their library, wherein both bread and books, both material and spiritual nourishment, were stowed; with a staff in the hand, and a leathern water-bottle by the side. As they journeyed, the biographer of Columbanus informs *Makes his way to Burgundy.*

us, "the venerable man took care to preach the word of the Gospel in whatever places they came to. . . . Whatever persons' houses he was staying in for any time, he was sure to turn the attention of all the inmates to their improvement in religion."[1]

Mistake of Milman.

It is in this connection that Milman makes the strange statement that Columbanus "at the outset was no missionary, urged by a passionate or determined zeal to convert pagan nations to the cross of Christ. . . . He and his followers seemed only to seek a safe retreat in which he might shroud his solitary devotion." But Milman in effect answers himself when he speaks of Ireland at that time as "a kind of Hesperian Elysium of peace and piety." If it was simply retirement that he sought for, Columbanus might have found it "not less secure against secular intrusion, as wild, as silent, as holy in the yet peaceful Ireland, or in the Scottish islands, as in the mountains of the Vosges or the valleys of the Alps." Milman is, in fact, misled by the circumstance that wherever they went the Irish missionaries first established a monastery in some secluded, lonely spot, because a cloister was the one fundamental feature of the church organisation with which they were familiar; but from that central point they never failed to extend their evangelistic operations over the surrounding territory. It was so in this case.

The wild region in which they settled.

Nowhere could they have found a region more in need of their civilising, Christianising influence than that into which our missionaries now came. It would be hardly possible to draw too dark a picture

[1] Jonas, c. iv.

of society in France under the Merovingian kings.
The Franks had indeed been nominally converted
under Clovis, but in their case the conversion seems
to have been even more superficial than the wholesale conversions of that time generally were. "The
Franks were sad Christians," says the eloquent
biographer of the Monks of the West. " While
they respected the freedom of the Catholic faith,
and made external profession of it, they violated
without scruple all its precepts, and at the same
time the simplest laws of humanity. After having
prostrated themselves before the tomb of some holy
martyr or confessor . . . we see them, sometimes in
outbreaks of fury, sometimes by cold-blooded cruelty,
give full vent to the evil instincts of their savage
nature. Their incredible perversity was most apparent in the domestic tragedies, the fratricidal
executions and assassinations, of which Clovis gave
the first example, and which marked the history
of his son and grandson with an ineffaceable stain.
Polygamy and perjury mingled in their daily life
with a semi-pagan superstition, and in reading these
bloody biographies, scarcely lightened by some
transient gleams of faith or humility, it is difficult
to believe that in embracing Christianity they gave
up a single pagan vice or adopted a single Christian
virtue."[1] The picture is drawn in dark and repulsive colours, but it in no way exaggerates the
evils of the society in which Columbanus and his
companions now found themselves on arriving
in Burgundy. They were indeed well received
by Guntram, the least vicious of the grandsons of
Clovis, and they might have found a comparatively

[1] "Monks of the West," by Montalembert.

pleasant and easy field of labour had they remained with him. But it was not ease or comfort they were in search of. "Over a range of sixty leagues and a breadth of ten or fifteen," says Montalembert, "nothing was to be seen but parallel chains of inaccessible defiles divided by endless forests, whose bristling pinewoods descended from the peaks of the highest mountains to overshadow the course of the rapid and pure streams of the Doubs, the Desoubre, and the Loue." It was here, amid the wild and desolate ranges of the Vosges Mountains, on the borders between Burgundy and Austrasia, now included in the department of Saone, in the province of Franche-Comté, that they found a congenial abode.

Fixes his abode at the old Roman fort of Annegray. In the ruins of the old Roman fort of Annegray they took up their residence. Nowhere could they have found better scope for self-denial or surroundings better fitted to inure them to privation and hardship. "It is an ugly thing," says Charles Kingsley, "even for an armed man to traverse without compass the bush of Australia or New Zealand, where there are no wild beasts. But it was uglier still to start out under the dark roof of those primeval forests. Knights, when they rode thither, went armed *cap-à-pie*, like Sintram through the dark valley, trusting in God and their good swords. Chapmen and merchants stole through it by a few tracks in great companies, armed with bill and bow. Peasants ventured into it a few miles to cut timber and find forage for their swine, and whispered wild legends of the ugly things therein, and sometimes, too, never came home. Away it stretched from the far Rhineland, wave after wave of oak and alder, beech and pine, God alone knew how far, into the land of night and wonder, and the infinite unknown, full of elk and bison, bear and wolf, lynx and glutton, and perhaps of worse beasts still."[1]

Amid such environments, then, in the solitary haunts of the bear, the lynx, and the wolf, did our missionaries now pitch their tents, clear a portion of the forest, and raise a monastery after the model with which we are already familiar. At first they suffered from a scarcity of even the barest necessaries of life, but Columbanus "bore in mind that man doth not live by bread only, but that they who satiate themselves with the Word of life enjoy an abundant and continual feast" (Jonas, c. v.). But sufficient land was soon reclaimed from the trees and brushwood of the forest to grow their corn, and produce at least the necessaries of existence. Very plain and scanty these were at the best. The ordi- His severe nary food of the community consisted of coarse discipline. bread, herbs, and meal and water. Columbanus himself was exceptionally abstemious in his mode of life. He would subsist for weeks on the herbs of the field and the wild berries of the woods. And the rule drawn up by him for his monks reflected the severity of his personal self-discipline. Here is a specimen of it: "Let the monk live under the discipline of one father and in the society of many, that from the one he may learn humility, from the other patience; from the one silence, from the other gentleness; let him never gratify his own wishes; let him eat whatever he is bidden; let him possess only what he receives; let him perform his allotted task with diligence; only when wearied out let him retire to bed; let him be compelled to rise before he

[1] "The Monks and the Heathen," *Good Words*, January 1863.

has slept sufficiently; when he is injured, let him
hold his peace; let him fear the head of the monastery as a master, and love him as a father; let
him believe that whatever he orders is for his
good, and obey him without question, seeing that
he is called to obedience, and to fulfil all that is
right; let his fare be homely and sparing, sufficient
to support life without weighing down the spirit—
a little bread, vegetables, pulse, or flour mixed
with water." To the question, "What are the
limits of obedience?" the answer is, "Even unto
death; for unto death Christ submitted Himself
to the Father for us." "If any brother be dis-
obedient, let him be two days on one biscuit and
water. If any say, 'I will not do it,' or break
a command or regulation, let him be two days on
one biscuit." In some cases corporal punishment
was inflicted. If any one failed to say "Amen"
when grace was said, the penalty was six stripes,
and any one who refused to observe the rule of
silence at meals was taught by the application of
the same number of lashes that silence, if not
golden, was preferable to a smarting back. "Whoever coughs at the beginning of the psalm, and
does not sing out well, six stripes; whoever smiles
during the prayer, six stripes." Probably, however, the disciplinary rules were for the most part
willingly submitted to, and the echoes of the
forest glades were awakened to the voice of hearty
praise and prayer, of measured chant and solemn
litany. And the brethren were never idle. While
some held the plough, others built the mill, or
trained the vine, or planted the apple-tree, and
others still transcribed and illuminated manu-

scripts, or educated the young, or tended the sick, or dispensed alms to the destitute. A time came when monasteries ceased to serve the purpose for which they were designed, and became haunts of laziness and nurseries of selfishness and vice. But in their earlier history, and especially in the hands of men like Columbanus, they were hives of industry, schools of self-discipline and self-denial, and, even on their industrial side, to the too often lawless and idle populations amidst which they were planted they afforded a stimulating and elevating example. It was this aspect of their work that impressed the great missionary, David Livingstone. " The monks," he says, " did not disdain to hold the plough; they introduced fruit-trees, flowers, vegetables, in addition to teaching and emancipating the serfs; their monasteries were mission-stations, which resembled ours in being dispensaries for the sick, almshouses for the poor, and nurseries of learning. Can we learn nothing from them in their prosperity as the schools of Europe, and see nought in their history but the pollution and laziness of their decay?" In the instance before us, the Franks, both heathen and nominally Christian, were profoundly affected by the example of Columbanus and his companions, came in large numbers to receive instruction, and were encouraged to follow their example. And before long they grew to such dimensions that they had to hive off and erect other similar institutions, one at Luxeuil (on the ruins of Luxovium, an old fortified Roman town), eight miles from Annegray, and another at Fontenay in the same neighbourhood. For some twenty years Colum-

What Livingstone thought of it.

banus and his monks laboured in those regions, making many disciples, and exerting a powerful and most salutary influence on the people among whom they lived. And all classes were reached by them. It is said that among the disciples of Columbanus the sons of the nobility were numbered by hundreds.

Comes in collision with the Frankish clergy. But he was not permitted to pursue his work in peace. He was too stern a disciplinarian and too faithful a monitor not to make determined enemies. His blameless life and stern discipline rebuked the laxity of the Frankish clergy and awakened their hostility; and particularly his attachment to the Irish method of observing Easter, and the other Irish usages, brought him into direct and sharp collision with their leaders. In 602 or 603 the bishops convoked a synod, and summoned him to appear. He did not attend their council, but sent a letter, which is still preserved, explaining and defending his action. "I am not the author of those differences," he said. "I came as a stranger amongst you, in behalf of our common Lord and Master, Jesus Christ. In His name I beseech your holinesses to let me live in peace and quiet, as I have lived for twelve years in the depths of these forests, beside the bones of my seventeen departed brethren. Let us live in the same land with you here as, if we are worthy, we hope to live together in the same heaven hereafter. . . . I have judged it better that you should know what are the subjects that we here handle and study with one another. For these are our canons, the commandments of the Lord and of the Apostles. In these is our faith; these are our arms, our shield and sword; these

are our defence; these it is that have influenced us
to leave our native land; these we struggle in our
lukewarm way to observe; in these we desire to
pray that we may persevere until death, as we have
seen our elders do before us." He suggests either
that each should abide in the mode of life wherein
he hath been called, "or else that the books should
be read on both sides with peace and humility,
and without anything of a contentious spirit, and
whatever system accords most with the Old and
New Testaments that that should be observed without ill-feeling on the part of any one."

He also addressed a letter to Pope Gregory the Writes to
Great vindicating his practices in very outspoken Pope
Gregory.
terms: "How is it that you with all your wisdom,
you, the brilliant light of whose sanctified talents
is shining abroad throughout the world, are induced
to support this dark Paschal system? I wonder, I
confess, that the erroneous practice of Gaul has not
been long since abolished by you. . . . You are
afraid, perhaps, of incurring the charge of a taste
for novelty, and are content with the authority of
your predecessors, and of Pope Leo in particular.
But do not, I beseech you, in a matter of such
importance, give way to the dictates of humility
or gravity only, as they are often mistaken. It
may be that in this affair *a living dog is better than
a dead Leo.* [He has the effrontery in writing one
Pope to pun on the name of another.]. . . . Let your
vigilance then be careful . . . that there be no dis-
agreement between yourself and Jerome. . . . For I
confess to you plainly that the man who contradicts
the authority of Jerome will be looked upon as a
heretic, and rejected with scorn by the Churches of

the West. For as far as the Divine Scriptures
are concerned, they entertain sentiments decidedly
and wholly accordant with his." This singular
epistle ends thus: "If, as I have heard from your
pious friend Candidus, you are disposed to give
me this answer, that what is established by the
authority of antiquity cannot be altered, certainly
error can lay claim to antiquity, but the truth which
condemns it is always of higher antiquity still."

Straight
talk to Boni-
face IV. In his letter to Pope Boniface IV., written later,
but which may be noticed here, Columbanus adopts
even the language of rebuke, and writes in a way
that must make the flesh of a modern Roman
Catholic creep. He calls on Boniface to "purge
the chair of Peter from all error." "And that I
may say out all (not to seem to flatter even yourself
unduly), it is also a painful thing to reflect on that
you, the party possessed of the legitimate power,
were not the first to come forward, influenced by
zeal for the faith, and, after first proving the purity
of your own faith, to condemn or excommunicate
the party that dared to defame the principal See
relative to the orthodoxy of its faith."

He calls upon the Pope to "remove the cloud
of suspicion from St. Peter's chair." "Convoke,
therefore, an assembly, that you may clear away
the charges alleged against you; for it is no child's
play that you are accused of. For it is the re-
ceiving of heretics, as I am informed, that you are
charged with, though far be it from gaining credit,
as a thing having occurred, or existing, or likely to
happen. They say, however, that Eutyches, Dios-
corus, Nestorius, old heretics, as we know them to
have been, were countenanced by Virgilius in some

Fifth Synod. See there the cause of the entire
scandal, as they say, if you, too, as they assert,
countenance the same persons; or, if you know
that Virgilius died so infected, why do you bring
forward his name in a manner at variance with a
good conscience?"

It does not appear from this that Columbanus
believed much in Papal infallibility. He evidently
thought the Pope as liable to error and as much
in need of wholesome advice as any one; nor is he
over-respectful in the terms in which he tenders it.

His collision with the royal court of Burgundy His collision
was, however, much more serious than his brush with the
royal court.
with the prelates and the Pope. It shows us very
clearly what manner of man he was—that he was
not a reed shaken by the wind.

When Clovis died, his realm was divided among
his four sons, but, on the death of three of them, was
re-united under the survivor, Clotaire, but again
distributed a second time among the four sons of
Clotaire, Charibert becoming ruler of that kingdom
of which Paris was the capital, Chilperic of Soissons,
Sigebert of Austrasia, the designation of the German
or eastern division, and Guntram of Burgundy. On
the death of Sigebert of Austrasia he was succeeded
by his son Hildebert, who, on the death of his uncle
Guntram, inherited Burgundy as well. But Hildebert also dying, his two sons succeeded him, Theodebert in Austrasia, and Theoderic (or Thierry) in
Burgundy. The sons were youths, however, when
their father died, and were entirely under the direction of their grandmother, Brunehild, who has been
described as another Jezebel. Ultimately expelled
from the court of the king of Austrasia, she took

up her abode with Thierry, who was living a licentious and immoral life. In order to retain her influence and power, and lest, should he wed a lawful wife, she should lose her ascendency, Brunehild encouraged him in his immorality, and opposed any attempt on his part to marry a lawful queen and put away his concubines. Columbanus had acquired considerable influence over Thierry, and more than once succeeded in getting him to promise to abandon his vicious habits. But in so doing he only incurred the displeasure of Brunchild. On one occasion, when he was at court, she desired him to bestow his blessing on the four illegitimate children of Thierry; but he indignantly refused to do so. Thenceforward she began a series of petty persecutions against Columbanus and his communities, and at length she succeeded in inducing Thierry to banish Driven from him from the kingdom. By a company of soldiers Burgundy. he was seized, and, with a few of his companions, taken down the Loire to Orleans and then to Nantes, where he was put on board a ship bound for Ireland. But driven back by a storm, he next found himself on the coast of Neustria. The king of Neustria, Clotaire II., besought him to remain, but, anxious no doubt to return to his community, he went to the court of Theodebert, king of Austrasia, who received him kindly. But finding return impossible, he and his associates embarked upon the Rhine, up which they made their way as far as the Lake of Zurich, and, after a short stay at Zug, they went on Passes to to Bregenz, on the Lake of Constance in Switzerland. Switzer- Here they found a ruined Roman city and the ruins land. of a Christian church. Callech, now better known as St. Gall, one of the companions of Columbanus, was able to preach to the people in their own language, and was so far successful that he ventured to break their idols and fling them into the lake. Many believed and were baptized, but others were filled with anger and a desire for revenge. For three years the missionaries tarried here, rebuilding the ancient church and founding a monastery. St. Gall was a skilful angler, and met the wants of the little community by fishing on the lake, which still abounds with a great variety of fish. One night while he was so engaged, he heard (we are told) the Spirit of the Mountains call to the Spirit of the Waters: "Arise and hasten to mine aid. Behold, strangers have come, and driven me from my temple. Come, and help me to expel them from the land!" To which responded the Spirit of the Waters: "Lo, even now one of them is busy on my surface, but I cannot injure him. Often have I desired to break his nets, but as often I am baffled by his invocation of the all-prevailing Name in which he is always praying."

Their human foes were not so easily defeated; one of the native chieftains formed a confederation of the heathen against the missionaries, and Columbanus determined on withdrawing. St. Gall fell sick and was left behind, and was the means ultimately of reclaiming the people of that whole region from barbarism, teaching them both the duties of religion and the arts of agriculture, giving his name to the town and canton of St. Gall, and becoming, in short, the apostle of Switzerland. *St. Gall becomes the apostle of this region.*

Meanwhile, Columbanus crossed the Alps into Northern Italy, went to the court of Agilulf, king of the Lombards, by whom he was cordially received, *Columbanus crosses the Alps;*

and granted territory on which he might reside. With the king's consent, he founded in a lonely defile of the Apennines, between Genoa and Milan, the famous monastery of Bobbio, which, with its precious library, rose into great celebrity, and continued till modern times, and where some most valuable manuscripts, both of the Bible and of other works, have been found. It was there that the famous Muratorian fragment on the canon of the New Testament was discovered; and Muratori, the scholar who discovered it, made out a catalogue of seven hundred manuscripts which the convent possessed in the eighteenth century. From this catalogue we learn that the library at Bobbio contained the writings of Origen, Cyprian, Athanasius, Eusebius, Augustine, Chrysostom, Hilary; Greek and Latin classics, such as Homer, Virgil, Horace, Lucan, Juvenal, Cicero; books on geography, mathematics, and the like; and, as might have been expected, works of Irish and English origin, such as "The Antiphonary of Bangor," the writings of Adamnan, and the works of Bede. The convent of St. Gall, founded by Callech or Gallus, was exceptionally rich in its manuscript treasures. Some valuable manuscripts of the New Testament have been found there, one of them containing the Epistles of the Apostle Paul. On the margin of this manuscript writing was observed which was for some time an enigma to Continental scholars; but the late Dr. John O'Donovan, an eminent Celtic scholar, found that the language of the writing was early Irish, the work no doubt of Irish monks. One of these marginal notes is at once amusing and suggestive. It was evidently written by some Irishman

and founds Bobbio.

268

COLUMBANUS

who had paid a visit to Rome, had called at St. Gall on his way home, and took the opportunity of noting down on the blank margin of the manuscript what he thought of the great ecclesiastical metropolis. His remarks were couched in verse, of which this has been given as a literal rendering :—

"To come to Rome, to come to Rome,
Much of trouble, little of profit ;
The thing thou seekest here,
If thou bring not with thee, thou findest not.

Great folly, great madness,
Great ruin of sense, great insanity,
Since thou hast set out for death,
That thou shouldst be in disobedience to the Son of
Mary." [1]

This Irishman, like Luther, and many another, went to Rome manifestly with great expectations, but returned home disappointed.

When Columbanus settled at Bobbio, the Arian heresy prevailed among the Lombards in Northern Italy. While he sought to diffuse the light of Christianity among those still in pagan darkness, he laboured to counteract error by setting forth the truth. It was now that he wrote to Boniface IV. But not even Bobbio was destined to see his end. On the opposite shore of Trebbia he found a cave which he transformed into a sort of church. There he spent his last days, and there his long, chequered, His death. and eventful pilgrimage ended on the 21st of November 615.

There is no doubt his influence went deep and

[1] See "Expositor" for June 1889.

far. His followers were numerous, were much devoted to his Rule, and propagated far and wide the
Irish type of Christianity which he transplanted to
the Continent.

His char-
acter.

He was a man of great strength of character, and
of great firmness and resoluteness of purpose. The
extraordinary boldness and energy with which he met
the difficulties and perils that beset his path, the
intrepid faithfulness with which he denounced vice
and crime, even in royal personages at whose mercy
he was, alike unsoftened by their smiles and unin-
timidated by their frowns, show that he was no
feeble reed shaken by the breeze, but rather, like
the rugged oak of his native Erin, standing firm
and fast, and holding its head erect against the
storm. The monastic rule which he promulgated
reveals the temper of a stern disciplinarian and a
strong and exacting ruler of men. But he was a
man of large nature and varied gifts and aptitudes,
in whom a love of his native country, which he
never forgot and never was ashamed of among
Franks or Lombards, a scholar's love of learning,
the sensitive and gentle genius of the poet, and the
resolute discipline of a strong ruler, blended with
the pitying compassion, continuous self-sacifice, and
unwearied activity and labour of a great missionary.
We must be strangely constituted if we refuse him
the tribute of our respect and admiration.

Other Irish
mission-
aries.

Here, however, our sketch of early Irish missionary enterprise must terminate. To touch, however
briefly, on the work of the other celebrated missionaries sent forth from the shores of Ireland; to sketch

COLUMBANUS

the labours of St. Dichuil (Deicolus), brother of St. Gallus, at Luthra, now Lure, in Besancon, where, under the patronage of Clotaire II., he reared a monastery and did an important work, and exerted an influence which causes his name to be still cherished there with veneration ; to accompany St. Fursa in his earnest and indefatigable mission, first among the East Angles, where, as Bede tells us, he was instrumental in converting many unbelievers and in confirming many Christians in the faith, and afterwards in France, preaching with such eloquence that Bede mentions the case of a monk who, when giving an account of his sermon, broke out into a profuse perspiration through the terror which the mere recollection of it created, though he was thinly clad and it was the coldest time of winter ; or to go with Mailduf to England, and see him rear a great monastic establishment at a spot which was called after him, *Maidulfsburg* or *Malmesbury*; or to follow St. Kilian in his missionary labours in Franconia, where, after leading multitudes, including not a few nobles, to forsake paganism and embrace Christianity, he at last, while engaged with others in the very act of worship, met with a martyr's death ; to note even in the briefest manner the outstanding events in the career of Fergil (Virgilius) in Bavaria, and his conflict with Boniface with regard to the administration of baptism, and touching the opinion expressed by him that the earth was round, and that men lived on the other side of it, and enjoyed, like ourselves, the benefit of sun, moon, and stars, an opinion which the "infallible" Pope Zachary declared to be "the wicked and perverse

doctrine of that individual," and directed Boniface
to "assemble a council and expel him from the
Church," having previously degraded him from the
honour of the priesthood ; how, nevertheless, later
he became, through the influence of King Pepin,
bishop of Saltzburg, and did a great work, not only
in Bavaria, but in giving the knowledge of the truth
to Carinthia as well, and thus gained the title of
"the Apostle of Carinthia ; " or to tell of Willibrord,
who, though born in Northumberland, went for education and inspiration to the Irish schools, where,
says his biographer, the illustrious Alcuin, he "attached himself to the society of the reverend persons "
who taught there, "in order that, like some very
skilful bee, he might be able to taste the honey-
dropping flowers of piety and build the sweet comb
of virtues in the hive of his own breast, and where for
twelve years this young man, that was afterwards to
become a preacher to many nations, received instruction from the first masters of devoted piety and
sacred learning, until he came to the state of a
perfect man, and to the age of the fulness of Christ,"[1]
and then went abroad to spread the Christian faith
among the heathen inhabitants of Batavia, Friesland,
and Westphalia ; or to follow those zealous and indefatigable missionaries to the region of perpetual
snow to which they penetrated, to accompany them
to Iceland, where the first Norwegian missionaries
who came there found that Irish missionaries had
been before them, and had left behind them Irish
books, bells, crosiers, and other traces of an early
Irish mission ; to relate the details of all this vast

[1] Alcuin, "Vit. Willibrord."

and widespread mission enterprise would carry us too far out of our way at present, and transgress the limits I have set myself, although the whole story of early Irish missions would make a volume as interesting as a romance, and would be well worth the telling.

CHAPTER XIV

DEFECTS IN THE CHURCH OF ST. PATRICK

So far we have regarded the Early Irish Church chiefly on its most favourable side. But history is worse than useless if it does not hold the mirror up to nature. Whether the facts agree or not with our own predilections, whether they are creditable or the reverse, the historian has no option but to represent them as they are. He is both short-sighted and disloyal to truth who tries to cover with his white-wash the defects and stains that disfigure ancient institutions. One of the chief uses of history, which is to note blemishes and to trace them to their cause, is thereby missed; and what should be one of our greatest and most effective teachers becomes thus a delusion and a snare. We have now before us, then, the disagreeable but imperative duty of noticing the deformities which too soon appeared in Irish Christianity.

We have seen that in at least one feature the Early Irish Church approximated to the Church of Apostolic times. It was comparatively evangelical in its teaching. Any one who reads the acknow-ledged writings of St. Patrick cannot but be struck with their evangelical tone, and their general freedom from the corruptions and superstitions which so soon began to debase mediæval Christianity. Yet

it must not be disguised that from an early date
even the Irish Church began to be adulterated with
base alloy. The ointment which the box of its
organisation held was soon spoiled by the presence
of more than one dead fly. From the very outset,
indeed, deleterious elements were admitted which
tended deeply and seriously to vitiate and corrupt
its practical influence for good.

How many of their old pagan customs and super- Irish Chris-
stitions the converts made by Patrick himself were teriorated
allowed to carry over along with them, we have from the
already had occasion to note. A considerable num- mixture of
ber of them survive to this hour. Then, in the pagan
monastic spirit, which from its start dominated the
Irish Church, a leaven was introduced essentially
at variance with New Testament Christianity, and
which could not but work injuriously. Again, in
spite of her independence, influences from without,
and especially from Roman ecclesiasticism, told on
the Irish Church ; and Irish Christianity deteriorated
—became less evangelical and more superstitious—
in proportion as she came under Roman domination.
One fact in particular is not to be overlooked. A
consensus of testimony bears witness that in the
sixth and seventh centuries there was a most serious
decline in the religion of the Irish, that, in fact, such
a relapse took place among the people generally to
their old pagan ways, that some writers do not
hesitate to call it an apostasy. It is noteworthy
that the same thing took place in England, and
from the same cause. In connection with the conversion of the Anglo-Saxons by Augustin and his
associates, Pope Gregory the Great expressly wrote
that pagan forms of worship might be profitably

preserved if modified to Christian uses, and that
even sacrifices of oxen might continue if they were
offered on saints' days. The result was what might
have been expected, that before long there was on
Relapse
into pagan-
ism.
the part of the people a wholesale relapse to paganism, and that it was with great difficulty, and chiefly
through the agency of Irish missionaries, that they
were at length reclaimed. An occurrence somewhat similar now took place in Ireland. In the
" Life of Gildas," a Welsh ecclesiastic, it is related
that in the time of Ainmire, king of Ireland (568–
571), almost all the people forsook the Christian
faith, and that Ainmire sent for Gildas and others
to recover them. From that relapse Irish Christianity seems never to have properly recovered, for
an immense number of the old pagan observances
continue to this day among the native Irish.
An inferior
type of
Christianity
survived.
It thus came to pass that the type of practical
Christianity that prevailed and became popular in
Ireland was a very inferior one. Both monks and
people came to be more than half pagan in their
ideas and ways. Irish Christianity was in a very
great degree paganism baptized, with saints in the
place of gods. It would certainly not be much
of an exaggeration to say that the saints were
Druidical priests with a slight Christian varnish.
Just as the Druids professed to possess preternatural
powers, and by means of spells and incantations
to work all sorts of wonders, similar miraculous
feats without number are ascribed to the Irish
saints in their Lives, written by the monks. Let
me give some specimens.

A thief stole Patrick's goat. He denied the
theft, but Patrick made the sign of the cross, and

the goat bleated from the thief's stomach. Patrick and his companions on their first visit to Tara are threatened with massacre; they instantly, at Patrick's word, take the form of deer and escape. At the same place a Druid dropped poison into Patrick's cup of ale. Patrick made the sign of the cross over it, and the ale became ice. He turned the cup upside down, and the poison dropped on the table. He made the sign of the cross again, the ale became liquid, and he drank it off. The monkish writers do not scruple to impute to the saint gross breaches of the moral law, and imagine that they are glorifying their hero. Thus the "Tripartite Life" represents him as going to Rome after he laid the foundations of Armagh, and as actually carrying off from thence, by what the Life calls "a pious fraud or theft, whilst the keepers of the sacred places were asleep and unconscious," a large quantity of relics of apostles and martyrs—" three hundred and three-score and five relics, together with the relics of Peter and Paul and Laurence and Stephen, and many others. And a sheet (or towel) was among them stained with Christ's blood, and some of the hair of the Virgin." "O wondrous deed! O rare theft of a vast treasure of holy things, committed without sacrilege, the plunder of the most holy place in the world!" the writer exclaims in rapt admiration of this gross violation of the eighth commandment. Returning from Rome after his first visit, the *Lebar Brecc* (thirteenth century) represents Patrick as entering a vessel on the strand of the sea of Britain. A leper sought permission to accompany him, but there was no room

A specimen of the miracles attributed to Irish saints.

277

for him on board. "So Patrick put out before him to swim in the sea the portable stone altar whereon he used to make offering every day. But for all that, God wrought a great miracle here, to wit, the stone went not to the bottom, nor did it stay behind them, but it swam round about the boat with the leper on it, until it arrived in Ireland."[1] A somewhat similar feat is attributed to Molaise. Molaise, sailing from Rome, met a leper on the open sea, sailing along complacently on a big stone. "Change places," said Molaise. They changed places, and Molaise sailed on the stone till he came to the island of Arran, where the stone may still be seen! St. Brendan sailing for seven years on a whale's back is a trifle compared to that.

One of the customs retained from Druidical times was the "perpetual fire." In the monastery of St. Kieran of Saigir, the sacred fire, from which all other fires were kindled, was allowed to go out, and the weather was bitterly cold. St. Kieran went forth, spread out his hands and prayed, whereupon there fell a thunderbolt by means of which he rekindled the fire. Another saint, Molua, wanted to see Rome. St. Aidan of Ferns took him up in his chariot, and they were both invisible till the following day. Molua was quite familiar with the eternal city from that day forward. Hugh, the swarthy king of Breifne, asked St. Caillin to make him fair, like St. Rioch of Inis-bo-finne. The saint prayed, and next morning he and St. Rioch were exactly alike. After Columba left Clonard, he went for a time, as the reader has seen, to the monastery of his friend St. Mobhi, of Glasnaoidhen

[1] "Tripartite Life," vol. ii. pp. 447, 448.

(Glasnevin), on the east bank of the Tolka. The huts of the pupils were on the west side of the river. One morning, when the bell rang for matins, there was a keen frost, and the river was frozen over, but Columba passed through it. "Bravely thou hast acted, O son of Niall," said St. Mobhi. "God is able to get us out of this difficulty," said Columba. And so, on the return of the pupils from church, they found all the huts removed and planted beside the church on the east bank of the river. But not earth only, but heaven and hell were equally at command, and a personal service to a saint secured the one, as a personal slight ensured the other. Columba gave heaven to the king of Ossory, because the king pulled off his boots! Adamnan threatened to send Finnachta, the king of Ireland, to hell, if he did not rise instantly from the chess-table at which he sat and come to him. Of course Finnachta at once rose and came!

Such is the sort of stuff with which the "Lives of the Saints" abound! Of course, the earlier saints did not themselves claim such supernatural powers. Patrick, in his genuine writings, never hints at his possessing them. But the legends that grew up around them in the minds of their monkish biographers show us what manner of persons those monks were, and the religious ideal which filled their imagination. The miracles attributed to the saints are at best capricious, prodigious, and grotesque, such as Puck might be supposed to delight in; but, as often as otherwise, they are spiteful, revengeful, and vicious in the motive that inspires them. Any one who looked crooked at those saints, according to their biographers, ran the risk of being struck dead on the spot.

Cursing
reduced to a
fine art. There was one accomplishment especially in which the Irish saints were adepts, and in which no one we have ever heard of could compete with them—except perhaps the Pope. They had reduced *cursing* to a fine art. The " Tripartite Life " represents St. Patrick himself as inflicting his curses on all who opposed him in any way, and as cursing localities, rivers, trees, and the like, as well as human beings. He curses Inver Domnan and Inver Ainge because he found no fish in them, and "both are barren ; " he curses even churches.[1] The cursing sometimes took the remarkable form of " fasting against " the person on whom it was desired to invoke the Divine judgment. In the " Tripartite Life " Patrick is described as " fasting against " a certain local king or chieftain called Trian, for oppressing his slaves. " And Patrick fasted against him. Trian did nothing for him. Patrick turned on the morrow from the fortress. He cast his spittle on the rock which lay on his road, and the rock broke into three. A third part of the spittle (or perhaps the rock) was then flung a thousand paces. Patrick said : ' Two-thirds of the fasting on the rock, a third on the king, and on the fort, and on the district. There will be of Trian's children neither king nor crown prince. He himself shall perish early, and shall go down to bitter hell.' "[2] It fell out accordingly. Dr. Whitley Stokes identifies this practice of " fasting against " persons with the Brahmanic practice called in Hindi *dharna*. Later saints employ the

---

[1] Stokes's " Tripartite," i. 159.   [2] Ibid., p. 219.

weapon with equal freedom. St. Kieran curses Kellach, and, in spite of the repentance of Kellach, he dies prematurely. Columba curses Black Hugh, and the curse takes effect. Ædh's son, Conall, flings mud at the clergy as they enter the assembly at Drumceatt. Columba rang his bells and solemnly cursed Conall, who was thenceforward stricken with insanity; and his mother and her maid, who encouraged him, turned into herons, condemned to be ever watching their prey at the ford of the river near Drumceatt. See too his curse upon the malefactor of "the royal race of Gabhran" recorded in Adamnan's "Life of Columba," ii. 22. Ruadan, again, curses Tara and its king, and from that day a blight falls on both. When we hear Erin glorified as "an island of saints" and as a sort of "Hesperian Elysium," the recollection of the character of these saints as portrayed by their admiring biographers is calculated to dispel some illusions.

Even the best of them, such as Columba, appear to have been passionate and vindictive, and to have given free rein to their passions at times. Witness Columba's action in forming a league against Diarmid, and in inciting the North to war against him; for it seems impossible to question that part of the story. The monks themselves shared in the feuds which raged between their tribes, were much addicted to fighting, were liable to be called out to military service, and were too apt to be swayed and agitated by those fierce and turbulent passions which such a life tended to inspire and foster. The bishop-king of Munster, Feidhlimidh (Phelim), devastated the sacred cloisters of Clonmacnois. In 673 a desperate battle was

The best of the saints passionate and vindictive.

fought between the monasteries of Clonmacnois and Durrow, and two hundred were slain. In 816 four hundred were slain in a similar engagement. "The clergy of Ireland went to their synods with their weapons, and fought pitched battles, and slew many persons therein." So the "Annals of MacFirbis" assure us.

The meaner vices, such as lying, and deception, gloried in.

Such scenes might at least cultivate vigour and valour, and the sterner and hardier traits of character generally. But alas! the meaner vices appear to have been rife among the monks, and to have been much admired by them. In the formation of strong character there are no traits more vital and fundamental than integrity and truth. Equivocation, deceit, lying, the monks appear to have cultivated as virtues. Ruadan and Molua, both great saints, gained their ends by equivocation, and gloried in it. Adamnan kept a monk to lie for him. Sir James Stephen, in his essay on Hildebrand, scornfully remarks that "nature has given horns to bulls, and to priests deceit and dissimulation." Certainly this was verified in the Irish clergy. And the bards, who still retained much of the old spirit, did not spare their double-dealing and general untrustworthiness.

Celtic Christianity in Ireland ethically weak.

The New Testament lays the utmost stress on the ethical part of Christianity. It demands truthful, honest, upright lives. Our Lord's word is, "By their fruit ye shall know them." And His servant requires the pursuit of "whatsoever things are true, whatsoever things are honest, whatsoever things are just, whatsoever things are pure, and whatsoever things are lovely." Tried by this standard, it must be confessed that Irish Christianity does not rank

high.   The fact is, that soon after Patrick's time it
became weak in the ethical department, strong in
the superstitious and ceremonial.   In his "Early
History of Institutions," Sir Henry Maine gives
ample proof of the low state of morals among the
Irish.   In the tenth century, the temporary coha-
bitation of the sexes, he shows, was part of the
accustomed order of society.   Not a moment too
soon did the Northmen come with a fresher, purer,
and more vigorous blood in their veins, more truth
on their lips, and more honesty in their lives.   No
true friend of Ireland can disguise these plain facts.

   It cannot be concealed either that the monks The monks
employed the power possessed by them to the poli- cause civil
tical ruin of their country.   How they came to ruin.
have such enormous political as well as ecclesiastical influence it is not hard to see.   To see it, it is
only necessary to remember that such a monastery
as Bangor had in connection with it many cells
and monasteries, not in Ulster only, but throughout
the other provinces of Ireland.   Many other monasteries were similarly extended, and the power of
their abbots reached to all the remote dependent
institutions.   The heads, or coarbs, of the mother-
houses thus came to wield an immense influence.
They not only ruled the Church, as we have seen;
they sat at the right hand of kings in all assemblies.
Possessed not only of much territory and great
wealth, but invested, as was supposed, with supernatural powers, no one dared to contradict or oppose
them.   The princes and kings thus found themselves
compelled to cultivate the good-will of the coarbs,
and dared not thwart their wishes even in secular
and political affairs.

Now there are some people who say that ecclesiastics as a class are indifferent politicians. They are too apt to look at civil affairs from one point of view, and incline to be narrow and impracticable. It is certain that the monks were the means of inflicting an irreparable injury on the best civil interests of Ireland. It came about in this way.

With so many petty kings and conflicting interests, public order and justice in Ireland depended on the central power, the power of the Ardri or over-king, being upheld and strengthened. King Diarmid, the over-king in the time of Columba, did obtain from his parliament a law enabling him to dismantle the fortifications of the sub-kings, so as to permit law and justice to run freely all through his realm. It is known that in this matter Ireland was in advance of all contemporary European nations. The system of Eric, that is, of atoning for wrongs and crimes, such as murder, by payment to the persons wronged, payment privately made, gave place to the maintenance of public justice at an earlier date in Ireland than elsewhere. It was this public justice that Diarmid was bent on maintaining. But in his attempt to execute it he was resisted by a provincial king called Guairé, who killed the king's officer. Thereupon the king of Ireland proceeded to chastise Guairé, and defeated and routed him in the encounter. Being now an outlaw, Guairé took refuge with Ruadan of Lorrha, one of the great abbots of the time. The very existence of the national life and the reign of law throughout his realm depended on Diarmid's being enabled to put down such rebellious opposition as that of Guairé, and any one who sought to shield the

284

latter was aiming a blow both at the national
life and the public justice of the country. If law
and order were to prevail, Ruadan was clearly
not entitled to protect an insurgent vassal of the
over-king, who very properly seized Guairé and
dragged him from his hiding-place. Now, however, enraged at what he called his right of sanctuary having been violated, Ruadan got all the
great coarbs and several discontented petty kings
to join him, unitedly demanding the surrender of
Guairé. Diarmid showed them that the great interests of public order and justice, and even their
own personal interests, were inconsistent with such
a claim, and forewarned them that if, instead of
supporting their over-king and upholding his hands
in such a case, they did all they could to weaken
and paralyse his efforts, the result would soon
be anarchy and internecine war. His warning,
although every word of it came out true, fell upon
deaf ears. They proceeded to curse the king of
Ireland and his army; and as Tara was the centre
of the royal power, and was regarded as being
peculiarly sacred, " Ruadan and a bishop that was
with him took their bells that they had, which they
rang hardly, and cursed the king and place, and
prayed God that no king or queen ever after should
or could dwell in Tara, and that it should be waste
for ever, without court or palace, as it fell out
accordingly." Such was the extraordinary power of
the monks, and such the dread in which their curse
was held, that Diarmid had no option but to submit. From that day a blight fell on the ancient
royal palace, on the power of the over-king, and
on the unity and strength of the national life of

Ireland. From that day the royal residence of Tara began to fall into decay, the kings had to live each in his own province, and the central kingly power was broken. Tara was blighted, and the national unity broken by the monks.

> " The harp that once in Tara's halls
> The soul of music shed,
> Now hangs as mute on Tara's walls
> As if that soul were fled."

With infinite and melting pathos that sweet air is sung. The patriot who sings it does not always remember whose hand it was that broke the chords of that harp, and ˦left it mute on Tara's palace walls; nor does he recall whose voice it was that brought desolation upon Tara. *It was the monks that did it!*

What remained of Diarmid's power was shattered by another monk, Columba, and in a way that has been told already in another connection. The great annual fair of Tailtenn was being held. On such occasions, to draw a weapon or inflict an injury on another was visited with death. A passionate young man, son of a petty king, drew his weapon and killed another. He then ran to Columba, who was present, and put himself under his protection. The king, however, quite properly insisted on inflicting the usual penalty for homicide on the offender. Columba was mortally offended, according to the story, stirred up a rebellion, got his royal relations in the North to league together, and at the battle of Cooldreevny they defeated Diarmid and effectually broke his power. Thus it was that among the worst enemies the national existence and prosperity of Ireland ever had were the monks. It would be hard to say whether they or Rome herself inflicted the most deadly blow on the growth of a true national life. But the part taken by Rome belongs to a later chapter in the history.

PART IV

LATER FORTUNES OF THE CHURCH OF
ST. PATRICK

CHAPTER XV

THE COMING OF THE DANES

WHEN Britain fell a prey first to the Roman and later to the Saxon invader, Ireland was permitted to go unscathed, and thus so long continued to retain her native laws and institutions intact, unaffected by the intrusion of either Roman or Teutonic civilisation. Her immunity was due in part, perhaps, to her supposed insignificance, but chiefly to her remote situation in the extreme west of Europe, from which she was isolated by the intervening sea, and lying out as she was amid the rolling Atlantic billows. But when the Danes, or Northmen rather, from their Scandinavian fiords began to move southwards into Gaul, and westwards into England, the sea, instead of proving a barrier, provided an easy and inviting highway for those adventurous sea-rovers, long inured to the perils of stormy oceans, and at an early date carried them to our Irish coasts. *The sea not a hindrance, but a highway to the Norsemen.*

These Norsemen we are apt to picture as mere savage and barbarous destroyers. In their own northern homes, on the contrary, they were not only industrious and thrifty, toiling hard to wring a scanty subsistence from a cold and barren soil under an ungenial wintry sky, and so living from year to year not far from the grim possibility of famine; *The Norsemen at home.*

but gentle, hospitable, and justice-loving, noted for fidelity to friends and a rare cleanness of life. But residing on the narrow strips of land that ran round their long-winding bays or fiords, and lay between the sea and the great mountain range which, near the western coast, runs up through the Scandinavian peninsula, they were accustomed from early years to a seafaring life, and were compelled to cultivate familiarity with danger, hardiness, and self-reliance, to which were soon added sturdy independence, strong individuality of character, and love of adventure. As their patches of land seldom yielded enough for their support, they had to betake themselves to the sea to supplement the produce of a niggard soil. It was soon apparent that beneath a calm exterior volcanic passion slumbered, needing only the occasion to be stirred into berserker rage, which found fierce enjoyment in the excitement, violence, and bloodshed of the battlefield. The basest of sins known to their moral code was the forgiveness of injuries, revenge the foremost of the virtues, and no indignity or cruelty was too humiliating to inflict upon an enemy. The brave who fell in battle went to Walhalla, where, in company with the gods, he would go forth to fight by day, and return to feast and carouse by night; and the cowardly would go to Niflheim, to sit alone as a shadow in presence of all that was fitted to excite disgust and loathing.

Unsettled by two causes.   Two causes at this juncture conspired to unsettle them in their Scandinavian abodes, and to send them forth on a predatory manner of life. One was the discovery that on other shores, within easy reach of their barks, was a richer harvest of plunder than their native haunts afforded, and the other was the setting up over them in their own country of an authority which they abhorred. They had been used hitherto to a free, self-regulated, independent mode of life. And rather than submit to the royal yoke which Harald Haarfagr sought to impose upon them, they rose in large numbers, left their fields and homesteads, and entered on that series of raiding incursions on the coasts and up the rivers of Germany, France, Spain, Sicily, as well as England and Ireland, which continued through so many generations. With their upbringing, it was nothing loath that they launched out upon the deep: they were used to it from childhood: it might be almost described as their native element. The name " Viking," by which they have been designated, is from *vik*, " a bay," and suggests the sort of life which they pursued and delighted in.

The Norsemen from whose ravages Ireland suffered "Finn-Galls," or for the first fifty years or so after their first coming "White were fair-haired Norwegians or Swedes, known as Strangers;" " Finn-Galls " or " White Strangers." About the Galls," or middle of the ninth century hosts of " Duv-Galls," "Black or " Black Strangers," swarthy in complexion and Strangers." dark-haired, began to come, attacking and overcoming the " Finn-Galls," who by that time had founded and established the commercial towns of Dublin, Limerick, Waterford, and Wexford. These were the Danars (*i.e.* the Danes properly so called) from Denmark. The two afterwards united and coalesced. The two hundred years and more through which the story of their efforts to obtain a firm footing in Ireland runs divide themselves into three periods: (1) The period of intermittent piratical
293

LATER FORTUNES [PART IV

Three periods in the Danish invasion.

incursion, during which they make sudden and unexpected raids, and having made a rapid descent on some monastery near the coast or on the banks of one of the larger rivers, they ravage it, carry off the spoils, and disappear. (2) The period when they have succeeded in effecting permanent settlements in the country, establish sea-board towns and colonies, and begin to carry on active commercial enterprise; and (3) The period when, under the great Brian Boroihme (Boru), the chief sections of the Celtic population unite to break the power of the Danes, and prove successful at the great battle of Clontarf. A brief and rapid survey must be given to each of these periods.

1. Period of disunited and desultory invasion.

1. The piratical expeditions of the first of these periods were directed chiefly against the monastic institutions, and it was they for the most part that suffered. The monasteries were the depositories of many valuable treasures, and being comparatively without defence, offered a strong temptation to such lawless plunderers. But it has been suggested that the raiders had other motives besides that of obtaining booty—that they were animated by positive and special hostility to the monasteries as Christian institutions. These pirates from the far north were not only heathen; they had just witnessed in their native regions a determined and ruthless attempt to force Christianity on the people at the point of the sword. Charlemagne had put forth a persistent effort, continued for thirty-three years, to subdue the Saxons who occupied what we now call Hanover, Oldenburg, Brunswick, and Westphalia, and to compel them to become Christians on pain of extermination. The most cruel atrocities were

294

inflicted on them in the name of Christianity. In
782, only a few years before the first appearance of
the Danes in Ireland, 4500 captive Saxons were
massacred at Verdun in a single day. No wonder
that the religion which came to them in the guise
of a tyrannical and cruel despotism, which laid
waste their territory with fire and sword, sought to
crush their independence, and even threatened their
extermination, was regarded with hatred and resent-
ment. Their king, Witikind, was son-in-law of
Sigefroi, the Danish sovereign, and, driven into
Danish territory as many of them were, they could
hardly fail to inspire their Scandinavian friends with
a feeling kindred to their own.

The first appearance of the Danes in Ireland of First
which we have any notice is thus recorded in the appearance
"Annals of the Four Masters" opposite the year 790.
790 : "Rechrain was burnt by the Gentile pirates,
and its shrines destroyed." By the " Annals of Ulster "
this event is connected with the year 794, which
would be 795 of the common era. It is noteworthy
that their first appearance in England is chronicled
under the year 787, when the crews of three pirate
barks from the North slew a king's officer who attempted to seize them. It was the premonitory
thunder - shower announcing a terrible and pro-
tracted tempest which would leave devastation and
ruin in its track. The name " Rechrain " was applied to three different islands—to what is now
called Rathlin, off the Antrim coast, near Ballycastle ; to an island in Lough Neagh, and to an
island off the coast of County Dublin, now known
as Lambay. Several historians take the place first
attacked by the Norsemen to be Lambay, off County

Dublin. Dr. Reeves, we think rightly, identifies it with Rathlin, off the Antrim coast.[1]

Their attacks increase in frequency. From this date onward the attacks of the Northmen increase in frequency, and are at first concentrated on the island monasteries, or on those near the coast; but soon they made their way up the larger rivers, such as the Bann, the Boyne, the Liffey, the Shannon, and penetrate far into the country, ravaging and destroying wherever they come. Here is a record in the "Annals of Innisfallen" opposite the year 810: "Bangor wasted by the Danes, and the shrine of Comgall broken open by them, and its learned men and bishops were smitten by the sword." Again, opposite the year 822, the "Annals of the Four Masters" say: "Bangor plundered by the Danes and its oratory destroyed, and the reliques of Comgall scattered from the shrine which contained them." Movilla, in County Down, suffered about the same time; and from this time forward we hear a continuous tale of burnings, plunderings, and slaughterings, whereby numerous monasteries and churches are pillaged and demolished, their shrines broken, their books or manuscripts "drowned" (*i.e.* thrown into river or lough), and their goods carried off.

2. Period of settlement and colonisation. 2. So far they came in small and detached parties, without any attempt at united action. But in 832, under a great leader called Turgesius, who has been identified (though not indubitably) with the renowned Scandinavian hero Ragnar Lodrog, they were combined together, and three fleets, apparently operating in concert under him, appeared, one on Lough Neagh, another in Dun-

[1] "Antiquities," p. 249.

dalk Bay, and a third on Lough Ree, on the Shannon. Armagh, the chief ecclesiastical centre in the north, was three times attacked by him in a single month, the abbot, Forannan, driven away to Munster, and the Christian form of worship displaced by the pagan. In the course of the next century and a half or so Armagh was again honoured by their unwelcome visits and ravages not much less than twenty times. We soon find Turgesius with his fleet on Lough Ree, where he plundered Clonmacnois, and set up his wife as a sort of priestess, and had pagan sacrifices offered upon the altar. He also pillaged the monasteries of Clonfert, Lorrha, Terryglas, and the numerous churches and monasteries in that region. Having ravaged the north, the west, and the south-west, he turned his hand to a more notable and fruitful achievement. Where Dublin now stands there was They found then nothing but a ford across the Liffey, with Dublin. perhaps a few scattered huts. It was then called Al-Cliath. Turgesius saw at once the importance of the position, and to guard the ford built a dún or fortress. The "Annals of the Four Masters" give the date as A.D. 840. Here, too, he laid the foundations of a Danish kingdom, and in due time the city of Dublin grew up around the fortress under the hands of the Danes. The real founder of Dublin was thus the Danish king, Turgesius. But strong ruler and conquering hero though he was, he fell before the charms that have laid so many strong men low. He fell in love with the daughter of Malachi, the king of Meath, and when he and his friends were being entertained by her on an island in Lough Owel, near Mullingar, they were slain by the daggers of fifteen young men disguised in female attire, and their bodies thrown into Lough Owel.

It may be asked, How was Turgesius enabled to gain such a footing in the country? Had anything in the nature of a combined effort been made by the Irish, they might have easily resisted him. But the answer is found in the dissensions and mutual jealousies of the native chiefs. It is significant that in many instances the feeling of hostility towards one another was more intense than against the foreign invader. This is well exemplified in the case of Feidlimidh (Phelim) MacCriffan, the king of Cashel, that is, of Munster, who, like some other kings of the same province, was a bishop as well as a king, but an ambitious and unscrupulous personage, who wished to be regarded as the supreme king of Ireland, and had on this account a special quarrel with the king of Meath. Instead of helping the latter against Turgesius, he took advantage of their prostration by the Norsemen to attack his brethren, and, strange to say, his worst depredations were committed against the monasteries and the ecclesiastics. In many instances grants of land had been given to churches and monasteries, and to many of these ecclesiastical territories (which were called Termon lands, from *terminus*, a boundary) the privilege of sanctuary belonged, so that they were regarded as sacred asylums which were safe against intrusion. But Feidlimidh more than once violated the Termon lands of Clonmacnois, burned down the monastic buildings, and slew the clergy; and the monasteries of Durrow, Kildare (where the Coarb of Armagh and his clergy had taken refuge), and even Armagh itself, were similarly treated by him. It is suggestive that his whole strength was employed exclusively against his brother chiefs, and in not a single instance against the Northmen.

In 852 a fleet of Black Strangers, or Danars, ^{The "Black} appeared at Dublin, and defeated the Finn-Galls, ^{Strangers"} or White Strangers, who had already settled there. ^{take the} Soon after, the struggle was renewed at Carlingford, ^{upper hand.} another Danish settlement, and after a desperate and bloody conflict, which lasted for three days, the Finn-Galls were again overthrown. After this the two sections of the Northmen for the most part united their forces.

Thus with varying fortunes affairs went on for ^{Red ruin} some 200 years, the Danes at times victorious, but the Irish chiefs at other times inflicting on them severe reverses. The history of Ireland during this period is a history of endless conflict and red ruin, when anarchy ran riot, and social disorganisation and moral deterioration went on apace. The Danish inhabitants of Dublin became Christians about the middle of the tenth century, but their conversion does not appear to have appreciably abated their fierce violence. We still hear of them continuing to plunder and demolish monasteries and churches, and carrying off captives and treasures.

Deadly must have been the terror spread amongst ^{and terror} the Irish by the cruel outrages of the Danes, a ^{caused by} dread the memory, or at least the tradition, of ^{the Danes.} which still lingers among the peasantry. The late Dr. Reeves in the *Ulster Journal of Archæology* relates an incident which serves to give us some idea of it. When early in the present century the Ordnance Survey began its operations in this

LATER FORTUNES [PART IV

country, a number of sappers and miners appeared suddenly one day on a little island which lies between Mourne and Carlingford, which had been a principal landing-place and colony of the Danes in early times. The news spread like wildfire throughout the district that the Danes were coming again, and the sensation and panic produced by the appalling tidings were immense!

Emigration to the Continent. In the early time the terror was not imaginary, but real, and one effect of it was that there set in a tide of emigration to the Continent, especially on the part of those devoted to the pursuit of learning. A Continental writer of the ninth century says that almost all Ireland, despising the perils of the sea, passed over to our shores with her crowd of philosophers.[1] Among these were

Dungal. Dungal, who became head of the great school of **John Scotus Erigena.** Pavia under Charlemagne, and John Scotus Erigena .(Erin-gena), the greatest genius and most profound philosopher of his day—in fact, the most remarkable man of his age. After leaving Ireland he became connected with the court of Charles the Bald (840–877), where he must have been on easy terms if the story told of him is true. When Charles once asked him across the dinner-table, " What is the difference between a Scot [an Irishman] and a sot?" his quick retort was, " The table, your Majesty!" But he was not merely the most brilliant wit of his time, but its most clever dialectician and deepest thinker. He was a diligent student of the Greek Fathers and of Neo-Platonism, had a tendency to pantheistic ideas, and anticipated not a little in Spinoza and Hegel; but his original,

[1] Haddan's " Remains," p. 285.

300

powerful, and naturally speculative intellect was too much held in bounds by the teaching of the Scriptures and the Christian view of the world to allow his philosophical principles to carry him to their natural conclusion. Even as it was, however, he surprised and disturbed the placid and stagnant thought of the ninth century with his nineteenth-century ideas. A great many of the statements of the Bible with regard to God which are apt to be taken literally, he ascribed to anthropomorphism, and according to him the true body and blood are not present in the sacrament, the bread and wine being only a memorial of Christ's body and blood. He thus rejected the doctrine of transubstantiation. Whereas the Schoolmen were, as a rule, sticklers for orthodoxy, this genuine and irrepressible Irishman was profoundly heretical. Hincmar, who had enlisted his service in a controversy on predestination, found him a very compromising and inconvenient ally, and denounced his teaching as a concoction of " Scotch porridge " (*pultes scotorum*); and at a later time Honorius III. described his great work *De Divisione Naturæ* as " teeming with the vermin of heretical depravity " !

It was in the lull that took place after the first great outbreak of the storm of Norse invasion that Cloicthcachs or Round Towers began to be erected, and that they were reared as a means of protection against the Danes, as places of refuge for the monks, and as keeps or safe storehouses for their books, bells, and other treasures, is now practically certain. Till then, stone buildings were very rare in Ireland. The earliest reference to the cloictheach thus occurs in the " Annals of the Four Masters," A.D. 948 :

Cloic-
theachs or
Round
Towers.

"The Cloictheach of Slane was burned by the Danes, with its full of reliques, with Caonechair, reader of Slane, and the crozier of the patron saint, and a bell—the best of bells." It was erected, possibly, a considerable time before the date mentioned. Respecting the origin and object of the Round Towers, there has been no end of conjectures, but the late Dr. Petrie in his work on the subject has put it beyond question that their purpose was what has been just indicated. "Though the abbey and all its buildings blazed around," he says, "the tower disregarded the fury of the flames; its extreme height, its isolated position, and the diminutive doorway, elevated so many feet above the ground, placed it beyond the reach of the destroyer." The case of Slane just mentioned, however, shows that in some instances even the Round Tower was not always proof against the fury of the Northmen. In the "Life of Tenenan" of Brittany, by Legrand, there is a statement which throws much light both on the object of the Round Towers and the date at which they began to be erected in Western Europe. Of St. Tenenan his biographer says : "He exhorted the people to penitence and amendment of life, and, providing for their defence and preservation, he appointed a chief man of their troop as their captain, recommending him to erect a little round tower near the church of Ploabennec, wherein to deposit the silver-plate and treasure of the same church, and protect them against the sacrilegious hands of the barbarians, should they wish to pillage the same church. This he accordingly did. Meanwhile the barbarians approached, and St. Tenenan hastily carried the sacred vessels into the tower, wherein the captain entered, and resolved to defend it at the cost of his blood."[1] Here we have not only the use of the Round Towers expressly defined, but their existence in Brittany as early as the seventh century recorded. The original type of the Round Tower, there is no doubt, came from the East, whence it was brought by Justinian to Constantinople in the sixth century. From Constantinople it was carried westwards to Ravenna, and a little later it is found at Pisa, Venice, Strassburg, in Switzerland and Belgium. The Cathedral of Aix-la-Chapelle, built under Charlemagne and Eginhard about A.D. 800, has two round towers. From Ravenna, too, the idea appears to have been carried to the north and west coasts of France, and thence to Ireland, with which France was at this time in close friendly relations. Merovingian and other French coins have been found in Ireland. Lord Dunraven seems to have traced the type from Ireland through France to Ravenna, and so to Constantinople and the East. It is just possible indeed, that the idea may have come still more directly from the East. It appears from the Litany of Ængus the Culdee that during the eighth century many Eastern ecclesiastics found refuge in Ireland. It refers to seven Egyptian monks as having been buried in one place.

The idea of them brought from the East.

In the beginning of the present century, according to Miss Stokes, 118 of these structures were still in existence; at present, according to Lord Dunraven, there are seventy-six still standing. The doorways faced the entrances of the churches to which they belonged, and the position of the tower

[1] See "Early Christian Art," p. 56, by Miss Margaret Stokes.

was, as a rule, about twenty feet to the north-west end of the church. They have been assigned to three periods :—the earliest from 890 to 927; the next from 973 to 1013; and the latest from 1170 to 1238; and these divisions are marked by a very distinct progress and improvement in the architecture. Miss Stokes has an interesting table classifying the Irish Round Towers according to their different styles, showing a gradual advance from the earlier to the later and more improved style.

3. The period of defeat and overthrow.

3. At length, at the close of the tenth and the opening of the eleventh century, there came a crisis in the history of the northern invaders. By the arrival of a great fleet of their kinsmen from across the sea, the Danes of Limerick had a large accession made to their number, and the south of Ireland was more than ever ravaged and oppressed by them. Danish kings and chiefs, stewards, and bailiffs were set over every territory, and a royal rent levied from the people. " And such was the oppressiveness of the tribute, that there was a king from among the foreigners over every territory, a chief over every chieftaincy, an abbot over every church, a steward over every village, and a soldier in every house; so that none of the men in Erinn had power to give even the milk of his cow, nor so much as the clutch of eggs of one hen, in succour to the aged or a friend, but was forced to preserve them for the foreigner; and though there were but one milk-giving cow in the house, she durst not be milked, but kept for the foreigner, and however long absent he might be, his share durst not be lessened. Although there was in the house but one cow, it must be killed for the meal of one night, if the means of supply could not be otherwise

obtained; and the tribute of an ounce of silver was
paid for every head, and he who had not the means
to pay himself went into slavery. No Irish chief was
able to give them deliverance from the foreigner
because of the excellence of their armour, the great-
ness of their achievements, their strength and valour,
and the excess of their thirst for the fruitful, grassy
lands of Erinn."[1]

One of the tribes that suffered most from these
oppressions was that of the Dal-Cais, in Munster,
whose chiefs were bound to support the king of
Cashel against invasion by the Hy Nialls, and were
also entitled to the kingship of Cashel at every alter-
nate succession. At the time of which I speak the
head of the tribe was Mathgamhain (Mahon), whose
younger and much abler brother was Brian, known
as Brian Boroihme (Boru). Rather than submit to
the Danish yoke, the two brothers led their followers
across the Shannon into the woods and solitudes of
Clare, whence they sallied forth in sudden and fierce
attacks on their oppressors. Mahon at length grew
weary of this sort of life, and, much to the vexation
of Brian, made peace with the Danes; but Brian
carried on the conflict till he was reduced to the last
extremity. Mahon sought an interview with his
brother, who pleaded that death was preferable to
submission, and that such was the motto of their
tribe. On an appeal being made to the tribe, they
gave their voice unanimously for war, for which they
rallied on their own tribe-land. The Irish fought
on very unequal terms with their opponents, who
were much better trained and disciplined, more compact, clad in coats of mail, and armed with superior

(margin note: Brian Borolhme.)

[1] "Wars of the Gaedhil with the Gaill," p. 49.

weapons. The latter, too, reinforced by some Irish chiefs, put forth all their strength. Yet in a decisive battle near the town of Tipperary the Danes were thoroughly defeated. Limerick was taken, plundered, and burned; those fit for war slain, and the rest enslaved, and the Danish power in the south shattered. Mahon having been treacherously assassinated by a conspiracy of Irish and Danish chiefs, the cause of the conspirators was not helped, but harmed by the treachery. In the person of Brian a much more powerful and formidable foe succeeded to the kingship, who speedily avenged his brother's death on both the native chiefs and the Danes, inflicting on them a crushing defeat. He received also the homage of the king of Leinster, who, however, in the year 1000 formed an alliance with the Dublin Danes. But the allies were completely overthrown by Brian in a great battle at Glen Mama in County Wicklow, and Maelmorda, king of Leinster, was captured by Brian's son Murchadh (Murrogh) in a yew-tree in which he was concealed. Dublin was taken and the Danes made subject to their conqueror. Here is how the result is described in the " Wars of the Gaedhil with the Gaill " (p. 117): " Ill-luck was it for the foreigners when Brian was born, for it was by him they were destroyed and enslaved. There was not a winnowing-sheet from Howth to Kerry that had not a foreigner in bondage, nor was there a mill without a foreign woman. No son of a soldier or officer of the Gaedhil deigned to put his hand to a flail or any other labour, nor did a woman deign to put her hands to the grinding-mill or to wash her clothes, but had a foreign man or woman to work for them.".

The titular king of all Ireland just now (1002) was Malachi II., but Brian by right of conquest became supreme sovereign of the country, and Malachi submitted without a struggle.

Brian proved a strong, wise, and just ruler, no less fitted for the piping times of peace than for the exigencies and stress of war. A strong central government was maintained by him; crime and disorder were repressed; vigorous steps were taken to repair the ruin that had been wrought by the Danes; and before long a reign of peace, order, and prosperity was established such as had not been known since the days of Cormac MacArt. " By him," says the work already quoted (" Wars of the Gaedhil with the Gaill "), " were erected in Erinn noble churches and their sanctuaries. He sent professors and masters to teach wisdom and knowledge, and to buy books, beyond the sea and the great ocean, because the writings and books in every church and sanctuary had been destroyed by the plunderers; and Brian himself gave the price of learning and the price of books to every one separately who went on this service. Many churches were built and repaired by him, bridges and roads were made, the fortresses of Munster were strengthened. . . . He continued in this way prosperous, peaceful, hospitable, just-judging, venerated, with law and rule among the clergy, with honour and renown among the laity; powerful, secure for fifteen years in the chief sovereignty of Ireland." The legend embodied by Moore in the song " Rich and rare were the gems she wore " of a young and beautiful maiden, richly clad, adorned with jewels, and having a ring of countless value on

(margin note: Brian's rule.)

307

her wand, passing alone and unattended through all Ireland from north to south unharmed, is intended to represent the secure and happy state of things under the rule of Brian.

But now, as ever, the worst foes to the prosperity and peace of Ireland and the best friends of anarchy were the local chieftains. Maelmorda, the hero of the yew-tree, was twitted by his sister Gormlaith for his pusillanimity in submitting to be Brian's vassal. This Gormlaith had had large matrimonial experience. She had been married first to the Danish king of Dublin, and was mother of the present Danish king, Sitric, then she became wife of Malachi, the king of Ireland, who divorced her, whereupon she united her fortunes with those of our hero Brian, but a short trial of her by Brian was enough. The Norse Saga describes her as very fair, but adds that "she did all things ill over which she had any power."[1] Soon after Maelmorda's interview with his sister, angry words arose at a game of chess between him and Brian's son Murchadh (Murrogh), who exasperated Maelmorda by stinging allusions to the incident of the yew-tree. The latter withdrew in deep wrath, roused Leinster into rebellion, and secured the alliance of the Danish king, Sitric, whose wife was a daughter of Brian (so mixed up by marriage were they), and Sitric in turn obtained the aid of Sigurd, the Danish king of Orkney, and his followers, as well as the assistance of other Vikings, to each of whom he secretly promised to give both his mother and the kingdom! While Maelmorda was organising the Leinster men in three great battalions in and around Dublin,

[1] "Burnt Njal," ii. 323.

and the black barques of the Danes were gathering and swarming in Dublin Bay, Brian and his son Donogh were not less alert and active. After relieving Malachi, who was first attacked, they marched to Dublin, burning and laying waste the territory of the enemy, and encamped at Kilmainham.

The field of battle extended from what is now Upper Sackville Street along the shore towards Clontarf. The Danes and their allies stood along the shore with their back towards the bay, and Brian and his army faced them. Brian was now an old man, and was induced to leave the chief command to his son Murrogh. It was Good Friday, 23rd April 1014. From sunrise till sunset, without a moment's pause, the battle raged. A body of 1000 Danes, clad in coats of mail, were literally hewed to pieces by the battle-axes of the Dal-Cassians. But the interest of the carnage centred in the feats of individual prowess. Fearful was the havoc wrought by Murrough, as, with a heavy sword in each hand, he mowed down the Danes, till he reached the bearer of the famous raven banner, and laid him low. It was seized by another Dane, who met with a similar fate. Others having refused to carry the fateful standard, it was grasped by Earl Sigurd himself, whose helmet was struck off by Murrogh's right-hand sword, while the left smote him dead. At length the Danes gave way and their host took to flight. They tried to reach their ships, but the tide had risen, and they were riding far out in the bay. At this moment Malachi, who seems not to have been engaged hitherto, swept upon them with his army, and the greater number of them fell before his onset, or were driven into the

The great battle of Clontarf.

309

sea, and perished in the waves. The Danish king, Sitric, had remained in the castle or fortress of Dublin to guard the city. As from the battlements they watched the progress of the struggle, and saw the first rush of Earl Sigurd's men, "Well do the foreigners reap the field; many a sheaf do they cast from them," cried Sitric. "The result will be seen at the end of the day," said his wife, Brian's daughter. When the Danes began to flee, her turn came. "It seems to me," she said, "that the foreigners have gained their patrimony." "What meanest thou, woman?" said the king. "Are they not rushing into the sea, which is their natural inheritance? They are like a herd of cows careering over the plain, maddened by the heat and the gad-flies, and not waiting to be milked." His unkingly answer was a blow upon her face.

But the victory won by the Irish was gained at a great cost. Murrogh, unarmed, was attacked by a Danish leader, described as "the head of valour and bravery of Lochlann," but he wrested from the Dane his sword, and thrust him through with it, though the other in falling inflicted a mortal wound on Murrogh. His heroic son, Turlough, a boy of fifteen, fought all day, and after the battle was found drowned at the fishing-weir of the Tolka, with his hands grasping the hair of a Dane whom he had pursued into the tide. A furious Viking leader, fleeing from the field, rushed with his battle-axe upon Brian himself. The brave old monarch cut him down with a single blow of his heavy sword, but the Dane as he fell clove the King's head in twain with his axe.

The fame of the battle and its horrors spread

rapidly over Europe. The "Annals of Ulster" Result of the victory. record that 7000 Danes and 4000 Irish were laid low, and almost all the leaders on both sides. Malachi resumed the sceptre of Ireland, and reigned, in name at least, for eight years. The power of the Danes was broken, but they continued to occupy the seaboard towns and colonies they had founded until, on the arrival of their Latinised kinsmen, the Anglo-Normans, in the twelfth century, they made common cause with them. They did not a little to promote commercial enterprise, and they brought an infusion of new blood, fresh energy, and the beginning of a new civilisation into Ireland. But for the present it availed little. No ruler arose strong enough to wield Brian's sceptre and to complete the work so well begun by him; and till the coming of the Normans the history of Ireland was one monotonous tale of intestine strife, anarchy, and chaos.

It remains to tell briefly the story of the Church during this period.

We have already seen that in the time of Patrick The Church and his successors there is no evidence of the slight-during the est value of submission to the Roman See, or of any period. organic connection with the Latin Church. On the contrary, there is abundant evidence of the free, independent spirit of the Irish Church, and of a long and most determined struggle against the efforts of ecclesiastics in sympathy with Rome to assimilate it to the Roman pattern. In many important matters Its diver-of organisation, doctrine, and ritual it differed widely gence from from the contemporary Church of Rome. In the early inde-comparatively evangelical character of its teach-pendence. ing, in the complete absence of episcopal jurisdiction and government, in the universal subordination

311

of the bishops and other clergy to the abbots, who were often presbyters, in the fact that the bishops were as numerous as the churches, and that in very many instances there were seven bishops connected with a single church, as well as in the rules affecting ordination, the Irish Church was widely divergent from the Roman. It is deeply significant in this connection that foreign Continental synods of the Latin Church are unattended by representatives of the Church of Ireland. But not less marked were the points of ritual in which they stood apart. Not only in the matter of the Easter celebration, and the tonsure, and the marriage of the clergy, and the scrupulous observance of the Lord's day, and the place given to the Scriptures, care being taken to supply each church with a copy, but even in the ritual of the Eucharist and of baptism, the Irish Liturgies and other records supply clear evidence of striking divergencies.[1] Even Irish ecclesiastics abroad were noted for their freedom and independence of thought and practice, and often appear in sharp collision with Roman ecclesiastics, and even with the Pope himself.

Organic connection repudiated on both sides.

It is, of course, quite conceivable that a remote and detached Church like the Irish might develop differences in minor matters, and yet maintain on the whole organic connection with and subordination to the Latin Church. But such connection was in fact repudiated on both sides. Thus Laurence, the successor of Augustin in the Archbishopric of Canterbury, in a letter addressed to the Irish abbots and bishops, and referred to in a previous chapter,

---

[1] See "The Church of Ireland," by the Rev. T. Olden, p. 139 *seq.*, for some of these differences.

says: "We have been informed by Bishop Dagan,
coming into this aforesaid island, and by the abbot
Columbanus in France, that the Scots in no way
differ from the Britons in behaviour; for Bishop
Dagan, coming to us, not only refused to eat with
us, but even to take his repast in the same house
where we were entertained."[1]   How Roman ecclesiastics were regarded by the British Church has
already appeared from a stanza I have given from
a poem written by the chief bard of the Britons;
and how, on the other hand, the Irish Church was
regarded by the Romanised Anglo-Saxon Church
I have shown by a decree of the English Church
Synod of Cealcythe in 816, refusing permission to
the Irish clergy to exercise their ministry in any
of their dioceses because it was uncertain by whom
they were ordained, or whether they were ordained
at all.

Candid Roman Catholic historians admit these
facts. Thus Baronius in his "Ecclesiastical Annals,"
referring to the time of Columba, affirms that "the
bishops of Ireland were all schismatics, separated
from the Church of Rome."

But from the seventh century onwards, intercourse
with the Continent, and with the ancient city on the
seven hills became more common, and the familiarity
of the Irish clergy with the ways of its great Church
increased. Laserian, abbot of Old Leighlin, for
example, visited Rome in the time of Gregory the
Great, and later in the time of Pope Honorius, by
whom he is said to have been ordained a bishop,
and commissioned to bring the Irish into submission
to the Roman See. Honorius himself wrote to the

Intercourse with Rome increases from seventh century.

[1] See Bede's "Ecclesiastical History," Bk. *iii.* c. 4.

Irish exhorting to conformity about the year 630; it was the first communication of a Pope with the Irish Church. But Laserian tried in vain to induce an Irish synod to conform. Cummian, too, a Columban monk, who had been educated at Durrow, but who had been brought into sympathy with the Roman usage, about the same time (630) attended a synod at Magh Lene for the same object, and in a letter to Segene, abbot of Iona, sought to justify his action. We cannot go into details, and must be content with stating that, as a result of the influences at work, the Roman method of observing Easter was adopted in the South of Ireland about A.D. 650.

The North holds out against Rome longest.

It is remarkable that the North held out against the change for more than half a century longer. From an early date Ireland was divided into two halves. The division is said to have been made by Conn of the hundred battles and Eoghan Mor in A.D. 166, although it was in some measure aided by nature. A range of gravel hills extends right across the centre of Ireland from Dublin to Galway, dividing it into two nearly equal parts. The northern part was known as Leth Chuinn, or Conn's half, and the southern as Leth Mhoga, or Mogh's half. Whatever the cause may have been, the people of the North were from early times distinguished from those of the South by marked differences of character. Giraldus Cambrensis, who was not an Irishman, and not partial to either, says of them: "We find the people of the North of Ireland were always warlike, while those of the South were subtle and crafty. The one coveted glory, the other was steeped in false-

hood; the one trusted to their arms, the other to
their arts; the one was full of courage, the other
of deceit." Others bear similar testimony, and
speak of the superior vigour and independence of
the Northerns, and of the national sentiment having
been more deeply rooted and more persistent in
them. Thus it was that in the great Easter controversy the clergy and people of the North were far
more stout and stubborn in their resistance to the
new custom than the more flexible and conciliatory
South, just as later, both in the attempt to subject
the Irish Church to Rome, and Ireland itself to the
English king, the North held out with greater
sturdiness and was the last to yield. But at length,
early in the eighth century, the opposition even of
the Northerns to the new method of observing
Easter gave way.

But as yet, be it observed, there was no general
submission to the jurisdiction of the Bishop of
Rome. In quite a variety of matters the Irish
continued to walk in their old paths. There is
as yet no trace of auricular confession or the invocation of saints, which first appears in the Litany
of Ængus in the tenth century, or of extreme
unction, the earliest reference to which occurs in
the opening of the twelfth century, or of the worship
of the Virgin, which is not fully developed till the
same century; and communion in both kinds still
continues to be observed.

But the conversion of the Danes marks a most
important epoch in the history of the Irish Church,
both in its relation to Rome and in its general organisation. The Dublin Danes became Christians, as
has been noted, in A.D. 948; and it was through

Conversion of Danes marks an epoch in history of relation of Irish Church to Rome. them that an organic connection was first established with the Roman Church, and that the hierarchical arrangements of that Church were introduced into this country. The first bishop of the Danes of Dublin of whom we hear was Donat or Dunan, whose appointment belongs to the year 1038. It was he who laid the foundations of the Church of the Holy Trinity, now Christ Church Cathedral, which was endowed by Sitric, the Danish king of Dublin, with certain lands in the territory of the Danes. Sitric had himself made a pilgrimage to· Rome. In 1072, Lanfranc, the Archbishop of Canterbury, a native of Pavia in Italy, claimed jurisdiction over the Irish Church at a synod in Winchester. Two years later, when, on the death of Dunan in 1074, the Dublin Danes elected a person named Patrick to be their bishop, he was sent to Lanfranc for consecration, and, on being consecrated in St. Paul's, promised submission to Lanfranc. It was quite natural that the Danes should thus desire connection with their

The Roman rule introduced through the Danes. Latinised kinsmen the Normans. *This was really the first step towards the formal introduction of the Roman rule into Ireland, and towards organic relationship with Rome.* The other Danish towns speedily followed the example thus set them. In 1096, Malchus, formerly a monk of Winchester, was sent from Waterford for consecration to Anselm (also an Italian), Lanfranc's disciple and successor in Canterbury; and in this case, Murtough, the king of Ireland, some Irish chiefs, such as the O'Briens, the great sept of the Dal-Cais, and several Irish bishops, united in the request. In 1106, Gillé, commonly called Gillebert or Gilbert, was similarly made

316

bishop of the Danish city of Limerick. He is noteworthy as the first person who held the office of
Papal legate in Ireland. And as Papal legate he
was the means of introducing a most important and
memorable measure for assimilating the Irish to the
Latin Church. It was he who called and presided
over the famous synod of Rathbreasil (1118), at
which diocesan episcopacy was first set up in Ireland.
The synod was attended, among others, by Celsus,
the Coarb of St. Patrick from Armagh. By this
synod the country was divided into twenty-four
dioceses, with two archbishoprics — Armagh and
Cashel—and church endowments were transferred
to the bishops. But Malchi O'Morgair, who was
first abbot of Bangor, then Bishop of Connor, and
afterward Archbishop of Armagh, the friend of St.
Bernard of Clairvaux, who has written his biography,
warmly espoused the Papal cause, became Papal
legate after Gillé, and, St. Bernard tells us, laboured
diligently, and was more successful than any of his
predecessors, in establishing in all the churches in
Ireland "the apostolic sanctions and the usages of
the Holy Church of Rome." He retired from the
primacy in 1137, and Gelasius was chosen to be his
successor at Armagh. Malachi at that date went to
Down, but died at Clairvaux in 1148. A few years
later, Cardinal Paparo arrived in Ireland with the
Palls, for which formal request had been made at a
synod called by Malachi. A "General Council of
the Church of Ireland" was held at Kells in 1152.
According to the "Four Masters," Gelasius and the
Cardinal presided at it, and it was attended by
twenty-two bishops, five bishops-elect, and three

Diocesan episcopacy set up by the Synod of Rathbreasil, A.D. 1118.

Cardinal Paparo brings the Palls.

thousand other ecclesiastics. It added two new archbishoprics—Dublin and Tuam—to those already founded, increased the number of sees to thirty-four, and passed enactments against marriage and the concubinage of the clergy.

It should be mentioned that Malachi was also the means of introducing the Cistercian order into Ireland; that in 1142 the Abbey of Mellifont, near Drogheda, was founded, and that before long other abbeys of the same order were erected.

Change of tone in Irish writers with respect to Rome.

In the writings of Irish ecclesiastics from the eighth or ninth century and onwards, there is, as you might expect from what has just been stated, a very manifest change of tone with respect to Rome, and a cessation of that freedom of speech, and even antagonism, which had previously appeared. Thus the writers of the "Lives of Patrick," from the time of the "Collections or Annotations of Tirechan," assigned by Dr. Reeves to the ninth century, are anxious to connect Patrick with Rome, and cannot conceive of him otherwise than as having received his commission from Rome, or from a source in sympathy therewith. This feeling, of course, deepens in the tenth, eleventh, and twelfth centuries, especially after organic connection has been established with the Roman See. It is significant, for example, that the Irish interpretation which in the eleventh century was put upon Patrick's vision of the light spreading from the north to the south, was that during the rule of Gurmund and Turgesius Ireland would be restored to the Roman obedience by Celsus of Armagh. During this period, too, there are many indications of a growing conformity to the Roman ritual. It is evident from the Stowe Missal that, at the time when it was composed, *i.e.* in the eleventh century, the Roman canon had already come into partial use in Ireland, and this Missal contains even a prayer for "our Pope." Bishop Donald, who was one of those concerned with the sending of Malchus in 1096 to be consecrated by Anselm, Archbishop of Canterbury, is described in the "Annals of the Four Masters" as "a doctor of both orders (or liturgies), Roman and Irish." In the opening of the twelfth century, Anselm writes to Gillé, the Bishop of Limerick and Roman legate in Ireland, pressing him to get the Irish to desist from their peculiar usages, and Gillé compiled a work, already referred to, the object of which was to supersede the "schismatical" Irish liturgies, and to secure that "one Catholic and Roman office" should take their place.[1] Ancient religious usages, even in the smallest matters of ritual and the like, are indeed always slowly and reluctantly given up. Some of the old Celtic customs still lingered even in the Anglo-Norman period. But their ultimate abandonment was a mere question of time. Vain is the attempt, when new influences are at work, to chain the future to the past. In human affairs, where life is, there is movement. One thing gives places to another; to-day is never quite as yesterday. It is so especially in such a crisis and cataclysm as Ireland had now been passing through. It was not possible that a vast and powerful institution like the Church of Rome, with her lustrous past and imposingly majestic and

Ancient religious customs slowly given up.

But impossible to chain the future to the past.

[1] Ussher's Works, iv. 274.

splendid present, and her world-wide, dominating
authority, could come in contact with a little community like the Irish Church without affecting it.
It was not possible that a strong people like the
Northern Vikings could land on Irish shores and
enter into Irish life and society without disturbing
it. But after all, even amid disturbance, the past
lives on. As Carlyle says somewhere, nothing that
is worthy in it perishes: it lives and works through
endless change. The body only dies; under the
mortal body lives a soul which is immortal. True,
the Danes brought anarchy, but what is anarchy
(as the same writer says in effect) but increased
resources which the old methods are not able to
administer—new wealth which the old coffers will
not contain? Even through anarchy the Danes
made an important contribution to Irish history.
They brought new blood, new life, new energy into
the Irish race, and some much-needed moral elements. For good or evil they did much to end
the isolation and singularity of Irish Christianity,
and to connect it with the great ecclesiastical empire whose seat is on the Tiber. For good or evil
they did much to prepare the way for the coming
of their relatives, the Anglo-Normans, and so to
link the destinies of Ireland with England. Such
events and movements as we have been rapidly and
imperfectly surveying, the superficial may regard
with unconcern and treat with flippancy. For our
part, as we contemplate the great turning-points
and crises, the decisive events and formative influences in our history, we feel ourselves in presence
of mysteries whose key is as yet hidden from us;

we are filled with awe and wonder as we follow the ways of Providence with nations as with individuals; but we await in faith and hope that spiritual emancipation and moral elevation that will give our country a larger life and a nobler destiny than she has yet known.

CHAPTER XVI

THE COMING OF THE ANGLO-NORMANS

After
Clontarf. THE state of Ireland—civil, social, and religious—
from the date of the battle of Clontarf was little
better, as has been indicated, than a state of
anarchy. The sceptre that fell from the hand of
Brian was, like the bow of Ulysses, so mighty an
instrument that no successor of his was found
strong enough to wield it; and the prestige of
the Niall dynasty had suffered such a blow from
him that to retrieve it was impossible. Whatever
show of national unity had persisted up till then
practically disappeared. There were, indeed, chiefs
who called themselves, and were recognised to some
extent as kings of Ireland, but they are signifi-
cantly dubbed in the Annals as "kings with opposition." From the date named till the coming
of the Anglo-Normans the history of Ireland was
little better than a series of petty conflicts between provincial chiefs, sometimes one and sometimes another in the ascendant. Amid the turmoil
and uncertainty of civil strife, violence, and bloodshed, which now became the normal condition of
the country, the pursuits of peace and civilisation
were impossible. The monasteries, where art and
industry, learning and religion, had hitherto found
an asylum, and where the tribes had set before

them an ideal, far from perfect, yet not altogether
sordid, or selfish, or violent, had been laid in ruin
by the Danes. It was a time of perpetual unrest,
of much evil, and of immeasurable social suffering
and misery—of both moral and material deterioration. It is not so strange, then, as has been suggested, that the Anglo-Normans came and took
possession of Ireland at the time they did, as that
they, or some other adventurers, did not seize so
tempting a prize sooner.

That the Anglo-Normans *would* come sooner or The Anglo-
later was almost inevitable. They were of the Normans.
same blood, stirred by the same spirit of enterprise and ambition, as the Norsemen or Danes
already settled in the country. In all directions
these sturdy Northmen had at this time been extending their dominions, and reducing even strong
peoples into subjection to their rule. Ruric and
his brothers, who penetrated to the interior of
what we now call Russia, and organised and ruled
over the Slavonic and Finnish tribes they found
there, and laid the foundations of the present
Russian Empire, were Northmen from the Baltic
coasts. Other bands of them had sailed northwards to the Faroe Islands, to Iceland and Green-
land, and thence to a region which they called
Vinland, but which is now believed to have been
the coast of New England, so that they anticipated the discovery of the American Continent
by Columbus nearly five hundred years later.
How they took possession of a large portion of
Gaul, and gave their name to the great province
of Normandy, is too familiar to need more than
to be mentioned. In France, it is true, they

underwent considerable change. They mingled, and to some extent intermarried, with the Franks, adopted the more civilised forms of life which they found prevalent among the Franks, and had grown into a great mail-clad aristocracy, residing in their castles, and welded together by the laws of feudalism. But, under a more civilised exterior, the old passion for adventure and conquest remains. In the eleventh century we find them making their way to Southern Italy, where, in 1059, Robert Guiscard is recognised by Pope Nicholas II. as Duke of Apulia and Calabria, and a little later as lord of all Lower Italy, while Sicily is conquered and occupied by his brother. When, in 1066, the Normans, under William the Conqueror, passed over from France and became masters of England, it was only a question of convenience when Ireland would be added to their dominions. The troubles and questions demanding urgent attention in their now wide-spread realm alone prevented William and his immediate successors from annexing Ireland. Henry II. was beset with the same difficulties. His realm had been even enlarged. He was not only king of England, but Duke of Normandy and Aquitaine, and Count of Anjou. That means that he was ruler of a third part, and that the finest part, of France. He had resided, in fact, much more in France than in England, could not speak English, and in all his ideas and sympathies was much more a Norman than an Englishman. But he was a strong, far-seeing ruler, intent on building up a firm and vigorous government. "There was something in his build and look," it has been said, "in the square, stout

Henry II.

frame, the fiery face, the close-cropped hair, the prominent eyes, the bull neck, the coarse, strong hands, the bowed legs, that marked out the keen, stirring, coarse-fibred man of business. ' He never sits down,' said one who observed him closely ; 'he is always on his legs from morning till night.' Orderly in business, careless in appearance, sparing in diet, never resting or giving his servants rest; chatty, inquisitive, endowed with a singular charm of address and strength of memory; obstinate in love or hatred, a fair scholar, a great hunter; his general air that of a rough, passionate, busy man, Henry's personal character told directly on the character of his reign."

It is not surprising that from the opening year of his reign such a ruler as we know Henry was had his eye on Ireland. Already, indeed, the relations between England and Ireland had been drawing the two countries closer to each other. Through the Danes in the first instance, the Churches of Ireland and England, as we have seen, had been brought into organic connection with one another, and a freer intercourse established between them. An active commerce was being carried on between the Danish cities in Ireland and some English towns, such as Bristol. One of the articles of commerce is rather remarkable. There was a considerable slave-trade between the two countries. Ireland is described as being full of Englishmen who had been kidnapped and sold as slaves into Ireland. An Irish synod, somewhat later, in accounting for the evils that had come upon their unhappy country, represent them as a judgment of Heaven for the iniquitous traffic in slaves which they had been

Henry II. has his eye on Ireland.

325

maintaining. In view of these facts—of the proximity of Ireland to the English shores, and of the unsettled and anarchical condition of the country— it was natural that Henry II. should desire to draw the bonds of union still closer. It is certain that at the very opening of his reign this purpose had

Obtains the Papal sanction to his project.

taken shape in his mind. He ascended the throne in 1154, and in 1155, only a few months after his coronation, he laid the matter before a council at Winchester, and sent his chaplain, John of Salisbury, to obtain the Papal sanction to his project of taking possession of Ireland. In a great measure through the gigantic efforts of Hildebrand, the Papal See had been raised to such a pitch of influence that even secular rulers were glad to obtain the countenance of the Pope to their larger undertakings. Thus even William the Conqueror was well pleased to have the approval of Pope Alexander II. in his conquest of England. In other cases also quite as striking, the Pope's blessing had been got. Over all islands in particular he claimed a special jurisdiction. Able and powerful ruler though Henry II. was, he therefore thought it prudent to have the Pope's assistance in the step which he contemplated. It was thus that he now applied to Pope Adrian IV.—Nicholas Breakspeare, the only Englishman who ever sat in the Papal chair—and received in response the following Papal Bull, which is of sufficient interest to be given in full :—

The Papal Bull.

"Adrian, the bishop, the servant of the servants of God, to his most dearly beloved son in Christ, the illustrious king of England, sendeth greeting with the apostolical benediction. Your Majesty laudably and profitably considers how you may best promote your glory on earth, and lay up for yourself an eternal reward in heaven, when, as becomes a Catholic prince, you labour to extend the borders of the Church, to teach the truths of the Christian faith to a rude and unlettered people, and to root out the weeds of wickedness from the field of the Lord. For this purpose you crave the advice and assistance of the Apostolic See, and in so doing, we are persuaded that the higher are your aims, and the more discreet your proceedings, the greater under God will be your success. For those who begin with zeal for the faith and love for religion may always have the best hopes of bringing their undertakings to a prosperous end. It is beyond all doubt, as your Highness acknowledgeth, that Ireland and all the other islands on which the light of the gospel of Christ has dawned, and which have received the knowledge of the Christian faith, do of right belong to St. Peter and the Holy Roman Church. Wherefore we are the more desirous to sow in them the acceptable seed of God's Word, because we know that it will be strictly required of us hereafter. You have signified to us, our well-beloved son in Christ, that you propose to enter the island of Ireland in order to reduce the people to obedience unto laws, and to root out from among them the weeds of sin; and that you are willing to yield and pay yearly from every house the pension of one penny to St. Peter, and to keep and preserve the rights of the churches in that land whole and inviolate. We, therefore, regarding your pious and laudable design with due favour, and graciously assenting to your petition, do hereby declare our will and pleasure that, for the purpose of enlarging the borders of the Church, setting bounds to the progress of wickedness, reforming evil manners, planting virtue, and increasing the Christian religion, you do enter that island, and execute therein whatsoever shall be for God's honour and the welfare of the same. And further, we do also strictly charge and require that the people of that land shall accept you with all honour, and reverence you as their lord, saving only the rights of the churches, which we will have inviolably preserved, and reserving to St. Peter and the Holy Roman Church the yearly pension of one penny from each house. If, therefore, you bring your purpose to good effect, let it be your study to improve the habits of that people, and take such orders by yourself, or by others whom you shall think fitting for their lives, manners, and conversation, that the Church there may be adorned by them, the Christian faith planted and increased, and all that concerns the honour of God and the salvation of souls be ordered by you in like manner; so that you may receive at God's hands the blessed reward of everlasting life, and may obtain on earth a glorious name in ages to come."

The Bull a genuine document. That for his invasion and subjection of Ireland Henry should have had the express authorisation of the Pope has been felt in certain quarters to be an ugly and awkward fact. Various attempts have therefore been made to represent the Bull as a forgery. But they have been signally unsuccessful, and are now practically given up as hopeless. The evidence of its genuineness is so clear and cogent as to leave no reasonable room for doubt. The grant of Adrian was expressly confirmed by his successor, Alexander III. Honorius III. in a letter to his legate speaks of "the English entry into Ireland by the mandate of the Apostolic See, and subjugating it to the obedience of the Roman Church." Indeed, candid Roman Catholics frankly admit its genuineness. "Never did there exist a more real or authentic document," says Dr. Lanigan. One cannot help reading the Pope's testimony, as given in this document, to Henry's piety in the light of his real character. People have come to take testimonials generally with considerable abatement. This one of Adrian to King Henry is absurdly beside the mark, and does not tend to strengthen one's faith in the Papal infallibility. Of Henry, history informs us that he "whispered, scribbled, and looked at picture-books during mass, never confessed, and cursed God in wild frenzies of blasphemy." But Henry undertook to bring Ireland into submission to Rome, to secure "from every house the pension of one penny to St. Peter," and "to reduce the people to obedience unto laws." How, therefore, could the Pope refuse to testify to the king's high religious character, or withhold his blessing from his "pious and laudable design"? Just then, however, Henry had quite enough business in hand in maintaining order both in his English and Continental dominions, and his "pious and laudable design" had to be postponed.

It was not, in fact, till 1171 that he found a fit occasion of carrying out his purpose, and it came about in this way. *Occasion of Henry's coming.*

Dermot MacMurrough, the king of Leinster,

The exile of
Dermot
MacMur-
rough.

was a chief of great ability, of huge size, and warlike propensities, whose voice had grown hoarse shouting his war-cry to his followers in battle, a man of tyrannical, cruel, and even savage and ferocious temper, whose fierce and repulsive aspect terrified both friends and foes. His character may be inferred from an incident related by the historian of the conquest, Giraldus Cambrensis. Turning over the heads of his enemies as he found them lying slain on the battlefield, " among them was the head of one he mortally hated above all the rest, and taking it by the ears and hair, he tore the nostrils and lips with his teeth in a most savage and inhuman manner." Early in his career he had attacked Kildare, slew the inhabitants of the town and the monastery, and forced the Abbess to marry one of his followers. Another feat of his was, but apparently with her own connivance, to carry off Devorgil, daughter of the king of Meath, and wife of Tiernan O'Rourke, king of Breifny, a tall, gaunt, powerful warrior, who had lost an eye in war, as Dermot had lost his voice. Her taste in men seems to have been peculiar. But O'Rourke, with the aid of Turlough O'Connor, king of Connaught, defeated Dermot, recovered his precious Devorgil, and returned home triumphant. Yet for all this Dermot was after the manner of the time highly religious, and had made what was then regarded as very exemplary atonement for his moral peccadilloes by founding quite a large number of abbeys and religious houses. At a later period he was not only hopelessly defeated, but driven across the sea an exile by this same Tiernan in conjunction with Turlough's son and successor,

Roderick O'Connor, the last Irishman who claimed
to be and was generally regarded as king of Ireland. In his desperate plight Dermot now deter- King
mined to seek the assistance of King Henry of Dermot
England against his enemies. For this purpose Henry.
he went to Bristol, but on learning that the king
was in Southern France, our distressed exile repaired thither. Henry was just then in the thick
of his conflict with Thomas à Becket, as well as
with the king of France, and could not personally
go to Dermot's aid, but he gave him letters patent
authorising any of his subjects to assist him in his
object. Dermot had done homage and taken the
oath of fealty to the king.

Richard de Clare, better known as Strongbow, Procures
was a Norman noble descended from the same line the assist-
as William the Conqueror, and consequently of the Strongbow,
same royal stock as Henry himself, but having
taken the opposite side from that of Henry, he
had lost the confidence of the king and been
deprived of his inheritance. He was now, therefore,
quite ready for any enterprise which might promise
to improve his fortunes. Dermot found him in
his castle near Bristol, besought his aid in the
effort to recover his lost kingdom of Leinster, and
by way of reward offered him his daughter Eva
in marriage, and the right of succession to the
kingdom of Leinster at his (Dermot's) death.
Richard of course closed with the bargain.

Robert Fitz-Stephen, a Norman-Welsh knight, and the
Maurice Fitz-Gerald, and other members of the Geraldines.
Geraldine family, Dermot secured by the offer of
the town of Wexford and the surrounding district
to be held in fee. To be sure this town and

territory were then, and had long been, in the possession of the Danes! But that made no barrier to either the giver or receiver. To be sure, also, Dermot had no right, according to the Irish laws, to dispose even of his own kingdom, from which his own tribe had deposed him, in this fashion, much less was he entitled to give away what never belonged to him. In this rude and systematic violation of Irish laws and usages, and the introduction of feudal principles now begun, we see one prolific source of the misery in store for Ireland. Indeed, according neither to Celtic nor to feudal ideas was it competent for Dermot to deal with the tribal rights and possessions as if they were his own private estate. Yet this was the manner in which he disposed of them. Having completed these arrangements and made other preparations, Dermot secretly returned to Ireland, and spent the winter of 1168–69 in seclusion in a monastery at Ferns, one of the monasteries founded by himself.

The Gerald-
ines take
Wexford.

The first of the foreigners to come were Robert Fitz-Stephen and the Fitz-Geralds. They landed at Bannow Bay, twenty-five miles from Wexford, on the 1st of May 1169. The next day they were joined by some others, and a little later by Dermot with as many followers as he could muster; and Wexford was attacked. In the slight attempt at resistance made by the inhabitants one picturesque, or rather one grotesque, incident is recorded. The attack was led by Robert de Barry, one of the Fitz-Geralds, and as he stood upon the wall which he had just scaled clad in splendid armour, and his helmet, shield, and battle-axe shone and sparkled with dazzling brilliance, the conspicuous figure which he made was as tempting as it was menacing to the citizens. One of them, no doubt an Irishman, whose unknightly ideas must have been very disgusting to the Normans, seeing the beautiful mark, seized a large stone, and taking careful aim, hit the proud armour-clad knight such a vigorous blow with it on the side of the head, that he fell headlong into the ditch, and his brother, Giraldus Cambrensis, relates that, in token of the vigour put into the blow, his double teeth all fell out at once many years after. The incident was one he was not likely to forget, and the Normans were so discouraged that for the time they retired, but only for a time. The inhabitants, soon perceiving that continued resistance was hopeless, surrendered, and town and territory were made over to the Fitz-Geralds.

Having left a garrison at Wexford, and Dermot having received considerable accessions to his forces from the Irish tribes, they marched against the king of Ossory, towards whom the king of Leinster had an old grudge. They suffered several reverses, but at length succeeded in crushing him, and in ravaging other districts as well. Roderick O'Connor, king of Connaught, and also king of Ireland, becoming alarmed at the success of Dermot and his allies, summoned what chiefs and followers he could gather, and set out to meet them at Ferns. It was highly characteristic that, while Roderick did his best by the offer of liberal bribes to induce Fitz-Stephen to withdraw, he made a secret agreement with Dermot that the latter should have all Leinster, and should submit to Roderick as Ardri, paying the annual homage and

[margin notes:] Dermot and the Normans attack the king of Ossory.

The king of Ireland meets them at Ferns.

333

service, and stipulating that no more foreigners should be brought over from England. It was about a year after the earliest invaders came that another band arrived under Raymond le Gros, a nephew of Fitz-Stephen. They were attacked by the men of Waterford, and were in great straits, when De Clare himself landed with two hundred men at arms, and other forces to the number of 10,000, marched on Waterford, and after a desperate struggle took it, and was soon after, in fulfilment of a previous promise, married to Eva, the daughter of King Dermot, who from this time forward was little more than a puppet in the hands of the Normans.

But Dublin, which had by this time risen into considerable importance, and whose commanding position was early recognised, was made the chief object of attack, and King Roderick, O'Rourke of Breifny, and the óther Irish chiefs, combined with the Danish inhabitants in its defence. It was, however, taken by the united armies of Dermot and the Normans, now raised to a formidable magnitude and strength, and although two successive and strenuous attempts were made to recover it by the Danes and the Irish, they were unsuccessful. Dermot soon after died, and De Clare, according to arrangement, succeeded to the kingdom of Leinster, and proceeded to organise it on feudal principles.

It is evident that the Irish people were beginning to take serious alarm at the state of servitude to which they were being reduced by the Normans; and this alarm found significant expression in a resolution passed by a synod of Irish clergy at Armagh. It is thus referred to by Giraldus Cambrensis : "It was unanimously resolved that it appeared to the synod that the Divine vengeance had brought upon them this severe judgment for the sins of the people, and especially for this, that they had long been wont to purchase natives of England, as well from traders as from robbers and pirates, and to reduce them to slavery; and that now they also by reciprocal justice were reduced to servitude by that very nation. It was, therefore, publicly decreed by the before-mentioned synod, and publicly proclaimed by universal accord, that all Englishmen throughout the island who were in a state of bondage should be restored to freedom."

But the English king had been noting with hardly less misgiving the progress of the Norman adventurers; he was very doubtful of their loyalty and fidelity to himself, and feared an attempt on their part to set up independent kingdoms in Ireland. He went so far as to cut off supplies and reinforcements and to recall their followers; and having at length recognised the expediency of coming over himself, he prepared an extensive armament for that purpose. De Clare, of whom he was specially suspicious, and who had been summoned to the king's presence in England, met him at Gloucester, renewed his oath of fealty, and undertook to hold Leinster as Henry's vassal. The king, after most elaborate preparations, landed at Waterford in October 1171 with a fleet of 400 ships, 500 knights, a large body of cavalry and archers, with great stores of arms and provisions—an army numbering probably altogether not less than 10,000 men. The express sanction already given to his enterprise in the Bull of Pope Adrian had borne good fruit

Misgiving of King Henry.

Henry lands at Waterford, October 1171.

335

in securing for him the good-will of the Irish clergy.

Roger de Hoveden informs us that "there came to the king at Waterford all the archbishops, bishops, and abbots of the whole of Ireland, and acknowledged him as king and lord of Ireland, taking the oath of fealty to him and to his heirs, and admitting his and their right of reigning over them for all time to come."

The king then marched to Dublin, where he was received with due state, where a temporary palace was erected for him just outside the walls of the city, and where with munificent hospitality and splendid pageantry he entertained and feasted both the Irish and Norman chiefs. Here the Irish chiefs, with the exception of O'Neill of Ulster, made submission, took the oath of fealty, and were confirmed in the possession of their several territories. No resistance whatever was attempted. Perhaps by some writers a little too much has been made of this. It has been said that he got possession of Ireland without striking a blow, that the chiefs voluntarily submitted to him, and that it is therefore wholly inappropriate to speak of his invasion as a conquest ; but a conquest it was for all that. The contemporary historians, who invariably so represent it, have a truer instinct than the modern political pamphleteers. Many hard battles had been already fought and won by the Norman knights and their armies who had preceded Henry. If the Irish, with the assistance of the Danes, were unable, after strenuous and stubborn attempts at resistance, to withstand the earlier bands of Norman adventurers, how could they hope to defeat Henry with such an army as he brought with him, and that army augmented by the Norman

forces already in the country? The Irish were too
quick-witted not to see that resistance under such
circumstances would be worse than useless. They
therefore at once, and wisely, submitted, because
they could do no otherwise. But while the rights
of the Irish chiefs generally were recognised, they
were required to hold their territories as vassals of
the king of England, while wide tracts were given
to the Norman knights without regard to the rights
of those already in possession. The ancient laws and
customs of the country were wholly disregarded and
completely set at nought.

Henry summoned a synod of the clergy, which _{The Synod}
met at Cashel in 1172, under the presidency of ^{of Cashel,}_{1172.}
Christian, bishop of Lismore, the Papal legate, and
was attended by three archbishops and other bishops
and clergy; the North only having no representatives
at it. The synod passed a series of resolutions, which
concerned for the most part minor points of discipline, and which were very particular in guarding the
temporal interests of the Church. The most important of these measures was the following: " That
Divine offices shall be henceforth celebrated in every
part of Ireland according to the forms and usages
of the Church of England. For it is right and just
that, as by Divine Providence Ireland has received
her lord and king from England, she should also
submit to a reformation from the same source.
Indeed, both the realm and Church of Ireland are
indebted to this mighty king for whatever they
enjoy of the blessings of peace and the growth of
religion; as before his coming to Ireland all sorts
of wickedness had prevailed among this people for a
long series of years, which now, by his authority and

care of the administration, are abolished." This last statement as to the religious prosperity consequent on the king's coming and administration was, to say the least, singularly premature. The decrees of this synod were, in fact, an undisguised attempt to Anglicise the Irish Church even more completely than had yet been done. From this time forward the English king found in the higher clergy in Ireland his most loyal servants and supporters.

Henry departs. Having spent the winter months at Dublin, Henry took his departure for England in the beginning of March. He left Hugh de Lacy as in some sense his Justiciary or Viceroy, but had taken no effective measures to carry out the principles which he had introduced. As Sir John Davies puts it : " He departed from Ireland without striking one blow, or building one castle, or planting one garrison among the Irish; neither left he behind him one true subject more than those he found there on coming over, which were only the English adventurers of before, who had gained the port towns in Leinster and Munster, and possessed some scopes of land thereunto adjoining, partly by Strongbow's alliance with the Lord of Leinster, and partly

Changes his policy. by plain invasion and conquest." Henry's earlier policy had been to play off the Irish chiefs against the Normans, to keep the latter in check by means of the former; and so he was at first quite friendly and conciliatory with the Irish, received them as his vassals, and treated them as on an equality with the Norman leaders. But for some reason, not very clear, his policy towards them was completely changed. From this time forward his aim was to rule Ireland through his Norman colonists, and to

338

govern the Irish, not by a conciliatory and friendly treatment, but by conceiving and designating them as " enemies," ignoring any rights possessed by them, and robbing and oppressing them by measures of the most unjust and violent character. He pro- ceeded to treat them as if they had no existence except as aliens, granting their territories as if those territories had no owners, or as if the owners had no right to them. In his grant of Meath to Hugh de Lacy, he ignores O'Rourke, the Irish chief of that territory. Similarly, although Roderick O'Connor had been allowed to retain Connaught as vassal to the king, and although O'Connor had been guilty of no treason, Connaught was now given to Fitz-Adhelm (De Burgo) and his heirs. In like manner the lordship of Ulster was granted to John de Courcy, a discontented follower of De Burgo; and, in the face of the most determined resistance on the part of the Ulidian chiefs and people, he proceeded through fire and slaughter to take possession of it. And so with other regions. And along with these conquests the feudal system was brought into operation, with all the evils incident to it, and bereft of all its advantages. The power of the Crown, for example, was not at hand to keep in check the excesses and oppressions of the Norman barons, who acted as independent princes. The general result was that at first the Anglo-Normans took possession of the plains and more fertile lands, and the native Irish were fain to retire largely to the boglands and mountainous regions, where they still retained their old social organisation and laws. With the exception of five Irish families who were known as the " five bloods "—namely, O'Neill, O'Melaghlin,

O'Connor, O'Brien, and MacMurrough—the Celtic population were henceforward regarded as aliens and enemies, and could not sue in the king's courts. A "mere Irishman" could not bring an action against an Englishman; he was "out of the king's peace," and to kill him was not recognised as an offence by the law: indeed, this plea was habitually set up. It is true the English Government still needed the Irish to enable them to keep in proper restraint their rebellious vassals, and often sought to employ them for this purpose, although the Government had done its best to make them both impotent and untrustworthy. The Normans, on the other hand, received no effective support from England, and soon the native Irish began to encroach on the districts occupied by the Normans, and to resume possession of them; and the power of the English Crown became little more than nominal in Ireland. The reasons why the English Government so completely failed to subdue Ireland are so well stated by the late Professor Richey in his "Short History," and so important, that it may be worth while briefly to summarise them:—

Reasons of the failure of the English Government to subdue Ireland.

1. The large extent comprised in the grants made to the first colonists led to such a dispersion of the Norman nobles over the fertile portions of the country, that the English colony never formed one compact body capable of combined action, while the districts occupied by the English were sparsely populated by the colonists, and had never been quite abandoned by the original inhabitants.

2. The military equipment of the Normans, and their mode of carrying on war, rendered their forces wholly inefficient, when, leaving the flat country,

they attempted to penetrate the fastnesses of the native tribes.

3. From the absence of any central government, civil wars continually arose between the several Norman lords, who often called in the assistance of the Irish. The power of the colonists was thus frittered away in dissensions.

4. The English Government continually called upon the Irish barons for aids and military service, to be employed in wars elsewhere than in Ireland.

5. Many of the estates of the Norman nobles descended to heiresses, who married Englishmen already possessing estates in England; hence arose absenteeism. The castles of the absentee lords became exclusively garrisoned by Irish mercenaries, commanded by an Irish seneschal, both of whom revolted on the first opportunity.

6. Even the lords who resided constantly on their Irish estates gradually lost their Norman habits, and tended to assimilate themselves to the manners and to adopt the language of the Irish. Thus arose intermarriages and fostering, which tended to fuse the Normans with the Irish, seduced them from their original allegiance, and taught them to regard their Celtic neighbours as friends and compatriots rather than hereditary enemies.

7. The Irish Channel, though wide enough to check colonisation and render military organisations in Ireland difficult and costly, afforded no insuperable obstacle to the passage and return of those who repaired to Ireland to seek their fortune, or who, having failed there, desired to return to England. Hence the constant arrival of fresh adventurers, who sought to enrich themselves by grants

from the Crown and legalised plunder, but rarely desired to make Ireland their permanent home. Unprincipled foreign speculators and beggarly court favourites afflicted Ireland, and were the instigators and sharers in the constant confiscations of the estates of Norman and Celt alike.[1]

As is suggested in the fourth reason given above, the condition of Ireland in its relations with England came to be much affected by the difficulties of England at home and her conflicts with other countries. The English sovereign, for example, was so much preoccupied by his struggle with the English baronage, and with the war of Scottish independence in the time of Edward I., as seriously to weaken his power in Ireland. In the war with Robert Bruce, Edward reinforced his army from Ireland, and the success of Bruce in asserting Scottish independence at Bannockburn not only lessened the prestige of England, but had other effects in Ireland. It was natural, too, that the Scottish king should adopt some means of cutting off the supplies sent to the English army from the Irish tribes, as well as find some occupation for his brother Edward, who might give trouble in Scotland. An agreement was thus come to between Bruce and the Irish chiefs to make a determined effort to overthrow the English power in Ireland, and to make Edward the Bruce, Robert's brother, king over the Irish. The Irish chiefs, however, in their design of freeing Ireland from English domination, thought it prudent to seek the aid of the Roman pontiff. With this object in view they addressed a remarkable letter to Pope John XXII.,

Invasion of Edward Bruce.

The Pope's sanction sought,

[1] See Richey's "Short History of the Irish People," pp. 179–186.

setting out their grievances. It begins: "To our most Holy Father in Christ, the Lord John, by the grace of God Supreme Pontiff, his attached children, Donald O'Neyl, king of Ulster, and rightful hereditary successor to the throne of Ireland, as well as the princes and nobles of the same realm, with the Irish people in general, present their humble salutations, approaching with kisses of devout homage to his sacred feet. . . . With loud and imploring cry we would convey to your holy ears in the contents of the present appeal an account of our first origin, and of the condition in which our affairs at this moment stand, and also of the cruel injuries to us and our forefathers, inflicted, threatened, and to the present hour continued, by successive kings of England, and their wicked ministers and Anglican barons of Irish birth." Referring to the state of their country under its native princes, they trace its subjugation and misery to "the unrighteous obsequiousness of Pope Adrian," and state that, as a result of his Bull, "upwards of fifty thousand persons of both nations had perished by the sword, independently of those who were worn out by famine or destroyed in dungeons." They then describe the evils inflicted on the Church, also how they have been deprived of their laws, and how, "with a view to the extermination of our people, infamous laws of the most abandoned and unprincipled character," which they proceed to specify, have been imposed on them. They point out how no Irishman can bring any action at law whatsoever; how when any Englishman kills an Irishman, even an Irish prelate, he is liable to no penalty, but is the more honoured, that it is held to be "no more sin to kill an Irishman

343

than a dog or any other brute animal." They state that an appeal had been made to the English king for the removal of these evils, but to no purpose; that they were inviting to their assistance "Edward de Bruce, the illustrious Earl of Carrick, brother-german of the most illustrious Lord Robert, by the grace of God king of the Scots, and descendant of some of the most noble of our own ancestors," and they conclude by praying the "Most Holy Father, out of a regard for justice and the public peace, mercifully to sanction their proceedings."

and refused. The Pope returned no answer to this appeal, except to send the letter of the Irish chiefs to Edward II., the English king, and to issue Bulls to the Irish bishops, requiring them to excommunicate all who should take up arms in behalf of Bruce or give him any help in Ireland.

Edward Bruce lands at Carrickfergus, and wins many victories. Edward Bruce landed at Carrickfergus in May 1315, with six thousand men, including many of the best Scottish soldiers, and in the following years inflicted a series of severe defeats on the Viceroy and on other leaders of the English colonists. At the close of 1316 Robert Bruce himself came over, and, in company with his brother and their Irish allies, entered on a new campaign, bent on exterminating the Anglo-Norman power in Ireland. Their progress from Ulster to Munster was one continuous career of devastation, in which they are described as "burning, slaying, plundering, sacking towns, castles, and even churches, going and returning." But Robert Bruce having gone back to Scotland, the colonists united under Jean de Bermingham, and, with a force much superior to that which Edward Bruce then commanded, took up a strong position at Faughard, near Dundalk. Bruce was advised to avoid a battle just then, but eighteen successive victories had made him over-confident. But is He suffered a severe and decisive defeat, he and defeated his chief officers were slain, and what remained of his army was glad to escape to Scotland. But is defeated and slain at Faughard.

The state of things in Ireland now became more deplorable than ever. The English power in that country, and its capacity to preserve order, grew even feebler than it had been; the Anglo-Norman lords become more independent and irresponsible, some of them without disguise throwing off their allegiance to the English Crown, adopting the Irish dress and language, and substituting the Irish laws for the English. Within sight of the royal garrison on the banks of the Shannon, the De Burgos of Connaught stripped off their Norman dress and arms, and put on the saffron robes of the Irish, becoming more Celtic than the Irish themselves. The Government had now to be content to confine its efforts to maintain order within the district afterwards known as the Pale, and which was already greatly circumscribed. Even Eastern Ulster, under the O'Neills, was practically withdrawn from English rule. The fact, already noted, that "many English of the said land (Ireland), forsaking the English language, manners, mode of riding, laws, and usages, live and govern themselves according to the manners, fashion, and language of the Irish enemies, and also have made divers marriages and alliances between themselves and the Irish enemies aforesaid," led to the passing of the famous Statute of Kilkenny, from the preamble of which the words just quoted are taken. This statute provided that "no The English power in Ireland feebler than ever. The Statute of Kilkenny.

345

alliance by marriage, gossipred, fostering of children, concubinage, or by amour, nor in any other manner, be henceforth made between the English and Irish of the one part, or of the other part; and that no Englishman nor other person, being at peace, do give or sell to any Irishman, in time of peace or war, horses or armour, nor any manner of victuals in time of war; and if any shall do to the contrary, and thereof be attainted, he shall have judgment of life and member, as a traitor to our lord the king." Every Englishman was required to use the English language, and the English custom, fashion, mode of riding and apparel; and any English, or Irish living among the English, not using these was liable to severe penalties. Irishmen were also prohibited from enjoying livings or being received into monasteries situated among the English; and many other prohibitions in a like spirit were included in the statute.

Its object: to make a wall of partition between the English and the Irish.

The object of this legislation was to build an impassable wall of separation between the English and the Irish, who all through the sections of the statute are designated " the Irish enemies "; " whereby it is manifest," says Sir John Davies in his " Discoverie," " that such as had the government of Ireland under the Crown of England did intend to make a perpetual separation and enmity between the English and Irish—pretending (no doubt) that the English in the end should root out the Irish; which the English not being able to do, did cause a perpetuall warre between the two nations, which continued four hundred and odd years."

But a dead letter.

As a matter of fact, the statute was little better than a dead letter. It could not be put into

346

operation. Human nature was too strong for it, and the fusion of races went on in spite of it. The colonists themselves found it intolerable, and obtained licenses enabling them to evade it.

"The English government during this period," says Professor Richey, one of the fairest and most moderate of historians, "was a source of unmixed evil to the country. The English kings had practically abandoned the exercise of sovereign power in Ireland. The English executive neither fulfilled the duty of a government nor permitted any other to be established. Their highest aim was self-preservation, and the means by which they sought it were the fomenting of civil war between the barons and chiefs outside the Pale, the rendering of assistance to any pretender who promised to embarrass or depose a tribal chieftain, and frequent razzias, equally barbarous and futile."[1] By the opening of the fifteenth century the "Irish enemies" had retaken a large part of the territory of which they had been deprived, and at this time parts only of the four shires of Dublin, Meath, Kildare, and Louth submitted to English rule. The lords of Kildare, Desmond, and Ormonde acted as independent sovereigns. "The stringent and ferocious statutes," says Richey, "which down to Henry VIII.'s reign are to be found in our statute-book, are evidence of fear and helplessness, not acts of overbearing force." And summing up the results at the accession of Henry VIII. he says, "The Celtic population had found the rule of England scarcely less injurious to them than the invasions of the Danes. . . . Every trace of English govern-

Character of the government.

---

[1] Richey's "Short History," p. 218.

ment, save the miseries which it had caused, had passed away from Ireland. The English king had no force in Ireland, nor any ally, save the heredi-
The English conquest a failure. tary enemies of the house of Kildare. The English conquest was confessedly a failure. The Anglo-Norman colony had disappeared, or been absorbed in the Celtic population. If the king of England were any longer to be lord of Ireland, the conquest of the island must be commenced again."[1]

The Church in the Anglo-Norman period. Some indications have been given as we proceeded of the condition of the Church in Ireland during this period, but a few words additional are necessary on the subject.

Foreign monastic orders introduced. Several foreign orders of monks were brought to Ireland, and many new monasteries, chiefly Cistercian, but some Benedictine and Augustinian, were founded, and the new establishments in most cases were erected on the sites of ancient Celtic monasteries, thus securing whatever advantage arose from the associations connected with them.

The political division created two sections in the Church. It was inevitable that the political division made between the two sections of the population by the Crown should create a like ecclesiastical division. They required each a separate clergy of its own, the one speaking French and English, and the other speaking Irish. Irish clergy and monks were, as we have seen, excluded from Anglo-Norman benefices and abbeys, and *vice versa.* "There was discord almost universally among the poor religious of Ireland," says Friar Clynn in his Annals, "some of them upholding and cherishing the part of their own nation, blood, and tongue ; others of them canvassing for the office of prelates and superiors."

[1] Richey's "Short History," pp. 238, 239.

Even the Pope himself gave his countenance, not only to the ostracism of the Irish generally, but to the exclusion of Irish ecclesiastics from English churches and monasteries. Thus a Bull of Leo X. in 1515 expressly excluded all of Irish blood and manners from St. Patrick's Cathedral in Dublin.

It is not to be inferred, however, that these two sections of the population constituted two Churches or communions. It is true that the Irish of this period still retained some of their old Celtic peculiarities and usages. But none the less they, as well as the English, acknowledged the Papal jurisdiction. In doctrine they were at one. In the numerous statutes against the Irish, neither Irish clergy nor people are ever charged with being heretics or schismatics. In fact, the stringent laws excluding Irish clergy from English livings were in cases of difficulty relaxed and Irish clergy admitted. Thus, an Act of the second year of Richard III., 1485, states that "as divers benefices of the diocese of Dublin are situated among the Irish enemy . . . and as no Englishman can inhabit said benefices, and divers English clerks who are enabled to have cure of souls are inexpert in the Irish language, and such of them who are expert disdain to inhabit among the Irish people, and others dare not inhabit among them, by which means Divine service is diminished and cure of souls neglected," it was enacted "that Walter Fitz-Symond, Archbishop of Dublin, for two years do collate Irish clerks to the said benefices, without any impeachment from the king, his heirs or ministers, provided that such beneficers be sworn to allegiance." Both the Rev. Thomas Olden and Professor G. T. Stokes frankly

(margin note) Not two Churches, but two factions in one Church.

admit this. Mr. Olden says: "They became divided
into two factions, though belonging to the same
Church, and in the main accepting the same doctrines." Again: "The two sections of the Church
stood apart, somewhat as those religious bodies in
America, who, though belonging to the same communion, are yet divided in North and South by the
question of colour." [1] "I do not intend to convey,"
says Professor G. T. Stokes, "that there were two
Churches in Ireland then, as there are two Churches
in Ireland now, with competing bishops in every
see, and competing incumbents in every parish. . . .
Henceforth there were two parties in the Irish
Church. There was the Celtic party, and there
was the Anglo-Norman party. They taught in the
main the same doctrines, acknowledged the nominal
supremacy of the same Pope, and yet were as distinct
from one another, and hated one another with as
perfect a hatred, as if they rejoiced in the designation
of Protestant or Papist, or the still more modern
one of Orangemen and Nationalists." [2]

The higher
clergy, with
the sanction
of the Pope,
political
agents for
the Crown.

But the higher clergy especially, who were generally
Anglo-Norman, were, as has already appeared, the
most loyal servants and supporters of the English
Crown. Inspired and encouraged from Rome, they
sympathised with the conquering race, aided them in
their political designs, and formed so many English
garrisons planted among the Irish. "The English
ecclesiastics appointed by the Crown or the Papal
See to bishoprics in Ireland were then, as subsequently," says Richey, "political appointments, and

[1] See Olden's "Church of Ireland," pp. 251, 289.
[2] "Ireland and the Anglo-Norman Church," Lect. xv. p. 343.

constituted part of the English garrison; they filled official positions; they sat at the council board; they furnished men and arms to the English deputy; they not unfrequently commanded them in the field; and, if it were necessary, they were ever willing and anxious to minister and exercise all kind of ecclesiastical censures against the wild Irish." While the Lord Deputy was engaged in "taming the Irish," the Dublin clergy twice a week prayed for his success.

And through the agency of the Church the Irish were made to groan under the burden of oppressive exactions in the shape of taxation. As early as 1229 a tax was levied on the Irish by Pope Gregory IX. to enable him to carry on his contest with the Emperor Frederick. With regard to this tax Hanmer says, "The clergy sent after their money Irish curses, for they were driven at the worst hand to sell unto the merciless merchants their cows, hackneys, caddows (*i.e.* blankets), and *aqua vitæ* to make present payment, and were driven to that extremity to pawn and sell their cups, chalices, copes, altar-cloths, and vestments." In 1240 an emissary came to Ireland from the same Pope demanding the twentieth of the whole land, besides donations and gratuities for the same war, under pain of excommunication. In 1251 there was a levy of "Saladin's tenths," as they were called, for the recovery of the Holy Sepulchre. Another levy was made in 1270 to enable the Pope to carry on war with the king of Arragon. In 1288 a grant of the six years' tenths which had been collected, as well as the tithes of the following

Oppressive Papal exactions.

six years, was made over to Edward I. It would be hard to say whether the Roman Pontiff and his clergy or the English Crown were most to blame for the iniquities and oppressions inflicted on the Irish throughout the Anglo-Norman period.

PART V

●

CHAPTER XVII

ON THE TITLE "THE CHURCH OF IRELAND"[1]

If in the course of this lecture a single word escapes me depreciatory of any Christian work which the Church that calls itself "The Church of Ireland" has done or is doing in this country, it will be very far from my purpose. For everything in it which consists with and makes for the progress of the kingdom of our common Master I am sincerely thankful. The one point with which I am here concerned is the propriety of the title assumed by it, and not so much the title itself as the exclusive claim that lies behind it, and which it is intended to assert; but even this question I hope to discuss in an academical spirit, and without any breach of Christian charity.

When the Church in question enjoyed the privi- *The title ex-*
lege of being a State establishment, and as such *cused while the Church*
had this title affixed to it, its members had a good *was estab-*
excuse for wearing the designation. But the justi- *lished.*
fication that could be pleaded thirty years ago is available no longer. From the place of privilege to which the State had raised it the same power has deposed it, and set it on a level with the other denominations. Yet to the old title and symbol

[1] This chapter and the next were given as public lectures at the opening and closing of a College session.

355

of superiority it clings more fondly and displays
it more obtrusively than ever. It may be said,
perhaps, "What's in a name?" and that "that
which we call a rose by any other name would
smell as sweet." But in the circles where this title
is current Juliet's philosophy in the matter of names
is not appreciated. It is evidently thought that
there is a great deal in a name. It is, in fact, the
claim which in this case underlies the name that
gives it importance. The claim is, that, in a sense
which is true of no other, which excludes every
other, the Episcopal communion *is* "The Church
of Ireland." When that Church was set up in this
country by Henry VIII., Edward VI., and Elizabeth,
we are told, it was no foreign institution imported
from England, but the revival and continuation of
the ancient Irish Church founded by St. Patrick;
that the modern Episcopal Church is thus identical
with the early Celtic Church and sole heir to its
prestige; that through St. Patrick, moreover, it is
lineally connected with the Apostles, enjoys the
priceless privilege of the true "Apostolical succession," and (although it includes but a fraction of
Irish Christianity) has thus an indefeasible and exclusive claim to the title "The Church of Ireland."
Other denominations are but unauthorised intruders
within the domain of the one legitimate Church of
the country.

The claim thus put forward is of course essentially a High Church one, advanced by men who
set vital store by "episcopal succession," and are
imbued with the Cyprianic idea which makes the
prelatical bishop of the essence of the Church, and
affirms that there can be no Church, and no Church

The claim underlying the title : that the modern Episcopal Church is identical with the early Celtic Church.

356

continuity, without him.   And yet I have repeatedly
heard it endorsed by Episcopalians who call themselves Evangelical, but habitually speak of members
of their own communion as " Church people."   They
profess to abhor sacerdotalism, but in thus implying
that the members of other denominations are *not*
" Church people," and in effect *unchurching* them,
they are most effectually disseminating sacerdotal
doctrine, and rolling its vocabulary as a sweet morsel
under their tongue.

The claim, a High Church one, based on the theory of Apostolical succession, unchurches other denominations.

   The aggressive boldness with which in recent
times this claim to be the lineal successor of the
ancient Celtic Church, and to be alone entitled
to the designation "The Irish Church," has been
advanced, must have struck the least observant.
The denominational organs of Episcopacy are never
tired of reiterating it.   At every Episcopal Church
Conference, as on the occasion of the last Conference
here in Belfast, a prominent place is assigned to it.
The newspapers are almost daily flaunting it in
our face.   A challenge is thus thrown down to the
other denominations which not only justifies but
compels examination into the grounds on which the
pretension rests.   If we now proceed to investigate
the merits of the claim, those who have flung down
the gage have the least reason to complain.   The
advocates of the view in question appeal to history.
It is fortunate that history has as little respect for
denominations as for persons.   At her bar ecclesiastical fictions meet with no more indulgence than any
other sort of fictions.   If the claim referred to has
any real basis in fact, if it is not a fond creation of
the ecclesiastical imagination, history will tell us.
To history then we turn.   It is not necessary to

A challenge is thus thrown down to other denominations.

The claim examined.

357

ask permission to state honestly and frankly the facts which history has recorded.

The contention is that the Church set up by Henry VIII., Edward VI., and Elizabeth was a continuation of the early Irish Church, and substantially identical with it. The first question for our consideration, then, is: How far were the essential features of the ancient Irish Church reproduced in the Church set up by the Tudors? Is the resemblance between them such as to justify the assertion of identity and continuity.

The fundamental features of the Celtic Church wanting in the Protestant Episcopal Church.

1. In reply to which I have to ask you to note first that the early Irish Church was a *self-governing community*. The shape assumed by it, and the laws by which its affairs were regulated, were not due to any external authority whatever. From the twelfth century onwards the English king, in conjunction with the Pope, did exercise control in the direction of its affairs, but in the early period the Irish Church was free from the interference of both Pope and king. Its independence of Rome, and its refusal for ages to submit to the Roman jurisdiction, is one of the commonplaces of history. The late Cardinal Newman describes it as " vehemently opposed " to the Roman Church. " It is not too much to say," he adds, " that through the influence of the Scottish Church and of the Celtic civilisation, of which Ireland was the centre, Christendom reached the very verge of a tremendous schism, almost reaching in extent to the unhappy sacrilege of the sixteenth century."[1] But what I desire here to emphasise is that the doctrine of the royal supremacy was as little recognised by the early Irish Church as the

1. The one self-governing; the other a creation of the State.

[1] " Life of Wilfrid, Archbishop of York."

doctrine of the Papal supremacy. The abbots sat
at the right hand of kings and often inspired their
policy, but no Irish king ever claimed to be the
supreme head or governor of the Celtic Church, or
to have power to legislate in its spiritual affairs.
This, I need not say, was the primary and fundamental feature of the Church set up by Henry VIII.
and Elizabeth—that to which it owed its creation
and the form assumed by it. Henry VIII. was constituted "the only supreme head on earth of the
whole Church in Ireland," with "full power and
authority" in spiritual affairs. Elizabeth took the
title of "supreme governor," with like authority.
Nor were these empty titles, worn for ornament;
they meant real governmental power. As Professor
Richey points out, the sovereign in this case "claimed
and exercised powers which the Papacy in the time
of its greatest influence had never pretended to
possess." "The king sitting in London, surrounded
by his English council, was to alter and modify the
creed and forms of the Church, according to his
varying views on these subjects, . . . and the
grounds proposed by him for such alterations in the
Church were not the principles of morality or the
teaching of the Scriptures, but simple obedience to
the will of the sovereign and the enforcement of the
statute law."[1]   Only once before in the history of
Christianity, Dr. Richey adds, had such arbitrary
interference been attempted by any sovereign, and
that was when the Isaurian Emperors sought to
impose their own will in matters of faith upon their
subjects.
   [Let me here say, parenthetically, that all the

[1] Richey's "Short History," pp. 367, 368, 371.

main statements I have to make in this lecture I
shall base upon the "Calendars of State Papers"
and other authoritative documents. Where these
are not expressly referred to, I shall support what
is advanced by Episcopal authorities of recognised
weight, such as Todd's "St. Patrick," and for the
later period Richey's "Short History." The latter
especially I shall cite often and of set purpose, as
an able, careful, and moderate writer, who supports
his affirmations by abundant quotations from the
original documents, and who was besides a professor
in Trinity College and an Episcopalian.]

Keep this in mind throughout, then—the new
Church set up in Ireland in the sixteenth century
was exactly what the will of the Tudor sovereigns
made it. We shall see by-and-by that the very
last thing they dreamt of was to revive the early
Irish Church or anything Irish.

2. ¶The hierarchical grades of the Irish Episcopal Church derived from Rome, and non-existent in the Celtic Church.

2. *Her graduated hierarchy, consisting of primate,
archbishops, diocesan bishops, deans, &c., the Irish
Episcopal Church derived not from the early Irish
Church, but directly from the Church of Rome.*
These hierarchical grades and dignities were absolutely unknown in the ancient Church of Ireland.
The new Irish Primate was described in the newspapers the other day as "the 111th successor of
St. Patrick in the primatial See of Ireland." Such
a statement is the result of a "plentiful lack" of
historical information. The Celtic Church of Ire

No Primate in the Celtic Church.

land had neither "archbishop" nor "primate" in
the modern sense. In his "Life of St. Patrick" Dr.
Todd demonstrates that the Abbot of Armagh had
no primatial jurisdiction, that "there was no
special jurisdiction in Armagh," that "there was

360

no such thing as a regular succession of bishops in No arch-
bishop. Armagh or elsewhere;" that, in fact, the coarbs or successors of St. Patrick at Armagh were abbots, many of them presbyters, some laymen, and at least one of them a woman.[1]

And the diocesan bishop was as conspicuous by No diocesan
bishop. his non-existence in the Church of St. Patrick as was the modern archbishop and primate. "The normal state of Episcopacy in Ireland was non-diocesan."[2] "Diocesan Episcopacy did not exist in the early Church," says the Rev. Thomas Olden, "and no attempt was made to introduce it until the Synod of Rathbreasil in 1118."[3] It was this Synod of Rathbreasil in the twelfth century, presided over by Gillé, the first Papal legate who appeared in this country, which made the earliest attempt to divide Ireland into dioceses and to set up diocesan Episcopacy. Diocesan Episcopacy was thus introduced into this country at the date named as an essential part of the constitution of the Church of Rome, and as an institution entirely new to Ireland.

And when you look at the bishops of the early Irish Church and compare them with the prelates of the Tudor Church, you see that the relation between them is not one of resemblance, but of contrast.

(a.) First, as regards *number*. Early authorities Celtic Epis-
copacy Con-
gregational. represent the number of bishops as corresponding with the number of the churches. Tirechan, in the "Book of Armagh" (eighth century), gives the number of bishops appointed by Patrick at 350.

---

[1] See Todd's "St. Patrick," pp. 16, 94, 171, 172.
[2] Ibid., p. 27.
[3] "The Church of Ireland," p. 117.

The Catalogue of Saints (supposed to be by Tirechan) mentions the same number, all founders
of churches. Nennius says Patrick founded 365
churches and ordained 365 bishops. The "Annals
of the Four Masters" represent him as founding
700 churches and appointing 700 bishops. Accordingly St. Bernard affirms that in his time "almost
every church had its separate bishop" in Ireland
("De Vita Malachiæ, c. x.). Lanfranc says that
"in towns and cities many (*plures*) bishops were
ordained."[1]   Hence Skene's remark that Patrick
"appears to have placed a bishop in each church
which he founded," and his designation of the system
as "Congregational Episcopacy." The facts collected by the late Dr. Reeves in his "Antiquities"
bear out these statements. From the documents
quoted by him we learn that in the neighbourhood
of Downpatrick there were not much less than half-
a-dozen bishops within a radius of a few miles, and
so in other districts. A state of things even more
remarkable still is brought out in some ancient
writings, from which we learn that a very common
arrangement was to have a group of seven bishops
connected with a single church. The "Martyrology
of Donegal" mentions six such groups with seven
bishops each, the seven being in each of three
of the groups sons of one father. "The Litany of
Angus the Culdee" (written before A.D. 800) gives
141 such groups of seven each to a single church,
and mentions in addition two sets of 150 bishops
each, and two more of 350. If in proportion to
the population, Ireland had as many bishops now
as she had then, she would have at the present time

Many
churches
had seven
bishops
each.

[1] Ussher's "Religion of the Ancient Irish," p. 322.

more than 10,000 bishops. Belfast alone would have probably not less than 1000 bishops—more than all the clergy of all denominations.

True, there were presbyters as well as bishops in the Celtic Church, but the difference between the Celtic bishop and the presbyters was certainly not greater than, apparently not so great as, that between the Presbyterian minister and his presbyters or elders. The Presbyterian minister alone can ordain and administer the sacraments, he preaches and presides, and in fact there can be no regular meeting of the presbyters without him in the chair, while of course he claims to be a New Testament bishop. But in matters of this sort we must not allow ourselves to be imposed on by mere words, but must look at things as they exist apart from the names applied to them.

(*b.*) And the bishops of the Celtic Church, as they had no dioceses, had no jurisdiction, no governmental power. The real rulers of that Church were the abbots, who were generally not bishops, but presbyters, often laymen, and even women. The bishops were in complete subordination to the abbots, and were regarded as inferior even to the lectors. In fact, as Skene shows, "the inferior functionaries of the community appear to have united the functions of a bishop with their proper duties." The bishop appears to have been a sort of "maid-of-all-work" to the community. You find him ploughing, carpentering, making shrines, teaching, sometimes even acting as the "champion" of the abbot, carrying him on his back when he journeyed, and when necessary fighting in his defence.

(*c.*) And bear another fact in mind. As Dr. Todd

The bishops had no jurisdiction.

And no 'succession" in the modern sense. shows: "There was no such thing as a succession of bishops" in the early Irish Church.[1] "Hence catalogues of successive bishops of Irish sees from their founder to the present day must be illusive."[2]   It is a fact of deep significance that for this reason the contemporary Churches in England and on the Continent refused to recognise the validity of orders in the Irish Church. The Council of Chalons-sur-Saone in 813 declared the orders conferred by the Scotic— that is, the Irish—bishops to be null and void, and questioned the validity of their episcopacy. In like manner, the synod of the contemporary English Church held at Cealcythe in 816, presided over by Wilfrid, Archbishop of Canterbury, enacted that no person of Scotic (*i.e.* Irish) race should be permitted to exercise his ministry in any English diocese, the first reason given being—*Quia incertum est nobis, unde et an ab aliquo ordinentur*—"because it was uncertain by whom they were ordained, or whether they were ordained by any one." The advocates of the theory under consideration are quite certain that they derive their orders from the Apostles through St. Patrick and the bishops who succeeded him. The contemporary Churches in England and on the Continent, which knew the facts vastly better, had no such confidence. On the contrary, they were uncertain by whom they were ordained, or whether they were ordained at all. In an inquisition taken at "Lymmavaddy" in 1609 by a jury on oath acting for the then County of Coleraine, the remarkable statement occurs that Donell M'Hugh O'Neale, king of Ireland, who reigned, according to the "Four

[1] Todd's "St. Patrick," pp. 171–172.
[2] Olden's "Church of Ireland," c. vii. p. 120.

Masters," from 624 till 639, "did *long before any bushopps were made in the said kingdom of Ireland*, give unto certain holy men whom they called *sancti patres* several portions of land and a third part of all the tithes," that certain proportions were given by them to tenants, called "Corbes" or "Herenaghs," and that this state of things continued "until the Church of Rome established busshopps in this kingdom." The inquisitions for Donegal, Fermanagh, and Cavan are to the same effect. These old jurors were men of discernment. The bishops of the earlier time were so different from the bishops constituted by the Roman Church that these ancient inquisitions refuse to call the earlier officials "bishops" at all, and reserve the title for the modern diocesan dignitaries.[1]

Note, then, that the ancient Irish Church had no primate, no metropolitan, no archbishop (in the modern sense), no diocesan bishop, and that the Celtic bishop differed from the modern diocesan bishop in almost everything but name.

3. The most fundamental and characteristic feature of the early Irish Church was its *monasticism*, which began with Patrick himself. "The entire Church appears to have been monastic, and her whole clergy embraced within the fold of the monastic rule."[2] Through the abbots or coarbs, as they were called, who were often presbyters, and sometimes laymen or women, and who, it should be carefully remembered, were the real rulers of the Irish Church, the whole Church was brought under the control of monasticism, leavened by its spirit and moulded to

(margin note: The Celtic Church based on monasticism; the Irish Episcopal Church set up on its ruins.)

---

[1] See Reeves' "Antiquities," &c., p. 161.
[2] Skene's "Celtic Scotland," vol. ii. Bk. ii. p. 42.

its forms. The great predominant feature in the organisation of the ancient Church of Ireland was its monasticism. To want this is to lack the most essential quality of the early Irish organisation, that which dominated and coloured everything, the keystone in the arch of its order, and the most distinctive note of its life. But not only does the Irish Episcopal Church lack this; in the act of creating that Church Henry dissolved the monasteries and abolished monasticism. The Church which overthrew monasticism can hardly be identical in form or order with that which cherished it as its most central, distinctive, and all-controlling institution.

Much which the Celtic Church prized the Church of Elizabeth demolished.

4. Closely akin to that just mentioned was another feature which distinguished early Celtic Christianity. "We know," says Dr. Todd, "that the ancient Irish ecclesiastics of the highest rank did not consider it beneath their dignity to work as artificers in the manufacture of shrines, reliquaries, bells, pastoral staffs, croziers, covers for sacred books, and other ornaments of the Church and its ministers.[1] Brigid's bishop, Condlaed, was a noted artificer of such ornaments. But by the agents of Elizabeth they were completely demolished. · All "monuments of superstition," and in particular "all shrines, and all other monuments of feigned miracles, pilgrimages, and superstition" were denounced and abolished by the 97th Irish canon. The Church which so treated them is not quite the same as that which prized them as her dearest treasures!

5. The last two points referred to suggest another, namely, that *the ideal of religious life* in

[1] "St. Patrick," p. 26.

the Celtic Church is not, I should hope, the ideal Their of our Protestant Episcopal brethren. Any one religious ideals who reads the acknowledged writings of St. Patrick different. cannot but be struck with the evangelical doctrine and spirit which pervade them, and their general freedom from the thaumaturgical and superstitious. Yet from an early date the Irish Church began to be debased and corrupted by these elements. Patrick's converts brought over with them from Paganism numerous Druidical customs and beliefs, many of which survive to this day. One result of this was a most serious relapse to the old Pagan observances—a relapse from which Irish Christianity seems never to have recovered. Thus it came about that the prevailing and popular type of practical Christianity in Ireland was decidedly inferior. As the Druids claimed preternatural powers, and professed to work wonders by means of spells and incantations, similar miraculous feats without number are attributed to the Irish saints by their monkish biographers. I wish I had time to give you a specimen of the miracles ascribed to them, which are not only childish and absurd, but capricious and prodigious, often spiteful and revengeful. There were two other accomplishments which they had reduced to a fine art, but which I can only mention in passing—*cursing* and *equivocation*. Sir Henry Maine, in his "Early History of Institutions," gives ample proof of the low state of morals amongst the Irish. They seem to have been as weak in the ethical line as they were strong in the superstitious and thaumaturgical. Do our Episcopal friends claim to represent the religious and moral ideal of the Celtic Church?

367

I trust not; and I repeat that the two Churches
— the ancient Irish and the Protestant Episcopal—are related to one another, both in organisation and moral ideal, by contrast rather than by
resemblance, and that the differences which distinguish them are broad, radical, and profound.

I must now advance to the second stage of the
inquiry, and invite you to look at the actual links
which are said to connect the modern Episcopal
Church with the Church of St. Patrick, and to
make the former the lineal descendant of the latter.
Several points here invite attention.

The theory
of two
Churches in
the Anglo-
Norman
period un-
tenable.

1. It has been alleged that from 1171 to 1535
two Churches existed in Ireland, one of them the
original Irish Church, to which the old Celtic
population adhered, and the other the Church or
Rome, introduced through the Danish and Norman
invaders; that these two Churches continued separate
till the Reformation, when Henry VIII. threw off
the Papal supremacy, expelled the foreign intrusive
Roman Church, and reinstated the ancient Irish
Church, which is none other than the Protestant
Episcopal Church of our time. The only drawback
to this representation is that it is pure fiction,
contradicted by the most patent facts.   In the
first place, it is not correct to say that from 1171
to 1535 there were two Churches in Ireland. There
were two factions of one Church, divided by racial
and political rather than by ecclesiastical differences.
Professor Richey, who pours deserved ridicule on
this pretension, points out that the Irish were
never reproached during this period for being
schismatics or heretics.   In spite of such enactments as those in the Statute of Kilkenny, special

licences were granted permitting Irishmen to accept
of benefices under the Anglo-Normans. In the
second place, to suppose that the Irish people
outside the Pale, or inside the Pale for that matter,
adhered to the new Anglican Church which it was
sought to force on them, is equally fictitious. It
was accepted only, as we shall see presently, by
the official class, chiefly Anglo-Norman, and even
by them only nominally, for they changed backwards and forwards with the sovereigns and govern-
ments they represented. But, as Mr. Brewer shows,
the immediate result of the dissolution of the
abbeys was to throw the whole spiritual guidance
of the Irish people into the hands of the preaching
Friars, a class of ecclesiastics who professed no
obedience to the bishops, who were at once the
greatest enemies of England and the warmest
friends of the Pope — "barefooted emissaries of
the Pope," Mr. Brewer calls them. By their
influence, and not less by the exactions, confiscations, treacheries, and attainders promoted by the
new Anglican Establishment, the Irish people were
effectually alienated both from it and from the
power that upheld it.[1]

2. But, we are assured again, the bishops and
clergy of the Irish Episcopal Church can trace their
lineal succession through indubitable links back to
St. Patrick, and through him to the Apostles. Now,
the main link by which this connection is held
to be maintained is the Elizabethan Archbishop
Curwin. Curwin was an Englishman, originally one
of Queen Mary's bishops, who had been consecrated

The lineal descent not traceable.

[1] See "The Calendar of State Papers," Carew, vol. ii. p. xxiii.,
vol. iii. p. xiv.

in London in 1555 by the infamous Bonner, Bishop
of London, Thirlby, Bishop of Ely, and Griffin,
Bishop of Rochester, all Englishmen. But among
the consecrators of Bonner was Richard Sampson,
Bishop of Rochester; among the consecrators of
Sampson was John Voysey, Bishop of Exeter, and
among the consecrators of Voysey was Thomas
Halsey, Bishop of Leighlin, an Irish bishop. Thus
when an English bishop, consecrated by English
bishops, and whose predecessors for three generations had been ordained by English bishops, goes
to Ireland as a bishop of the Anglican Church, set
up there by the will of the sovereign, that Church,
composed almost entirely of Englishmen, is transformed into " The Church of Ireland," and the
legitimate daughter and heir of the ancient Irish
Church, by the remote touch of an Irish bishop's
hand upon a predecessor of his in England four
generations back!—an attenuated thread of connection truly! A friend to whom I was mentioning
the point described the amount of Irish virtue thus
percolating as homœopathic! But alas! even that
is not available; for the late Dr. Maziere Brady
has shown that the said Halsey was an Englishman,
that he had been ordained at Rome, and that he
never once visited his Irish diocese, or had the least
connection with the Irish episcopate.[1]

As to that precious link, Curwin himself, it may
be added that he was an unprincipled time-server,
who was able to meet the varying demands of Henry
VIII., Edward VI., Mary, and Elizabeth, and was
branded by Archbishop Loftus as a man guilty of

[1] See Brady's "Irish Reformation," Introduction, xix. ; Harris's
" Ware," i. 460.

"open crimes." But even supposing it proved to demonstration that an Irish bishop had consecrated Curwin, or any other bishop of the Anglican Church set up in Ireland, that would be far from proving lineal descent from Patrick, and from making that Church "The Church of Ireland." For (1) many of the Irish bishops, from the eleventh century on-wards, were consecrated some in England and others in Rome. (2) As Dr. Todd shows, "the Irish bishops had no regular succession," and the attempt to make out a succession at Armagh or elsewhere is absurd. (3) Besides, it would prove too much for the purpose in view. The succession in such a case would be derived *through Roman bishops* in Ireland. If Roman bishops have the true suc-cession, and if Church continuity depends on that succession, then the Church of Rome both has the succession and has the vast majority of the Irish people, and therefore on this theory must be "The Church of Ireland," and the true successor of the ancient Church. But this raises the question— Wherein, according to New Testament teaching, does Church continuity consist? And the discus-sion of that question I must reserve for another occasion—perhaps the beginning of next session.

3. Just one other point remains for considera-tion—What were the *source and model* of the Church set up in Ireland by Henry VIII. and Elizabeth? Was it the early Celtic Church revived and reinstated? or was it simply Anglicanism transferred to Ireland? I have said enough to convince any candid mind that it was not the former—that the new establishment created by the Tudors differed widely and profoundly from the

The model of the Church set up by the Tudors not the Celtic Church but the Angli-can.

Celtic Church of Ireland. On what pattern, then, was it fashioned? We have not to travel far to discover. What the central and steady aim of the Tudor policy, both civil and ecclesiastical, in relation to this country was is too notorious to require demonstration. Even the most superficial student of the history of the period knows—*it was to Anglicise Ireland:* to extirpate and proscribe everything Irish, and to impose the laws, customs, and institutions of England upon Ireland. It was no new policy on their part, but the continuation of the old policy begun on the conquest of Ireland by the Normans under Henry II. in 1172. The object of the Anglo-Norman rulers was to bring Ireland under the control of English ideas and laws, and so displace the old Irish laws and customs; and the aim of assimilating Ireland to England extended to ecclesiastical as well as to civil and social affairs. By the Synod of Cashel (1172), at which a Papal legate presided, it was decreed, at the instance of the king, that "the Divine offices shall henceforth be celebrated in every part of Ireland *according to the laws and usages of the Church of England.*" For, remember, the policy of " Anglicising " Ireland was carried on with the warm approval and express sanction of Rome and the Irish Roman Catholic hierarchy. But it was a complete failure. Even the Anglo-Norman settlers became more Irish than the Irish themselves. Then came the famous Statute of Kilkenny (the first of a long series on the same lines), which outlawed the Irish, described and treated them as " enemies not in the King's peace," deprived them of all legal rights, so that it was held to be "no more sin to kill an Irishman than to kill a dog or any other brute animal;" prohibited all marriage, gossipred, fostering of children, and commerce of every sort with the Irish, and required the Irish living amongst the English to dress and shave like the latter, and to assume English names and usages. The chief supporters of this statute were the Roman Catholic hierarchy, who in the Act itself pledged themselves to excommunicate its violators.

Now the Anglicising policy of Henry II. and his successors was continued and extended by Henry VIII. The Parliament of 1536 repeated the worst provisions of the Statute of Kilkenny, and extended them to the whole country. Irish laws and customs were to be displaced by English law, English land tenure, the English language, English dress, and English modes of life.[1] "Indifferent to the condition, the wants, and the wishes of the broad mass of the population," says Mr. Brewer, "the Tudor sovereigns merely sought how to force the Irish into compliance with English manners, English habits, dress, and customs, and when the task proved impossible, nothing remained except to retreat or to ride rough-shod over all obstacles to good government and improvement.[2] The weight of the law was brought to bear against forelocks and moustaches; it regulated the size of noblemen's and gentlemen's shirts, and took under its protection hats, caps, French hoods and tippets. Saffron cloth and embroidery were little better than constructive treason." No maid or single woman was permitted "to wear or put any great roll or kercher of linen cloth upon

[1] See Act of 28 Henry VIII., c. 15, as given by Richey, p. 39.
[2] Carew, "Calendar of State Papers,"1575-1588, p. 27.

their heads, neither any great smock with great sleeves, but to put on hats, caps, French hoods, tippets, and the like."[1]

This included the "Anglicising" of the Church there.

But one of the main items in the "Anglicising" process, as Mr. Brewer also points out, was the setting up of the Anglican Church in Ireland. The preamble of the Act establishing ,it shows that the primary object was to assimilate the Church in Ireland to that of England. "Peace, religion, loyalty, or civility could not exist in Ireland[2] until the whole religious and social state of the country had been completely changed from the Celtic to the English mode." The revival or continuation of the Primitive Celtic Church was the very last thing intended by the sovereigns and their agents. They had as much idea of reviving the Celtic Church as they had of setting up Mahommedanism! Their aim was to extirpate and abolish everything Celtic. The Irish language itself was proscribed. Instead of the Bible being translated into Irish, or pains being taken to address the people in their own tongue, its use was forbidden, and only such as could speak English appointed to livings. This was much the same as to enact that only Englishmen were eligible. "The Anglicising system," says Richey (p. 389), "was extended to Church preferments, and an attempt made to substitute an English for the native priest-

Henry VIII. hood. By the 28th of Henry VIII., c. 15, sect. 7, it was enacted that all persons possessing Church patronage should appoint to such persons as can speak English, and to no other person or persons, unless there be no person or persons who can speak

---

[1] "Calendar of State Papers," as before.
[2] Richey, "Short History," p. 319.

English that will accept and take the same." And the English clergy instituted were, as a rule, the most worthless of their class. "Those of the clergy of England who could be induced to take livings in Ireland were neither the best nor the most eligible for the task," says Richey. Henry's chief agent, Archbishop Browne, Richey describes as "a mere official tool, whose writings, conduct, and actions were admirably adapted to discredit the principles and mar the success of the Reformation in Ireland." He accompanied the judges on circuit, and made it his chief business to publish the king's injunctions and the king's supremacy. As Mr. Brewer remarks, the Gospel offered to the Irish appeared to them " garbed in the guise of the executioner, armed with manacles and instruments of torture."[1] "Could a country be evangelised," asks Richey (p. 383), "by a process which equally resembled a gaol delivery and an episcopal visitation?" After a detailed review of the ecclesiastical action of Henry VIII. and his representatives, the latter concludes: "Thus the Protestant Episcopal Church was planted in Ireland, not by any Irish party, nor for the benefit of any Irish party, nor with reference to Irish interests, but as a portion of the policy of England, and as part of the great scheme of Anglicising this country."[2]

After Henry VIII. had been "gathered to his wives," the same policy was continued under Edward VI. The English Prayer-Book was introduced by an order of the king. "This measure" Richey describes as " part of the established policy of assimilating Ireland to England, without the slightest

Edward VI

[1] Carew, "Calendar of State Papers," 1575–1588, p. 25.
[2] "Short History," p. 386.

reference to the feelings or wants of the people."
The Deputy called together the Irish bishops, "not
for the purpose of taking their opinions, but simply
to receive his Majesty's orders."[1] "The Government
willed that Ireland should be reformed according to
the English pattern. This change was not to be
effected by persuading or winning over the masses;
it was to be accomplished by the appointment of
English Protestant bishops, and the promulgation of
English formulæ. No argument was addressed to
the people save the simple declaration, 'The king
so wills it.'"

Elizabeth.   The process of "Anglicising" Ireland was "acce-
lerated and completed" under Elizabeth. "Ireland
was to be a second England . . . in which the
sovereign's will or caprice was supreme, in which
every subject, with slavish adulation upon his lips,
altered his creed, political and religious, with the
opinions of the ruler."[2] The Earl of Sussex, the
Viceroy, was ordered to "set up the worship of God
as it is in England, and to make such statutes next
Parliament as were lately made in England, *mutatis
mutandis*." Sussex had acted as the agent of Queen
Mary in restoring Roman Catholicism, but he was
now equally ready to carry out the will of Elizabeth.
He might have said with another official of that
age, *Ortus sum ex salice, non ex quercu*—"I am sprung
not from the oak, but from the willow!" Now,
as before, the Government "aimed rather at the
introduction of English forms than the establishment of an Irish Protestant Church."[3] Only such
as could speak the English tongue (which virtually

[1] "Short History," p. 400.   [2] Richey, p. 492.
[3] Richey, p. 497.

meant only Englishmen) were eligible to livings.
It was enacted that none could act as masters
in the diocesan schools but Englishmen or men
of English birth. "The Government which passed
this statute," says Richey, "desired to establish
not a Protestant, but an English Church—not to
convert the people from Romanism, but from
Irishism" (p. 499). Yet the Church whose origin
and history are such is alone exclusively entitled to
the designation "The Irish Church"! The clergy
appointed appear, as a rule, to have been, if possible,
even more worthless than those of Henry VIII.
Their chief aim seems to have been to seize the
revenues of the Church and appropriate them
permanently to their own use and that of their
families. The poet Spenser describes the bishops
in remote parts as "not bestowing the benefices
which are in their own donation upon any, but
keeping them in their own hands, and letting their
own servants and potboys take up the tithes and
fruits of them." "Whatever disorders you see in
the Church of England, you may find there (in
Ireland) and many more," says Spenser—"namely,
gross simony, greedy covetousness, fleshly incon-
tinency, careless sloth, and generally all disordered
life in the common clergyman."[1]

Later still, the Thirty-nine Articles were, at the Charles I.
instance of Charles I., Wentworth, Laud, and
Bramhall, accepted in 1634 "for the manifestation
of agreement with the Church of England in the
confession of the same Christian faith and the
doctrine of the sacraments." Ussher and others
demurred and opposed, but in vain. Wentworth

[1] "State of Ireland," p. 529.

"would not endure that the Articles of the Church of England should be disputed." "Some hot spirits, sons of thunder," moved to petition the Deputy "for a free synod; but, in fine, they could not agree among themselves who should put the bell about the cat's neck!" So Wentworth had his way.

Charles II.   Froude states that in the time of Charles II. "there were not a hundred episcopally ordained clergy in Ireland," and Richey affirms that "but for the Plantation the Established Church would have gradually died out." "The Anglicanism which in England had a meaning," says Froude, "in Ireland was never more than an exotic; and until the newcomers in the North of Ireland had introduced another spirit, the Church of Ireland had existed only to give point to the sarcasm of the Catholics."

The Anglican Church in Ireland never the Church of the *Irish* people.   The Anglican Church in Ireland, in short, was never in any real sense the Church of the *Irish* people, never in any true sense *national*. "National religion, as I understand it," said the late Lord Selborne, then Sir Roundell Palmer, in the Irish Church debate in Parliament on March 22, 1869, "is not the profession of forms and ceremonies made by those at the head of the Government, but *it is the religion of the people*, who constitute the Church." On this principle the Anglican Church in Ireland was never in any true sense the "National" Church of the country. The Irish people as a body were, and still are, outside of it. As Richey shows, its doctrine was not "preached by missionaries, or supported by any popular movement; it was introduced into the country officially by Acts of Parliament and bishops acting

378

under royal authority."[1] So far as the mass of the population was concerned, the statutory measures were a dead letter. In the words of Richey, "they were Acts of Parliament sitting in Dublin, and had no more result than numerous other Acts of similar Parliaments relative to secular affairs" (p. 361). So far as membership was concerned, the new Church extended very little beyond the Government officials, and was very far from including even the whole of these. "The great majority of offices continued to be filled by Roman Catholics; for had it not been so, they had remained empty."[2]

Thus the Anglican Church in Ireland was wanting in the essential element of a National Church— namely, the people. It consisted of a staff of officers who had no regiments to follow them, a set of shepherds without flocks, who, however, enriched themselves by fleecing the alien flocks of "the Irish enemy." And, as it was not the Church of the Irish people, it never showed the slightest sympathy with their condition as a people. On the contrary, it was one of the most active agents in crushing and oppressing them with the terrible penal laws. As Privy Councillors and Lord Justices, and also as members of the House of Lords, the bishops took a most active and influential part in riveting the galling chains of those penal statutes on the limbs of the Irish, and to the last resisted every attempt to relax them.

Such is the history of the Church that claims to be alone deserving of the title "The Church of Ireland!" I suppose that never since history began has a claim been set up and a title assumed with

[1] "Short History," p. 360.   [2] Richey, p. 362.

so little warrant, or a fiction foisted on the world as history with so infinitesimal a nucleus of fact. The case sought to be made for it is at every stage in the history contradicted, discredited, and made ridiculous by the real facts. If there be one title more absurdly inappropriate than another from every point of view it is the one in question. When you want to flout or ridicule a person, you fasten on him some designation which conveys the reverse of what he is. To apply the title "The Church of Ireland" to the institution set up by the Tudor sovereigns seems to any one who knows its history like a cruel attempt at irony or satire. It recalls a past which its best friends should desire to have forgotten.

The Church in question will act more wisely to take its stand upon its modern rather than upon its ancient history. Its career in recent times is at least respectable. Its ministers and people have been doing good work, which gives them an honourable place among the denominations of the country. Let them be content with that. Let them give up the childish attempt to grasp at superiority and exclusiveness, and at a title that denotes them. It is certain that in no sense that consists with truth or reality can the institution whose creation and early career I have been tracing be called the Church either of St. Patrick or of Ireland. Not St. Patrick, but a "saint" of a very different pattern, namely, Henry VIII., is its true parent and founder, and if it wants a name that will record its real origin and history, that name is "The Anglican Church in Ireland."

In a single sentence let me say in closing, that

in no modern Church have we an exact transcript of the organisation of the old Celtic Church. It was ruled by abbots, and governed by them neither as bishops nor as presbyters, for in some cases they were neither the one nor the other, but only laymen, and, as I have said, women. But according to the New Testament, external organisation is not of the essence of what constitutes the Church. The Church is the body of Christ. This it is that continues from age to age; and the body of Christ is the whole community of believers, by whatever name they are called. Every Christian Irishman who has the same Lord and the same faith as St. Patrick, the same baptism, the same God and Father, who is above all, and through all, and in all; who is animated by the same Spirit of life and . love, and sustained by the same immortal hope, is a member of the one body of Christ, which continues through all the ages, and belongs, therefore, to the same Church as the great apostle of Ireland.

No modern Church reproduces exactly the Celtic Church.

CHAPTER XVIII

"APOSTOLICAL SUCCESSION"

In the public lecture which it fell to me to give at the close of last session, I discussed from a historical point of view the claim of the Protestant Episcopal Church of this country to be the lineal successor and only modern representative of the ancient Celtic Church of Ireland, and to be alone entitled to the designation " The Church of Ireland."

Is "Apostolical succession" the true bond of Church continuity? In that lecture I promised to discuss now, at the opening of this session, the theory of Church continuity which underlies the claim in question. Now the bond by which, according to this view, Church continuity is maintained is that with which we are familiar under the name of "Apostolical or episcopal succession." As defined by the leading exponents of this doctrine, the Church is a visible corporate unity which continues through all the ages, and the continuity of this one visible body depends on an unbroken episcopal succession coming down from the apostles to the prelates of our own time. The Holy Spirit and the grace which He imparts, including fellowship with God and with the life of God, are transmitted only through this succession, and through ministers episcopally ordained, who constitute thus a special and privileged priest-

382

hood.[1]   Of "Apostolical succession," thus defined, Canon Gore affirms that it is "a permanent and essential element of Christianity," and Palmer that it is "a note of the true Church," and that "no community which is without it can be a Church of Christ." If this theory is sound, the larger half of Protestant Christendom is unchurched by it, and cut off from fellowship in the grace of the Spirit, the life of the Son, and the love of the Father, which the Church can enjoy only through the medium of this succession.

In the brief time at my command to-day an exhaustive treatment of this subject in all its bearings is impossible.   I can only glance rapidly at some of its more important aspects and assumptions. But before proceeding to do so, two remarks of a general and preliminary kind suggest themselves.

1. The theory is incapable of proof.   It requires that we should be able to trace the succession link by link from the prelates of our own time up to the Apostles.   Ignorance respecting a single link would be fatal to that certainty about the true Church which the succession is supposed to give.   Yet no competent and candid historian would affirm that every link is traceable by sound historical evidence to Apostolic times.   The earliest successors of the Apostles at Rome and elsewhere were, as we shall see by-and-by, presbyter-bishops.   Then, who would undertake to trace the successions, and to prove that there is no flaw in them, through the wild ecclesiastical disorders of the tenth century, including the time of "the Papal Pornocracy," when

Incapable of proof.

---

[1] See Palmer on "The Church of Christ," Part i. c. viii., sec. 5 ; Haddon's "Apostolical Succession," c. i. ; Carter's "Doctrine of Priesthood," c. v. p. 31 ; Gore's "Ministry of the Christian Church," c. ii. pp. 70, 94, 120.

for a long series of years three women "of highest
rank and lowest character" filled the Papal chair
with their paramours and bastards, and when in-
trigue, lawlessness, rapine, lust, and murder everywhere ran riot both in Church and State? Precious
links in the chain of succession truly! Singular
channels for the conveyance of the Holy Spirit
and His grace, even if we were sure that there
was no flaw in their consecration! But who can
guarantee that their ordination in every case was
regular? And, remember, a single break in the
chain would vitiate the whole succession. What
folly to rest the very existence of the Church on
an external act which, human nature being what
it is, might easily fail to be performed! The late
Cardinal Newman gave up the task of tracing the
succession as hopeless, and found the warrant of the
true succession in the present living authoritative
voice of the Church. When Canon Gore admits
the weakness and inadequacy of the "antiquarian"
or "genealogical" proof, but relies upon a special
Providence to preserve the succession, Newman has
answered him by anticipation. "If it is presum-
able," says Newman, "that a special Providence
precludes such flaws or compensates for them, they
(the Anglicans) cannot take the benefit of that presumption to themselves; for to do so would be
claiming to belong to the true Church to which
the high Providence is promised, and this they
cannot do without arguing in a circle, first proving
that they are in the true Church because they have
valid orders, and then that their orders are valid
because they are in the true Church."[1]

[1] "Essays Critical and Historical," vol. ii. p. 89.

2. The so - called "Episcopal succession" fails Fails to to secure the very object for which the theory has secure visible been framed. Its advocates are for ever insisting corporate on the *visible corporate unity* of the Church, of unity. which prelatical succession is the bond. Has it, however, secured such unity? Three different com- munions claim to possess the Episcopal succession —the Roman, the Greek, and the Anglican. But these do not constitute one Church, or even three " branches " of one Church having visible corporate union and communion ; they are three Churches com- pletely severed from one another, not only not in com- munion with one another, but refusing, most of them, to recognise the others as true Churches at all. The " visible corporate unity " and continuity are con- spicuous by their absence. Now, if there is but one visible corporate body, separation from it under any circumstances is of course quite unlawful ; separation from it is schism.

But we have deeper and more serious objections to this doctrine. If, as Canon Gore affirms, Epis- copal succession is "a permanent and essential ele- ment of Christianity," we may expect to have it clearly and emphatically inculcated by the authori- tative exponents of Christian truth. But not only is there not a solitary word or line from our Lord or His Apostles that lends countenance to this theory : I must now proceed to show you that it goes right in the teeth of the most vital and fundamental teaching of the New Testament, and that the clear testimony of early Christian history equally condemns it.

1. No one can read the New Testament without perceiving that Christianity is pre-eminently a

SUPPLEMENTARY [PART V

This theory reverses the New Testament principle, which sets supreme value on the spiritual and moral, secondary value on forms. spiritual religion, a " ministration of the Spirit," [1] and that Christian ministers are " ministers of the new covenant, not of the letter which killeth, but of the Spirit which giveth life." It sets supreme value on the spiritual and the moral, and reduces external forms to a minimum. If there is one thing which Scripture affirms more plainly than another, it is the sovereign, free agency of the Divine Spirit, who " divideth to every man severally as He will," [2] and of whom it is written, " Where the Spirit of the Lord is, there is liberty." [3] " As many as received Him, to them gave He power to become the sons of God, even to them that believe on His name; which were born, not of blood, nor of the will of the flesh, nor of the will of man, but of God." [4] For as " the wind bloweth where it listeth, and thou hearest the sound thereof, but canst not tell whence it cometh, and whither it goeth; so is every one that is born of the Spirit." [5] We shall see in a moment that the Holy Spirit was given to the Church as a whole, and is promised to " them that ask Him," irrespective of any connection on their part with a prelate. To affirm that the grace of the Spirit and all the blessings of salvation can reach the Church and its individual members only through the manual touch of a prelatical bishop, or rather only through an unbroken series of such touches reaching back to the Apostles, is to set a value on the external and the arbitrary which the New Testament sets only on spiritual and moral action; it is to put the Church and all its members at the mercy of

[1] 2 Cor. iii. 8. [2] 1 Cor. xii. 11. [3] 2 Cor. iii. 17.
[4] John i. 12, 13. [5] John iii. 8.

386

a few weak and erring men, and to seek to enslave the infinite, sovereign, free Spirit of the
living God to the will of ecclesiastics, who are
frail at the best, often capricious, and sometimes
have been even wicked and depraved.

2. This doctrine contradicts the New Testament
idea of the *Church.* "No bishop, no Church."
How contrary this is to the teaching of the New
Testament, wherein the office-bearers, as such, are
distinguished from the Church or Christian community, and the Christian community apart from
the officers is designated the Church.[1] "Where two
or three are gathered together in My name, there
am I in the midst of them," says Christ.[2] Their
being gathered together in the name of Christ, not
their being gathered around a prelatical bishop, is
what secures Christ's presence and constitutes them
a part of His Church. "I am the door [the door,
i.e. of the sheepfold, which is another name for
the Church]; by Me if any man enter in [not if
any man enter through the bishop], he shall be
saved, and shall go in and out, and find pasture."[3] Who are described by Paul as being "no
more strangers and foreigners, but fellow-citizens
with the saints, and of the household of God"?
Those who connect themselves with an Episcopal
community? Nay; but those who "in Christ Jesus
are made nigh by the blood of Christ, and through
Him have access by one Spirit into the Father."[4]
The doctrine of Episcopal succession perverts the
Scriptural idea of the Church.

3. What is worse, it perverts the *terms of salva-*

*It contra-
dicts the
New Testa-
ment idea of
the Church.*

---

[1] See Acts xx. 28; 1 Cor. xii. 28; 1 Tim. iii. 15.
[2] Matt. xviii. 20.   [3] John x. 9.   [4] Ephes. ii. 12-22.

387

It perverts *tion,* and adds a new condition of which there is
the terms of
salvation. no hint in the Bible. All through the New Testament salvation is made to turn on faith in Christ
and union with Christ by faith. "If any man be
in Christ, he is a new creature." "There is, therefore, now no condemnation to them that are in
Christ Jesus." "Come unto Me, all ye that labour
and are heavy laden, and I will give you rest."
"Believe on the Lord Jesus Christ, and thou shalt
be saved." "Whosoever shall call on the name of
the Lord shall be saved." The refrain of the High
Churchman, on the other hand, is—" No salvation
without subjection to the bishop." "As well might
one out of the ark of Noah have escaped the flood
as one out of the Church [*i.e.* the Episcopal fold] be
saved, because she alone is the bearer of the Holy
Spirit and of all grace. *Extra ecclesiam nulla salus.*"
Such is the teaching of Cyprian in his *De Unitate
Ecclesiæ,* the Magna Charta of High Churchmen.
Voluntary separation from the Episcopal Church
Palmer describes as "a sin which, unless repented
of, is eternally destructive of the soul." And this,
too, is substantially the teaching of Canon Gore
in the work referred to. Where Scripture puts
Christ, the High Churchman puts the Church, the
Episcopal organisation. He thrusts the bishop, the
priest, between the sinner and his Saviour. What
an audacious perversion of New Testament teaching! It is not Christianity, but, as it has been
well called, *Churchianity,* and the great apostle of
it is not Peter or Paul, but Cyprian.

4. The idea of *the ministry* which this theory
involves is equally at variance with Scripture.

(1.) It represents the Christian ministry as a

sacerdotal caste, through whom alone the gifts of
Divine grace are transmitted.   Now in the New
Testament there is no trace of, and no room left
for, a sacerdotal caste.   The word "priest" (*hiereus*)
is never applied in it to Christian ministers.   They
are called "elders," "bishops," "pastors," "ambas-
sadors," "stewards," but never "priests."   They
are to teach, preach, watch, tend, rule; but they
are nowhere invested with exclusive "guardianship
of the grace by which Christians live" (Gore).   The
spirit of all grace is given not to officials merely,
but to the whole Church.   The passage in John xx.
21, 23—"As my Father hath sent Me, even so send
I you.   And when He had said this, He breathed
on them, and saith unto them, Receive ye the Holy
Ghost: Whose soever sins ye forgive, they are for-
given," &c.,—is often cited in support of the claim
in question.   It is certain, however, that others
besides the Apostles were present on the occasion,
for in Luke's account of the incident we hear not
only of "the eleven," but of "them that were
with them."   "The commission must be regarded
as the commission of the Christian society," says
Bishop Westcott, "and not as that of the Christian
ministry."[1]   "It must be noticed," says Plummer,
in his Commentary in the Cambridge Bible for
Schools and Colleges, "that it (the gift of the
Holy Ghost) is given to the whole company present,
not to the Apostles alone. . . . The commission in
the first instance is to the Christian community as
a whole, not to the ministry alone."   So also Alford,
Lightfoot, Plumptre, Maclear, and, indeed, exegetes
generally.   We thus see on what solid Scriptural

[1] See his "Commentary on the Gospel of John," p. 295.

ground the Reformers based their teaching that all Church power resides in the last resort in the Christian community as a whole, and not in the episcopate. Even Hooker grants this, that "the whole Church visible is the true original subject of all power."[1] Were it otherwise, did the Church depend upon the episcopate, and were the episcopate to become, as it has often been, heretical and corrupt, the chief Shepherd would be leaving His sheep in the power of persons described by the Apostle as "wolves." He has not done so; nor has He anywhere invested the Christian ministry with an exclusive priesthood, or informed them that to offer propitiatory sacrifice is one of their prerogatives. The great propitiatory sacrifice has been offered "once for all," and does not need to be repeated.[2] Hooker also admits that the offering of sacrifice is "no part of the Church ministry."[3] "The word presbyter," he says, "doth seem more fit, and in propriety of speech more agreeable than priest with the drift of the whole gospel of Jesus Christ."[4] I may add that in the sub-apostolic literature there is just as little trace of a sacerdotal ministry as in the New Testament. It is only, as Lightfoot well shows, "towards the close of the second century we discern the first germs appearing above the surface." "But," he adds, "as Cyprian crowned the edifice of Episcopal power, so also was he the first to put forward, without relief or disguise, these sacerdotal assumptions." And the rise and rapid growth of sacerdotalism Lightfoot traces to heathen influences, and to "the increasing mass of heathen con-

[1] "Eccles. Pol.," vii. 14.   [2] Heb. ix. 28 ; x. 12-14.
[3] "Eccles. Pol.," v. 73.   [4] Ibid., v. 73.

verts who were incapable of shaking off their sacerdotal prejudices and appreciating the free spirit of
the Gospel."[1] It was only two years after his conversion from heathenism that Cyprian became a bishop.

Now the great English Reformers who founded the Sacerdotal-
Church of England repudiated sacerdotalism. The ism repudi-
ated by the
conception of Christianity as a sacramental and sac- English
rificial system, and of the ministry as a sacerdotal Reformers
also.
caste, they emphatically rejected. In the "Institu-
tion of a Christian Man," drawn up and signed by
Archbishop Cranmer, the Archbishop of York, eleven
bishops, twenty-three doctors of theology and professors of canon law, and approved by the king and both
houses of Parliament, this order was issued: "As
touching the sacrament of holy orders, we will that
all bishops and preachers shall instruct and teach our
people . . . that in the New Testament there is no
mention of other degrees but of deacons or ministers,
and of presbyters or bishops," and that "power and
authority of any one bishop over another were and
be given them by the consent, ordinances, and positive laws of men only, and not by any ordinance of
God in Holy Scripture."[2] With good reason, then,
the Pope's Bull, issued the other day, directs attention to the view entertained of the Christian ministry
by the English Reformers, and to the action taken by
them in the new ordinal which they framed. The
question which the Pope had to determine was, Does The Pope's
the Anglican Church possess true sacerdotal orders? recent Bull
based on
He answers by an exceedingly emphatic "No," and this repudia-
one reason he assigns is that "whatever set forth the tion.

[1] Dissertation on "The Christian Ministry" in "Commentary
on Philippians," pp. 244-269.
[2] See Burnet's "History of Reformation," vol. i., Appendix.

dignity and office of the priesthood in the Catholic rite was deliberately removed from the Edwardine ordinal at the Reformation." " In the whole ordinal," he says, " not only is there no clear mention of the sacrifice, of consecration, of the *sacerdotium*, and of the power of consecrating and offering sacrifices, but every trace of these things which were in the Catholic rite was deliberately removed and struck out," and the rite of episcopal consecration was also " stripped of the words which denote the *summum sacerdotium*." The addition in 1662—a century later—of the words " for the office and work of a priest," only shows " that the Anglicans themselves perceived that the first form was defective and inadequate." But even if this latter form had been sufficient, which, according to the Pope, it was not, he points out that it came too late, for during the previous century the hierarchy had become extinct. The Pope's Bull, therefore, " pronounced and declared that ordinations carried out according to the Anglican rite have been and are absolutely null and utterly void." In fact, as Cardinal Vaughan reminds them, "neither Jansenist, Russian, Greek, nor any of the Eastern sects who possess valid orders, had ever been able or willing to recognise the validity of Anglican orders." It is highly edifying in these circumstances to hear the soft-hearted Cardinal express his deep concern and profound sympathy with those who thus stand " shivering in their insular isolation, disowned within their own communion, as well as by the immense majority of the English people "! How cruel is the irony of history! Here are those who have been wholesale unchurching others themselves severed from the Catholic corporate unity, and left shivering

in the cold, in the position of miserable schismatics!
No wonder Dr. Parker recently congratulated himself
and his hearers on this immense accession to the
ranks of the "dissenters" in England.

(2.) But this doctrine is equally at variance with
New Testament teaching with respect to *Church
organisation.* The place held by the Apostles as
founders of the Church was in many respects unique.
(*a*) They had their commission immediately from
Christ. (*b*) It was essential that they should have
seen Christ after He had risen from the dead, to
enable them to bear witness of His resurrection.
(*c*) The gift of working miracles was also possessed
by them; (*d*) and as Lightfoot indicates, their commission was chiefly missionary in its import. "The
opinion," says that great scholar, "that the officers of
the Church who were first called apostles came afterwards to be designated bishops is baseless. If the two
offices had been identical, the substitution of the one
name for the other would have required some explanation. But, in fact, the functions of the apostle
and the bishop differed widely. The apostle, like the
prophet or the evangelist, held no local office. He
was essentially, as the name denotes, a missionary
moving about from place to place, founding and confirming new brotherhoods. . . . *It is not, therefore, to
the apostle that we must look for the prototype of the
bishop.*"[1] It is obvious that in most of their essential characteristics the Apostles had no successors;
but in so far as they had successors in the work of
administering and governing the Church, those successors were presbyter-bishops. In this connection

This theory
at variance
with New
Testament
teaching on
Church or-
ganisation.

[1] Lightfoot's dissertation on "The Christian Ministry" in his
"Commentary on Philippians," pp. 195, 196.

they take the position of elders, and so designate
themselves. "The elders which are among you I
exhort, who am also an elder."[1] John also calls
himself an elder.[2] Accordingly, in matters of Church
government, as at the Council of Jerusalem, the
Apostles associate the elders with themselves, and
co-operate with them.[3] Hence, before the Apostles
had passed away, the power of governing the Church,
including ordination, had been given to presbyters,
and descended from them to other presbyters. For
observe that the presbyters are not only called
bishops, but exercise the so-called episcopal functions of ordaining and ruling. Peter exhorts the
elders to "feed the flock of God, taking the episcopate thereof."[4] Timothy is ordained by "the laying
on of the hands of the presbytery"[5] as Paul and
Barnabas are ordained to their missionary work by
the laying on of the hands of the "prophets and
teachers" at Antioch.[6] The only local office-bearers
regarding whose appointment directions are given in
the pastoral epistles, wherein the Apostle is making
provision for the future government of the Church,
are presbyter-bishops and deacons. No directions
whatever are given with regard to prelatical bishops,
no provision is made for their appointment or continuance, nor is there any trace of them in the
literature of the first century. Timothy and Titus
were of course not local office-bearers at all. As
Lightfoot says, "It is the conception of a later age
which represents Timothy as bishop of Ephesus and
Titus as bishop of Crete. St. Paul's own language

[1] 1 Peter v. 1.   [2] 2 John i.; 3 John i.
[3] Acts x. 44, 47; Acts xv. 6, 22; Acts xxi. 18, 19.
[4] 1 Peter v. 1, 2.   [5] 1 Tim. iv. 14.   [6] Acts xiii. 1-3.

implies that the position which they held was only temporary." As Hooker puts it, "Timothy and Titus were presbyters of principal sufficiency, whom the Apostles sent abroad and used as agents in ecclesiastical affairs wheresoever they saw need."

If we pass for a moment from the New Testament into the literature of the sub-apostolic period, we find all this abundantly confirmed. Scholars generally agree with Lightfoot when he says: "*The Episcopate was formed not out of the apostolic order by localisation, but out of the Presbyteral by elevation,* and the title which was originally common to all came at length to be appropriated by the chief among them."[1] What a demolition, what a collapse the "Apostolical succession" theory suffers from this one unquestionable fact, stated and proved by Lightfoot, that the episcopate was a development out of the presbyterate! Its significance in this connection has not been sufficiently accentuated. That the fact was so is put beyond peradventure by the evidence. We have this to begin with, that all through the New Testament period "bishop" and "presbyter" were names for the same officer, and used interchangeably. Then, from the Epistle of Clement and from other sources, we know there was no bishop in the later sense at Rome at the end of the first century, but only presbyter-bishops and deacons. Bishop Lightfoot admits that Linus, Anacletus, and Clement were nothing more than presbyter-bishops. Lipsius, who has made the list of Roman bishops a matter of special study, concludes, after a careful and critical examination of the evidence, that Linus, Anacletus, and Clement

The Episcopate a development from the Presbyterate.

[1] Lightfoot's "Philippians," p. 196.

395

before the close of the first century, and Evaristus
and Alexander in the early part of the second
century, were presbyter-bishops in the Roman
Church, and that it was only after A.D. 139 that
monarchical episcopacy appeared there. Langen,
an Old Catholic, carries the line of presbyter-bishops
at Rome down to Alexander (A.D. 109–119). Such
also was the state of things at Corinth, as Clement's
Epistle puts beyond doubt, at the end of the first
century. Similarly, the *Didache* knows only of the
two orders of local officials in the region to which
it belongs. Polycarp's Epistle proves that there
were only the same two orders at Philippi, that
monarchical episcopacy was non-existent, and that
Polycarp saw no need for it at Philippi; and the
researches of Professor Ramsay in Asia Minor dis-
close a similar state of things there so late as at
the middle of the second century. Even in the
time of Irenæus and Clement of Alexandria, towards the end of the second century, the transition
to monarchical episcopacy is still in progress. As
Lightfoot says, though Irenæus "views the episcopate as a distinct office from the presbytery, he does
not regard it as a distinct order." He constantly
speaks of the succession from the Apostles as "a
succession of presbyters." As the same scholar
points out, "the same estimate of the office appears
in Clement of Alexandria. The functions of the
bishop and presbyter are thus regarded as substantially the same in kind, though different in
degree, while the functions of the diaconate are
different from both."[1] To other facts equally important and significant the scholarly Bishop directs

[1] Lightfoot's "Philippians," pp. 226, 282.

attention. "At Alexandria," he says, "the bishop was nominated and apparently ordained by the twelve presbyters out of their own number." Jerome states that "from the days of St. Mark the Evangelist down to the episcopate of Heraclas and Dionysius, the presbyters at Alexandria used always to appoint as bishop one chosen out of their number and placed in the higher grade."[1] Hilary and Eutychius take this appointment as including ordination. Hilary elsewhere affirms that "there is one ordination for the bishop and the presbyter," the bishop being simply *qui inter presbyteros primus est*. Jerome, the greatest scholar in Latin Christendom, positively affirms that "among the ancients presbyters and bishops were the same; but little by little, that all seeds of dissension might be plucked up, the whole care was devolved on one. As, therefore, the presbyters know that by the custom of the Church they are subject to him who is their president, so let bishops know that they are above presbyters more by the custom of the Church than by any actual ordinance of the Lord."[2] All these facts, and others of a like kind, put it beyond reasonable doubt that the monarchical episcopate was a development out of the presbyterate. If this was so—and scholars generally accept of it—then the first links in the chain of succession after the Apostles were *presbyters*, and thus the theory of an "unbroken episcopal succession" breaks down at the very outset.

Unable to resist the force of these facts, Canon Gore candidly succumbs to them. "No one, of whatever part of the Church," he says, "can main-

[1] Ep. 146 ad Evang. [2] Jerome on Titus, 1-5.

397

Canon Gore admits the true episcopacy of presbyter-bishops. tain that the existence of what may be called, for lack of a distinctive term, *mon-Episcopacy*, is essential to the continuity of the Church" (p. 73). Referring to "the view (which is undoubtedly supported by the Epistle of Polycarp, taken alone) that the Churches in the West were governed simply by a council of presbyters, who had no superiors over them, and who therefore must be supposed to have handed on their own ministry," Canon Gore says that "there is no objection on the ground of principle to this conclusion, viewed in the light of the Apostolical succession, as has been sufficiently explained already. These presbyter-bishops legitimately 'ordained' and fulfilled episcopal functions because those functions belonged to the equal commission they had all received. Subsequently, at later ordinations, this full commission was confined to one of their number, and the rest received the reduced authority which belonged to the presbyterate of later Church history" (p. 324). Referring again to Jerome's testimony that one of the presbyters at Alexandria succeeded to the episcopate by the appointment of his fellow-presbyters, Canon Gore explains that "this would only mean that the Alexandrian presbyters were by the terms of their ordination bishops *in posse*" (p. 339).

And thus surrenders his central position. Thus by the irresistible force of stern facts Canon Gore is driven to surrender the very centre and citadel of the position which his book was written to defend. His argument in behalf of "Episcopal succession" comes to grief and utterly collapses the moment it comes into close quarters with the evidence. If all through the first century and far into the second presbyterial ordination was suffi-

398

cient, it cannot be inadequate now, nor can prelatical ordination rise higher than its source in
presbyterial ordination.

5. The idea of *Church continuity* which this
theory assumes is not the Scriptural idea. Far be
it from me to deny continuity in the Church; on
the contrary, I affirm it; only I maintain with
Scripture that it depends on the persistence not of
external accidental matters, but of things spiritual
and essential. The idea of continuity has taken
large possession of modern thought. It has been
called "the law of laws," the law by which other
laws act. We see it in the principle of the con-
servation of energy, according to which the amount
of energy in the universe is constant, although its
form may vary; in the law of gravitation, by which
matter is affected wherever it exists; and in the
law of biogenesis, the law of life from pre-existent
life, and the law by which the plant or animal
preserves its type. It operates in the still higher
domain of character, which persists through the lifetime of the individual, and raises (as the authors
of the "Unseen Universe" maintain) a strong presumption in favour of its continuation beyond the
grave, while it is bequeathed to future generations.
It enters the field of history, and secures that each
successive epoch is in great measure the result of
antecedent influences and forces, making history
thus a living growth, and not a mere mechanical
succession of events manipulated by kings or govern-
ments. It would be strange if it did not obtain
also in the sphere of religion. There has undoubtedly been a continuity of the Church of
Christ from the beginning of its history till now.

*The Scrip-
tural idea of
continuity.*

Amid many external divisions, through profound
convulsions and vast changes, in the dissolution
and fall of empires, through times of weltering
chaos, when the foundations of society seemed to
be giving way, even in seasons of eclipse, when its
own light grew dim and its own life ebbed low, its
continuity has not been broken. But the Church
or Body of Christ which is thus continuous is the
society of the faithful. Pastors and teachers have
been given "for the edifying of the body," but it
would continue to exist although not a prelate or
presbyter remained on earth, for every member of
it is himself a priest, with as full and immediate
access through Christ to God as that enjoyed by
the venerable tenant of the Vatican. Let no one
say that the Church, thus regarded, is a body with
out an organism, and therefore a contradiction
in terms. It has an organism more perfect and
effective than any external one could be, and of
which that of the natural body is but a faint and
imperfect image. It is "knit together" or arti-
culated by "joints and bands," but its ligaments
are not an unbroken Episcopal succession, but
faith and love. The one essential bond of union
is the indwelling of the Holy Spirit, who unites the
members by faith to Christ, the Head, animates
them with one life from Him, makes them one
family or brotherhood, and fills them with love to
one another. It is "by one Spirit they are all
baptized into one body."[1] The unity is, therefore,
Spiritual—"the unity of the Spirit"—"the unity
of the faith and of the knowledge of the Son of
God." "There is one body, and one Spirit, even as

[1] 1 Cor. xii. 13.

ye are called in one hope of your calling, one Lord, one faith, one baptism, one God and Father of all, who is above all, and through all, and in you all." The unity is Spiritual, and real just because it is Spiritual; whereas the unity secured by any external organisation is only seeming. While it excludes great multitudes whose characters and lives prove that they are true disciples of Christ, genuine members of His body, the external organisation, by the admission of the exponents of Episcopal succession, embraces large numbers who are not true Christians at all, not real members of Christ's body. But while the "unity" of this theory is only seeming, that which Paul expounds is real and genuine. Being thus a living organism, the Church "increases with the increase of God," grows up into Him in all things which is the Head, even Christ, "from whom the whole body fitly joined together and compacted by that which every joint supplieth, according to the effectual working in the measure of every part, maketh increase of the body unto the edifying of itself in love."[1] This is the Church or body of Christ which continues from age to age, and these are the essential elements of its continuity. It is beyond question that a ministry has been instituted in the Church by our Lord and His Apostles, that clear directions have been given for their continuance, and that ordinarily that continuance is secured by their election by the people and their ordination by ministers already duly constituted; and, further, that the only *local* office-bearers of whom we have any trace in the New Testament are presbyter-bishops and deacons. But this ministry is not a

[1] Eph. iv. 16.

2 C

sacerdotal caste, and has no other or higher priest-hood than that which belongs to Christians generally. The transmission of the Holy Spirit and His grace is not confined to them, but, with all Church power, belongs to the whole Church, so that should a ministry fail or become corrupt, the Church could originate and appoint a new one. Thus, while the Christian ministry exists for the well-being of the Church, it is not essential to its being, nor any necessary part of its continuity. The essential elements of its con-tinuity lie, as we have seen, deeper.

The Scriptural test of a true Church.   6. The *test* of a Christian society which the doctrine I am examining requires is not the test which Scripture recommends. Scripture does not ask you by antiquarian research to find a Church whose prelatical succession you can trace back step by step through nineteen centuries to the Apostles; for Scripture does not expect you to perform an impossibility. The most erudite historian that ever lived would not be equal to the task, for the necessary evidence is not extant; or rather, there is more than ample evidence to disprove the assumption. A much more simple and effective criterion is prescribed. "A good tree cannot bring forth evil fruit," says our Lord Himself, " neither can a corrupt tree bring forth good fruit. . . . Wherefore by their fruits ye shall know them."[1] " By this shall all men know that ye are My disciples, if ye have love one to another."[2] "If any man have not the spirit of Christ, he is none of His."[3] Not any mere external, mechanical qualification, such as circumcision or prelatical suc-cession, but qualities spiritual and moral—a "new creation," "faith working by love," and the "keep-

[1] Matt. vii. 15-20.   [2] John xiii. 35.   [3] Rom. viii. 9.

ing the commandments of God"—are the evidence
required to prove that men are "in Christ Jesus."
"The individual life can enjoy fellowship with God
only through membership in the one body and by
dependence on sacraments of regeneration, confir-
mation, communion, absolution, of which ministers episcopally ordained are the appointed instruments;" this is the teaching of Canon Gore. "If
we say that we have fellowship with Him, and walk
in darkness, we lie, and do not the truth; but if we
walk in the light, as He is in the light, we have
fellowship one with another, and the blood of Jesus
Christ His Son cleanseth us from all sin;" this is
the teaching of the Apostle John.[1]   He adds—
"Hereby we do know that we know Him, if we keep
His commandments;"[2] "We know that we have
passed from death unto life because we love the
brethren;" and much more to the same effect.

What a splendid opportunity is thus offered to
the advocates of this doctrine! They allege that
prelates only, and those prelatically ordained, are
"guardians of the grace by which Christians live";
that we can have the life of Christ and fellowship
with God only through them.   If this be so—if
they only are the Divinely authorised channels of
Divine grace, if they only can give Christ's body
and blood to men for their life and nourishment, the
fact will be glaringly apparent in the lives of those
who enjoy this privilege—apparent in their pre-
eminent faith and love and holiness, and self-
sacrificing zeal, and no less apparent in the moral
degradation and spiritual barrenness of those miserable beings who live in communities where prelates

[1] 1 John i. 6-7.   [2] 1 John ii. 3.

are unknown. Here is a short, practical, and decisive method of settling this question. Is the Word of God quick and powerful, fruitful in faith and holy living *only* when preached by men ·prelatically ordained? Are they who enjoy their ministry, and *they only*, good and true, gentle and patient, temperate and virtuous, self-sacrificing and Christ-like? I make bold to affirm that in Christian faith and love, in purity of life, in philanthropic labours, and in missionary enterprise, and in missionary *success* too, the non-Episcopal communions will bear favourable comparison with those which possess the extraordinary advantage of prelatical ordination.

Appeal of Archbishop Alexander. In connection with this question I cannot but refer in closing to some words spoken the other day by the venerable primate, Dr. Alexander. "Are we for ever to hold out hands in vain," he said, "to our separated brethren?" We are not sure whether Presbyterians are included in this appeal, for, of course, as they never belonged to the Episcopal Church, they never "separated" from it, and cannot appropriately be called "separated brethren" any more than Episcopalians themselves. If the genial Primate meant to include us, I must frankly own that I for one was not previously aware that his hands and those of his clergy generally had been so warmly and so wistfully held out to us, unless the offer to absorb us into the "historic Episcopate" be so regarded. In fact, some of us were under the impression that till very lately many hands were being held out in quite a different direction. If, however, the good Primate and his brethren are now ready to hold out friendly hands, and on equal terms, I

CHAP. XVIII] "APOSTOLICAL SUCCESSION"

believe there is not, as there never has been, any obstacle on our side to friendly Christian fellowship and co-operation. But we should like to know more definitely what the kindly Primate means by holding out his hands. Does he mean that he is ready to recognise the ordination of our ministers as valid, and to admit them to his pulpits? Or does he mean that before they can be admitted they must be reordained, and so brought within the pale of the "Apostolical succession"? If that is what he means, I fear that for some time yet his hands will be held out in vain. He speaks in glowing terms of Protestantism, but it is open to grave question whether any one who holds the doctrine of "Apostolical succession" is in the original and proper sense of the term a Protestant. The principles involved in that doctrine are just the principles which lie at the root and basis of the Papal system, the very principles against which the Reformers protested and battled with all their might. The so-called Protestant who accepts of them is not the genuine article; his is not the Protestantism of the Reformers; he has already surrendered and betrayed what the Reformers regarded as the fundamental principles of Protestantism. The one serious and insuperable barrier to union and communion between Anglicanism and the non-Episcopal Churches is just this doctrine of "Apostolical succession," and the denial of the validity of the orders of the latter by the former. It is a denial, indeed, which affects Anglicans themselves much more than it does us. As we don't believe in "prelatical succession," we cannot regard it as any great loss or hardship to be without it. If some Continental State denied to

England the right to call herself a nation, England would not be much the worse, and if that State presumed too much on the denial, she might discover, to her surprise, that England is not without some of the essential attributes of a nation. In the same way the denial that we are a Church of Christ really does not trouble us since we are quite convinced of it ourselves. But such denial does affect those who unchurch us. " To refuse to recognise those as Christians who are Christians; to refuse communion with those in whom Christ dwells by His Spirit; to unchurch the living members of His body; to with-hold sympathy, fellowship, and co-operation from those devoted to His service and crowned with His blessing and recognition, is a great sin. It is that sin of schism which all churchmen profess to regard with special abhorrence." Besides, such excommunication cannot but react injuriously upon its authors. It tends to foster spiritual pride and a sense of superiority which is not salutary. The Jews regarded themselves as special favourites of Heaven because of their descent from Abraham, and irrespective of character and life, and that belief made them proud, self-righteous, bigoted and intolerant. And the moderns who repeat the old cry, " The temple of the Lord, the temple of the Lord, the temple of the Lord are we," are in imminent peril of being as exclusive and contemptuous as those who first uttered it. How momentous in every point of view, gentlemen, that you should rise above the narrow, exclusive, materialistic conception of the Church on which I have been commenting—a conception which owes its genesis and debasement to Pagan influences—that you should learn to think of Christians everywhere, by whatever name they are called, as brethren in Christ, of the Church as the whole company of believers, and, like the great Apostle, widen and enlarge your sympathies till they include "all that in every place call upon the name of Jesus Christ our Lord"—the only sense in which the Church can be properly called "Catholic."

APPENDIX

NOTE TO CHAPTER XVII

In a paper read before a clerical society by the Rev. L. A. Pooler, M.A., and afterwards published, an elaborate attempt is made to neutralise the facts set forth in the lecture contained in Chapter XVII. Not because of the intrinsic importance of the arguments presented in that paper, but because complete silence with regard to them would be misunderstood, it may be proper here briefly to exhibit their real character.

The method adopted by the critic in reviewing the first part of the lecture in question is to minimise and obscure as far as possible the numerous and fundamental points of difference, and to magnify to the uttermost the infinitesimal and almost invisible points in common between the ancient Celtic Church of Ireland and the Irish Protestant Episcopal Church.

I had pointed out that Henry VIII. was declared by statute to be the "supreme head," and Elizabeth the "supreme governor" of the Church set up by them in Ireland in the sixteenth century. My critic does not see how this affects the matter at issue. It affects it in this way. The titles thus assumed by them were not nominal merely, but meant real "headship" and "government." The Church set up by them was their own creation. The form given to it was due, as Richey amply proves, not to the Irish people and clergy, but simply to the will of the sovereigns (see *ante*, pp. 359, 373–376, and the references to authorities in proof of it). And attention was called to this to prepare the way for what is fully demonstrated in a subsequent part of the lecture (pp. 373–377, *ante*), namely, that what Henry VIII. and Elizabeth attempted was not to revive the Celtic Church,

APPENDIX

but to "Anglicise" the Church then existing. As Professor
Richey shows, "The Protestant Episcopal Church was planted
in Ireland, not by any Irish party, nor with reference to
Irish interests, but as a portion of the policy of England, and
as part of the great scheme of Anglicising this country."[1]
The critic is wisely silent on this most vital part of the
question.

I had shown that the ancient Irish Church had no hierarchical grades — no primate, no archbishop, no diocesan
bishop; that these came into Ireland from a Roman source
in the twelfth century; that the Celtic bishop was connected
with a single church, and that his position at best was no
other than the presiding minister of a congregation. This,
it seems, is quite immaterial. The addition of a hierarchy,
including diocesan Episcopacy, was, however, a tremendous
change upon the Celtic Church. Let it be done away with
in what now calls itself "The Church of Ireland;" let primate, archbishop, diocesan bishop be abolished, and the
bishops be at the utmost ministers of congregations, and what
vital difference will then remain between that Church and
the non-Episcopal Churches, whose ministers are bishops,
ordain, and administer the sacraments? It is this systematic
attempt to conceal the magnitude of the change from the
organisation of the Celtic Church to the modern hierarchical
organisation, and thus to hoodwink the public, that makes
much in Irish ecclesiastical history so worthless.

Ah! but the essential thing is that the Celtic Church had
the three orders of bishops, priests, and deacons, says Mr.
Pooler. Let us not delude ourselves with mere words; let
us rather scrutinise closely the things denoted by them.
Now the Celtic bishop was not a diocesan; he had no jurisdiction over other clergy; he was associated with a single
church, and was not more, at highest, than a congregational
bishop. True, a difference was made between him and the
presbyters. But in non-Episcopal Churches—in the Presbyterian Church, for example—quite as great a difference is
made between the minister and his elders or presbyters.
True, the Celtic bishop ordained; but in like manner in the
Presbyterian Church the minister only may ordain. It is

[1] Richey's "Short History," p. 386.

his prerogative not only to ordain, but preside in the congregation, preach, and administer the sacraments. He is, in fact, a congregational bishop, and bears a much closer resemblance both to the second-century bishop and to the Celtic bishop than the modern diocesan bishop does. It has been shown, moreover, that the later diocesan bishop was a development from the presiding presbyter-bishop of the first century (see *ante*, pp. 393–398).

"Although the diocesan system did not exist, and could not have existed," says Mr. Pooler, "yet there arose a state of things more or less corresponding to it." But the ruler of the so-called "spiritual diocese" in this case, that is, the abbot, was not necessarily a bishop, but as often a presbyter.

"Gradually," Mr. Pooler adds, "a further approximation was made to the diocesan divisions, when bishops began to be appointed to tribes." Then he quotes the "Lebar Brecc" to the effect that "there was to be a chief bishop for every chief tribe in Ireland for ordaining ecclesiastics, consecrating churches, &c. Now the "Lebar Brecc" is a compilation, according to Professor O'Curry, of the end of the fourteenth, according to Dr. Whitley Stokes, of the fifteenth century. It is a compilation of documents of various dates. The particular extract quoted by Mr. Pooler is assigned by Dr. Whitley Stokes to the thirteenth century! Diocesan Episcopacy had been already introduced in the beginning of the twelfth century, although the earlier state of things persisted more or less even after that. A document of this sort belonging to the thirteenth century is not of much value in determining the state of things in the fourth or fifth! In the study of history it is of vital importance to attend to the dates of documents.

I had shown that there was "no regular succession of bishops in the Irish Church," and that, in the words of Mr. Olden, "the catalogues of successive bishops of Irish sees must be illusive." This is admitted by all scholars, nor does Mr. Pooler attempt to deny it; but he goes on to affirm that "Armagh was never without a bishop." It is a pity that he simply makes the statement, and gives not a particle of evidence in support of it. I challenge him to produce the evidence. Dr. Todd in his "Memoir of St. Patrick" gives from a MS. in the "Book of Leinster" a list of the kings

APPENDIX

of Ireland, with notices of the deaths of the abbots and bishops at Armagh. In a few instances the coarbs of Patrick in this catalogue are described as bishops, and in one or two other cases the names of bishops occur, but in the great majority of the records in this list there is no mention whatever of a bishop, and no trace of one having existed. Dr. Todd states that four ancient lists of the coarbs of St. Patrick have been preserved, and in fact gives the lists, but says, "They all bear evidence of having been drawn up at the close of the eleventh or beginning of the twelfth century, when archiepiscopal and diocesan jurisdiction was introduced; and it is probable," he adds, "that their authors were influenced by a wish to establish a claim to a regular episcopal succession, at least at Armagh;" but the only semblance to such a succession they could make out was a list of coarbs, who, as a rule, were not bishops at all. Indeed, both Dr. Todd and Dr. Reeves admit that there is no record of a series of bishops at Armagh.[1]

The enactment of the Synod of Cealcythe that "no person of Scotic (*i.e.* Irish) race should be permitted to exercise his ministry in any English diocese, the first reason given being 'because it is uncertain by whom they were ordained, or whether they were ordained by any one,'" Mr. Pooler construes as a precaution against cases of fraud or imposture. This only shows that Mr. Pooler has not really examined the record of the decree on which he pronounces. It is true that some four centuries later than this we do hear of pseudobishops, pretending to be Irish, undertaking to perform episcopal functions in England; but in this case there is absolutely no suspicion or suggestion of fraud. The reasons for the enactment are expressly mentioned, one being that given above, and the other because their orders are not derived from metropolitan or diocesan bishops.

I had shown that the fundamental feature of the early Irish Church was its monasticism; that its real rulers were the abbots; that to lack this is to lack the most essential feature of early Irish Church organisation; and that the Church which overthrew monasticism can hardly be identical

---

[1] See Todd's "St. Patrick," p. 172, and Reeves's "Antiquities," p. 136.

411

in form or order with that which cherished it as its most distinctive and all-controlling institution. Mr. Pooler's crushing reply is the somewhat peevish query, "How can this affect the question?" We rather think that most people not blinded by prejudice will admit that it affects it a good deal.

I had referred to the value set on shrines, relics, and the like in the Celtic Church, and to the 97th Canon of the Church set up by the Tudors, which denounces these as "monuments of superstition." I of course touched on this in passing to show that not in organisation only, but in deeper matters still the modern Church differs from the ancient one. To notice it at all was, it seems, to "mistake accidents for essentials."

For the same purpose I had spoken of "the moral and religious ideal of the Celtic Church" as different, happily, from that of our Protestant Episcopal brethren. Though I imagined I had made clear what I meant by this (see p. 367, ante), Mr. Pooler has some strangely irrelevant remarks on the subject. What the ideal was appears in the legends that grew up in the minds of the monks as to the spiteful miracles, and the lying, deceit, cursing, &c., which they impute to the "saints." Then he adds : "It will be a great day not merely for the Church of Ireland, but for Christendom at large, when the ideal of Christendom shall be again as high as was the ideal" of certain Irishmen whom he mentions. Any one who turns to Chapter XIV. of this volume will see what I meant by "the moral and religious ideal of the Celtic Church," how inadequate Mr. Pooler's knowledge of that Church seems to be, and how foolish are his aspirations. Of course I do not deny that in such men as Columba and Columbanus there is much to admire.

In the critic's remarks on the Anglo-Norman period there is nothing that calls for notice. It is satisfactory to find him admitting that there was only one Church in Ireland during that period. On the subject of what, from the New Testament and Christian point of view, constitutes Church continuity, I refer to Chapter XVIII. of this volume. It is there shown that it is certainly not "apostolical succession." We come now to the Reformation period.

I had shown that Curwin, the fountain of orders for the

APPENDIX

Tudor Church, was an Englishman, and ordained by Englishmen. Mr. Pooler answers: "Irish orders are not distinct
from the orders of the Christian Church. What we have to
show is not that Irish orders are distinctively Irish without
intermixture, but that they are Christian; and when a man
holding Christian orders works *legally* [italics not mine] in
the Church of Ireland, he is a member of the Church of
Ireland, and of the ministry of the Church of Ireland." Mr.
Pooler thus abandons the citadel of the position, that to which
all the advocates of the theory I was meeting attach vital
importance. In writings and speeches without number it
has been asserted that the Protestant episcopal succession is
traceable through Irish bishops up to St. Patrick, and on
this alleged fact the claim to be truly "Irish" is based. If
this claim is abandoned, I have of course nothing more to say
on this part of the subject. I am not now concerned to deny
the derivation of orders from an English bishop or bishops.
Even if the orders had been derived from an Irish source,
that would not constitute a handful of English officials into
an Irish Church. But if they are not Irish, and the great
body of the Irish people remained outside it, as they did, on
what ground does the Tudor Church claim the title "The
Church of Ireland"? Is a mere *legal* enactment, forced on
Ireland by the will of despotic rulers, enough to make such
a handful of English officials "The Irish Church" in any
real sense? Is the basis of the claim then a mere "legal"
fiction?

Passing by some things that are irrelevant, I now come to
what is by far the choicest morsel in the paper I am reviewing. Mr. Pooler says: "There was no schism in the Church
of Ireland during the reign of Henry VIII. There was only
one Church, and Browne the Reformer, and Cromer and Dow-
dall, who opposed the Reformation, were members" (p. 17).
Again, "We now come to the first schism in the Church
of Ireland. Elizabeth came to the throne in 1558, and for
eight years the only Church in this country was the Church
of Ireland. But in the year 1567 the Pope established a
branch of the Roman Church in this country, under the
control of persons who are known as 'titular bishops,' and
who are the origin of the Roman bishops as at present existing in this land" (p. 22).

413

APPENDIX

Many amusing attempts have been made to make out a case for the Church set up in Ireland by the Tudors. For a good while it was a favourite expedient to maintain that from 1171 to 1535 two Churches existed in Ireland, one of them the Celtic Church, to which the native Irish adhered, and the other the Church of Rome, the Church of the Anglo-Norman invaders; and that what Henry VIII. did was to push aside the intrusive Anglo-Norman Church, and to reinstate the old Irish Church. But the facts were too stubborn for this theory, and it had to be abandoned. Mr. Pooler himself has thrown it over. To say that the new theory announced by Mr. Pooler is the most ridiculous and puerile of all, and a most barefaced perversion of the patent facts of history, is a mild way of putting it. It is the last desperate shift of a cause *in extremis*.

In the first place, both Henry VIII. and Elizabeth had broken off from the Roman Communion. If there is anything at all in the principle of "unbroken visible corporate unity," a principle which is the very core and centre of High Churchism, the complete severance both in England and in Ireland from Rome was a violation of that "visible corporate unity," and, from the High Church point of view, a case of gross and palpable schism.

In the next place, the Church set up in Ireland by Henry VIII. and Elizabeth was, as I have shown already (see *ante*, pp. 369, 379 *seq.*), accepted only by the official class, chiefly English, and only nominally by them. The great body of the Irish people and clergy never for a moment ceased from communion with Rome, and all through stood completely aloof from the Tudor structure. As Professor Richey shows, the statutory measures were a dead letter as regarded the mass of the population. "They were," he says, "Acts of Parliament sitting in Dublin, and had no more result than numerous other Acts of similar Parliaments relative to secular affairs."[1] The new Church, as he points out, extended ittle beyond the Government officials, and was far from including the whole of these. This is put beyond doubt by the Calendars of State Papers edited by Mr. Brewer.[2] In

---

[1] "Short History," p. 361.
[2] See the vol. for 1515–1574, and the vol. for 1575–1588.

his Introduction to the second of the volumes mentioned below, Mr. Brewer shows that "preachers and people remained equally obstinate." As regards "the mass of the population," he says : "In their estimation it was reason sufficient to condemn whatever England approved, to hate a doctrine propagated by English bishops, to whom they had never been accustomed to listen, and with whose residence among them they had associated much of their miseries and misfortunes. If Irish Catholics had been lukewarm before, this alone was enough to inflame their zeal in defence of their ancient faith ; to bring out in prominent relief the Papal tendencies of Ireland ; to induce them to regard their priests, whether of their own nation or of other nations, with a veneration and respect they had never paid even to their chiefs." [1] Again, "Is it surprising that the mass of the Irish people, who had never known what it was to be ruled by a king, to whom the supremacy of the Pope had been the mainstay of their religion, above all, who had never been prepared for the change, should have obstinately resisted ? Is it strange that their obstinacy should have grown in proportion to the severity of the measures employed to enforce the obnoxious maxim ? In vain the highest ecclesiastical preferments in Ireland were offered to the most able and most uncompromising advocates of the new doctrine. Few in number, unaided by their clergy, coldly supported in general by the Deputy, the cardinal doctrine of English Protestantism fell unheeded from the lips of a few right reverend preachers. Received with menaces and defiance even in the Cathedral of Dublin, guarded as it was by the Deputy and his soldiers, it found no hearers beyond those walls, it made no proselytes." [2]

But now, what about the Irish bishops? Mr. Pooler, referring to Mr. Froude's assertion on this subject, describes him as an imaginative writer. Here is what Mr. Froude wrote in a letter to Dr. Maziere Brady : "I have examined, I believe thoroughly, all the Irish State Papers in the Record Office during and from the time of Henry VIII. to 1574, and it is from them, in connection with the voluminous

---

[1] "Calendar of State Papers (Carew), 1575-1588," Introd. p. xvii. [2] Ibid., p. xix.

APPENDIX

MSS. in Spain on the same subject, that I draw my conclusion respecting the supposed conversion of Irish bishops and clergy to the Reformation. *I am thoroughly convinced that (with the exception of the Archbishop of Dublin) not one of Queen Mary's bishops, nor any one of the clergy beyond the Pale went over to the Reformation"* (italics not mine). The mere assertion that Mr. Froude was imaginative is not enough, without some evidence, to set aside this statement of his. The case of Field will be referred to in a moment.

But Mr. Pooler writes as if we depended in this matter on the sole testimony of Mr. Froude. It is not so. The late Dr. Maziere Brady investigated the question with great learning and industry, and has given the result in several treatises, especially in his work "The Alleged Conversion of the Irish Bishops to the Reformed Religion at the Accession of Queen Elizabeth; and the Assumed Descent of the Present Established Hierarchy in Ireland from the Ancient Irish Church Disproved" (Longmans, Green & Co., 1866). In this work the old stale misstatements on this subject, which are repeated afresh by Mr. Pooler, are completely refuted. In the preface Dr. Brady says that in collecting materials for the "Clerical and Parochial Records of Cork, Cloyne, and Ross," he was engaged for many years in examining the published works and unpublished archives relating to the Reformation period, and could not fail to remark that no documentary evidence was forthcoming to verify the received opinions touching the asserted conversion of the Irish bishops, and the descent of the Reformed Episcopate from the ancient Irish Church. He sought admission, he says, to the archives at Rome, found the researches of Theiner, and had the use of unpublished transcripts from the Roman archives by Dr. Moran, then Vice-Rector of the Irish College at Rome. In Cotton's "Fasti Ecclesiæ Hibernicæ," in the State Paper Office in London, in the Patent Rolls of Ireland, and in Theiner's "Vetera Monumenta," he found much assistance; and the evidence of the Roman archives he was able to verify by manuscripts in the Bodleian Library and the State Paper Office. In minute detail he goes over all the Sees, adducing clear evidence with regard to each, and the general result he sums up in the declaration that "there is not a particle of

416

APPENDIX

evidence upon record to prove that any of the Marian bishops, except Curwin, became Protestants. . . . I am thoroughly convinced that (with the exception of the Archbishop of Dublin) not one of Queen Mary's bishops, nor any one of the clergy beyond the Pale, went over to the Reformation. Of the clergy scarcely any within the Pale went over. . . . Not one of Queen Mary's prelates, except Hugh Curwin, can be proved to have had any part in the consecration of an Elizabethan bishop. Indeed, Usher, Ware, and Harris, although fully alive to the importance of such a discovery, were unable even to name a single Irish bishop who could be said to have assisted Curwin, and to have thus transmitted a dubious claim to the Irish succession. . . . As Curwin was English by consecration and birth, the present episcopate of the Reformed Anglican Church in Ireland cannot now be connected, as far as consecrations are concerned, with the pre-Reformation Irish hierarchy. All the more modern bishops in Ireland, except those who have been translated from English Sees, must trace their ecclesiastical pedigree backwards to one or other of those eight bishops who formed at the Restoration in 1660 the entire episcopate of the Established Church in Ireland." Then he traces the consecration of each, and finds as a result that "of the eight bishops of 1660, some were Scotsmen, some were Englishmen, one was a Welshman, but not one was of an Irish family." He shows that "of the twenty-six bishops alive in 1558, twenty-five were natives of Ireland, and continued Roman Catholics."

Even in the case of those who took the oath of supremacy, and were put on commissions by Elizabeth, Dr. Brady proves that they continued Roman Catholics. This was so even as regards Field or O'Fihel of Leighlin, mentioned by Mr. Pooler. He, with the other Marian bishops, except Curwin, is denounced as "Irishe" by a Royal Commission. Dr. Brady adds, that "the oath of supremacy and abjuration was offered and taken within the Pale, but with modifications, and a free use of the maxim that oaths are to be interpreted *ex animo imponentis*. Outside the Pale it was not offered during the first part of Elizabeth's reign, for enough law did not prevail beyond the limits of the English colony." He quotes many authorities in support of these various statements; and also of the fact that bishops deprived by the Queen continued to act as bishops, and ruled their dioceses, and that, although

417   2 D

employed by the Queen in various ways, bishops continued Roman Catholics. As an introduction to the study of this subject, I recommend to Mr. Pooler the perusal of this and other treatises by Dr. Maziere Brady.

Mr. Pooler wrote to Mr. Gladstone to ask whether he intended to interfere with the title of the Church disestablished by him. Here is Mr. Gladstone's answer : " In approaching the question of Irish disestablishment my leading idea was this—We were about to carry the Established Church of Ireland out of an existence defined by statutory conditions into one purely voluntary and severed from State authority. Our duty, as it appeared to us, was this—(1) To make that severance complete. (2) To take care that, in effecting it, we did not lacerate nor in any way impair the means of action belonging to her as a Church, and we left her the fullest liberty to assert any and every claim she might consider herself to possess *on other than statutory grounds*. So far as our intention went, it was not our business to provide her with a title." (Italics mine.) Mr. Pooler is entitled to all the comfort he can extract from these words ! But observe, Mr. Gladstone's duty was to " make the severance from State authority complete," and to take care in effecting it to give her the fullest liberty to assert any claim she might possess " *on other than statutory grounds*." I have shown that " on other than statutory grounds " she has no claim whatever to the title " The Church of Ireland." I may add that Earl Spencer, as Lord Lieutenant of Ireland under Mr. Gladstone's Government, stated to a deputation from the General Assembly of the Irish Presbyterian Church, that the Attorney-General for England and the Attorney-General for Ireland had both given the Irish Government the opinion that the disestablished Episcopal Church was not entitled to the designation " The Church of Ireland," and that the Irish Government could not use it. When the Conservatives came into power a counter-opinion was got from their law-officers. Any one who reads the latter opinion, as given by Mr. Pooler, will see on what flimsy " statutory " grounds the opinion is based—namely, on incidental references to the disestablished Church in the Irish Act of 1869 and subsequently, references which, to be understood, had to describe the Church in such terms as are employed. What a basis on which to rest the justification of the title, " The Church of Ireland " !

INDEX

ABBOTS, the real rulers of the Irish Church, 167, 177
Abbot's Knoll, 236
Adamnan, 22, 58, 139, 221, 279
Adrian IV., Pope, Bull of, 326; his obsequiousness, 343
Ædh, king of Ireland, 241
Ædh, Bishop, 63
Ædh Dubh, ordination of, 184
Ædilhun, 210
Ængus, king of Munster, 174
Africa, proconsular, 200
Aidan, the apostle of England, 4; his ordination, 185 seq.; his work in England, 248
Aidan, king of British Dalriada, 241
Aileach, Hill of, 21
Ailech, monastery of, 218
Ailcluaide, 59, 71
Alban or Caledonia, 20
Alban, St., 74
Albanian Picts, 10
Albinus, 213
Alcuin, 58, 213, 214, 272
Aldfrid, 211
Alexander, Archbishop, 404
Amator, 94
Anamchara or "soul-friend," 181
Anglican Church in Ireland, 192, 378
Anglican orders, Pope's Bull on, 391

Anglo-Norman Church, two sections of, 348, 368
Annadown, 218
Annegray, old Roman fort of, 258
Annoit, the, 145
Anselm, 88, 319
Antiphonary of Bangor, 124, 158
"Antiquities" of Bishop Reeves, 64
Aodh Finn, 35
Apostles, their place in primitive Church, 393; had properly no successors, 393
Apostles, twelve, of Erin, 157
Apostolic canons, 199
"Apostolical succession," the theory defined, 382; incapable of proof, 383; Newman on, 384; corporate unity not secured by, 385; contradicts New Testament, 385; repudiated by the Reformers, 391
Archbishops, modern, unknown in Celtic Church, 360
Architecture, 31
Ardbishops, 168
Ardnamurchan, 239
Ardri, 16
Argyleshire (Airer Gael), 20, 234
Argyll, Duke of, on Columba, 222
Arles, Synod of, 75

INDEX

Armagh, 116, 212, 297
Armoy (Airther Maige), 114
Arran, 35
Aryan tribes, 26
Aspect of ancient Ireland, 40
Attacotti, 71
Augustin, his mission, 72 ; his interview with the British bishops, 165
Aulus Plautius, 73
Auricular confession, 124, 315

BALLYBETAGH, 40
Ballyligpatrick, 82
Ballyshannon, 42
Bangor, 157, 296
Bannavem Tabernæ, 68-69
Banshee, 42
Baronius, 164, 313
Basel Hymn, 58
Bede, 55, 56, 91, 165, 177, 249
Beehive houses, 36
Beltane, 42
Benen, 27, 151
Berct, 79
Bernard, St., 164, 173, 317
Bishops in Celtic Church, 170-205
Biur, the river, 226
Bobbio, 268
Book of Acaill, 26, 45
Book of Armagh, 63-64, 182
Book of Ballymote, 44
Book of Durrow, 182
Book of Kells, 182
Bregenz, Columbanus at, 266
Brehon laws, 24 seq., 75, 139
Brehons, 24, 29
Brendan (of Birr), 157
Brendan (of Clonfert), 157, 216
Brian Boroimhe, 17, 80, 305, 307
Bricriu, 18

Bright, 104, 172
Brigid, St., 152 seq., 157
Britains, the (Britanniæ), 60, 70, 83
British Christianity derived from East, 74
Britons, the early, 10 ; when Christianised, 72-75
Brocan, 152
Broccaide, 152
Bruce, Edward, 80 ; his invasion of Ireland, 342, 344 seq. ; defeated at Faughard, 345
Bruce, Robert, 342
Brude, 235, 239
Brugh-na-Boyne, 34, 108
Brunehild, 265
Buckna, 82
Buid chonaill (yellow plague), 225
Bull of Adrian IV., 326 ; its genuineness, 328

CAERMARTHEN, Black Book of, 71
Cæsar, 12
Caillin, St., 35, 278
Cain Patrick (Patrick's law), 27
Cainnech, 229
Cairbre Riada, 20, 80
Cairnech, 27
Caledonia or Alban, 20
Callech (see Gallus)
Calpornius, 72
Canice, 157
Canon Patraic (Book of Armagh), 64
Cantyre, 235
Carlingford, 299, 300
Carlyle, dictum of, 53
Carns or tumuli, 33, 34
Cashel, decree of Synod of, 337
Cashels (or Cathairs), 36

INDEX

Castletown Fort, 18
Catalogue of Saints, 58, 170
Cathbad, 115
Catholicism, Professor Sohm on, 142
Cato on Celts, 12
Cealcythe, Synod of, 168, 411
Celestine, Pope, 47, 55, 75, 89
Celsus, 317
Celtic Church, its story interesting, 4
Celts, 8, 9, 10, 11, 12, 13
Champion, 183
Cheetham on primitive Episcopacy, 202
Chorepiscopi, 197
Christ Church Cathedral, 316
Christian, Bishop of Lismore, 337
Chronicle of Prosper, 47
Chronicon Hyense, 186
Chronology of Patrick's life, 67
Church, true test of the, 402
Church continuity, 399
"Church of Ireland," claim to the title examined, 355
Church organisation, 142
Cianan, 152
Cinnenum, 78
Cists (or cistvæns), 33
Clann, 14
Claudian, 23
Claudius, 73
Clement, 213
Clergy, married, in Irish Church, 75; held secular offices, 76, 232
Clonard, 155, 223
Clonmacnois, 160, 232
Clontarf, battle of, 309, 322
Coarb (heir or successor), 143-145
Coarb, Patrick's, 167
Coilbad, 115

Colcu, 213
Coleraine, 172
Colgan, 65, 93, 94
Colman, Bishop, 25
Colmenar, 7
Columba, Lives of, 220; his birth, 222; education, 223; erects three hundred churches, 229; sets out for Iona, 230; his motive, 230; visits Brude, 240; his death, 244; his character, 245; reputed miracles, 278, 279
Columba (son of Crimthan), 157
Columbanus, Life of, by Jonas, 253; birth, 253; education at Cleenish and Bangor, 254; sets out on mission and reaches Burgundy, 255; appearance of the missionary band, 255; region where settle in Vosges Mountains, 256-258; his severe discipline, 259, 260; collision with Frankish clergy, 262; letter to Gregory, 263; letter to Boniface IV., 264; expulsion by Brunehild and Thierry, 265, 266; at Bobbio, 268; death, 269; character, 270
Comber, 116
Comgall, 157
Commemoratio Laborum, ascribed to Patrick, 59
Committee to revise laws, 27
Communion in both kinds, 124, 315
Compairche, the, 145
Conaire II., 20, 80
Conall Gulban, 35, 110
Conall Kernach, 18
Conary the Great, 17
Condlaed, 155
Conchessa, 77
Conn-Ced-Cathach (Conn of the Hundred Battles), 20, 314

INDEX

Conn of the Poor, 76
Connaught, Patrick visits, 111
Connor, 115
Conor MacNessa, 17, 18, 30
Constantius, 74
Contra Collatorem, 48
Cooldreevny, battle of, 147, 231, 235
Corc, 27
Cormac MacArt, 21, 26, 40, 44–47 ; a Christian, 43 seq., 71
Coroticus, 59
Crann, 38
Crannogs, 38
Crimthann, 71, 72
Criterion of historical testimony, 85
Croagh-Patrick, 113
Croghan, 18
Crom Cruach, 43, 110
Cromdubh, 110
Cromlech (or dolmen), 32, 33
Cronan, 159
Cruithne or Picti, 10
Cruithnechan, 223
Cuailnge (Cooley), 18
Cuchullin, 18, 31, 35
Culbrandan, 218
Culfeightrin, 115
Cumine, Life of Columba by, 220
Cummian, 57, 314
Curnan, slain by Diarmaid, 146, 231
Cursing in Irish Church, 280, 281
Curwin, Archbishop, 369

DABONNA, 152
Dagan, Bishop, 166
Daire, 27, 116,
Daire-Calgaich, 226
Dalaradia, 10, 79, 115
Dal-Cais, the, 305

Dalriada, 80, 115; British, 242, 243
Dalta, the, 145
Danars, 293, 299
Danes, the coming of the, 291 ; first appearance in Ireland, 295; aided by Irish dissensions, 298 ; terror caused by, 299; oppressions of, 304; defeated by Brian Boru, 306; conversion of, 315; Church under, 311; unite with Church of Rome, 316
Danish invasions, three periods in the, 294
Darcachein, the Hui, 116
Darerca, 78
Dathi, 24
De Barry, Robert, 332
De Burgo, 339
De Burgos, the, don saffron robes, 345
De Courcy, 117, 339
"De Rerum Natura" of Bede, 56
Decurio, 60, 76
Dedannans, 6
Deis or rights, 15
Deer's cry, 62
Dermot, 23
Dermot MacMurrough, king of Leinster, 329, 331
Derry, 226, 227
Diarmaid, 147, 230
Dichuil, 213, 271
Dignitaries, three free, 146
Dimman, 115
Diocesan Episcopacy, unknown in early Irish Church, 168, 361 ; Todd, Skene, Olden on, 169
Diocletian, his persecution, 74
Doctrine, Patrick's, 120–124 ; of Scripture, 121 ; of the Trinity, 122 ; of grace, 123 ; of Lord's day, 123; of the Lord's Supper, 124

INDEX

Dolmens (or Cromlechs), 32, 33
Domhanghard (Donard), 104, 105
Donaghmore, 103
Donald, Bishop, 319
Donaldson, Dr., on historical evidence, 85
Donogh, 309
Dowth, 34
Druada or magi, 42, 46
Druidical priests, 109
Drumceatt, Convention at, 241
Drumcliffe, 229
Drumeeny, 115
Drumtullogh, 115
Dubhthach, 27, 109, 110
Dublin, founding of, 297 ; taken by Normans, 334
Duffack, 153
Dumbarton (Ail Cluaide), 59, 70
Dunan, 316
Dundalgan, 18
Dundalk Bay, 299
Dungal, 300
Dun-leth-glass (Downpatrick), 117
Dunlugaidh, 35
Dunraven, Lord, 106
Duns, 35, 36
Dunsverick, 115
Durrow, 228, 232
Duv-Galls, 293, 299
Dysart, Souterrains at, 37

EASTER Controversy, 165, 167, 251
Easter Eve, 42
Ecbatius, 77
Ecgbert, 210
Ecgfrid, 79
Education in early Ireland, 207
Edward I., 342
Edward II., 344

Egypt, monasticism first appears in, 134
Eithne, mother of Columba, 223
Elysium, Irish, 41
Emain or Emania, 18, 21
Eoghan Mor (or Mogh Nuadhat), 20
Epic literature, Irish, 30
Episcopacy in early Irish Church 173 ; St. Bernard on, 362 ; Lanfranc on, 362
Episcopate developed from the Presbyterate, 395
Erc, Patrick's disciple, 138
Erc's sons, 115
Eric, 25
Eriu, 10, 11
Etchen, 224
Ethnea the Fair, 111
Eusebius on British Church, 74
Extreme unction, 315

FAUGHART, 153
Fedelma the Ruddy, 111
Fedhlimidh, father of Columba, 223
Feidhlimidh, bishop-king, 281
Feidhlimidh MacCriffan, king of Cashel, 298
Feis, the, established by Ollamh Fodla, 19, 23
Fergil (Virgilius), 212, 271
Fergus, 35, 115
Ferguson, Sir Samuel, 47
Ferleighinn, 213
Fiacc's Hymn, 58, 65, 70, 91, 151
Fianna, 31
Fileadh, 30
Findchan, 184
Finn-Galls, 293, 299
Finnian (of Clonard), 155, 223
Finnian (of Maghbile), 160
Finn MacCumhaill, 23, 31, 44, 45

INDEX

Firbolgs, 5
Fitzgeralds, the, 332
Fitzstephen, Robert, 332, 333
Five Bloods, the, 339
Flaiths (or nobles), 15
Foclut, 84
Fomorians, 5
Fontenay, 261
Forests, 40
Forradh, 22
Fothrad, 115
Franks, 50; and Romans, 125
Friar Clynn, 348
Fursa, St., 271

GAELS, two branches of, 10
Gailiuns of Liogarne, 6
Gallus (St. Gall), 159, 266, 268
Gartan, 222
Gartnaidh, 243
Gelasius, 317
Gemman, 148, 223
Germanus, 75, 94
Giant's Causeway, 5, 71
Gildas, 74
Gillebert, 164, 316
Giraldus Cambrensis, 168, 314
Glasnevin, 160
Glen Mama, 306
Gluaire, 116
Glynn, 116
Gore, Canon, admits the episcopal
    functions of presbyters, 398
Gormlaith, 308
Graine, 23
Great men, influence of, 53, 54
Gregory IX., Pope, 351
Grimm, 8
Guntram, 257

HADDON and Stubbs, 74, 75
Harald Haarfagr, 293

Harnack, Dr. Adolph, on primi-
    tive Church organisation, 199
Harris, 104
Henry II., 324 seq.; gets Papal
    sanction to his conquest of
    Ireland, 326; occasion of his
    coming, 329; lands at Water-
    ford, 335; welcomed by the
    clergy, 336; at Dublin, 336;
    change of policy, 338
Henry VIII. supreme head of
    Irish Church, 359; his aim to
    Anglicise Ireland, 372, 373;
    which included the Angli-
    cising of the Church, 374 seq.
Herenaghs, 365
Hiberio, 10
Hiberionaces, 10
Hiberni, 10
Hierarchical grades of modern
    Church unknown in Celtic
    Church, 300
Hildebrand, 326
Hill of Slane, 42, 108
Honorius, Pope, 313
House of Heroes, 22, 23
Hymn of St. Cummine Fota, 58
Hymn of St. Patrick, 62

IBERIAN origin, some Irish of,
    17
Iceland, Irish mission to, 272
Ideal of moral and religious life
    in Irish Church, 276, 366
Ierne, 10
Inchaguile, 78
Inis Banba, 11
Inis Ealga, 11
Inis Fail, 10
Inis Fodla, 11
Inis-na-Beeva, 11, 40
Invocation of saints, 124, 315
Inverness, 240

INDEX

Iona, name and aspect of island, 235 ; Duke of Argyll on, 236 ; its monastery, 238 ; centre of influence, 243

Ireland, early names of, 10, 11

Irish Christianity, early, defects in, 274 ; relapse into paganism, 276

Irish Church, relation to Rome in early period, 163-167, 311-320 ; wherein it differed from Rome, 312 ; early independence, 163, 312, 358

Irish clergy excluded from English livings, 349

"Irish enemies," 306, 340, 349

Irish liturgies, 164

Irish missionaries, 270

Irish races, 6, 8

Island Magee, 116

Ita, St., 216

JARLATH, St., 216

Jerome on British Christians, 75 ; on Pelagius, 75 ; on episcopacy, 397

Jocelyn, 66, 95, 114

John XXIII., Pope, 342

Johnson, Dr. Samuel, on Iona, 238

KELLACH and St. Kieran, 176

Kells, founding of, 228 ; Synod of, 317

Keltar, Rath, 18

Keltar of the Battles, 18

Kieran, St., of Saigir, 139, 157, 278

Kieran, St., the Artificer, 157

Kilbally, 212

Kilbrandan Sound, 218

Kilbride, 154

Kildare, 152 seq.

Kilkenny, Statute of, 345 ; its object, 346

Killinchy, 104

Killmacrennan, 222

Kilroot, 172

Kinship, root idea of Irish social system, 14

Knowth, 34

LACY, Hugh de, 338, 339

Lamartine, saying of, 3

Lambay, 229

Landlordism in Ireland, origin of, 15

Lanfranc, on Irish ordinations, 88 ; claims jurisdiction in Ireland, 316

Langen on early Roman bishops, 396

Lanigan, Dr., 69, 124, 319

Laoghaire, King, 24 ; his daughters, 111

Lascrian, 313

Laurentius, 165, 166

Laws, ancient, 24, 25, 26

Leachta, 32

Learning in pre-Christian Ireland, 28

Lebar Brecc, 71, 171

Lecale (or Maghinis), 102, 103

Ledwich, 55

Leth Chuinn, or Conn's Half, 20, 314

Leth Mogha, or Mogh's Half, 20, 314

Lewis, Sir G. Cornewall, his test of credibility, 85

Lia Fail, 22

"Liber Pontificalis," 90

Lightfoot, Bishop, on Aidan, 4 ; on Pomponia Græcina, 73 ; on early Roman bishops, 395

INDEX

Limania, or Liamain, 78
Lindisfarne, 248
Lipsius on early Roman bishops, 395
Lis, 36
Lismore, 160
Lissanisky, 36
Litany of Ængus, 174
Liturgical Tract, 58
Livingstone, David, on early monasticism, 261
Lochaber, 239
Loire, 23
Lough Corrib, 78
Lomman, 151
Lorica (or Hymn) of Patrick, 62, 109
Lorne, 234
Lough Neagh, 296
Lough Owel, 297
Lough Ree, 297
Loughbrickland, 18, 172
Love of country, 3
Lugnaid, 78, 152
Lupait, 78
Luxeuil, 261
Luxeuil Calendar, 58
Lymmavaddy, Inquisition at, 364

MacERC, 103
MacFirbis, his Book of Genealogies, 6
MacNisse, Bishop of Connor, 115
Macroig, Fergus, 18
Maelmorda, 306, 308
Magh Lene, 314
Maghera, 104, 172
Magheramorne, 116
Maghinis (Lecale), 103, 119
Mahee Island, 103, 104, 151
Mahon, 305
Mailduf, 271
Maine, Sir Henry, 26

Malachi, Archbishop of Armagh, 165, 317
Malachi, king of Ireland, 307, 308, 309, 311
Malchus, 316
Malmesbury, 271
Manis, 152
Marcus, Life of Patrick by, 93
Marriage of Patrick's father and grandfather, 61
Martin, St., of Tours, 134
Martyrologium, Bede's, 56
Martyrology of Donegal, 174
Meath, 16, 172
Mebh (Maive), 17, 18
Mel, 152
Mellifont, 318
Merovingian kings, 257
Metropolitan jurisdiction, early Irish Church without, 167
Milesians, 6, 8
Miliuc or Milchu, 79, 82, 102, 103
Milman, 256
Miracles, absence of, from Patrick's " Confession," 61
Miracles by Irish saints, specimens of, 277, 278, 279
Missionary achievements, 215
Mobhi, 157, 225
Mochay, 151
Mochta, 151
Mogh Nuadhat, 20
Molaise, 157, 225
Molua, 278
Mommsen on characteristics of Celts, 12, 13
Monasterboice, 160
Monasteries, Irish, 136–149
Monasticism in Irish Church, 131 seq., 365
Moronus on monastic school of Lismore, 211
Morven, 239

426

INDEX

Mound of Cow, 22
Mound of Hostages, 22
Movilla, 160, 296
Moylinney, 80
Moyslecht, 43, 110
Muckamore, 172
Mugenog, 152
Muintir or familia, 140
Muirbhech Mil, 35
Muirchu, his memoir of Patrick,
58, 63, 90
Mull, 236
Mullaghshee, 42
Mur Tea, 22
Murrogh, 306, 308, 309, 310

NATHI, 48
Nationality, Irish, 16, 17
Navan Fort, 18
Neambuach, 22
Nektan, 152
Nemedh, legend of, 8
Nemedians, 5
Nemthur, 70, 71
Nendrum, 103, 137
Nennius, 93
Neo-Platonism, 133
New Grange, 34, 108
Niall of the Nine Hostages, 17,
23
Ninnine's Prayer, 58
Ninnian, 75
Ninnidh, 157
Norman conquests, 323, 324
Norsemen at home, 291 ; how
driven away, 292 ; Irish towns
founded by, 293
Northern Hy Niall, 23

O'CONNOR, Turlough, 330
O'Curry, lectures on MS. materials, quoted, 6 ; on education,
207 seq.

O'Donnell, Manus, his Life of
Columba, 221, 230
O'Donovan, Dr., 126
Ogham inscriptions, 37
Olcan, Bishop of Armoy, 114
Olden, Rev. Thomas, 178, 350
Ollamhs, 28, 29, 242
Ondbahum, 77
Oran's, St., Chapel, 236
Ordination in early Irish Church,
87, 184, 241
Organisation of early Irish
Church, 16, 162, 163, 192
O'Rourke, Tiernan, 330, 339
Ossian's picture of Finn Mac
Cumhal, 45
Oswald, King, 248
Oswy, King, 251

PALLADIUS, 47, 48, 49
Papal exactions, 351
Papal jurisdiction, early Irish
Church free from, 163
Paparo, Cardinal, 317
Partholonians, 5
Patrick, the true apostle of Ireland, 49, 53 ; his existence
questioned and proved, 54–56 ;
names of, 68 ; birthplace, 69 ;
how he came to be a Christian,
72 ; his mother, 77 ; his sisters,
78 ; captivity, 68, 78, 81, 82 ;
escape, 83 ; his call, 84 ; source
of his commission, 84 seq. ; alleged residence on Continent,
95 ; by whom ordained uncertain, 96 ; his character, 101,
127 ; his usual policy, 107 ;
often in peril, 107 ; interview
with King Laoghaire, 109 ;
with Laoghaire's daughters,
111 ; his death, 117, 119 ;
where buried, 117 ; his doc-

INDEX

trine, 120 *seq.* ; causes of success, 125, 126 ; reputed miracles, 276; and curses, 280

Patrick, a Danish bishop, 316

Pelagius, 75

Perpetual fire, 155

Petrie, Dr., 19, 78

Petty, Sir W., on population of Ireland, 172

Picts, 10, 75, 79

Pig, the, 41

Pomponia Græcina, 73

Pope, was Patrick commissioned by the, 84 *seq.*

Potitus, 72

Primatial jurisdiction, early Irish Church without, 167

Promised land, 217

Probus, 65, 93

Prosper of Aquitaine, 47, 49, 55, 89

QUERNS, 40

RADIANCE, a year's, after Patrick s death, 119

Raholp, 172

Ramoan, 172

Ramsay, Professor, 31

Raphoe (Rath-Both), 228

Rashee, 116, 172

Rath Caelchu, 23

Rath Graine, 23

Rath Laoghaire, 22

Rath Muirbhuilg, 104

Rath of Synods, 22

Rathbreasil, Synod of, 169, 170, 317

Rathlin, 136, 172, 295

Rathmore, 79

Rath-na-Riogh, 21

Raths, 36

Raymond le Gros, 334

Red Branch Knights, 18, 31

Reeves, Bishop, 57, 58, 64, 80, 82, 193

Reilig Oran, 237

Religion of pre-Christian Ireland, 41 *seq.*

Restitutus, 78

Ri or king, 16

Richey, Professor, on ancient Irish laws, 27

Rights, Book of, 26

Rioc, 152

Roads, 40

Roman coins found in Ireland, 71

Roman See, change of tone towards, 318

Romans withdrawn from Britain, 72

"Romish wolves," 166

Rossa, 27

Ross-na-Righ, 47

Round Towers, 301, 303

Route, 80

Ruadhan, 147, 157

Ruric, 323

SAINTS, Irish, their character, 281 *seq.*

Saladin's tenths, 351

Salisbury, John of, 326

Saltair of Tara, 45

Saman, 19

Sanday, Professor, on primitive Episcopacy, 201

Sannan, 78

Saul, 102, 117

Scanlan Mor, 242

Schools, endowed secular, 207–209

Schools, monastic, 209-211

Scoti, 10, 11

Scotia, ancient name of Ireland, 10, 11

INDEX

Scotia Major, 11
Scotia Minor, 11
Scotland, origin of name of, 20
Scots from Dalriada go to Cantyre, 223
Scotus Erigena, 159, 213, 300
Scribe, 182
Scribings, 34
Secundinus (Sechnall), 57, 90, 152
Sedulius, 212
Senchus Mor, 26, 27
Sept, a group of families, 14
Sepulchral mounds, 33, 34, 108
Serpents, legend of expulsion of, 113
Seven bishops, groups of, 174
Shane, 42
Shrines, &c., 366
Sidh (Shee), 41
Sigefroi, 295
Sigerson, Dr., 81
Sigurd, 308, 309
Sinnell, 157
Sitric, 308, 310
Skene, Dr., 66, 69
Skelligs, 105, 106
Skerry, 82
Slane, 108, 302
Slany, the river, 102
Slavery in Ireland, 325
Slemish, 79, 81, 102
Slieve Donard, 104
Slieve Slainge, 105
Social organisation of early Irish, 14
Solinus, 114
Sources for Patrick's life, 59 seq.
Souterrains (subterranean houses), 37, 38
Southern Hy Niall, 23
Stilicho, 23
Stokes, Dr. Whitley, 66
Stokes, Margaret, 32

Stokes, Professor G. T., 59, 350
"Stowe Missal," 124, 319
Strongbow (Richard de Clare), 331-334
Succession in Irish Church, law of, 188; no regular succession of bishops, 190, 364; St. Bernard on, 191; alleged lineal descent of the modern Irish Episcopal Church from St. Patrick, 369
Suffragans unknown in early Irish Church, 194
Sullivan, Dr., on early Irish races, 7
Sullivan's Introduction to O'Curry's "Manners and Customs of Ancient Irish," 8
Sun-worship, 42
Sweat-houses, 39
Swords, 229

TACITUS, 6, 73
Tailltenn, 19, 35, 110, 232
Tain-bo-Cuailnge, 18
Tanist, 16
Tara, 17, 19, 21-22, 107, 147, 284-286
Teach-an-alais (sweat-houses), 39
Tenenan, 302
Termon lands, 298
Tertullian on evangelisation of Britain, 74
Theodosius, 72
Theodosius, the Emperor, 92
Thierry, King, 265
Thierry on characteristics of the Celts, 12
Tigris, 78
Tirechan, Collections of, 64, 92, 111, 113, 118
Tiree, 218
Tithes, 140

INDEX

Tlachta, 19, 42

Todd, Dr., his memoir of St. Patrick, 66, his chronology of Patrick's life, 66

Tonsure, Irish, 87

Torques, 22

Torr Abb, 236

Torvean, 239

Tory Island, 229

Transition in architecture, 40

Trebbia, death of Columbanus at, 269

Trias Thaumaturga, 65

Tribal constitution of society impaired the central sovereignty, 17

Tribe, the, 14–15

Tribe-land, right to, 14

Tripartite Life of St. Patrick, 49, 66, 94, 113

Tuath, 14, 146

Tuathal, King, 19

Tubernacool, holy well, 82

Tumuli (or Carns), 33, 34

Turgesius, 296, 297

Turlough, 310

Types, two distinct, of early Irish, 7

ULIDIA, 30, 127

Ulster patriotism, M. Arnold on, 3

Ultan, Bishop, 64, 92

"VATICANISING" antiquity, 162

Vaughan, Cardinal, on Anglican orders, 392

Viking, 293

Vinland, 323

Virgin, worship of the, 315

WALHALLA, Scandinavian, 41

Wasserschleben's "Irish Canons," 87, 89

Watermills, 40

Wattled houses, 36

Whitby, Synod at, 251

Wicklow, Palladius lands at, 48; Patrick lands at, 101

Wilde's, Sir W., "Beauties of the Boyne," 108

Wilfrith, 251

William the Conqueror, 326

Willibrord, 272

Witikind, 295

YELLOW plague, 225

ZIMMER on genesis of the legend of a Roman Mission of Patrick, 95

Zug, Columbanus at, 266

Printed by BALLANTYNE, HANSON & CO.

Edinburgh & London